Wisdom, Wit, and Will:
Women Choral Conductors On Their Art

Wisdom, Wit, and Will: Women Choral Conductors On Their Art

Compiled and Edited by
Joan Catoni Conlon

Contributors

Hilary Apfelstadt, Marguerite Brooks, Joan Catoni Conlon, Sharon Hansen, Ann Howard Jones, Melinda O'Neal, Doreen Rao, Kathy Saltzman Romey with Emilie Sweet and Shekela Wanyama, Harriet Simons, Beverly Taylor, Joan Whittemore, Lori Wiest, Sue Williamson

Additional Editors

Sarah Deveau
Laurie Ongley
Gordon Paine

GIA Publications, Inc.
Chicago

G-7590

GIA Publications, Inc.
7404 S. Mason Ave., Chicago, Illinois 60638
www.giamusic.com

ISBN: 978-1-57999-760-1

Contents

Our Lives

Wisdom, Wit, and Will

Introduction

Joan Catoni Conlon

In *Wisdom, Wit, and Will: Women Choral Conductors On Their Art,* over a dozen American women choral conductors present significant insights into the choral arts and, in particular, into the contributions of and challenges to women in the field. These chapters, while diverse in content and focus, all represent a fresh call for the artistic and professional development of all choral conductors, both men and women. Each author has a different focus in her work, yet each is committed to the quality of the choral music experience in the twenty-first century, and to preparation of the next generation of conductors. These chapters are not written for women only, but for all readers. *Wisdom, Wit and Will* is divided into three subject areas: **Our Music**, **Our Teaching**, and **Our Lives**.

Our Music consists of "Analyzing the Choral-Orchestral Score," by Ann Howard Jones with Timothy Westerhaus and Sarah Deveau; "Building Bridges: Choruses Engaging Communities," by Kathy Saltzman Romey with Emilie Sweet and Shekela Wanyama; "Conducting the Choral-Orchestral Work," by Beverly Taylor; "Passion and Authenticity: A Conversation with Marin Alsop," by Melinda O'Neal; and "Must We Sing of Women Only as Men Have Sung?" by Joan Catoni Conlon.

Our Teaching includes "Women Conductors As Leaders and Mentors," by Hilary Apfelstadt; "Women, Conductors, and the Tenure Process: What's Up In The Academy?" by Sharon Hansen; "Feminine Perspectives on Conducting and Teaching Choral Music," by Doreen Rao; "Teaching Graduate Conductors," by Marguerite Brooks; and "Artistry Through Improvisation in the Choral Rehearsal," by Sue Williamson.

The section entitled **Our Lives** contains "Finding Balance: Professional and Personal," by Hilary Apfelstadt; "Nadia and Me," by Harriet Simons; and "Biographies of Selected American Women Choral Conductors: Charlene Archibeque, Tamara Brooks, Elaine Brown, Fiora Contino, Lorna Cooke deVaron, Jane Hardester, Margaret Hawkins, Iva Dee Hiatt, Margaret Hillis, Eva Jessye, Colleen Kirk, and Alice Parker," by Joan Whittemore and Lori Wiest.

Each of the essays herein imparts information both carefully researched and distilled from life experience. The chapters by Brooks, Simons, and Rao discuss conducting and conducting pedagogy; Jones and Taylor, score preparation, programming, analytical methodology; Rao, O'Neal, Romey, and Williamson, educational goals for the twenty-first century and outreach strategies—topics of interest to all conductors. These essays will be immediately applicable by all conductors.

Some authors do focus primarily on women's issues (Apfelstadt, Conlon, Hansen, Whittemore, Wiest and, to a lesser extent, Rao and Taylor), yet hold insights of great importance for both men and women readers. These chapters provide data on the current and past states of affairs for women; review the life work of a dozen eminent women choral conductors; give counsel to both men and women conducting students and professionals; describe career paths taken by some women conductors; or reflect on the logistics for pursuing a path that includes career and family.

As discussed by Apfelstadt, Hansen, Rao and Taylor, women do encounter a different set of circumstances in the profession than do their male counterparts. These authors address those differences and how to cope with the resulting consequences.

Did You Know?

Many of the disparities of treatment between men and women choral conductors cited here date back to the days prior to work-place initiatives against sexual harassment. For example, Margaret Hillis, who conducted the Chicago Symphony Chorus, was told that although she was good enough to study conducting at the conservatory, she would be not admitted because she would be taking the place of someone who could get a job. The reader may consult chapters by Whittemore and Conlon for more descriptions of similar slights to women in the recent and distant past.

However, other narratives, alarmingly, suggest a persistence of attitude that threatens to be an ongoing, abiding concern. First-hand accounts in the writings of Hansen, Rao, and Taylor indicate that such disparities endure to the present day. An agent seeking a conducting engagement is told, "Do not send a woman conductor!" A woman is asked, "Why did you want to become a conductor? Men do not like to take directions from women." Another is told, "We never have had a woman conductor before, so I think we will ask somebody else."

Unity of Concern

The authors' insights into some professional and personal issues may reflect a view different from the norm because they are women, but the objective of each author is to see beyond such past events as those cited above and to turn to those goals that concern all conductors today. However significant and disturbing is the evidence of gender discrimination, the authors of these essays invariably embrace as their ultimate mission the broader goal of enhancing or improving the choral arts. Each of the book's essays has a slightly different function, but each chapter advocates for professional growth and increasing awareness of professional possibilities for both women and men conductors.

The Contributions Within This Volume

One concept that appears in various chapters is the role of collaboration in the choral culture. Conductors typically think of collaboration as combining forces, choral, or choral and instrumental, or perhaps co-teaching. In the essays by Romey, Rao, and Williamson, however, collaboration takes on heightened meaning. Romey addresses the larger aspects of collaboration, of disparate communities not simply performing with one another, but of being co-creators in non-hierarchical initiatives for social good. Rao speaks of eschewing self-assertive enterprise and instead of opening lines of communication and understanding between cultures and societies in the post-9/11 world. Williamson amplifies on collaboration through the activity of choral improvisation that relies upon trust, listening, risk-taking and awareness of the resulting whole.

The authors' specializations are quite varied, and, in addition to conducting, conducting pedagogy and score preparation, also include developing a knowledge of choral literature and of performance practice, preparing conductors to work with choirs and orchestras, expanding the conductors' awareness of other cultures and other cultures' expectations, inspiring the next generation of choral conductors and choral classroom teachers, and reaching out to communities—both to teach them and to learn from them.

The Chapters: Insights, Advice, Accounts

Apfelstadt draws on both personal experience and on significant research in her two essays, one on balancing career and family, entitled "Finding Balance: Professional and Personal," and one on styles of leadership and mentoring, entitled "Women Conductors as Leaders and Mentors." Her chapter on finding balance offers with honesty and integrity her inspiring reflections on her own life experiences. Of great significance is her invaluable advice for efficiently organizing one's time and schedule—information of critical importance for all readers. Her essay on the subjects of leadership and mentoring discusses with great resourcefulness mentoring—especially mentoring women students, as well as conducting pedagogy, and styles of leadership. The data she has assembled regarding our lives in the twenty-first century will prove to be revelatory. Did you know, for example, that people now speak more quickly than they once spoke?

Hansen's chapter is a groundbreaking examination of the tenure process for women, especially for women choral conductors. Hansen presents data on numbers of men and women in choral conducting academia, as well as their comparative earnings and ranks. Like many of the book's chapters, this is a must-read for anybody in academia. Her essay distills cogent advice and counsel from many authors on the subject of women seeking tenure. Hansen includes important updating of information on gender-related issues in higher education, data unfortunately neglected of late by various professional organizations. Because of this neglect, Hansen's report presents the latest data on the subject. She intersperses within her research some powerful anonymous narratives by women who reflect on their pursuit of tenure. One potential author refused to submit her story; she didn't wish to revisit painful memories. Another related breezing right through the tenure process. Most of the narratives relate circuitous paths to tenure, frequently encumbered by small-minded ritual from a past generation.

Rao's provocative and highly original chapter explores new goals for those who prepare choral conductors in the post-9/11 world. Rao avers that as the world has changed and has become smaller, society too has changed in such a way as to limit our interdependence upon one another and the necessity of collaboration, whether nations, cultures or peoples. In this new world, conductors must see that they exist within the context of the smaller, interdependent cultures of the globe. As conductors become less insular in their outlook and in their regard for others, they must eschew the limited goals of an earlier generation.

Romey's "Building Bridges: Choruses Engaging Communities," written with Emilie Sweet and Shekela M. Wanyama, sets out an innovative and splendid plan for collaborating and forging alliances with communities beyond the traditional chorus and beyond academia, for seeking positive social change through choral singing, for creating opportunities for shared activities by people of different races, religions and cultures. The Bridges program of the Minnesota Chorale has creative and non-hierarchical strategies for reaching out to disparate communities, strategies that necessitate joint planning and programming so that participants learn from and about each others' traditions. The organization, with the motto, "Art for the greater good!" has generated and sponsored inclusive dialogue and discussion, interdisciplinary performances, concerts and lectures, and poignant human outreach that combines "Habitat for Humanity" and choral singing. This valuable chapter also includes helpful detailed objectives for any choir wishing to pursue community engagement.

Taylor's "Conducting the Choral-Orchestral Work" confronts the issues faced by any choral conductor, male or female, who conducts an orchestra. She addresses the issue of the orchestra's attitude toward a choral conductor, and gives extremely helpful advice for using the choir to teach the orchestra, especially for imparting appropriate phrasing or concepts in the text. From her background of frequently conducting major choral-orchestra works, this seasoned, highly-experienced conductor focuses on how to prepare singers, the orchestra and the score for rehearsal and performance. She describes how to work with the orchestra, what the conductor should expect from the orchestra, and she discusses in detail what the conductor should accomplish before working with the orchestra. She speaks to refining one's listening skills, baton technique, and she also addresses practical concerns, such as budget preparation. Of particular importance is her essay's coda, a personal narrative that encapsulates the essence of every conductor's work.

Jones presents her remarkably thorough methodology for score preparation and analysis, a chapter that should be a *vademecum* for every conductor. As long-time assistant to the late Robert Shaw, she was witness to the plethora of techniques he employed in analyzing and rehearsing a score. Jones clearly articulates the details of her score preparation methodology, a procedure applicable to any score, but particularly helpful for understanding the largest and most complex of choral-orchestral scores. Particularly helpful is her description of the accompanying chart to which a conductor ultimately adds all the information necessary to conduct a score from memory. Jones presents an approach for appreciating the large musical gestures of a work, as well as details that make up the whole. The over-arching lesson of this modus operandi is that there is no closure to score study. Rather, there always will be more to discover in a great masterpiece.

Brooks has written a chapter outlining both her philosophy and her method of teaching graduate conductors. In customizing a course of study for each grad student, Brooks can address the student's strengths and weaknesses. In encouraging each student to study with more than one conducting colleague, she ensures abundant feedback on the student's conducting technique and style. In promoting reading outside of music—in addition to sources on music—she can nurture the student's awareness of language, and of the role of a composition's text in expressive conducting. In insisting that both she and her students work on score memorization, she stresses the importance of thorough score preparation.

In conversation with **O'Neal**, Marin Alsop, conductor of the Baltimore Symphony Orchestra, also emphasizes score preparation (being "two-hundred percent prepared"). Alsop stresses the need for continuing one's professional growth, and for being "the best conductor you can be." Further, Alsop emerges as ardent enthusiast for educating young conductors, audiences, and children. At her encouragement, the BSO directs ten percent of its budget into Research and Development. The resulting innovations have set the BSO and Alsop on a unique course of outreach and community interaction. Winner of the prestigious MacArthur Fellowship, Alsop donated her own award funds toward increasing the BSO's visibility and involvement in its community.

Whittemore and **Wiest** present biographies of selected women choral conductors from the present and from earlier generations (Archibeque, Brooks, Brown, Contino, Cooke deVaron, Hardester, Hawkins, Hiatt, Hillis, Kirk, Jessye, and Parker). Whittemore has assiduously pursued insights into the work of these leading choral conducting luminaries. Some of them also have conducted opera (Contino), have conducted major works with major orchestras (Hillis, Hawkins, Brooks), have focused, reshaped and elevated their choral milieu (Jessye, Hiatt), have been president of the American Choral Directors Association (Kirk), have been synonymous with all that we call Americana (Parker), have seen choral music as a bridge between all peoples (Brown and Philadelphia's Singing City), have published an important choral repertoire list (Hawkins), have conducted frequently at ACDA conventions (Archibeque, Brown, Cooke deVaron, Hardester). Each has had enormous impact on leading choral conductors today; each has left a legacy of choral excellence.

Williamson's chapter provides fresh ideas on how to teach choral improvisation in the classroom. Although improvisation was named in 2000 as one of the National Standards for Music Education, many conductors still avoid incorporating improvisation into their teaching. For those who remain wary of sharing control of the choral classroom, Williamson gives specific instructions for teaching choral improvisation, for small classes and large. Starting with the most immediately accessible musical materials—such as a descending octave scale, Williamson describes a procedure that builds on simple unison singing, and guides the way to creating elaborate inventions. The process generates and is generated by trust, interdependence, and, ultimately, listening. Williamson also demonstrates the benefits of improvisation to the individual student and to the entire choral program. Her chapter includes reports from a middle-school teacher, a high-school teacher, and a college conductor, all of whom give step-by-step instructions for teaching improvisation.

Simons describes in "Nadia and Me" her studies with Nadia Boulanger in the summer of 1959 at the American Conservatory, held in the Louis XV wing of Fontainebleau Palace outside of Paris. Simons' narration describes Mlle. Boulanger's rigorous expectations, high standards and famously difficult requirements. Simons tells of Boulanger's techniques for teaching both mental and physical discipline while teaching score reading, harmony, ear training, voice leading, and basso continuo realization. Students also studied chant, and were expected to have detailed knowledge of the scores they conducted that summer, preferably from memory, i.e., Stravinsky's *Dumbarton Oaks* and the Fauré Requiem. Simons describes some of Boulanger's teaching materials and techniques. Of special interest is Boulanger's pedagogical use of the piano to learn scores, to increase concentration, to teach independence of hands, fingers and mind.

Conlon's chapter "Must We Sing of Women Only as Men Have Sung?" examines texts about women set to choral music through the ages. The chapter presents the poems of some relatively unknown Italian, French and German women poets of the Renaissance—some of whom depict women as strong and independent, as persons who question their lot in life. These representations of women differ markedly from male poets' typical representations of women, i.e., as creatures who speak only of love, longing, lamenting and loss. Most composers throughout history have managed to ignore the voices of women as sung by women poets. These poems run the gamut of expression—ribald, loving, funny—and some voice complaints that they are regarded as lesser beings than their male counterparts or their male siblings. Still others are vindictive as they demand equality from their husbands. But they are not content with expressing only love, longing, lamenting and loss.

First Steps

During a 1995 American Choral Directors Association national convention panel dedicated to women's issues, approximately a dozen women panelists presented in two sessions widely divergent points of view regarding their roles as women in choral music. The panelists spoke either in general terms or told of personal experience. Some panelists averred that women were assuming more visibility and responsibility in the world at large and in the choral conducting profession.

Others cited frustrating instances when they had not been treated as equal to their male colleagues. Another described teaching techniques she employed with all her students regardless of gender, and one woman described how she was pursuing a doctorate in choral conducting while being mother to a young child. On the other extreme, some panelists stressed that their primary importance in life was to be wife, mother, and homemaker, and that involvement in choral music was simply a way of keeping active in music.

In the course of the sessions, each of the women simply spoke for five minutes apiece. The divergent panel presentations concluded without a single coordinated message or voice, or without stating any mutual concerns, or proposing further discussion, or mentioning career strategies that may or may not have included motherhood and a career in conducting or in higher education. A great deal was left unsaid.

At the same ACDA convention, conductor Sandra Willetts presented an Interest Session on choral music of contemporary women composers conducted by women conductors. Hilary Apfelstadt, Charlene Archibeque, and Norma Raybon conducted Willetts' University of Alabama University Singers in the presentation. Since that 1995 convention, women choral conductors' matters have not been systematically addressed by ACDA.

Writing more than a decade after that first ACDA women's panel, contributors to the present volume acknowledge that many career pathways in choral music are valid, and that each person has different priorities and experiences. The contributors to this volume refrain from passing judgment on any course that women have taken, or will take, to reach fulfillment. Each essay is intended to share knowledge learned by the authors over their careers. Some of the authors have focused on career only, while others have combined family and distinguished career, and are mothers and grandmothers. Most are, or have been, Directors of Choral Activities at a college or university.

♦♦♦

In the 1970s, the literature about choral music was tremendously enhanced by the appearance of the book *Choral Symposium* by Harold Decker, Julius Herford, and other highly distinguished leaders in the choral profession, all of whom were male. Since that time, the profile of the academic and of the conductor has changed significantly. As Hansen has demonstrated, numbers of women recipients of advanced degrees have greatly increased since that time. Will these new women professionals be regarded as colorful novelties or serious colleagues? Will the likes of such world figures as Madeline Albright and Condoleeza Rice significantly benefit the lot of women in their respective fields, and will women choral conductors ultimately be recognized as equals with their male colleagues?

Although the present volume offers a history of some significant women in the field, the substance of the book focuses on developing future strong choral conductors of any gender. To quote from the opening, the book has a single concern: developing the professional and artistic choral conductor and teacher. These thoughtful, reflective essays offer options, and discuss those qualities and skills that any conductor should embody to create the best of all experiences for their choral conducting students and for their singers. This volume shares an extraordinary amount of knowledge, as did the *Choral Symposium* of the 1970s. Only the context is different, because the world is now different.

The Database

In conjunction with this printed volume, the American Choral Directors Association sponsors an online database of women conductors that lists each conductor's contact information and interests, and that describes the nature of her professional position. Rachel J. Samet, editor of the database, is responsible for updating the content. All women choral conductors are encouraged to become part of the database, the web site address for which is *Women in Choral Music, An International Database of Women Choral Conductors*, http://www.womeninchoralmusic.org/. Additionally, two Co-Site Administrators, Giselle Wyers and Gabrielle Dietrich, have established a Facebook site entitled "Women Choral Conductors."

♦♦♦

I express my profound gratitude to each author for her dedication to her art and to her profession, and for her artistry and creativity that have enriched and inspired so many. I gratefully acknowledge the kind assistance and support of Steve Brooks and the late Gene Brooks, of Carroll Gonzo, Hilary Apfelstadt, and William Belan for their support of the present volume and for their ongoing support of the database. I also am indebted to the late Dr. R. Lynn Whitten for his inspiration and generous support, to the University of Colorado for the Kayden Award book subvention, to Dr. Andrew Kuster for his design, layout and editing of the book, and to my husband Frank Conlon, who has provided technical and moral support beyond measure.

Joan Catoni Conlon
Seattle, January 2009

Our Music

Analyzing the Choral-Orchestral Score

Ann Howard Jones
with Sarah Deveau and Timothy Westerhaus

Introduction

Conductors, teachers and clinicians continually and strongly emphasize two things: first, the necessity and the critical importance of choosing music carefully; and, second, thorough knowledge of the score before the first rehearsal. In the matter of choice of music, few would disagree that the conductor should attend to the aesthetics of taste and, further, that rigorous standards of compositional craft, text-setting, and a successful union of the two are of prime importance when selecting choral music for performance. Careful consideration of these elements of music is the conductor's most important challenge.

When selecting repertoire, the conductor should explore and utilize the whole range of literature and include examples from the historical past. A concert program that includes only music written in the last twenty-five years certainly can be justified, but a conductor always must strive for a balanced selection of repertoire.[1]

Once the music has been chosen, the conductor's task moves to learning the score, i.e., learning as much as possible about every piece that we will conduct. This necessitates time and devotion to the task. Julius Herford, the teacher of a generation of choral conductors in the United States in the middle of the twentieth century said, "(A personal concept) implies a quality of reading that conceives thought and, ultimately, conceives the work as a whole. It demands a long, even ceaseless, process of learning." (Decker and Herford 1973, 199.)

This work is time spent by the conductor alone with the score. Quoting Helmuth Rilling, "If you want to be a good conductor, score preparation will require much work ahead of time—much *solitary* work." (Hansen, 99.) The conductor must develop a systematic approach to the study of the musical score, and insure that prime time is set aside for this essential part of the process. "Score study is a catalyst for the ultimate artistic and unified whole composition." (Marvin in Webb, 98.) Score study should not be the last thing on the list, coming after committee meetings, program planning, fund raising, and travel arrangements, for example.

In my role as Robert Shaw's assistant with the Atlanta Symphony Choruses, I observed first hand Mr. Shaw's careful and thorough score preparation. He would pore over the score note by note, chord by chord, word by word, and often would mark nearly every note with some sign affecting dynamics, articulation or balance that would result from his meticulous study of the score and his mental imaginings of the music. It was remarkable to see the editing and re-editing for every performance no matter how many times he had conducted the work. In commenting about his general approach to score study, he wrote: "First, there are the technical considerations. . . . pitch[es] which are right or wrong; . . . rhythms, meters, tempos and durations [which] are precise or imprecise; . . . loudness [which] is proportioned or disproportioned; . . . articulation [which] is just or unjust; . . . and colors and textures which are appropriate or inappropriate. These . . . are not nearly so mysterious as those of us who are mystified by [them] would have you believe." (Blocker, 384.) Shaw often said that the composer frequently made only the broad stroke and we were to make the composer's idea work with the musical resources we had at our disposal. He would "fix" the composer's dynamics to correct issues of balance, add articulation marks to clarify a line in the texture, add rhythmic impulse to breathing and consonants, and provide a variety of additional editings. He was always striving to take the composer's ideas from the page and put them into the performance in the best possible way.

Conductors work to discover what makes each musical composition unique, and a love of this process is essential. A knowledgeable and prepared conductor is more effective in rehearsal, and it clearly is to everyone's benefit that the conductor is thoroughly familiar with every detail of the score before the rehearsing begins. This does not mean that the conductor will not change his or her mind in the rehearsal process; but it does mean that many decisions have been made and much work on the score has taken place before the first encounter with the ensemble. This must be a priority for the conductor.

Many methods are available to assist in this process. Authors disagree about various parts of it—the order of steps through which the process moves, the necessity of keyboard skills as an aid in the reproduction of the score, the ability to hear the music silently, the need for visual representations of the score, the ability to dramatize the text, harmonic analysis, the use of recordings—but no one denies its importance. The conductor, the performer and the composer are inextricably intertwined with the score and the only effective way to uncover each work as a whole is to strive to know in the most minute detail what the composer was trying to say. This can then be communicated, dramatized and illuminated in rehearsal and performance.

This chapter explains and presents the approach to score study that has been the most useful to me. This is by no means the only way such preparation can be done, nor is it recommended that it be followed assiduously. After all, such a system is only useful if it works for the person who uses it. Remember that analysis leads the conductor to a thorough knowledge of the music, to start the learning process for the conductor. These ideas are suggestions for an approach that will shape the rehearsal. Jameson Marvin counsels, these ideas "will enhance every part of the learning of the work, and will ultimately save you time and effort as you work. . . ." (Webb, 98.)

Conductors need help and even instruction in the area of analysis. Most conductors learned to conduct before learning how to study a score. They start to conduct before developing any ideas about the music (Battisti and Garofalo, iii). As a result, few conductors can create compelling musical performances precisely because they have learned conducting techniques before they have learned how to analyze and prepare the score. (Ibid., 23.)

In this chapter, I will suggest an approach to the score that focuses on improving the conductors' grasp of the music. Through that knowledge and understanding, the conductor enhances the quality of the performance by discovering the composer's intention.

The Basics of the Score

Look at the piece. Note the fundamental details of the work and write them down: the composer, the composer's dates, the opus number and the date of composition, the catalogue number, (BWV or NMA number for Bach or Mozart, respectively, for example), the text and its source, the presence of a translation and a guide to pronunciation if the work is in a foreign language, the timing, the presence (or absence) of rehearsal letters, numbers or measure numbers (adding them if they are not present and being sure the choral parts and the orchestral parts are marked with the same rehearsal letters or numbers), the publisher and the publisher's number, and the editor.

Next take note of the musical facts: the key of the work, the number of movements and their respective harmonic centers, the range of the voice parts and their distribution, the timing of the work as a whole and of each movement and, finally, the instrumentation.

To save time and to avoid adding a step to the process, write all of this information on the piece of paper that ultimately will become an analytical "graph" in the manner described by Julius Herford (see Decker and Herford, 199–265). Some conductors prefer to put all of this information in the score itself. Although that is perfectly acceptable, the score can become cluttered. More importantly, conductors need to create a visual representation of the score apart from the music itself for purposes of literally seeing each work's structure and for assisting in the learning of the work. Eventually, all the analytical material will be included on this "graph"—from the basic facts of the composition to the length of the phrases and the harmonic analysis.

Understand that studying this graph will be most productive if one has the full score at hand while digesting the analytical material.

Soundless Listening and Reading

Once the critical elements of a work have been written down, the next step is to define the basic sound of the composition. What are the musical elements of the piece? How does the music move? What gives this composition its "voice"? What is the composer trying to say? Page through the piece with these questions in mind. Become aware of tempos, meters, harmonies and rhythms. In this phase, think only about the music. Try not to think about issues of performance or even how you will conduct some passage. Just think about the score. Let your imagination work.

Next, read the music soundlessly. Read in a tempo that will allow the music to be read in speeds proportional to the final tempo and in a tempo that allows you to read the music without stopping. This usually means selecting a slightly slower tempo than that of the performance. During this part of the process, take in as many details as possible, but try to get a general idea of the outline of the score without stopping and starting.

Early in the process of learning a work, one is tempted to jump ahead and to begin to work on conducting problems, difficulties with particular pitches and rhythms, rehearsal planning, for example, but, as Battisti and Garofalo teach, this part of the process is "looking for the broad gesture, the landscape of the work." They warn against looking at too much detail in this reading stage. "If detail is explored too early, it is difficult to judge whether the particular detail being examined is important or not." (Battisti and Garofalo, 23.) Battisti and Garofalo also suggest avoiding the piano or recordings at this phase in order to cultivate the ability to hear with the eyes. "Listening to a recording, the conductor doesn't read the music, he or she follows it." (23–32.) Certainly recordings can be of assistance, but at a later stage. "Score reading is like walking down a path through the woods with an alert, concentrated mind and an observant, perceptive attitude. Each time you do it, you discover something new in the environment. If you do it three, four, or five times every day, eventually you will get to know the path and its environment so well that you will be able to walk through it with your eyes closed, yet see, hear, and smell the surroundings." (23.)

If one does not have sufficient score reading skills to hear the music without sound, then one must address and practice this skill. If the conductor's skills are insufficient or if music is so complex that silent reading is nonproductive, play one part at a time at the piano to get an idea of the whole. Then, combine parts to see how the voices fit together. Start with what you have determined is the melody and then add the other parts to it in some order of importance. The bass part might be added next if the soprano is judged to be the melody. If the conductor does not have enough keyboard ability to manage this at some level, then a recording may be the only choice. The conductor, however, needs to be able to imagine the sound without the sound actually being present.

The Process of Analysis

The next step then is the analytical process itself. Start with pitch, and pitch as it is organized into *melody*. The conductor should think carefully about words to describe the melody and melodic motion. Rather than focus exclusively on theoretical aspects, this examination of the ideas of the melodic material should take into account at least the following practical characteristcs:

- the scale reference (major, minor, chromatic, modal, etc.)
- the shape of the melody
- the tessitura and range
- the presence of decorative elements, melismatic passages and embellishments
- the relationship to the harmony beneath it, especially noting non-chord tones, suspensions, etc.
- the relationship to any accompaniment

- the way the notes are organized (step-wise, leaps, melismas, etc.)
- the melody's changes throughout the composition (sequences, ostinati, repetition and any combinations)
- the shifting of the melody from one part to another, as in fugue or counterpoint, for example

Next study the *rhythm*, and the related matters of tempo, meter and harmonic rhythm.[2] Note if and how the composer indicates tempo. Are there tempo words that need definition? Even after the individual words are defined, the composer's meaning may be obscured. Think, for example, of Beethoven writing these words at the beginning of the Kyrie of the Mass in C: "*Andante con moto assai vivace quasi allegretto ma non troppo.*"

Are there metronome markings? What are all the ramifications of the speed of the piece: study the fastest notes and their rhythms, look at the long sustained passages thinking about vocal endurance and control, and decipher any difficult rhythms in each line. Mark all the variations of tempo that are indicated as ritardando and accelerando or as changes, and look for any interruptions of tempo such as a fermata or a grand pause. Techniques used by the composer to affect rhythm might also be examined in this phase: hemiola, syncopation, augmentation, diminution, the absence of meter and bar lines, and the use of silence, for example. Finally, take careful note of meter changes and devise a way to mark your score to make those changes easy to see as you are eventually rehearsing the work.

Identify the architecture of the piece on the basis of its *harmony*. Find the key or pitch center of the work first. Then start with the big shapes of the piece and move down to the level of the phrase from there. Decisions about a work's structure are based on the way the composer uses harmony and harmonic motion. First, mark the clear cadences that delineate large divisions first.

Then, look for modulations, pedal points, and other harmonic devices that shape the larger structure. Only after that is clear, analyze the smaller subdivisions, phrases and individual chords. Conductors must know how a piece is put together harmonically so that they can determine the work's structure, but some can find themselves mired in individual chordal analysis or in the text divisions too early in the process. Instead, identify the large shape as determined by major harmonic arrivals and departures. Look also for modal changes, the speed of the harmonic rhythm, the relationship of harmony to melody, and other elements of harmonic analysis.[3] Then, devise a system that works for you to indicate the major turning points in the harmony. Mark these not only in the score, but also note them in the form of an analytical graph. For a sample of such a graph, see Example 1 below.

The next level of analysis is of *form*. In creating the overview of the work, take into account the number of different kinds of forms that the work might include. In large multi-movement choral compositions, for example, there might be sonata-allegro form, variation, binary, and through-composed forms. In a small octavo, you may encounter verse and refrain, fugue, strophic, and others that are integrated into the composition. Each movement requires analysis of its most minute detail, and each movement requires a separate sheet of paper so that the form and internal structures are visible to the eye and not just marked in the score. No matter what the size of the form or the complexity of its organization, look for clearly delineated sections in the work and mark them with a vertical line.[4]

Place a vertical line below the music at each major point in the structure. Perhaps the music does not fall into easily described structures. If the form is freer, determine why that is the case. What is the relationship of the form to the text? "Kyrie eleison, Christe eleison, Kyrie eleison" lends itself to an A–B–A form, for example. Other texts do not readily suggest form. Composers may present the Credo of a Mass text in a variety of ways, from continuous variation to A–B–A form. After making decisions about the overall form and the divisions of the music or movement, then mark phrase lengths and, finally, groupings within the phrase.

Two examples follow that provide models for your own score study and preparation: the Kyrie from Schubert's Mass in G (Example 2) and the fourth movement of *Ein deutsches Requiem* by Brahms, "Wie lieblich sind deine Wohnungen" (Example 3). Note that in these examples, the *overall form* is at the top of the graph. In the score, this level is marked with a vertical line underneath the music, but as your ideas grow more and more certain, you can mark all the way down through the music. You might consider using a ruler to keep the score looking neat and uncluttered.

At the next level down are the *divisions*. Such divisions may include a three part structure within the A part of an A–B–A form, for example. Mark them with a wedge (^) in the score, at the bottom edge of the music and exactly on the bar line where the material stops and starts. In Example 1, note that the divisions are lined up under the proper place in the *overall form*.

Next are the *subdivisions*. Mark these with a bracket [ ] . Within the first part of the A section, perhaps there are two larger collections of material. Within those two large parts are smaller (but still considerable) subdivisions. The subdivisions then are broken down into *phrases* and the phrases are divided further into groups of measures called *bar groupings*. The abstract idea of these levels is illustrated below and specific application to a composition is shown in the examples provided.

Example 1

Overall form:	A . . . . B . . . .
Division:	a . . . . | b . . . . | a . . . .
Subdivision:	1–16 ^ 17–33
Phrase:	[1–8]
Bar grouping:	(2 + 4 + 2)

When determining the length of a phrase, consider these comments that Robert Shaw wrote in a letter dated 29 October 1969:

> Phrasing is a sort of punctuation. We use commas, parentheses, dashes, and assorted devices to group together those words in a sentence which make in passing a sense unto themselves, even though it be subordinate and qualifying to the sense of the whole. . . . These punctuations imply varying degrees of pause before proceeding to other, but related, ideas.

How do we know what notes are to be grouped together in the musical phrase? Shaw suggests the following:

> 1. Explore the varieties of sequence and imitation . . . and let them be heard.
>
> 2. Grant to adjacent scale-wise motion one sort of articulation and to its interruption another sort.
>
> 3. Convey the inner and hidden dialogue, the yin and yang, the up and down, the question and answer, male and female, boy-girl, tension and relaxation.
>
> 4. Be considerate of the text. It might just coincide with melodic or harmonic accentuation-and this moment is the Pentecost of song.
>
> 5. An up-beat is a spring-board. The higher you have to bound the harder you must hit the board.
>
> 6. Cultivate the forward look. Melody is a vagabond, incorrigibly searching the world for a place "really" to settle down. Even punctuation is not a pe-

riod of retrospect, but of marshaling strength and scanning the horizon. The last note we sing is the one to which all others lead. (Shaw cited in Blocker, 69–70.)

Learning a work is greatly facilitated by the visual representation provided by this kind of analysis. The conductor will see the various sizes of the divisions and the subdivisions, for instance, and if there is an unbalanced phrase, this also becomes clear because it is visible on the analytical graph. The graph thus becomes a condensed representation of the work.

Julius Herford's ideas about score analysis have been taught through various conductors, including Daniel Moe and Don V Moses, and through Robert Shaw. The ideas suggested here come from the work of Julius Herford, but they have been modified over the years and are assembled into this mental picture, this visual guide to the work, called an analytical graph. Two examples are provided in this chapter. (See Bruce Chamberlain in *Teaching Music Through Performance*, Volume I, 513 ff. for more examples of deciphering the graphs—which he calls "analysis charts.")

As may be seen in Example 2, the basic facts of a work appear at the top. Down one level is the *form* of the piece divided into sections: *overall form*, *division*, *subdivision*, *phrase*, and finally *bar grouping*. The *overall form* is a description of the big structure: A–B, A–B–A, exposition, development and recapitulation, verse and refrain, etc. The next level, called the *division*, is the designation for the smaller units within the overall form but a larger level than either the subdivision or the phrase. If the composition being studied is in A–B *overall form*, for example, the first "A" section might divide into three *divisions*. Each *division* then might divide into *subdivisions* and, ultimately, each *subdivision* into groups of *phrases* and each *phrase* can be broken into measures which are put together into *bar groupings*. Decisions about each of these formal divisions should be supported by the key, harmonies, cadences or turning points utilized by the composer.

The description of the harmonic motion of a work appears under the architectural description, for this determines the formal designations. If text, harmony and form do not coincide, let harmony be the deciding factor in determining the length of the *phrase* or the *bar grouping* and not the words. The most skillfully written pieces will tie text to harmonic motion and to form, but the composer does not always observe such unity.

The use of graph paper facilitates the visualization of all of this material. I recommend that the conductor use graph paper with small enough squares

Example 2

Mass in G, no. 2, D 167 (1815), Kyrie
Franz Schubert (1797-1828)

Prepared by Tim Westerhaus

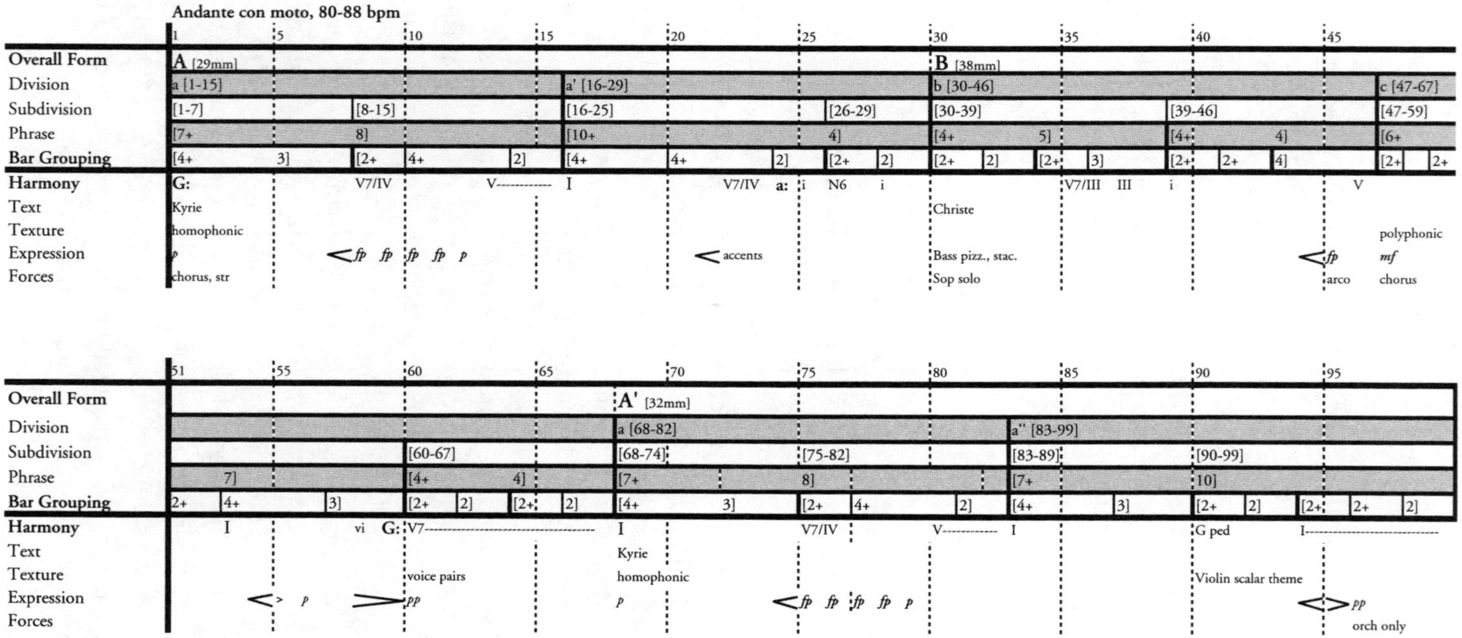

Example 3

Ein deutsches Requiem, op. 45 (1868), IV "Wie lieblich sind deine Wohnungen"
Johannes Brahms (1833-1897)

Prepared by Tim Westerhaus

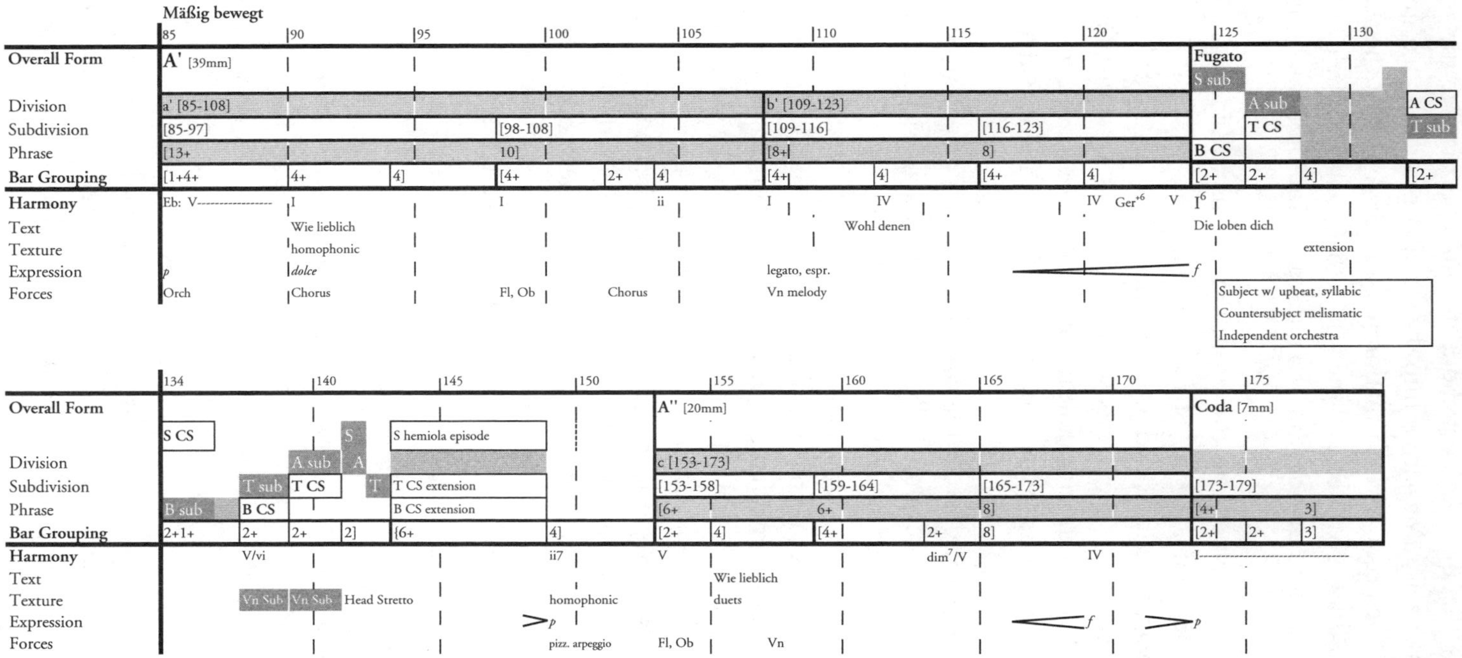

so that one square can equal one measure, pursuant to the goals of condensing all of this information into the smallest possible space, and, two, including all the necessary information to spatially represent the actual score.[5]

Now draw a bold line all the way across the graph. Below the line are such things as chord progressions, text, texture, expression, and special notes about forces.

If you do not reprint the entire *text* on this analytical graph, at least write in the first and last word of each new *division*.

Dynamics are indicated on the graph if there is a special purpose in the dynamic gesture or the composer uses dynamics for something sudden or unusual. The guiding principle is not to clutter the graph with too much detail. Some conductors make elaborate markings to indicate dynamic levels to assist them in learning the work.

The term *texture* tells the conductor whether the music is moving homophonically or polyphonically. In contrapuntal music, space the entries of the specific voices of the chorus on the graph, showing the measure in which the voice enters, keeping accurate the order and distance of the voices' entries. Below the line, write specific notes about style, thematic transformation, repetitive rhythmic figures, pedal points, ostinati and any other information that will help the conductor learn the detail of the score.

"Wie lieblich sind deine Wohnungen," the fourth movement of Brahms' *Ein deutsches Requiem*, requires a more complicated graphic analysis (see Example 3). On this graph, note the formal analysis, the harmonic analysis, and the texture, text, dynamics and all the other elements of the movement. The *fugato* is clearly designated on the graph by order of entries and the nature of the content of each line (subject, countersubject, etc.) with the bar groupings underneath.

The Orchestration Chart

If the work being analyzed includes instruments, create an *orchestration chart* as a separate document to accompany the analysis, a chart that will show which musicians are involved at which points in a work.

The process of creating an orchestration chart for choral-orchestral works imparts a general understanding of the work's overall construction to the conductor and, most importantly, reveals information necessary to plan and pace rehearsals. This orchestration chart is achieved by scanning through the entire work, noting each instrument's participation and overall characteristics.

Example 4

Ein deutsches Requiem, **Op. 45 (1868)** Tim Westerhaus, 2008
Johannes Brahms (1833-1897)
Orchestration Chart

Timings	I. Selig sind, die da Leid tragen	II. Denn alles Fleisch es ist wie Gras	III. Herr, lehre doch mich	IV. Wie lieblich sind deine Wohnungen	V. Ihr habt nun Traurigkeit	VI. Denn wir haben hie keine bleibende Statt	VII. Selig sind die Toten
John Eliot Gardiner	09:50	13:10	08:55	05:25	07:05	11:20	09:35
James Levine	09:30	16:30	10:15	05:20	06:50	11:20	10:30
Robert Shaw	10:10	15:00	09:30	05:40	07:10	11:00	11:15
Forces							
Piccolo		X				X	
Flute (2)	X	X	X	X	X	X	X
Oboe (2)	X	X	X	X	X	X	X
Clarinet (2) - A, Bb		X	X	X	X	X	X
Bassoon (2)	X	X	X	X	X	X	X
Contrabassoon *ad libitum*		X	X			X	X
Horn (1, 2) - F, Bb basso, D, Eb	X	X	X	X	X	X	X
Horn (3, 4) - C basso, E		X	X			X	X
Trumpet (2) - Bb, D, C		X	X			X	
Trombone (3)	X	X	X			X	X
Tuba		X	X m. 173 ped			X	
Timpani (3)		X	X			X	
Harp (2+)	X	X					X
Soprano Solo					X		
Baritone Solo			X			X	
Chorus (SATB)	X	X	X	X	X	X	X
Violin I		X *div*	X *div*	X	X	X	X
Violin II		X *div*	X *div*	X	X	X *div*	X
Viola	X *divisi*	X 3-*div*	X *div*	X	X *div*	X	X
Cello	X 3-*div*	X	X *div*	X	X *solo*	X	X
Contrabass	X	X	X *div*	X	X	X	X
Organ *ad libitum*	X	X	X			X	X
Notes						opt. *attacca* VI to VII	

On the vertical axis, all the instruments are listed in score order, and on the horizontal axis, all the movements are listed in the order in which they occur. If consistently functioning in pairs or groups, woodwind and brass instruments need not be listed individually, although the number of each should be indicated. Include transpositions of instruments, where applicable, and performer doublings (e.g., third oboe doubles English horn) on the vertical axis.

Soloists should be listed individually, the process of which identifies movements that require coaching in advance of the first rehearsal with orchestra and soloists. The chorus may be listed as one unit if all voice parts consistently participate together but listed separately if one or more movements do not require the full choral ensemble. For example, in J. S. Bach's "Wachet auf, ruft uns die Stimme," BWV 140, the fourth movement involves only the tenors. In Brahms' *Ein deutsches Requiem*, however, the choir participates throughout as a unit.

The orchestration chart must be adapted to accurately reflect the ensemble and performance practice of the work. For example, in a Handel oratorio, the strings may divide into *concertist* and *ripienist* groups for entire movements, and, thus, the chart should reflect those personnel contrasts. Concerted Baroque works require enumeration of the basso continuo players and should be grouped into two categories: those that provide a harmonic realization and those that play the bass line. For example, the former group may include theorbo, harpsichord, and organ while the latter may include bassoon, cello, and contrabass. Listing the continuo instruments in such a way demands that the conductor make decisions about the various continuo instruments participating in each movement before contracting the orchestra. The terms "play" or "tacet" then must be written into the individual continuo performance parts.[6]

Having created this matrix, the conductor performs a broad scan of the music and indicates each instrument's participation for every movement. General characteristics are considered through this process. Integral and incidental *divisi* markings should be included, as these will have important implications for the forces needed for a performance. Additionally, take account of notable solos, such as the cello solo in the fifth movement of the same work, "Ihr habt nun Traurigkeit." Throughout this process, note each instrument's general characteristics. For example, one would note in Mozart's Requiem that the trumpets and timpani primarily function as tonic and dominant punctuations. Therefore, their presence at early orchestra rehearsals may be unnecessary. Lastly, relevant relationships between movements must be incorporated into the chart, such as the *attacca* segue between the opening Introit and the ensuing Kyrie in Mozart's Requiem.

The general observations gleaned from this process make efficient and respectful rehearsals possible. The general principle in rehearsals is that one starts with movements with the largest number of performers and rehearses in such an order that one ends with the smallest number of personnel. For example, one should not begin the rehearsal of Brahms' *Ein deutsches Requiem* with the opening movement, during which both violin sections and many brass players sit idly. Rather, a respectful conductor starts with movements that employ the largest number of musicians, namely the second, third, or sixth movements and ends with movements that employ smallest number, the fourth movement.

Movements that include *attacca* transitions must be rehearsed as such; in this way, orchestral musicians will make any necessary accommodations to make as seamless or brief a connection as possible. Because pacing is crucial in precious, limited orchestral rehearsals, include the timing of each movement on this chart to ensure that each movement will have the necessary and adequate rehearsal time. A useful starting point for planning rehearsals is to take the performance time required for each movement and double or triple that length of time for rehearsal. If the end result is more time than one has available for rehearsal, problems of inadequate rehearsal time will become clear.

Once the orchestration chart is completed, design a seating chart for the forces involved in the performance. Each time a work is rehearsed, the rehearsal space needs to be set up according to that design. The stage set up for certain works in the choral-symphonic repertoire needs careful thought because the orchestration is unusual or because the instruments required for the performance need special consideration for sight-line or acoustical reasons. *Symphony of Psalms* of Stravinsky is one such example because of the absence of upper strings and the presence of two pianos. The conductor must determine in advance how the orchestra is to be displayed on the stage to achieve maximum acoustical effect and the optimum positioning of all of the players.

Similarly, any choral music of Bach that includes a continuo group requires special care with the seating arrangement. As a general guide, the continuo cellist and the continuo keyboardist prefer be able to see one another and to be in close proximity to one another and to the Evangelist, if the work is a Passion.[8]

Note that the analytical graphs and charts discussed in the last two sections represent one individual's ideas about the way the work is put together. Occasionally there will be differences of opinion about where a phrase begins and ends, whether or not there is a coda and where it begins, or whether a form is rounded binary or ternary, for example. Performance is always improved, however, by completing the analytical graph and charts because these provide a level of understanding of structure and its components that will enhance the conductor's understanding of the composition. In his insightful book *How Does a Poem Mean*, the famous poet and author John Ciardi wrote:

> By nature, analysis is plodding at best. . . . Analysis is never in any sense a substitute for the poem. The best any analysis can do is to prepare the reader to enter the poem more perceptively. By isolating for special consideration some of the many simultaneous elements of the poem, analysis makes them more visible in one sense, and less interesting in another. It is up to the reader, once the analysis is completed, to re-read the poem in a way that will restore the simultaneity and therefore the liveliness and interest of the poetic structure. The only reason for taking a poem apart is that it may then be put back together again more richly. (Ciardi, 1959, 663–664)

Marking the Score

After the analysis is complete, the graph is prepared and the orchestration chart is made, the other activity in which most conductors become absorbed is the personal marking of the score. Most conductors have a very individualized way of indicating events and calling attention to important things in the score. Sometimes a well-used and often-performed score simply will not allow any more metronome markings, any more ideas about text translation or pronunciation, or any more metric indications. If that is the case, purchase a new score and start afresh.

There are, however, certain things that the experienced conductor wants in the score. The following list contains those things which are important:

- *Metronome markings.* Conductors must study and rehearse music in a tempo to be able to recreate a desired tempo again and again. A metronome marking that is checked frequently is the only way to assure this. Some think that the most important thing a conductor does for an ensemble is to set a proper tempo, and to be able to repeat it consistently. Managing to find the marked tempo and to then adhere to it is one of the most important skills the conductor must acquire.

- *Translation.* Word-for-word translation is better than poetic translation. Write it directly into the score beneath the original words. The translation volumes of Latin and German texts prepared by Ron Jeffers and published by Earthsongs are invaluable for understanding text in those two languages (see bibliography).

- *Important entrances.* Some conductors mark every entrance. I think it is most useful to mark only the most important ones or the ones that you want to be most prominently heard. Some would advocate for the marking of every cymbal crash. I believe that it is critical to mark the first entry of an instrument or a voice after a long rest. Mark important entries that duplicate or support one another, and those that are independent. A bracket or an arch from one part to another will guide the conductor's eye.

- *Analysis.* Add a short-hand analysis to the score from the analytical graph. This will help you in guiding the shaping of the phrases and will serve as a reminder of the structure within which you will rehearse. Any structural seams must be clearly marked and must be carefully practiced by the conductor in advance of the rehearsal. Often, especially in works that instrumentalists have played many times, a conductor may not find it necessary to rehearse a movement from beginning to end. The orchestra needs to see the beginning for the tempo, the ending for the ritardando, if appropriate, the length of the last note, its relationship to the starting note of the next movement, and any and all changes of tempo or style in the interior of the work. If pressed for time in rehearsal, never neglect those items.

- *Breaths.* When you are thinking about phrasing, mark breathing places in the parts. Robert Shaw taught that a breath mark that has no rhythmic implication is almost useless. When a breath mark is inserted, it must have a precise rhythmical value attached to it. This is especially helpful when the chorus is trying to place consonants at the ends of phrases. Because music requires split second precision and enunciation, the rhythmic placement of breath is essential.

- *Correct diction.* Learn the International Phonetic Alphabet (IPA) and use its symbols to assist with the precision of the language.[9]

- *Meter changes.* Some conductors simply print in large numbers the number of beats in each measure at the beginning of each measure, especially when the meter changes. Others use symbols above the measures—triangles for triple meter, squares for a 4/4 meter, and large "L" shapes for duple meter. The numbers indicating the beats in the measure are difficult to see when there is time for only a quick glance. The faster the tempo and the smaller the unit of division, the more need for the symbols.

- *Dynamics.* Edit dynamics where necessary. If you know from studying the score that the brass, who are marked *fortissimo* by the composer, are going to overbalance the chorus, mark the part and your score with an alternate dynamic. This kind of detail is especially important when the composer has indicated dynamics only with a broad gesture. The conductor has to anticipate balance problems and mark the score and the parts accordingly. Mark the high and low points of *crescendi* and *diminuendi* with a specific dynamic marking. Some musicians think that all crescendos open to *forte* and all diminuendos end at *pianissimo*. A marking disabuses them of that incorrect assumption. Also, mark the principal and the accompanimental parts in contrapuntal material. This information will also be useful when marked in the parts for the instrumentalists and vocalists, but must be marked in the score from which you conduct. Sometimes the acoustics of a performance venue will require that more bass strength is needed, for example. That could be marked in the score ahead of time. If one examines a score edited for performance by Robert Shaw, one will see a variety of markings in the parts to indicate a change in dynamic from the score as the composer or editor prepared it. Shaw also liked to indicate a certain number of voices going up to support a higher part or a certain number of voices going down to strengthen a lower voice. He was extremely conscious of balancing voices in the chorus by numbers of voices on a part and not by certain parts being asked to sing louder. By the end of his career, he was expert at anticipating those kinds of problems, and those singers sitting on the edges of each section knew that they had to be alert to go up or down as the marking in the part required.[7]

- *Standing and sitting cues.* There is rarely the need to take precious time between movements in performance for the soloists or the chorus to stand and sit. Plan for the singers to stand or sit on a musical cue, and then, except in rare cases, the responsibility is the singer's and not the conductor's. More importantly, the heartbeat of a performance is not disturbed when the music comes to a halt and unmeasured time is spent getting the singers into position to sing the next movement.

Conclusion

There can be no doubt that preparation of a score requires a formidable amount of work. The reason for such preparation is for the conductor to know a composition in its most minute detail. Careful marking of the score allows the conductor to keep the composer's intention clearly in mind, and can help the conductor keep a firm hold during the performance. In the final analysis, a performance is less about the detail than it is about the larger gesture; but if the detail is missing, the larger gesture might not be able to be heard. If a conductor allows "squishy" rhythms, imprecise diction, imbalances, undifferentiated dynamics, unimaginative articulations, and inattention to appropriate tone and tone color, a performance is surely seriously flawed. The musicians who give so generously of themselves to sing in our choruses and play in our orchestras need to know that we are passionate about the music, that we have thought about it a great deal, that we have analyzed its content, and that we have imagined how it might sound; in short, that we know the music. In the end, the performance is less about the musicians and the conductor than about the composer. Much depends on that understanding. Performers should not perform because the conductor imposes his or her self on the music. Instead of the conductor saying, "give me more" of this or that, the conductor who has prepared the score functions more as a conduit for the composer's ideas. We rehearse and perform to reveal the detail of what the composer is trying to say. Music demands no less.

There are other elements that contribute to the conductor's success in preparation of the score. While thorough discussion of each of them is outside of the scope of this chapter, these are some of the essentials that should be in place before a conductor begins to study scores:

- Excellent aural skills. From the podium, the conductor must be able to identify errors, correct balances, adjust dynamics, hear good diction, and insist on accurate rhythm.

- An understanding of style. Each piece fits in an historical context and in the context of the composer's output. The thoroughly prepared conductor has a grasp of the appropriate style for the work at hand and how the piece represents the composer.

- A working knowledge of the demands of the performance practices appropriate for the repertoire.

- A basic concept of the possibilities and limitations of the instrument called "the voice." One must know as much as possible about the voice and vocal production if one is conducting a chorus. Ideally, the conductor should provide healthy vocal modeling for the choir, and it is best if one can sing well. Many conductors cannot. That does not mean that the conductor is not well-informed about what a singer can do and what is appropriate for the voice and what is not. The same is true of the instruments. The conductor is not expected to be able to play all the instruments of the instrumental ensemble, but is expected to have a working knowledge of what the sonorities of the various families are, some of the vocabulary that speaks to the players, and what it is like to sit in an orchestra or a wind ensemble is ideal. One gains enormous sympathy for the cymbal player that counts many measures and plays one crash, for example, or the flutist who is expected to play very high and very softly with excellent intonation, or for the brass player who is constantly admonished to play softer. Some knowledge of string techniques is very helpful, but most concertmasters will be happy to assist with bowings and with articulations that are appropriate for the conductor's performance ideas. Remember that phrasing is transmitted through the bowings. The concertmaster will be greatly helped if you have a solid idea ahead of time of the phrase lengths and the stylistic expression of the work.

  The ability to demonstrate is important, and it should be noted that the more inexperienced the musicians are, the greater the need for frequent demonstration and for "coaching" the musicians.

- A well-grounded knowledge of formal analysis and the definition of phrases. This is the means by which the piece is brought to life. Without an excellent background in harmony, counterpoint and analysis, the conductor is compromised. (See Lawson and Stowell, *The Historical Performance of Music: An Introduction* in the bibliography.)

- Control of tempo. Robert Shaw's example would certainly support the idea that setting a proper tempo is one of the most important things a competent conductor should do. Work at this carefully and consistently. A metronome is an invaluable aid. Tempo changes must be intentional.

- A conducting technique that supports the musicians and works effectively to bring the composer's ideas into being. Conductors assume that the instrumentalists need from the conductor, first and foremost, a clear beat. Clarity is certainly important, but linked to the conducting gesture itself is the whole idea of podium presence. A conductor must convincingly convey eloquence, passion, ideas, dynamics and the imaginings which have resulted from study. The conductor is respectful of all the musicians, and his or her passion and love for the music and for the process of bringing it to life must come through the conducting gesture. Different people have different ways of accomplishing all of this, but the successful conductors have much in common: love for what they do and care and concern for the musicians and the composer are their prime concerns.
- A cultivated imagination. A conductor best encourages the musicians' creativity by presenting imaginative ideas, and by being well-informed, competent and well-prepared. The conductor, who is in the position of encouraging musicians to express themselves through the composer, can help the individual musician in that expression by providing well-prepared and thoughtful guidance.

Biography

Ann Howard Jones, Professor of Music and Director of Choral Activities at Boston University, where she is an award-winning teacher, conducts the Boston University Symphonic Chorus and Chamber Chorus, administers the Master of Music and Doctor of Musical Arts degrees in choral conducting and teaches advanced choral conducting.

Recognized for her expertise in conducting technique, choral and vocal pedagogy, rehearsal procedures and performance practice, Dr. Jones has recently appeared as guest lecturer for the American Choral Directors Association Division and National Conventions, the American Guild of Organists Region I Convention, the Long Island Choral Festival, the Tennessee Arts Academy, on the summer session faculty in the Central Connecticut State University's graduate music program and at Westminster Choir College. She was invited to deliver presentations at the national convention of the Music Educators National Conference and to lecture on rehearsal techniques at the International Federation of Choral Music Symposium. She has been a guest faculty member at the University of Missouri, Miami University, Drake University, San Diego State University, the University of Missouri at Kansas City, Michigan State University, and the University of North Texas. Dr. Jones has also conducted the Mormon Tabernacle Choir in live broadcasts. In 2003, she delivered a lecture on score preparation for a Professional Training Workshop at Carnegie Hall, and the following year she was invited to prepare the chorus for Charles Dutoit's performance of Stravinsky, Poulenc, and Fauré at Carnegie Hall. She was invited by Chorus America to lead a workshop for conductors of Children's Choruses on the campus of Northwestern University and in SanFrancisco with the San Francisco Girls Chorus, and she was invited to lecture on vocal technique in the choral rehearsal at Juilliard in the summer of 2005. She has served on panels for the Chorus America National Convention in Washington, D.C. and for the Conductors Guild.

Equally acclaimed as a conductor, her guest conducting appearances have included many All-State, district, regional and festival choruses. Dr. Jones is conductor of the Boston University Tanglewood Institute Young Artists Choruses, a summer program for high school musicians.

Dr. Jones was Assistant Conductor for Choruses with the Atlanta Symphony Orchestra from 1984–1998 where she was closely associated with the late Robert Shaw, Music Director Emeritus and Conductor Laureate. She was the first Conductor of the Atlanta Symphony Youth Chorus. She served as Musical Assistant with the Robert Shaw Chamber Singers and Festival Singers, whose performances led to numerous recordings on TELARC and critical acclaim at Carnegie Hall. As one of the organizers of the Robert Shaw Institute, she assisted Mr. Shaw in the musical preparations for the Institute, which rehearsed, performed and recorded in France from 1988–1994.

Dr. Jones' degrees are from the University of Iowa. She has been a member of the faculty at the Universities of Iowa, Georgia, and Illinois, and at Wittenberg and Emory Universities. While a Fulbright Senior Lecturer in Brazil, she consulted in the development of a university choral program and taught choral and vocal pedagogy.

Bibliography

Adler, Samuel. *The Study of Orchestration.* Third edition. New York: W. W. Norton & Company, 2002.

Battisti, Frank, and Robert Garofalo. *Guide to Score Study for the Wind Band Conductor.* Galesville, Maryland: Meredith Music Publications, 1990.

Blocker, Robert, ed. *The Robert Shaw Reader.* New Haven, Connecticut: Yale University Press, 2004.

Buchanan, Heather J., and Matthew W. Mehaffey, eds. *Teaching Music through Performance in Choir.* Volumes 1 and 2. Chicago: GIA Publications, Inc., 2005.

Cadwallader, Allen, and David Gagné. *Analysis of Tonal Music: A Schenkerian Approach.* New York: Oxford University Press, 1998.

Ciardi, John. *How does a Poem Mean?* Boston: The Riverside Press, 1959.

Daniels, David. *Orchestral Music: A Handbook.* Fourth edition. Lanham, Maryland: Scarecrow Press, 2005.

Decker, Harold A., and Julius Herford, eds. *Choral Conducting Symposium.* Second ed. Englewood Cliffs, New Jersey: Prentice Hall, 1973.

Demaree, Robert W., Jr., and Don V Moses. *The Complete Conductor: A Comprehensive Resource for the Professional Conductor of the Twenty-First Century.* Englewood Cliffs, New Jersey: Prentice Hall, 1995.

Glenn, Carole, ed. *In Quest of Answers: Interviews with American Choral Conductors.* Chapel Hill, North Carolina: Hinshaw Music, Inc., 1991.

Green, Jonathan D. *A Conductor's Guide to Choral-Orchestral Works.* Metuchen, New Jersey: Scarecrow Press, 1994.

Hansen, Sharon. *Helmuth Rilling: Conductor-Teacher.* Dayton, Ohio: Roger Dean Publishing Company, 1997.

Jeffers, Ron. *Translations and Annotations of Choral Repertoire: Volume I, Sacred Latin Texts.* Corvallis, Oregon: Earthsongs, 1988.

Jeffers, Ron and Gordon Paine. *Translations and Annotations of Choral Repertoire: Volume II, German Texts.* Corvallis, Oregon: Earthsongs, 2000.

Lawson, Colin, and Robin Stowell. *The Historical Performance of Music: An Introduction.* Cambridge: Cambridge University Press, 1999.

Mussulman, Joseph A. *Dear People . . . Robert Shaw.* Bloomington, Indiana: Indiana University Press, 1979.

Neuen, Donald. *Choral Concepts.* Belmont, California: Schirmer/Thomson Learning, 2002.

Rudolph, Max. *The Grammar of Conducting: A Practical Study of Modern Baton Technique.* Second ed. New York: G. Schirmer, 1980.

Schuller, Gunther. *The Compleat Conductor.* Oxford: Oxford University Press, 1997.

Wall, Joan. *International Phonetic Alphabet for Singers: A Manual for English and Foreign Language Diction.* Redmond, Washington: Caldwell Publishing, 1989.

Wall, Joan, et al. *Diction for Singers: A Concise Reference for English, Italian, Latin, German, French and Spanish Pronunciation.* Redmond, Washington: Caldwell Publishing, 1990.

Webb, Guy B., ed. *Up Front! Becoming the Complete Choral Conductor.* Boston: ECS Publishing, 1993.

NOTES

1 I once advised a group of conductors to keep a record of all the works sung in a given year, and to do that over a period of years just to see which works were repeated, which works appeared once and never again, and which works were never performed again. This is a useful way to track a commitment and a responsibility to the music of the past, to the very music that has laid a foundation for the music of the future.

2 Bear in mind for rehearsal the technique learned from Robert Shaw called "count-singing" to hammer home the idea that the ensemble itself generates pulse, rhythm and tempo. Begin the work on a piece by sight reading "on the numbers," as he used to say—no text, no dynamics—just rhythm. The chorus member, ably guided to sing the correct pitches by a remarkably accurate accompanist who always played along quietly, sang the pulse and its division from the beginning to the end of a work many times until the rhythmic motion was secure. Only after rhythm was well established and sung exactly were text and dynamics added. As we used the system, and I must admit we modified and adjusted it as we went along, we learned to add the final consonants in rhythm while we counted. This proved a very helpful time-saving device as we rarely had to rehearse final consonants once we added text. (There is an illustration on p. 89–90 of the Blocker book.)

Quoting from Mr. Shaw, count singing establishes the following:

> l. There is absolutely no doubt as to the instant—the beat of its fraction—on which sound is supposed to begin.
>
> 2. There can be absolute certainty as to the instant upon which sound is supposed to stop—upon which silence (rest value) is supposed to begin.
>
> 3. Because each pitch is articulated for as many pulse divisions as its duration specifies (a whole note will have usually eight eighth-note phonations), the pitch itself is defined eight times per measure—which is the world's greatest aid to intonation.
>
> 4. Since, in two-, four- or more, part writing, pitches may be of varying length in the different voices, count-singing on the pulse divisions aligns all counterpoint in meticulous detail, and allows harmonic changes to be precise and apparent to all.
>
> 5. Since problems of crescendo and diminuendo are problems of amount and timing (of "how much" or "how little," "how rapidly" or "where") the sung eighth- or sixteenth-note pulse offers the only convenient time-scale by which to measure increase or decrease of sonority.

> 6. The alternations of English vowels "uh, ee, oo, oo-uh" (as in "one, two, three, four") give a range of vowel sounds wide enough to avoid tiring the voice (unless done to psychotic excess), and wide enough, more importantly, to stimulate a continuity of tonal core (vocal color, vocal line) through changing pitches and vocal ranges. . . . (Blocker, pp. 89–90)

> [Count singing] forces the common perception of Pitch and Duration; and thus is the principal means to the clarification of counterpoint and harmony. It facilitates the control of Dynamics and Articulation—and thereby, expressivity. It feeds variety of vowel and successive redefining of pitch into vocal line, and thus reinforces tonal qualities. And—when merged gradually with text qualities and word disciplines—it finally teaches people to sing together the text from which the composer drew his inspiration. (Blocker, p. 90).

Of course there are variations of the principles of count singing. A neutral syllable can be chosen to articulate rhythms ("doo" or "noo" are my preferences, depending on style) or one can tap while singing, but in my experience nothing works quite as well as counting.

After everyone count-sings several times through the score, then it can be alternated with text, or half of the chorus can sing text while the other half counts (and the counting should dominate). Here, two principles are paramount: consonants must be executed ahead of the beat, quickly and with precision; and the vowel sound must arrive on the beat. Count-singing in the background of rehearsal of text can help those principles become firmly established.

One of the first works I sang with Mr. Shaw and the Atlanta Symphony Chorus was the Berlioz Requiem. We rehearsed the *a cappella* section of the work, "Quaerens me," without the text until the week of the performance! The problems that resulted when the words were added were significant, despite the rhythmic security of that large chorus and the precision of the execution of the pitches. It took several repetitions before we could pronounce text with quick consonants ahead of the beat without accent or disruption of the vowel while still retaining the style of the one movement of the work that is for chorus alone.

In my own experience, I have found that there is the rarest piece that cannot profit from the stabilization of pulse and the unifying of rhythmic impulse that count-singing can provide. Sometimes singers are slow to come to the realization that count-singing is a benefit to them, but they can be persuaded and the music will be the better for it. I use the technique in almost every rehearsal and find that it solves more problems than it creates—even if the singers don't love every minute of it! However, it does tax my own patience. I want the ensemble to pass through this stage quickly and get on to the text. But, I have found if I rush this part of the process, I almost always regret it. Count-singing, because of its rhythmic reinforcement, becomes one of the basic disciplines that I come back to again and again as a foundation from which the rest of the music can be built.

3 For the conductor who might need a review of tonal analysis, see Kostka and Payne *Tonal Harmony: With an Introduction to Twentieth-Century Music*, McGraw Hill, 2003.

4 I usually do not mark all the way through the music the first time I am analyzing form. If I change my mind, the marking can be difficult to alter and the erasures can get messy.

5 Some are clever enough to use the computer for all of this, as was the case with Boston University doctoral student Timothy Westerhaus, who assisted me with this project. Note that these graphs are not a "reproduction" of the score, but a visual representation.

6 For an in-depth look at Bach *basso continuo* practice, see Lawrence Dreyfus. *Bach's Continuo Group: Players and Practices in His Vocal Works*. Cambridge, Massachusetts: Harvard University Press, 1987.

7 Balance problems may be solved in a variety of ways. For example, where voices cross, consider what will be required to keep the high voices from protruding unintentionally. Sometimes a voice ventures into a range that is less than optimal and that will require some adjustment to keep the parts balanced. Shaw believed that there are more effective ways to achieve balance than simply by telling one part to sing louder and another to sing softer. Mr. Shaw always numbered the singers in his choruses from the lowest voice of each section to the highest. The basses, for example, would be numbered from 101 up, with the higher number indicated not only the highest voice in the bass section, but the total number of singers in the section. The tenors' numbers would start with 201 and go up, the altos 301 and the sopranos 401. When a balance problem occurred, the voices whose numbers were the closest to the part that needed reinforcing would be added to strengthen the part. Similarly, nearby voices could be subtracted. In this way, Mr. Shaw balanced by numbers, and the choral scores he edited are full of arrows suggesting that a specific number of singers move up or down to attempt to achieve better balance.

8 The *Robert Shaw Reader*, includes some of the diagrams used by Mr. Shaw for the Bach Mass in B Minor (pp. 124–125), the Berlioz Requiem (pp. 189 and 203), the Britten *War Requiem* (p. 238), Handel's *Messiah* (pp. 281–282), Mendelssohn's *Elijah* (p. 303) and Stravinsky's *Symphony of Psalms* (p. 320).

9 See Joan Wall, *International Phonetic Alphabet for Singers: A Manual for English and Foreign Language Diction and Diction for Singers: A Concise Reference for English, Italian, Latin, German, French and Spanish Pronunciation.*

Must We Sing of Women Only as Men Have Sung?

Joan Catoni Conlon

Some choral texts feature women as targets of violence. Women, of course, have rarely been the authors of such texts. Perhaps composers ought to know more poetry by women.

All works of art are products of the time in which they were created, so not all choral texts reflect the sensibilities of our own century. Some sentiments remain the same; some are different. Each generation understands love, caress, flirtation, beauty, devotion, and honor. Each generation does not need to dwell on assault, abuse, maltreatment, exploitation or objectification of women. Today's conductors should confront the magnitude of some of the damaging texts that we frequently program, and address the issues raised by such texts. The conductor who selects questionable texts should devise a *modus operandi* for interpreting them with singers or audience to place the texts into cultural or historical setting.

Most famous poets throughout history have been men, just as most famous composers have been men. Primarily male poets have authored the misogynous texts we sing. This essay seeks to discover and listen to the missing voices of women poets—poets whose works are missing from the choral canon. Further, the essay presents poetry and sources of poetry by women poets, mainly from the Renaissance, since the artistic flowering of that era influenced musical and poetic gestures in following centuries. That era, which established patterns and standards of artistic expression, offers a rich body of texts, of affirmative repositories by women that should be explored by modern composers.

The Prominent Male Voice

Why are women's voices missing? Are those unheard texts written by women equal in quality and similar in subject matter to those we know? Will the same sentiments be expressed, or will they be different? Would those poems by women have offered to the early composer equal opportunity for pictorial madrigalisms, for example? For affective musical gesture? Would women's poems include contrasting imagery to stimulate the composers' imagination? If Italian Renaissance male composers had noticed the poetry of their women contemporaries, would their music have sounded the same as their settings of poems of their contemporary male poets? Were poems by Vittoria Colonna (1490–1557)—an acquaintance of Michelangelo, Veronica Gambara (1485–1550), Gaspara Stampa (1523–1553), Chiara Matraini (1514–1597), Laura Terracina (1519–1577), Isabella Di Morra (1520–1546), Veronica Franco (1546–1591), or Modesta dal Pozzo (1555–1592), the artistic and technical equivalents of Livio Celiano, Filippo Alberti, Scipione Agnelli, Ercole Bentivoglio, Antonio Allegretti, or Girolamo Casoni?

Women's poetry probably was dismissed because it was assumed to be one-dimensional, due to a woman's limited life experience. Since women poets were encouraged by society to write only on certain acceptable subjects, would the scope of their poems also be limited? The answer is a resounding, "*No.*" Women poets clearly understood very well that poetry is the interaction between meaning, rhythm and sound. They understood how vocabulary energizes verse and how energy and rhythm are co-dependent. But, historically, poetry by women simply has not been sought out, examined, or set to music.

In poems by men, women's expression is limited mainly to love, longing, lamenting and loss. By contrast, in early poems by women, as will be seen below, the authors speak earnestly, expressively, and with sophistication on many subjects. Early women's poems cover a wide array of topics. Although their worlds may have been circumscribed, their thoughts were free to express nuanced observations on their lives, their loves, their culture, and their social milieu.

Choral Music for Mixed Voices: No Women Allowed

Historically, sacred music in earlier centuries was performed only by men, or by men and boys. Following the directive of St. Paul, women were to be silent in church. Cloistered nuns sang for themselves, as did cloistered men in the monastic tradition. If nuns performed publicly, they sang behind screens; never were they both seen and heard. In the mid-eighteenth century in Germany, female sopranos began to sing publicly in some cathedrals, and to sing in concerts of sacred music held not in churches but in civic halls. Paintings of the Venetian *ospedali* from the time of Vivaldi show young women performing in full view of the audience, but at a distance from their listeners.[1]

The all-male ensemble was not limited only to sacred music, however. Scholars reveal that all-male ensembles frequently performed secular music and that men sang SATB repertoire.[2] Most certainly, some secular texts seem intended for men singers rather than women, such as texts that celebrate male virility. Doubtless, no educated woman, no woman taught how to read music, no woman with a sense of propriety would likely sing or be physically able to accomplish what is said in the words of di Lasso's *Matona mia cara*: "mi ficcar tutta notte / Urtar, urtar . . ." Likewise, in later centuries, the explicit texts in rowdy rounds by Purcell and Mozart suggest performance by male ensembles.

Whereas women traditionally were sheltered from pursuing such studies as politics, science, or mathematics, women could pursue the study of the fine arts, painting, music and poetry. The extraordinary and wealthy woman could become significant patrons of the arts.[3] Isabella d'Este and Elisabetta Gonzaga, two of the most notable women patrons of the Italian Renaissance, who were admired in court, supported a remarkable group of artists in the plastic and graphic arts, in music, and in poetry and literature.[4] These women, wealthy, highly influential, literate, and knowledgeable about the fine arts, have been in an unusually small minority throughout history, however. Many wealthy and literate women came from commercial middle and upper classes, and had neither contact with the fine arts nor interest in supporting them.[5] The Gonzaga and Este women simply were extraordinary in their support of the arts.

Treatment of Women in Music

Guilty? Off with their heads!

In her book, *Feminine Endings: Music, Gender and Sexuality*,[6] Susan McClary discusses how throughout music history women typically have been treated, or maltreated, as lesser beings than men. She points out that in Monteverdi's 1607 opera *Orfeo*, Euridice, pondering life without Orfeo, sings a passage that has lost completely its harmonic grounding. The chord progressions sound like a series of unrelated chords, portraying that without Orfeo poor Euridice is lost.

But at least the besotted Euridice has been faithful to Orfeo, so she escapes being murdered on stage. Unfaithful women in the history of opera have faced far worse fates. McClary cites unfaithful women in opera plots who are murdered, such as Lulu and Carmen. They are, after all, fallen women, so the proper bourgeois audience response to their murders would be that the women had it coming to them.[7] Berg's opera *Wozzek* closes with an equally unhappy fate for the heroine.[8] In real life and in earlier centuries, two very real unfaithful wives also were killed by their musician husbands. Composers Don Carlo Gesualdo da Venosa (c. 1561–1613) and Bartolomeo Tromboncino (c. 1470–1535) each escaped punishment for the crime of murdering his unfaithful wife.

Interestingly, the theme of murdering a woman who challenged norms of decency persists beyond musical settings. In earlier decades of American film, the unfaithful woman frequently suffered the deadly fate of Carmen and Lulu; she routinely died at the end of the film.[9] For fallen women who did not die, there existed the alternative death through censorship. Characters portrayed by the popular icon Mae West, for example, escaped the fate of Carmen and Lulu, but Mae West's films were routinely censored by the Production Code Administration.[10]

In addition to film and the operatic stage, certain popular texts in choral music actually glorify the use of force against women. One finds evidence of texts of oppression and of celebrating in song the abuse or punishment of women. Why do choirs sing words that reinforce such behavior? Does the passion inherent in profound musical expression, composed in most cases by men, excuse such acts? To whom do such texts speak? If a woman's destiny rests not only in the hands of her man, where are the musical settings of texts that celebrate a woman's agency?

Unfaithful women are not the only women to suffer in literature or in song. Certainly, faithful women in literature also died at the hands of those who "loved" them, long before male composers began setting murderous texts to music. Furthermore, musical settings are rife with faithful women abandoned and left to die, in both early and late music. Otello kills Desdemona in a jealous rage. Theseus leaves Ariadne for dead in Ottavio Rinuccini's *Lamento d'Arianna* (see Monteverdi's Book 6). In Torquato Tasso's epic *Gerusalemme liberata*, Rinaldo abandons Armida to certain death.[11]

Yet another faithful woman dies in Tasso's *Gerusalemme liberata* when Tancredi mistakenly slays his beloved Clorinda in battle during Holy War,[12] as in later centuries the unlucky jester Rigoletto mistakenly slays his beloved and only daughter Gilda. Is this mere tragic titillation? Other interpretations are possible, and one woman poet described the killing of Clorinda quite differently.

Petronilla Paolini Massimi (1663–1726) writes the following poem about the Saracen Clorinda, much loved by Tancredi, but killed by Tancredi while she is disguised in her battle armor. In Massimi's poem, Clorinda is described as preferring the taking up of military arms to more feminine roles. Massimi's perception of Clorinda is important because it differs radically from Tasso's narration, written a century earlier. If a male composer ever thought to set Massimi's thoughtful story of Clorinda's death, no finished product has survived. In Massimi's seventeenth-century poem, Clorinda slain by her beloved becomes a metaphor for woman oppressed by man.[13]

Sdenga Clorinda a i femminili uffici	To female duties Clorinda scorned to turn
chinar la destra, e sotta l'elmo accoglie	her hand, and beneath her helmet gathered
i biondi crini e con guerrieri voglie	her blond tresses and with warlike arms
fa del proprio valor pompa a i nemici.	herself displayed her worth to enemies.
Così gli alti natali e i lieti auspici	Likewise for lofty birth and joyful auspices,
e gli aur'ei tetti e le regali spoglie	for golden palaces and royal regalia
nulla curando, Amalasunta coglie	caring no whit, Amalasuntha won
de' fecondi Licei lauri felici.	felicitous laurels from Athens' fruitful schools.
Mente capace d'ogni nobil cura	A mind apt for every noble care
ha il nostra sesso: or qual potente inganno	our sex possesses: so what mighty fraud
dall'imprese d'onor l'alme ne fura?	diverts our souls from deeds of honor?
So ben che i fati a noi guerra non fanno,	I well know the fates war not with us,
Né i suoi doni contende a noi natura:	nor does Nature to us deny her gifts:
sol del nostro valor l'uomore é tiranno.	the sole oppressor of our worth is man.[14]
	(Translation by Muriel Kittel)

Words We Actually Sing in Choral Music

Suitors always have known the persuasive powers of carefully crafted poetry to win the heart of the beloved. In early musical settings, virtuous women were extolled. And the seducing males who penned the eloquent poems to seduce women, aren't they were equally venerated? Such compelling, graphic and powerfully amorous pleadings are spoken to a willing listener who succumbs to love in Heinrich Isaac's setting of *Donna di dentro*.

Donna, di dentro dalla tua casa	Lady, within your house,
son rose, gigli e fiori. . . .	are roses, lilies and many flowers. . . .
Dammi una rosa.	Give me a rose.
"Totela, o perla pretiosa."	"Take it! . . ."[15]

In Josquin's *Bergerette Savoysienne*, the seducer indicates he will not take "No" for an answer.

Bergerette savoysienne,	Little Savoyard shepherdess . . .
Qui gardes moutons aux praz,	
Dy moy si vieulx estre myenne:	tell me if you will be mine;
Je te donray uns soulas,	I will give you great fun,
Et ung petit chapperon;	and a small bonnet;
Dy moy se tu m'aymeras	Tell me whether you will love me,
Oupar le merande ou non.	whether it is deserved or not.
Je suis la proche voisine	I know the nearby priest very well
De monsieur le cura,	
Et pour chose qu'on me die	and, whatever I am told,
Mon vouloir ne changera . . .	you will not change my wish . . .[16]

Gilles Joye (c. 1424–1483), who wrote *ballatas* and *rondeaux*, is forthright in his intention to seduce and, by quoting the Old Testament, even promises forgiveness of the fallen women's sins by an authority greater than himself. That authority increases because the poet speaks both in French and in Latin, the language of authority.

Ce qu'on fait a quatimini	What is done behind closed doors
Touchant multiplicamini	about increasing and multiplying,
Mais qu'il soit bien tenu secré	if it really is kept secret,
Sera tenu pour excusé	will be forgiven by the Almighty.
In conspectus Altissimi.	
Et pourtant operamini	And so get to work,
Mes filles, et letatimini	my lasses, and be joyful,
Car jamais il n'est revelé.	because no one will know.
Et se vous engrossemini	And if you become pregnant . . .
Soit in nomine Domini . . .	
Vous avés a proufit ouvré	you still will have something
Qui vous sera tout pardonné	for all your suffering,
	which will be completely forgiven
Mais que vous confitemini.	if you but confess.[17]

In *The Ballad of Little Musgrave and Lady Barnard* (anonymous author, *Oxford Book of Ballads* and famously set by Benjamin Britten), Lord Barnard kills his unfaithful wife, whom he finds lying with her footman, Little Musgrave. The deaths of both Lady Barnard and Clorinda may be accidental killings in the contexts of the ballad and epic from which they are excerpted, but these slayings are not unique in the literature. With the exception of the biblical Judith who leads her people after slaying the evil Holofernes, there are not many equivalent poetic settings by male composers in which the male is killed and the woman survives.

If misogyny is defined as distrust of or hatred of women, examples certainly occur in both the classics and in popular genres as well. For example, in performances of Handel's oratorio *Samson*, conductors sometimes omit the bipartite chorus (No. 55):

To man God's universal law
Gave pow'r to keep his wife in awe.
Thus shall his life be ne'er dismay'd
By female usurpation sway'd.

Such language, of course, simply reflects biblical precedent:

I permit no woman to teach or to have authority over a man.
(Timothy 2:12)[18]

Offenbach's "The Neighbors' Chorus," popular today with high school choruses, exalts prurient gossip about a misbehaving gentlewoman. Unfortunately, the neighbors enjoy too much the gory details when asking, "Did you beat her, try to choke her? and knock her all about?"

Please excuse us, mister, we don't want to bother, we only want to know.
All of us are neighbors, so were very curious, why do you look so low?
Give us all the lowdown, Did you reach a show-down with your last lady love?
. . .
Did she keep you waiting, did she break your date?
Please elucidate, please elaborate.
Did she treat you badly, was she very bad?
Did she make you mad? Are you very sad?
Was she a very rich man's daughter
who showed that she was not all you thought her?
When with your songs of love you sought her,
were you dowsed with water poured down from above?

Did you beat her, try to choke her till you made her pout?
Did her father take a poker, did he throw you out?
Did you beat her and choke her and knock her all about?[19]

The biblical story of the assault upon Susanna by two elders has intrigued composers from the time of Lassus[20] in the Renaissance to Dominick Argento in the twentieth century. In some early settings of the story, Susanna takes her life rather than succumb to the assault. Such a suicide was sanctioned by St. Jerome, who said:

> In persecutions, it is not lawful to commit suicide except when one's chastity is jeopardized.[21]

In other tellings of the story, Susanna does not submit. Rather, she is praised for her stoic refusal to yield to the elders who threaten to accuse her of adultery if she does not surrender. The innocent Susanna is defended by Daniel, and the perpetrators are stoned to death. In his acclaimed composition for choir and piano, *Peter Quince at the Clavier*, Argento sets Wallace Stevens's poem about Susanna's beauty, her singing, her bathing, her attracting the attention of the elders, and their attempted assault upon her. In the Stevens poem, the elder perpetrators flee "with a noise like tambourines." In Stevens's final stanzas, the body dies, the garden dies, and maidens die, but Susanna's immortal music "plays on the clear viol of her memory, / And makes a constant sacrament of praise." Both the poem and Argento's evocative setting immortalize Susanna, her loveliness, her strength, and the beauty of her music.[22]

French chansons such as *Au joly jeu* and *Margot labourez les vigne* salute the conquest of woman and treat that conquest as a game.[23]

Au joli jeu du pousse avant	How pleasant to play the game
Il fait bon jouer.	of getting it in!
L'autrier m'aloie ébaloier,	The other day, when I was looking for
Je rencontrai la belle au corps gent,	amusement, I met a comely maiden.
Souriant doucement, la voix baiser.	Smiling sweetly, I tried to kiss her.
Elle en fait doute,	She objects,
Mais je la boute.	But I press onward, saying,
Laissez, laissez, laissez, trut avant,	Let yourself go, let yourself go, come on!
Laissez, laissez, trut avant,	Let yourself go, let yourself go, come on!
Au joli jeu du pousse avant	How pleasant to play the game
Il fait bon jouer.	of getting it in!
Pour un refus me faut laisser	When she refused, I should have let her go,
Propos lui tiens amoureusement,	but I held her closely, and
Souriant doucement, la voix baiser,	Smiling sweetly, tried to kiss her.

Elle riotte	What a fuss she makes,
Dance sans notte.	wriggling around.
Au joli jeu du pousse avant.	How pleasant to play the game of getting it in!

In *Margot labourez les vignes*, the lonely and unhandsome Margot is outnumbered by three captains who will force her to "forfeit":

Margot labourez les vignes,	Margot, go to work in the vineyards,
Vignes, vignes, vignolet.	
Margot labourez les vignes,	Margot, go to work in the vineyards
Bientôt.	Early.
En revenant de Lorraine, Margot,	Coming back from Lorraine,
Rencontrai troi capitaines.	I met three captains,
Ils m'ont salue vilaine, Margot,	They called out "homely maiden"
Je sui leu fièvre quartaine	and shunned me like the plague.
Ils m'ont donné pour ètranne,Margot,	They gave me, to gain my favor,
Un bouquet de marjolaine.	A bouquet of marjoram.
S'il fleurit je serai reine,	If it flowers, I'll be queen,
S'il y meurt je perds ma peine.	And if it dies, I'll have to forfeit.[24]

In *Il est bel et bon*, husband might be wife beater.

Il est bel et bon,	"He is handsome and kind,
Commère, mon mari.	My dear, is my husband."
Il etait duex femmes	There were two women talking,
Toute d'un pays,	both from the same village.
Disant l'une à l'autre:	Said one to the other,
Avez bon mari?	"Do you have a good husband?"
Il ne me courrouce	"He never angers me,
Ne me bat aussi,	Nor does he beat me,
Il fait le mènage;	He does the housework,
Il donne aux poulailles,	He feeds the chickens,
Et je prends mes plaisirs.	While I enjoy myself.
Commère c'est pour rire,	My dear, it makes me laugh
Quand les poulailles crient:	When the chickens squawk:
Co co co co co co dac	*Co co co co co co dac*
"Petite coquette, qu'estce ci?"	'Oh, little chickie, what's the matter?'
Il est bel et bon,	He is handsome and kind,
Commère, mon mari.	My dear, is my husband."

Author Gender in Choral Music Texts: The Missing Voice

Women poets wrote during the Middle Ages and Renaissance; women poets doubtless have existed for as long as women have been literate. Yet, women's voices have never been heard as often in musical settings, and their works are curiously absent from most anthologies. Women composers may have been inclined to set poetry by women, but until recently, male composers rarely have set that poetry to music.[25]

Today, women's poetry certainly is more difficult to locate than poems by men. Womens' poetry was neither reprinted nor anthologized regularly, while writings by men consistently have been more often preserved than those by women. Fortunately, recently published poetry collections tend to include more poetry by women.

Writing poetry has hardly been considered a radical activity for women. In fact, poetry historically was considered a safe field of study for educated women, unlike other studies. Leonardo Bruni expressed the popular view to Battista Malatesta in Verona in 1443 that "public proficiency in advanced studies is indecorous for women," and that rhetoric should not be pursued by women at all, "for if a woman throws her arms around while speaking, or if she increases the volume of her speech with greater forcefulness, she will appear threatening, insane, and requiring restraint."[26] Deprived of other intellectual pursuits, many schooled women wrote poetry, and their poems and their essays often give valuable insight into their lives and into their families' expectations. The early women poets' voices speak a multitude of ideas, some of resisting, some of embracing, traditional womanly roles. The rich palette of women's worldly observations explores, for example, modesty and vulnerability; arranged marriage; a longing for love; unhappiness in a convent; equality among lovers; oppression; writing, spinning and weaving (endeavors women could respectably pursue); jealous men; freedom; and, occasionally, passionate defenses of good women who were scorned, unappreciated, or punished.

The Case of Italy: Alternative Voices

Italian culture has fostered a particularly strong bond between literate women and poetry. The reader of early Italian women's poetry need not suspend aesthetic judgment. These poems resemble in quality those written by their male counterparts. The vocabulary in both is rich and subtle; both make abundant use of symbolism, imagery and metaphor. Rhyme schemes in both follow traditional patterns, and the Italian poets observe the expected sette-syllabic (seven syllable) and hendecasyllabic (eleven syllable) verse lengths. But the subjects about which women wrote, or did not write, sometimes differed markedly from men. The array of subjects yields insights into a literate woman's life in Renaissance Italy, or France, or Germany. Few women poets, for example, celebrate their amorous bravado, as male poets frequently boast.

Both genders of poets lament unrequited love. But not all women speak confidently of their destiny being in their own hands. Some voices, as in the poem by Laura Terracina below, apologize for their meager artistic efforts. This apologetic tone was considered proper for a suitably modest woman author. Male poets and composers typically adopt such an apologetic tone when submitting a volume of works to a dedicatee. Nevertheless, as will be seen below, some women poets stray from the approved poetic subjects of family, sentiment, love, the eternally feminine, and religion.[27]

An anonymous thirteenth-century Italian poet laments the marriage her father has arranged to a man other than the man she loves. The structure of the poem is notable for the change from bright to covered vowel colors as she details the reasons for her grief, and for the return of the opening thoughts at the poem's conclusion.

A la stagion che'l mondo foglia e fiora	In the season when the world's in leaf and flower
acresce gioia a tuti fin' amanti:	the joy of all true lovers waxes strong:
vanno insieme a li giardini alora	in pairs the go to gardens at the hour
che gli auscelletti fanno dolzi canti;	when little birds are singing their sweet song;
la franca gente tutta s'inamora,	All gentle folk now come beneath love's power,
e di servir ciascun trages' inanti,	and the service of his love is each man's care,
ed ogni damigella in gioia dimora;	while every maid in gladness spends her hours;
e me, n'abondan marimenti e pianti.	but I am filled with weeping and despair.
Ca lo mio padre m'ha messa 'n errore,	For my father has treated me most ill
e tenemi sovente in forte doglia:	and keeps me often in the sorest anguish:
donar mi vole a mia forze segnore,	he would give me to a lord against my will,
ed io di ciò non ho disio né voglia,	And this I neither do desire nor wish,

e 'n gran tormento vivo a tutte l'ore;	and every hour I pass in sharpest grief;
però mi relagra fior nè foglia.	and so receive no joy from flower or leaf.
	(Translated by Muriel Kittel[28])

Even the earliest of the women writers lament their culture's low expectations of women, no matter how well born. The poet Modesta dal Pozzo (1555–1592) in her poem "Women's Worth," laments that as a girl she was not challenged as a boy was challenged. Had she been equally challenged, her accomplishments would be greater, and she, her life, and her work would be more valued.

Il Merito della Donne	Woman's Worth
Le donne in ogni età fur da Natura	Women in every age by Nature were
Di gran giudicio e d'animo dotate,	With sound judgment and brave hearts endowed
Nè men atte a mostrar con studio e cura	And no less fit to demonstrate with zeal
Senno e valor degli nomini son nate.	Men's wisdom, care, and worth, were born,
E perchè, se commune è la figura	And why then, if they bear a common stamp,
Se non son le sostanze variate,	If their substances be not different,
S'hanno simile un cibo e un parlar, denno	If they have one food, one speech alike,
Differente aver poi 'ardire e il senno?	Should they then differ in good sense and courage?
. . .	
Se quando nasce una figliuola al padre,	If, when a daughter to a father is born,
La ponesse col figlio a un'opra eguale,	He were to set her with his son to equal tasks,
Non saria nelle imprese alte e leggiadre	She would not in lofty enterprise or light
Al frate inferior nè disuguale;	Inferior or unequal to her brother be;
O la ponesse in fra le armate squadre	Or were he to place her in armed squadrons
Seco o a imparar qualch'arte liberate;	With him, or allow her to learn some liberal art;
Ma perchè in altri affar viene allevata,	But because she is reared to other things,
Per l'educazion poco è stimata.	Small esteem her education brings.[29]
	(Translated by Muriel Kittel)

Not all early Italian women writers felt powerless. In the fourteenth century, St. Catherine of Siena composed passionate, powerful and persuasive arguments that ultimately led to the return of the Papacy from Avignon.[30] Neither were all women of wealth only privately tutored. A very few sixteenth-century Florentine academies were open to both male and female students. Yet, the plight of most women is described by Laura Terracina (1519–1577), who wrote that her life as woman constantly put her at a disadvantage:

Commiato	Envoi to Poem to the Virgin
Qualunque sia che per caso o per forza	Whoever may by chance or of necessity
legga giammai questo mie incolte rime	read some day these uncouth lines of mine,
benchè é il giudicio lo sforza	though he may be compelled by honor and good sense
sì, che convien ch'assai poco le stime;	to consider them in rather low esteem,
pur lo pregh'io che non passi la scorza,	I beg that he probe not beneath the skin,
chè l'ignoranza mia dentro s'imprime:	because my ignorance makes its mark within:
e, se giovane, indotta, e donna io sono,	and if I am young, unlearned, and a woman,
nè principio nè fin posso aver buono.[40]	I can have no good beginning nor good end.
	(Translated by Muriel Kittel[32])

The Case of France: Alternative Voices

Some, but not all, poetry by early women does celebrate the approved themes of love, family, sentiment and loss. Long before women began asserting freedom in modern times, other voices claimed social independence from commonly-held mores. The Comtesse Beatrice de Die (twelfth century) even claimed a woman's prerogative to sexual pleasure.

Joan Kelly-Gadol claims that the Renaissance woman was worse off than her male counterpart and than her medieval predecessor because classical culture—reintroduced during the Renaissance—has "patriarchal and misogynous bias."[33] Women's sexuality became more regulated during the Renaissance, as were women's political and economic roles.[34] In the world of medieval courtly love, celebrants could separate love from marriage, and the married wealthy medieval woman had great power in life and in love in several ways. She had her own vassals to do her bidding, and her lover was her peer, not her master. If she had an inheritance on which her husband was dependent, her husband cared less about legitimacy of heir than about securing his tenure, as long as his wife was discreet.[35] The Comtesse de Die explains in the following forthright declaration of a medieval lady's freedom:

Bel amics, avinens e bos,	Handsome, charming, kind friend,
Cora us tenrai en mon poder?	Will you be within my power soon?
E que jagues ab vos un ser	I wish to lie beside you
E qu'ie.us des un bais amoros!	And lovingly embrace you!
Sapchatz, gran talen n'auria	Know ye this: I would give anything
Qu'ie.us tengues en luoc del marrit . . .	To have you in my husband's place . . .[36]

Later than the Comtesse de Die, a less powerful and more unhappy young woman sent to become a nun complains in an anonymous poem entitled, *Motet*:

Je sui joliete,	I am merry,
Sadete, pleisans,	Pretty, pleasing,
Joine pucelete:	A young maiden;
N'ai pas quinze ans,	Not quite fifteen;
Point mamalete	Little breasts swelling
Selonc le tans:	In keeping with the season:
Si deüsse aprendre	I should indeed be learning
D'amors et entendre	Of love, and discovering
Les samblans	Its charming
Deduisans;	Face.
Mès je sui mise en prison.	But I am put in prison.
De Diu ait maleïçon	God's curse on
Qui m'i mist!	Him who put me in this place!
Mal et vilanie	Evil and villainy
Et pechié fist	And sin did he
De tel pucelete	To send to a nunnery
Rendre en abiete.	Such a maid as I.
Trop i mefist, par ma foi;	I'faith, he did too great a wrong;
En religion vif en grant anoi;	In religion I live in misery,
Dieus! can trop sui jonete;	O God, for I am too young.
Je sens les doz maus desoz ma ceinturete:	I feel beneath my belt the sweet pain:
Honis soit de Diu qui me fist nonnete!	May God curse him who made me nun.
	(Translated by Muriel Kittel[37])

A more independent anonymous poet vows that two may play the game of infidelity in marriage in *Motet*:

Hé Dieus! je n'ai pas mari	My husband is not worthy of me,
Du tot a mon gré:	not suitable.
Il n'a cortoisie en li	He is not courteous,
Ne joliveté!	and he is not happy.
Jone dame est bien traïe,	They treat a young girl badly

Par la foi que doi a Dè,

Pour faire sa volenté;
Ce fu trop mal devisé.
De mari sui mal païe:
D'ami m'en amenderai,

Et si m'en savoit mal gré;
Mon mari, si face amie,
Car, voelle ou non, j'amerai!

when they give her such a churl,
and leave her at his mercy.
By my faith,
I know this is unfair.
Since I know my worth,
I shall even up the score
with another friend,
and so should he.
It must be so; . . .
my loving heart will have its way.
(After a translation by Patricia Terry[38])

Christine de Pisan (1364–1430) took exception to the descriptions of women handed down by the poet Ovid and by men of the Old Testament in her *L'Epistre au Dieu d'Amours* (Epistle to the God of Love).

En vers dient, Adam, David, Sanson,
Et Salemon et autre a foison
Furent deceuz par femme main et tart;
Et qui sera donc li home qui s'en gart?
Li autres die que moult sont decevables,
Cautilleuses, faulses et pou valables.
autres dient que trop sont mençongieres,
Variables, inconstans et legieres.
D'autres pluseurs grans vices les accusent
Et blasment moult, sanz qui riens les excusent
Et ainsi font clers et soir et matin,
Puis en français, leurs vers, puis en latin,
Et se fondent dessus ne sçay qualz livre
Qui plus dient de mençlonges qu'uns yvres.
Ovide en dit, en un livre qu'il fist,
Assez de maulz, dont je tiens qu'il meffist,
Quil appella le Remede d'amours,
Ou leur met sus moult de villaines mours,
Ordes, laides, pleines de villenie.
Que telz vices aient je le luy nye,
Au deffendre de bataille je gage

Adam, David, Samson, Solomon,
And myriad others say in verse
They were deceived by woman,
early and late:
What man, then, can protect himself?
Some say that many women are deceitful,
Wily, false, of little worth;
Others that too many are liars,
Fickle, flighty and inconstant;
Still others accuse them of great vices,
Blaming them much, excusing
them nothing.
Thus do the clerics, night and day,
First in French verse, then in Latin,
Based on who knows what books
That tell more lies than drunkards do.
Ovid, in a book he wrote and called,
"Love's Remedy" speaks of many faults,
But I believe he gravely erred.
He assigns to women base habits,
Makes them unclean, ugly, villainous.
I deny they have such vices;
In their defense I'll wage battle

Contre tous ceulz qui giter voldront gage;	With any who'll accept the challenge;
Voire, j'entens des femmes honnorables,	Of course, I mean honorable women;
En mes contes ne metz les non valables.	The unworthy have no place in my tales.
	(Translated by Sarah Spence[39])

As early a poet as Marie de Ventadour (c. 1222) engages in poetic dialogue on the topic of lover as an equal.

'Vuoill qe'm digatz si deu far egalmen	I want you to tell me if a lady should
Dompna per drut, can lo quier francamen,	Treat her lover as her equal, when he asks openly,
Cum el per lieis tot cant taing ad amor	As he does in all that pertains to love,
Segon los dreitz que tenon l'amador:	Under the law that lovers obey.
. . .	
'E respon vos de la dompna breumen	And I answer you, briefly, that the lady
Que per son drut deu far comunalmen	Should treat her lover as he does her,
Cum el per lieis ses garda de ricor:	Without any thought of wealth,
Qu'en dos amics non deu aver major.	For between two such friends there should be no master.
	(Translated by Joan M. Ferrante[40])

The Case of Germany: Alternative Voices

Of Renaissance sources regarding women, one of the most interesting was the 1595 debate in Germany between Valens Acidalius and Simon Gediccus, "Are Women Human?" Although this anonymous essay, entitled *Disputatio nova contra mulieres, qua probatur eas homines non esse*, actually was mere satire directed against the Anabaptists, the debate that ensued from the *Disputatio* lasted nearly two hundred years. The author of the satirical *Disputatio* contended that if the Anabaptists could believe that Christ and the Holy Spirit were not divine, then he, the author, could believe that women were not human. Unfortunately, the longevity of the debate greatly outlasted the author's original intention. Clearly, such writings and the resulting debate did nothing to improve regard for women.

Man, according to the *Disputatio*, was *causa efficiens*, woman merely *causa instrumentalis*. "If a smith forged a sword with the help of a hammer, the hammer remained his tool. It did not become a member of his body. Similarly, "woman did not become part of mankind when man used her to perpetuate the human race."[41]

Hildegard of Bingen (1098–1179) was only one strong woman artist whose writings survived in German cloisters. The devotional love poems written by Mechtild von Magdeburg (1210–1285) were tolerated because she was a nun writing for other women. Her writings, it was thought, could be excused as diary entries by a deranged nun.[42] Because her poems were thought to be highly erotic love poems to God, she at first was threatened with her manuscripts being confiscated. But she kept them within the confines of the cloister, where they were preserved by later generations of women. Mechtild, among her lengthier poems, also penned this passionate sacred couplet, entitled, *Wie Gott kummet in die Seele.*

Ich kumm zu meiner Lieben
Wie ein Tau auf die Blume.

Outside the cloister, secular women poets were persecuted. One, Annelein von Freiburg, was burned at the stake. Catholic men attacked Argula von Grumbach (1492–1554), whose poetry, written during the Reformation, supported the Protestant cause. Secular poets writing during the Renaissance were accused of "neglecting their household responsibilities," and of upsetting the "moral order of the universe."[43] A much later poet, Anna Ovena Hoyers (1584–1655), penned the following poem, written in a rather innocent, unaffected manner:

For the Christian Reader

Dieses Buch dürch eine Fraw bescheibn,	This book, by a woman writ,
Wird man gwiss darumb meht beliebn,	Is the better because of it.
Weiln dergleichen nie gesehn,	Because its like has ne'er been seen;
Von Frawn so geistreich ausgehn.	Wit and sense from woman's pen.
Man wolls nur lesen und betrachtn	Just consider what you read
Und auff der Spötter Red nicht achtn,	And to the scoffers pay no heed,
Die da sagen: es sey nicht fein.	Who say it isn't right.
Christus hameist Mariam preist,	For Mary Christ his special praise reserved,
Ob schoen Martha ihm kocht und speist,	Even though Martha cooked and served,
Weiln sie erwehlt das beste Theil,	Because she chose the better role
In dehm sie gesucht der Seelen Heil.	In that she chose to save the soul.
Wie diese Frau auch hat gethan,	So does the present woman, too,
Als darvon diss Buch zeugen kan,	As this book will prove to you
Das auch die Weisheit nicht zuholln	That wisdom is not to be found
Von Welt-Gelehrten und Hohen-Schuln,	In colleges and learned rounds,
Sondern vom Heyligen Geist allein	But from the Holy Ghost alone

Mus erbeten und gelernet sein.	Can the highest things be known.
Gott woll das sich niemand wol schämm	God would have you feel no shame
Von Frawn guth Exempel zu nehmn.	If he speaks in woman's name.
Wollst nur leser diss perlegirn	And should you, readers, peruse this work,
Und darnach darvon Iudicirn.	And thereupon decide its worth,
Der Heyliger Geist dich illustrirn	The Holy Spirit will illuminate
Und dich zum Reich Gottes recht führ.	And lead you to God's kingdom.[44]
Amen.	Amen.
	(Translated by S. L. Cocalis[45])

A poem by Sibylle Schwarz (1621–1638) is a great deal more secular and sophisticated in its vision, and likens the beloved's inpenetrable heart to the laurel (Daphne) bush that withstands all assaults from thunder and lightning.[46]

Ist Lieb ein Feur, und kan das Eisen schmiegen,
If love is a fire, and shape iron,
bin ich vol Feur, und voller Lieben Pein,
If I am filled with fire and love's anguish,
wohrvohn mag doch der Liebsten Hertze seyn?
Of what substance then is my beloved's heart?
wans eisern wär, so würd ess mir erliegen,
If it were iron, then it should yield to me;

wans gülden wär, so würd ichs können biegen,
Were it of gold, then I could mold it
durch meine Gluht; solls aber fleischern seyn,
With my ardor, but if it is made of flesh,
so schliess ich fort" Ess ist ein fleischern Stain:
Then I conclude: it must be a stone of flesh,
doch kan mich nicht ein Stein, wie sie, betriegen.
Yet a stone could not beguile me as she does.

Ists dan wie Frost, wie kalter Schnee und Eiss,
And if it be like frost, of cold snow and ice,
wie presst sie dann auss mir den Liebesschweiss?
Then why does it make me sweat with passion?
Mich deucht: Ihr Herz ist wie die Loorberblätter,
I think her heart must be of laurel leaves,

die nicht beru:hrt ein starcker Donnerkeil,
That a mighty thunderbolt leaves unscathed.
sie, sie verlacht, Cupido, deine Pfeil;
She, O Cupid, mocks your arrows,

und ist befreyt für deinem Donnerwetter
And remains untouched by your thunderstorm.
(Translated by Kandace Einbeck)

The poet Catharina Regina von Greiffenberg (1633–1694) claims indifference to Cupid and freedom from Cupid's powers over her.

Gegen Amor
Anti-Cupid

Der leine Wüterich mag mit den Pfeilen spielen
That ruthless little tyrant can trifle, flirt, and fling
und tändeln, wie we will: er gewinnet mir nichts ab,
his arrows as he pleases: I'll ward off his caress
weil gegen seine Pfeil ein Demant Herz ich hab.
For in this case, you see, a heart of stone I do possess.
Er machet mich nicht wund, ich darf nit Schmerzen fühlen.
He cannot wound me; I will not feel the sting.

Er mag mit tausend List auf meine Freyheit zielen
With a thousand tricks and ruses he wants my independence.
Ihm ich, dem blinden Kind, ein Zucker-Zeitlein gab:
To him, that blind child, I have given a confection:
er meint', es wär mein Herz. O leicht-geteuschter Knab!
He thought it was my heart, did not suspect deception!
Ich will mein Mütlein noch an deinen Einfalt Kühlen.
But I will vent my anger on his inexperience.

Schau, wie gefällt dir das! trotz, spra:ng mir diesen Stein
Look, how do you like that! Defy me; split this stone for me
mit deinem goldnen Pfeil. Der Lorbeer soll mich zieren,
With your golden arrow. I'll be adorned with laurel leaves,
nicht deine Dornen-Ros' und Myrten-Sträuchelein.
Not with your myrtle boughs and roses that are thorny.

Du meinst es sey nur Scherz, ich wolle mich vexiren.
You think its just a joke, that I wish to tease.
Nein! Nein! die süsse Ruh soll mir das Liebste seyn,
No, no! Sweet repose is the most precious thing to me.
mein dapfers Herz soll nichts als Ruh und Freyheit spüren.
My brave heart is made for freedom and for peace.
(Translated by S. L. Cocalis and G. M. Geiger[47])

Conclusions

Scene: A most convivial college choral concert. A men's chorus was singing a specially-arranged satire based on Andrew Lloyd Weber's "Music of the Night" with clever words that parodied the famous Alfred Hitchcock film *Psycho*. When they reached the film's notorious scene where Janet Leigh is slashed to death in the motel shower, the men sang words that rhymed with "the music of the night," i.e., "Did she put up a fight?" The audience erupted into a sudden, hysterical spurt of nervous laughter at the outrageous parody. I later reflected on that nervous laughter. On one level, the spoof was completely innocent. But on another level, the incident reinforced how on occasion our society, as well as many other societies in the world of today and of yesteryear, laugh off and accept a high threshold of violence, especially force expressed against women.

The following question arises: Has violence against women become universalized and normalized just when our society has begun to accept women conductors and women in other leadership positions formerly held by men? Impressive women have held important national and international offices and positions. Yet, misogyny is plainly evident in popular culture. According to media scholars, Hip-Hop and misogynistic rap, with their attendant acceptance of degrading depictions of women, enjoy wide appreciation in our culture, especially among the young. Certainly, the contemporary coexistence of Hip-Hop, misogynistic rap, and the recognition of women in positions of leadership casts a curious juxtaposition. Are conductors simply adding to a widespread phenomenon when we program texts that are demeaning to women? True, probably different listeners attend Hip-Hop performances than attend choral concerts. Nevertheless, examples less graphic than Hip-Hop, but examples nonetheless, also are found in some musical works frequently performed today.

In addition to being mindful of texts in choral works, today's conductors should be aware of recognizing the many powerful compositions and texts by women. The assignment is not an easy one. Poems by women, although an abundant resource, have been underused by both male and female composers throughout the centuries.[48] Male composers either have not known about them, or they have not sought out these poetic works because women's contemplations and experiences were suspected of being too narrow and limited in scope to fully reflect the human experience. Societal norms dictated the range of subjects about which women poets were to write, and in some instances dictated the acceptable forms for women to write in as well. Such strictures, of course, usually were defined by males. But the question remained: could the woman poet, narrowly defined by men, transcend her environment to speak in a language that would interest all composers? Early men and women had different perceptions of reality because they were assigned different roles; they performed rather different jobs and had different expectations. Renaissance men believed that the ancients had established these different roles. Men were free to travel; women were expected to run the home; women were subjected to a stricter code of behavior.[49]

Women poets, however, did read, and many of those who carefully observed society crafted equally thoughtful commentary on their condition in life, on their culture, and on their immediate social and physical surroundings. In a later century, Emily Dickinson (1830–1886) would pen her now famous poem, "Wild nights!" a poem that certainly transcends the reality of her life in ninteenth-century Massachusetts. Dickinson, a poet who lived the last half of her life as a recluse, shunning visitors and dedicating herself only to writing, produced this rapturous poem that exudes passionate longing for escape from her solitude. Here, her isolation breeds the feared darkness of her soul, the storms of the sea that she calls her "wild nights." Were she "in port," or with a cherished lover, she would be "rowing in Eden" and could not be harmed by storming winds. She would be "done with the compass, done with the chart."

Wild nights! Wild nights!
Were I with thee,
Wild nights should be
Our luxury!
Futile the winds
To a heart in port,
Done with the compass,
Done with the chart.
Rowing in Eden!
Ah! the sea!
Might I but moor
To-night in thee!

Gender bias in the selection of poems by early composers prevented them from discovering a body of literature rich in personality, spirit and character, in imagery, in metaphor, and in narrative styles. When the voices of the women poets could avoid being tempered by patriarchy, they spoke with extraordinary insight and sensitivity. Their astute observations might have been omitted in early anthologies very nearly in a ratio inversely proportional to the amount that women have written. The world of today does not really know the extent of women's writings, a body of literature that has gone unrecognized until recently. The now-recognized abundant body of literature by women authors should serve as a much-appreciated repository for today's composers.

When programming works that students will learn from and will enjoy, today's conductors should take time to note the gender of poets and composers. Fortunately, in the late ninteenth, the twentieth and the twenty-first century, we have begun to recognize brilliant poets and composers who are women. Yet, such esteemed choral standards as "Neighbors' Chorus," "Au joli jeu," and "Il est bel et bon" currently are extremely popular with young singers. High school students who today blog on line about those titles invariably are enthusiastic that their choirs are singing them.

Surely, however, in all of choral literature—among the rich spectrum of Gilbert and Sullivan choruses and French chansons—there are other admirable selections to perform.[50] Are those naughty French chanson texts simply "boys-will-be-boys" raciness that enlivens our appreciation of a music from the past? Should conductors just not perform such works?

JUST SAY, "NO"?

Not programming certain works, of course, is one option. On the other hand, if conductors and scholars boycott every work of music and literature that deals insensitively with women, much of the legacy of western classical choral music, to say nothing of great monuments of literature, suddenly would be unavailable to today's students. Should women not attend Shakespeare's *Taming of the Shrew* and the musical on which that play is based, *Kiss Me, Kate!* ? Should the music be overlooked? Should men not attend performances of *Princess Ida* for its anti-male rhetoric? Should Jews resent Bach's setting of the *Passion According to St. John* because that gospel dates from a later era than the gospels by Matthew, Mark and Luke, and it speaks in a language that widens the gulf between Christians and Jews?

Michael Marissen[51] has written about the troubling origins of Handel's famed and revered *Messiah*. According to Marissen, Handels librettist, the scholar Charles Jennens, was heavily influenced by the writings of the Anglican bishop Richard Kidder, who claimed in a 1690 treatise that Jesus was the Messiah that the Jews ought to have recognized long ago. The 1726 edition owned by Jennens of Kidder's treatise bears on its title page the text, "A Demonstration of the Messias in which The Truth of the Christian Religion Is Proved, against all the Enemies thereof, But especially against the Jews." Marissen further avers that the "Hallelujah" chorus, because of the texts that directly precede it at the end of Part II of *Messiah,* does not celebrate the birth of Christ at all, but the destruction of Jerusalem and the second temple by the Romans in AD 70.

In response to Marissens article, which appeared in the New York Times on Easter Sunday, 2007, most published letters to the editor agreed with one another that listeners should not be forced to hear Handel's great work only in its Anti-Semitic historical context. "Would Marissen plumb every belief of Mozart, Leonardo, Monet, et al." Art was, after all, created by human beings who were "subject to the influence of time and place," and the beauty of great art is that it "transcends the sins of its creator."[52] Likewise, in an era closer to our own, Brahms longed for a strong and just German nation, and stated a preference for musical elements that were *deutsch und echt*, yet the words "German" and "pure" resonate very differently today than when Brahms used them.

Accepting this premise, we regard these debatable texts as period pieces that simply reflect acceptable mores of their times. They do not reflect attitudes of our times, but the ethos of the times in which they were created. Rather than damning these works with guilt-by-association,[53] understand that beliefs and customs described in such texts represent to the modern listener a throwback to an earlier time, and, as such, can become topics of constructive dialogue between conductor and singers.

Another conductor states that for her the boundaries are somewhat fluid:

> Regarding the question of whether conductors should refrain from programming pieces with overtly sexist texts or accept that they are period pieces and treat them as such, I think that most conductors wrestle with this sort of question when considering any text that is potentially offensive for whatever reason. For me the boundaries are somewhat fluid, depending upon context. I usually decide what I am comfortable with on an individual basis. Some pieces, I just will not program at all (e.g., many of the texts quoted in this article would fall into that category.). And I hate Wagner's penchant for sacrificing women to redeem men, but I still listen to Wagner and the opera because I love the music and the art form in spite of the fact that so much of it is grounded in a socially less-enlightened past. I believe much of this is a personal choice, but it is important for all of us to be challenged and to think deeply about what we are communicating or endorsing before we pro-

> gram anything with a somewhat questionable text.
>
> I also find that questions such as these arise in other contexts. For example, a few years ago I programmed a piece about the horrors of the war in the former Yugoslavia. It was a very powerful and gut-wrenching piece and the programming of the entire concert was exceptional in its statement about the importance of peace, reconciliation and the ability of choral and vocal music to draw people together. A couple of my singers were unable to sing portions of the text of the one piece, which had to do with the death of children. It was emotionally too difficult for them. I absolutely respected and supported them in their decision to not sing that piece, but to participate in the remainder of the concert.[54]

Questionable texts exist, and may exist in a ravishingly beautiful piece of music, in music that is well-crafted, is inspiring, and is important for students to know to gain an understanding of many styles and periods of music. Questionable texts provide all conductors with food for thought, and a conductor should not program them without preparing for the consequences. Conductors should provide all corollaries: If I select this text, I must explain its historical and/or cultural context. The conductor may wish to interpret such texts to both singers and audience. Such contextualizing may occur with program notes, pre-concert lecture, or introductory commentary by conductor or singer. In the meantime, wise editors in conjunction with knowledgeable publishers just might be able to get into student hands texts and music that the students will enjoy, that they can learn from, that represent an historically well-rounded perspective of choral literature, and that are not offensive to women of today's world. They may even find some texts by women.

Biography

Joan Catoni Conlon is Director of Graduate Choral Research in the College of Music at the University of Colorado—Boulder. Before teaching at CU, Dr. Conlon was Professor of Choral Music and Conducting for the University of Washington, and Conductor of the Northwest Chamber Chorus in Seattle.

She is active as an editor, arranger, conductor, and presenter. A noted scholar of choral music, she has published numerous choral editions in her areas of research and performance interests, which include the choral music of Georg Philipp Telemann and of Claudio Monteverdi.

Following research travel to Frankfurt, London, Brussels, and Italy, she conducted performances with the Northwest Chamber Chorus of Telemann choral cantatas, unheard since the eighteenth century, which she had transcribed from manuscripts. Her editions and arrangements have been published by Alliance Music, Augsburg, Lawson-Gould, and Southern Music. Her articles and reviews have appeared in the *Choral Journal*, and in the *Music Educator's Journal.*

On two sabbaticals, she studied Hindustani classical vocal music in India, and she also lectured in India. In 2001, she was guest professor at the China Conservatory in Beijing, and she has traveled internationally with her choirs.

In 2001 she published the book *Performing Monteverdi: A Conductor's Guide* with Hinshaw, Chapel Hill. Dr. Conlon has chaired the Research and Publications Committee of the American Choral Directors Association.

Acknowledgements

The author gratefully acknowledges the kind assistance of friends, students, and colleagues who read her chapter "Must We Always Sing of Ourselves As Men Have Sung?" and who shared their ideas: Professor Mary O'Neil, Dr. Darlene Lawrence, Professor Elissa Guralnick, Karen Thomas, Miriam Espeseth, Alexa Doebele, Professor Larry Kaptein, Professor Jeremy Smith, Matthew Potterton, Dr. David Kates, and Professor Frank Conlon.

NOTES

[1] Landon, H. C. Robbins, *Five Centuries of Music in Venice.* New York: Schirmer Books, 1991. pp. 104–105, 121.

[2] Denis Stevens, p. 51, *The Letters of Claudio Monteverdi*, translated by Denis Stevens. Oxford: Clarendon, New York: Oxford University Press, 1995.

[3] In urban Italy of the Renaissance, the place of most women "was in the home and the place of men out in the world of affairs." (p. 15) Likewise, reading stimulated the imagination, which made for unhealthy moods and immoral inclinations." In "A way of looking at women in renaissance Florence," *The Journal of Medieval and Renaissance Studies*, DIII/5681, Vol. 4 (1974).

[4] Similarly, in modern times, many women continued the tradition of patronage, including such lesser known but extraordinary figures as Winnaretta Singer ("Tante Winnie"), sewing machine heiress, later Princesse de Polignac, patron of Kurt Weill, Igor Stravinsky, Gabriel Fauré, Nadia Boulanger and Igor Markevitch.

[5] *The Journal of Medieval and Renaissance Studies*, DIII/5681, Vol. 4, "A way of looking at women in Renaissance Florence," Lauro Martines, UCLA, 1984. p. 18.

[6] McClary, Susan, *Feminine Endings: Music, Gender and Sexuality*. Minneapolis: University of Minnesota Press, 1991.

[7] McClary, when interviewed on National Public Radio, Saturday morning, 22 September 2007, averred that Carmen had to be killed because she was a threat, just as "Dracula has to be killed." Denyce Graves, the mezzosoprano who frequently has sung the role of Carmen on the opera stage, stated in the same interview that each time she performs the role, she gains strength from Carmen's strength and self-determination.

[8] Marie, murdered at the end of Alban Berg's opera *Wozzek*, falls victim to her deranged male companion. The opera ends as her young son is skipping off into the woods where he will discover her dead body. Contrarily, some composers gave extraordinary power and challenges to their women characters. Mozart famously empowered servant girls when he reversed roles between servant and aristocrat, male and female. In both *Cosi fan tutte* and *Marriage of Figaro*, servant girls abandon their usual stereotypical role. Despina and Susanna, respectively, act with imagination, good sense, intelligence, independence, and strong will to influence the operas' plots to good effect. In each of the two operas, the resolution, fashioned by the negotiating servant girl, is beneficial to all parties—aristocrat and servant alike.

[9] Lea Jacob, *The Wages of Sin: Censorship and the Fallen Woman Film, 1918–1942.*

Berkeley: University of California Press, 1997.

[10] Gregory D. Black, *Hollywood Censored: Morality Codes, Catholics, and the Movies.* Cambridge: Cambridge University Press, 1994.

[11] They later are reunited.

[12] *Il Combattimento di Tancredi e Clorinda*, in Monteverdi's eighth book of madrigals, tells the story of Tancredi's mortally wounding the Saracen Clorinda, and of baptizing her before she died. The unintended death of Clorinda at the hand of Tancredi and his remorse also appears in Monteverdi's third book of madrigals, in the three-madrigal set "Vivrò fra I miei tormenti," "Ma dove, o lasso," and "Io pur verrò."

[13] Amalasuntha was a strong historic figure, the daughter of Theodoric, king of the Ostrogoths. Upon her father's death in 526, she obtained the throne for her son, Atalaric, who died in 534. She was killed in 535 by her cousin Theodatus, whom she had made king. Amalasuntha was respected as a literary scholar.

[14] *The Defiant Muse: Italian Feminist Poems from the Middle Ages to the Present, A Bilingual Anthology*, edited by Beverly Allen, Muriel Kittel, and Keala Jane Jewell. Introduction by Beverly Allen. New York: The Feminist Press of the City University of New York, 1986, pp. 26–27. This series, entitled "The Defiant Muse: Women Poets from the Middle Ages to the Present," addresses the lack of women poets in anthologies, and dedicates one volume to women poets writing in the Italian, Dutch, Hispanic, Flemish, French and German languages.

[15] From *Food, Wine, and Song*, Orlando Consort. After a translation by Leofranc-Holford Stevens. Harmonia Mundi, France, 2001.

[16] From Josquin des Pres, *Missa fortuna desperata; Songs; Motets by Isaac, Senfl, and Greiter*. The Clerks Group, conductor and editor, Edward Wickham. After a translation. London: Gaudeamus, 2001.

[17] From *Armes, Amours: Songs of the 14th and 15th Centuries*, by Alla Francesca with Alta, co-directed by Emmanuel Bonnardot, Pierre Hamon and Brigitte Lesne. After a translation by Louise Riley-Smith. Paris: Opus 111, 1998.

[18] In recent times, misogyny's latest incarnation may be found in rap artists and in those popular Hip-Hop performers who glorify negative attitudes toward women. Observers of Hip-Hop claim that the entire phenomenon is caused by media moguls for materialistic gain. For whatever reason, today's Hip-Hop performers peddle racial, homophobic and gender stereotyping. At the present time, while racial and homophobic hate language is outlawed, hate language directed toward women is not classified as hate speech. Young women with whom misogynistic Hip-Hop is popular say they just like a particular artist or beat, and they do not believe the artist is talking about them personally, but about other women, when the performer uses abusive language.

Some defenders of Hip-Hop think critics are too hard on it, as quoted in PBS documentary, "Hip-Hop: Beyond Beats and Rhymes" by Byron Hurt, premiered 20 February 2007 in Independent Lens Series, PBS. (Consult: http://www.pbs.org/independentlens/hiphop/film.htm, accessed 11 August 2007.) Instead, such critics blame "American popular culture, which has trafficked in racist and sexist images and language for centuries and provides all sort of incentives for young men of color to act our a hard-core masculinity." Such critics aver that the media, not the popular performers are blamed for the current coarsening of language (Jeff Chang, editor, *Total Chaos: The Art and Aesthetics of Hip-Hop*, New York: Basic Civitas Books, 2007).

Further, some rap is political, and the words avoid misogyny. Defenders claim that some Hip-Hop has positive effects. Certain women authors promote a different Hip-Hop discourse by replacing Hip-Hop's misogynous language and imagery with language that empowers rather than assails young women. This new empowering use of Hip-Hop is meant to reverse the negative rap videos that especially portray black women negatively.

Nevertheless, in some places, the coarsened misygyny of Hip-Hop has entered the consciousness of popular culture. The Canadian telephone carrier Bell Mobility considered one Hip-Hop performance ("Pimp Tones") to be sufficiently popular and attractive to offer it as a ringtone option. The woman activitist Valerie Smith sued the Ontario Human Rights Commission over the use, saying that it further normalized violence toward women. The ringtone option was subsequently withdrawn.

[19] Offenbach, Jacques, "Neighbors Chorus" from the comic opera *La jolie parfumeuse*, translated By Jan Meyerowitz. New York: Broude Brothers Limited, 1954.

[20] Lassus published his setting of the story of Susanna in 1560. The first setting probably dates back to 1548 and the composer Didier Lupi.

[21] Mary Beth Rose, *Women in the Middle Ages and the Renaissance*. Syracuse: Syracuse University Press, 1986, p. 52.

[22] Throughout Argento's remarkable setting, the composer incorporates a twelve-tone row in many guises, remaining ever attentive to the expressive context of each appearance of the row.

[23] *Kings Singers Madrigals*, Volume I, edited by Clifford Bartlett, translations done by Silvia Dimiziani, London: Faber, 1984.

[24] According to Joan Kelly-Gadol, in "Did Women Have a Renaissance?" from *Becoming Visible: Women in European History*, 1977, ed. R. Bridenthal and C. Koonz, the twelfth century theorist of the "Art of Courtly Love," Andreas Capellanus, encouraged Andreas the knight who wanted a peasant girl "not to

hesitate to take what you seek and embrace her by force." (p.141) Toward the lady, however, "a true lover considers nothing good except what he thinks will please his beloved."

[25] Two well-known examples from the twentieth century are Ned Rorem and Ildebrando Pizzetti, both of whom set texts from Sappho. Other twentieth-century composers who have set texts of Emily Dickinson include John Adams, Samuel Barber, and Daniel Pinkham.

[26] From *Humanism to the Humanities: Education and the Liberal Arts in 15th and 16th century Europe*, Anthony Grafton and Lisa Jardine. Cambridge: Harvard University Press, 1986. Chapter 2, "Woman Humanists: Education for What?"

[27] *The Defiant Muse: German Feminist Poems from the Middle Ages to the Present, A Bilingual Anthology*, edited and with an introduction by Susan L. Cocalis. The Feminist Press at the City University of New York: New York, 1986. p. xv

[28] *The Defiant Muse: Italian Feminist Poems from the Middle Ages to the Present, A Bilingual Anthology*, edited by Beverly Allen, Muriel Kittel, and Keala Jane Jewell. Introduction by Beverly Allen. New York: The Feminist Press of the City University of New York, 1986. pp. 2–3.

[29] *The Defiant Muse: Italian Feminist Poems from the Middle Ages to the Present, A Bilingual Anthology*. pp. 22–23.

[30] *The Defiant Muse: Italian Feminist Poems from the Middle Ages to the Present, A Bilingual Anthology*. p. xvi.

[31] *The Defiant Muse: Italian Feminist Poems from the Middle Ages to the Present, A Bilingual Anthology*, pp. 10–11. Included in the Italian volume of the "Defiant Muse" series are dozens of women poets not listed above, including Petronilla Paolini Massimi (1663–1726), Faustina Maratti Zappi (1680–1746), Diodata Saluzzo (1774–1840), Maria Guaci Nobile (1808–1848), Caterina Bon Brenzoni (1813–1856), and Guiseppina Turrisi Colonna (1822–1848).

[32] *The Defiant Muse: Italian Feminist Poems from the Middle Ages to the Present, A Bilingual Anthology*. pp. 10–11.

[33] Joan Kelly-Gadol, "Did Women Have a Renaissance?" *Becoming Visible: Women in European History*, 1977, ed. R. Bridenthal and C. Koonz.

[34] Ibid. Gadol maintains that women in the Renaissance were educated by humanists who did not teach chivalry and romance, but taught classical culture. p. 149.

[35] Ibid.

[36] *The Women Troubadours*, trans. and ed. by Meg Pogin, New York: Paddington Press, 1976.

[37] *The Defiant Muse: French Feminist Poems from the Middle Ages to the Present, A Bilingual Anthology*. Edited and with an Introduction by Domna C. Stanton.

Feminist Press at CUNY: New York, 1986. pp. 6–7.

[38] *The Defiant Muse: French Feminist Poems from the Middle Ages to the Present, A Bilingual Anthology.* pp. 4–5.

[39] *The Defiant Muse: French Feminist Poems from the Middle Ages to the Present, A Bilingual Anthology*. pp. 14–15.

[40] *The Defiant Muse: French Feminist Poems from the Middle Ages to the Present, A Bilingual Anthology*. pp. 10–11.

[41] Manfred P. Fleischer, "'Are Women Human?' The Debate of 1595 Between Valens Acidalius and Simon Gediccus," *The Sixteenth Century Journal*, XII, No. 2 (1981).

[42] *The Defiant Muse: German Feminist Poems from the Middle Ages to the Present, A Bilingual Anthology*, edited and with an introduction by Susan L. Cocalis. The Feminist Press at the City University of New York: New York, 1986. p. xvi. Samuel Pepys, on discovering his wife's diary, was so upset that he ordered her to tear it up. He then allowed her to keep it, because only other women presumably would read it.

[43] *The Defiant Muse: German Feminist Poems from the Middle Ages to the Present, A Bilingual Anthology*. pp. xvi–xvii

[44] The Cocalis translation ended with the words "and lead you to the Pearly Gate."

[45] *The Defiant Muse: German Feminist Poems from the Middle Ages to the Present, A Bilingual Anthology*. pp. 8–9.

[46] Some scholars attribute this poem to Anna Ovena Hoyers (1584–1655), the author of the previous poem.

[47] *The Defiant Muse: German Feminist Poems from the Middle Ages to the Present, A Bilingual Anthology*. pp. 8–9.

[48] Women playwrights have suffered the same fate. One Englishwoman, Elizabeth Cary, born 1585, wrote plays in which she discussed "the contradictions and claustrophobia of the early modern household, as well as intermarriage between classes, and gender roles." She converted to Catholicism but had a Protestant husband.

[49] Martines, p. 24.

[50] Some Gilbert and Sullivan texts are equally offensive to modern ears, such as the Mikado's aria, "My object all sublime," in which he explains that a woman "who stains her gray hair puce, or pinches her figger is [punished by being] blacked like a nigger with permanent walnut juice."

[51] "Unsettling History of That Joyous Hallelujah," *The New York Times*, 8 April 2007 (Easter Sunday).

[52] Letter written by David E. Feldman, Long Beach, NewYork, 15 April 2007.

[53] In his 15 April 2007, letter to the editor of *The New York Times*, Clifford Crouch of Brookside Village, Texas, maintains that Handel just worked with the texts presented to him, as he did in many "inane librettos of countless operas now forgotten." This brings to mind the certainly puzzling type of da capo aria in a Baroque opera in which the soloist sings in part "A" of the aria that all lives are threatened with certain death, then sings in part "B" that they are saved from destruction, but then must repeat part "A" again because of conventions of performance practice. Certainly the text in such circumstances ranks below the music in importance to the composer.

[54] Email correspondence with Karen Thomas, conductor of the Seattle Pro Musica, 20 July 2007.

Building Bridges: Choruses Engaging Communities

Kathy Saltzman Romey
with Emilie Sweet and Shekela M. Wanyama

Introduction and Acknowledgments

Choral organizations throughout the United States extend their performance activity beyond the concert hall to include a myriad of creative efforts that utilize music as a tool for community building and education. Yet current programming and outreach models are often ineffective in bridging the gap between art and twenty-first century society. Additionally, the separation between composer and conductor furthers the challenge of connecting performers and listeners to the creative process that inspires the realization of any musical score. What role can programming, outreach, and presentation play in surmounting these obstacles and broadening the scope of the collective musical experience, both on- and offstage?

As choral artists, we are motivated by the deep connection between text and music, which illuminates what it means to be human. Within the rehearsal process, we seek to uncover and reveal the essence of our art and eventually to communicate this understanding to the listener through our music making. The ultimate goal, however, should not be limited solely to sharing these insights with audience members in a concert presentation. Rather, we have the opportunity to include the community in a more purposeful exploration of larger issues throughout the entire process of program conception, rehearsal, and performance. This approach, we believe, deepens our relationship with the music and one another, and inspires us to more actively engage with the world around us.

Consideration of the common practices in our field reveals the universal potential for rewarding partnerships within our communities. The outreach programs discussed in this chapter reflect a growing movement to link disparate partners within collaborations based on a lateral rather than hierarchical relationship model. The equalization and expansion of such relationships serve as a multilayered approach to programming and provide greater intentionality to musical selection, the rehearsal process, and the concert event itself. Using dynamic programming as a vehicle for social engagement and dialogue, the choral art can thus connect more directly with issues relevant to contemporary society. We hope that through examination of trends in programming, collaboration, outreach, and the role of the conductor, we can develop a more meaningful approach to cultivating community and positive social change through choral singing.

While many have influenced our personal journeys, we wish to collectively acknowledge the following organizations and individuals for their contributions to this document: The Minnesota Chorale, Conspirare, the University of Minnesota, Temple University, Judy Arnstein, Larry Fuchsberg, Craig Hella Johnson, Alan Harler, Camille Kolles, Matthew W. Mehaffey, Gordon Paine, and H. Royce Saltzman.

The Past is Prologue: A Critical View of Contemporary Choral Programming and Outreach Practices in the United States

In considering the future direction of choral music in the twenty-first century, we must pause to reflect on our history and to assess the efficacy of our current practices. Through careful examination of the legacy of choral music, we can begin to understand the current position of the choral field in larger society and alter the trajectory of its path accordingly. If choral music is to reclaim a position of artistic relevance and significance within our communities, both the work of art (the thing, the object, the noun) and the artists' work (the craft, the process, the verb) need to play a deep and meaningful role in the lives of the performers, the audience, and the greater community. Two questions require our attention as we position the field of choral music to reach this goal: Have we considered the role of the conductor in relationship to the score, the composer, the ensemble, the audience, and especially our communities? And have we responded creatively to the evolving conditions in which we live, adapting our traditions to embrace the traditions of others?

The conductor plays a special role in the performance event. As the only musician on stage who makes no sound, the conductor must fully understand the scope of her position before taking the podium. What does a conductor do in a performance? Without diminishing the contributions of the ensemble or the audience, she provides musical leadership, both in the form of interpretation or in the literal realization of the musical notation in the score.

She filters the musical energy of the performers and connects it to the audience. She, in turn, is the focal point for the audience and links *their* experience to the performers. As the facilitator of the musical event, she plays all of these roles and makes choices in the best interests of the composer, the work, the performers, the space, the audience, and herself. She is an advocate for many people, not the least of whom is the composer, yet her advocacy extends far beyond this.

In considering the multi-layered role of the conductor, it is important to acknowledge that for many, the identity of the conductor is built on historical character archetypes from the early twentieth century that are often incongruent to the musical sensibilities of the modern musician. This incongruence is clearly seen in the following two oppositional views of the conductor's relationship to the score. The idea of the "composer's advocate," as proposed by conductor Erich Leinsdorf in his polemic book of the same title, has inadvertently suggested the demotion of all participants in the performance experience to a subservient position to the object of music. Perhaps unknowingly, Leinsdorf has transferred the concept of universal deference to the composer's voice and the compositional process to the physical object of the score. This overemphasis on the score is dangerous, as it strips from music that which is most valuable to artistic expression—our humanity—along with the processes of composition, rehearsal, performance, and audience participation that make up the choral art.

In his book *Musicking: The Meanings of Performing and Listening*, musicologist Christopher Small offers a counter to Leinsdorf's approach. Small discusses the linguistic significance of the word "music" and interprets it to mean the processes of hearing or making music. He writes, "The act of musicking establishes in the place where it is happening a set of relationships, and it is in those relationships that the meaning of the act lies."[1] In Small's estimation, music is not an object, but rather, a verb. By considering "music" in its gerund form, "musicking," we can acknowledge the dynamic process of music making that exists in all cultures and assert that the music of one culture is not inherently superior to the music of another. Likewise, because music is so intimately linked to the relationships and identities of its participants, we must recognize that our programming practices impact individuals and institutions within our communities in a deep and meaningful way. We must take care when conceiving concert programs—just as we care for the people and relationships in our lives—not to inadvertently serve the enduring hegemony of a singular music heritage and thereby unintentionally marginalize the music or members of any given community. The methodology and content of a dynamic programming philosophy must reflect critical thinking, collaborative relationships, and the expression of an active artistic voice. By thoughtfully selecting choral repertoire with this relational impact in mind, we can more actively build our ensembles and audiences to reflect all of our community.

Some outreach initiatives may unintentionally do more harm than good. In theory, the construction of outreach programs utilizes broad education platforms and an increased accessibility to arts events to include populations unfamiliar with classical music. Outreach also serves to build an appreciation for the cultural heritage of both the masterworks of choral music and the special ritual that is the rehearsal and concert process. In practice, however, the cultural gesture of outreach can further marginalize members of our community. Differentiating populations based on their appreciation of art music and its rituals may inadvertently demote the value of other cultural expressions; what was intended to be welcoming and inclusive can easily convey something altogether different.

Understanding this, we must embrace an active relationship with our concert programming following a dynamic, responsive model that does not promote a hierarchical valuation of one music over another, but rather explores and integrates the musicking of all humanity. Additionally, we must expand the purpose of our outreach programs beyond the role of audience building. By recasting arts outreach as community engagement, we will discover that choral musicians have as much to learn from our community as our community has to learn from us.

The program examples that follow explore this methodology in practice. Kathy Saltzman Romey discusses the Minnesota Chorale's Bridges program, and Emilie Sweet describes the genesis of her Bridges-inspired program, The Alchemy Project. Shekela M. Wanyama then frames the efforts of the Bridges program and The Alchemy Project within the context of choral activism in the twenty-first century.

Our Voices, Our Tools: The Minnesota Chorale's Bridges Program

Kathy Saltzman Romey

"There is a vitality, a life force, a quickening," said dancer-choreographer Martha Graham, "that is translated through you into action. And because there is only one of you in all time, this expression is unique. If you block it, it will never exist through any other medium and be lost. The world will not hear it."[2]

It is no simple matter to connect to this "life force" and "translate it into action." Each time we lift our batons, we have the opportunity to study ourselves and the larger world through the cognitive and emotional lens of choral literature. The preparation and presentation of this music can be a provocative exploration of artistic expression as shaped by language, ethnicity, history, religion, philosophy, and individual experience. The process of music making, however, is not only a means for study and personal growth. It can also be a critical vehicle for social inquiry and change—the "action" of which Martha Graham speaks.

The 250-voice Minnesota Chorale serves as the principal chorus and primary choral resource of the Minnesota Orchestra. As its Artistic Director, I am most widely known for my preparation and advocacy of symphonic choral music. In addition to working with the orchestra, the Chorale holds an overarching goal of reaching a broad community of audiences by performing an ever-widening repertory of choral music. This range of activity supports the ultimate mission of the organization to celebrate the human voice and its power to educate, enrich, unite, and inspire.

Like many symphonic choruses, the Minnesota Chorale is defined more by music's past than by its future. As a choral organization, we struggle in our search for relevance and seek creative ways to expand our reach beyond the traditional repertoire, audiences, and concert stage. I have always been inspired by the work of Singing City, which was founded in 1948 by Dr. Elaine Brown as an integrated choir in the inner city of Philadelphia. "The Choir was born out of the Fellowship House movement, which believed that differences between races, religions, and cultures could be bridged by ordinary people coming together in shared activities."[3]

Similarly, the Minnesota Chorale has developed a series of educational programs that augment our symphonic performance activities to connect with the greater community through unique artistic partnerships. While these efforts are often categorized as "outreach," the programs are also an important form of "choral inreach." With every project, the singers have an opportunity to explore a new body of repertoire and engage in both individual and collective exploration of their role within contemporary society.

Since 1994, the Minnesota Chorale's flagship community series, Bridges, has employed choral music and the sheer magnetism of singing to cultivate and deepen relationships with diverse populations. In annual concert programs, the Chorale collaborates with guest artists to explore music from around the globe. Concert presentations usually occur outside of conventional venues and are frequently interactive and non-traditional in nature. The thrust of each Bridges project challenges the chorus to examine music and culture anew, and stimulates organizational thinking to move beyond western classical repertoire. Past Bridges programs have focused on collaborations with specific ethnic populations, youth, social service organizations, and enthusiasts of other art forms. Informing these ventures is the belief that the power of song and the powerful social symbolism of the chorus—in which heterogeneous voices combine to achieve a common purpose—can call attention to worthy causes, promote cooperative endeavor, and help mend a divided world.

In its first decade, Bridges focused on connecting with different facets of the local Twin Cities community, such as the growing Russian immigrant population and Jewish-Christian faith communities. An eighteen-month community partnership with inner city African-American church choirs was especially memorable. The program featured weekly sessions led by different clinicians in the study of African-American sacred song. This culminated first in a sing-along concert entitled "Lift Every Voice," and later in a multi-choir concert, "God's Trombones." Art Sidner, a singer from one of the partnering church choirs, reflected on this experience in the program notes for the 1998 "God's Trombones" concert:

> As African-Americans, it's not often that we have gotten to sing certain kinds of music that aren't in the popular media, and to share that with non-African-American singers. Lots of times we perform for white audiences, but haven't had a chance to sing with white people. We were reaching out to each other in a way that we normally don't. One of the facts about being a minority in a majority culture is that you know more about the majority

> culture than they know about you. This was a rare opportunity to focus on something that is not, and probably wouldn't be, well known by the majority culture unless they had an opportunity like this.

Partnerships such as this Bridges collaboration place all participants—regardless of cultural background—in positions of learning and teaching. While the challenge of negotiating cultural differences cannot be underestimated, the creation of a level playing field between members offers the potential for more constructive dialogue and creative exchange.

In its second decade, Bridges became increasingly concerned with using choral music, both new and old, to illuminate ideas and issues. One such example was "Musical Chi: East-West Convergences," a 2004 collaboration exploring the close connection between music, body, and spirit. This program was built around a residency with *t'ai chi* master and author Chungliang Al Huang, who is a Bach devotee and an authority on East-West cultural synthesis. In a week of residency activities, this remarkable teacher related music to traditional Chinese movement and images in assemblies presented to more than one thousand school children. Culminating concerts featuring Chungliang Al Huang, Chinese pipa virtuoso Gao Hong and the Minnesota Chorale were presented at the Minneapolis Museum of Art and The Marsh, a Twin Cities health and wellness center. The program explored parallels between musical and bodily flow, and revealed surprising connections between Western classical music and traditional Eastern disciplines of the body and mind.

The 2007 Bridges program was the most ambitious and unique endeavor to date. Symphonic choruses seldom sing about people like Somali émigré Mohamed Hadi, his wife, and their four children. "Sing Me a Home," however, had the Minnesota Chorale singing about the Hadis and five other families in a partnership with Habitat for Humanity, inner-city high school choirs, student writers, and Minnesota composers. The partnership focused on issues of affordable housing, family, and community. In collaboration with Twin Cities Habitat for Humanity, whose stated mission is "to eliminate poverty housing from the Twin Cities area and to make decent, affordable shelter for all people a matter of conscience,"[4] the project pursued the following goals:

- to express the feelings of hope, pride, and community that surround the idea of "home"

- to deepen public awareness of issues relating to affordable housing and poverty
- to advance the goals of both organizations by harnessing the synergies between them.

Mohamed Hadi and his family live on the east side of St. Paul, Minnesota. They fled Somalia—"a beautiful country," he says, "when it is peaceful"—in the early 1990s, traveling first to North Dakota. After moving to Minnesota in 1996, he applied to Twin Cities Habitat for Humanity and together with Habitat volunteers, helped build the St. Paul house that he and his family have owned since 2000. He recalls sitting outside the house, soon after moving in, and watching his children play. "Look," he said to his wife, "is this a dream, or what?"

Six such families, representing the rich diversity of Twin Cities Habitat homeowners, were interviewed over a two-month period. Their stories served as raw material for prose texts written by students from four partnering inner-city high schools under the guidance of mentor/writer Heid Erdrich. The students' poems were then given to prominent local composers, who were each commissioned to produce a choral setting for one of the partnering high school choirs.

The culminating performance, encompassing both familiar and the newly-composed works, featured a spoken-word presentation of one student's text accompanied by traditional Hmong flute; the four high school choirs premiering their commissioned songs; and a larger, final work for the combined choirs entitled "Sing Me a Home," with text by Heid Erdrich and music by former Chorale composer-in-residence Janika Vandervelde. The concert program was complemented by projected photographs of the participating families, Habitat homes, and building projects from the greater Twin Cities area. Both music and images represented the vital work in which Habitat is engaged and embodied the Chorale's belief in using song as a force for social good. Mohamed Hadi and his family recognize the responsibilities attendant upon their good fortune. "Our house," he says, "is a place where we welcome Somalis who don't have a house. We have got two rooms downstairs, so Somalis, when they come here, don't have to end up on the street. We always have someone in our house."

A similar spirit of responsibility inspires the Minnesota Chorale. We believe our voices are a powerful tool that can help envision a new reality, much like the story of the Hadi family captured in this poem by student writer Anne Goetz from St. Paul Central High School:

Here We Can Dream

The warm sun in the deep-dyed azure sky
Traveled evenly each day, constant as the way
We welcomed foreigners with open arms.
This was home. *Kani waa gurigii.**

But one day I came from work to see the children
All holding guns. Each night I heard the fighting getting closer
And I knew we had to leave.

But here we can dream, here we have hope.
Here we can open our doors to those still waiting in the cold,
And our home becomes their home, too.
This is home.

The sky is bleached to gray;
A bitter wind tears leaves from the trees.
Darkness swallows up the day.

But here we can dream, here we have hope.
Here we can open our doors to those still waiting in the cold,
And our home becomes their home, too.
This is home. *Kani waa gurigii.*

* "This is/was home" in the Somali language.

In its collaboration with Twin Cities Habitat for Humanity, the Minnesota Chorale harnessed the energy and eloquence of its art in the service of pressing community needs. Following "Sing Me a Home," or indeed any Bridges program, we invite our singers to serve as advocates for the project; carrying songs back to their respective communities; sharing them with friends, students, and colleagues; and performing them at similar events. The ripple effect produced by these many acts of "singer advocacy" can be powerful and sustained, touching many more people than any single chorus could otherwise reach.

In the Twin Cities, as in many communities in the United States, poverty stems largely from the unmet need for adequate and affordable housing—a problem often invisible to those not directly touched by it. In partnership with Habitat for Humanity or a similar organization, any chorus can embrace the task of calling attention to this basic and enduring need, or any other issue present in the surrounding community.

As conductors and educators, we must continually engage in a dialogue that examines the role and relevance of choral music in an ever-changing society. Through programs like Bridges, choirs around the world are expanding the scope of their programming, using music as a vehicle for building new relationships and heightening awareness of social issues important to the greater community. This broadens and deepens the artistic experience for everyone involved.

To recall the words of Martha Graham: "And because there is only one of you in all time, this expression is unique. If you block it, it will never exist through any other medium and be lost. The world will not hear it." But the world should hear our voices. We have a responsibility, I believe, to share our unique expression through the medium we champion—the compelling medium of song.

> Included in the appendix are written resources from the Minnesota Chorale's "Sing Me a Home" project, which may be used freely by choirs interested in mounting similar programs. To view additional "Sing Me a Home" program materials, including the complete commissioned poems and songs, visit www.minnesotachorale.org.

Building on "Bridges": The Birth of The Alchemy Project

Emilie Sweet

As a young conductor, I have recently realized that my career path has paralleled my personal development as an adult. The challenges of developing my own musical identity and contributing to the choral community have stretched me just as adolescence did all those years ago. Those pervasive teenage questions—Who am I? Why am I here? What is the meaning of what we do?—have re-emerged in a new context professionally. Searching for the answers to these questions and planning for the future have required a bit of reflection about where I have come from and the relationships that have most inspired me.

It is no surprise that my identity as a musician and my own musical work synthesize the ideologies and practices of my mentors with my own point of view. Though I have certainly been influenced by teachers, colleagues, and friends too numerous to name, I feel most indebted to Craig Hella Johnson and Kathy Saltzman Romey for their work with their respective organizations, Conspirare and the Minnesota Chorale. I consider my own work to be a hybrid of the programming and engagement practices of their ensembles.

I studied with Craig Hella Johnson and sang with his Austin, Texas-based ensemble Conspirare from 2003 through 2005. "Conspirare" means "to breathe together," and Johnson deliberately chose that moniker to reflect his uniquely collaborative leadership style and programming philosophy. Both the ensemble and their performances have been praised as meaningful and provocative music making.

Because of Johnson's orientation toward collaborative leadership and artistic programming, I was challenged to invest personally in each program. As both his student and as a professional singer in his ensemble, I felt truly valued musically. I was no longer just one anonymous voice among many—my voice and point of view mattered.

Johnson's exploration of this leadership model was no empty gesture. As his conducting student, I was challenged to explore musical relationships laterally as opposed to hierarchically. My experiences with Conspirare confirmed for me that the collaborative nature of the music-making experience must be cultivated in every relationship and with every musical selection. Singing and studying with Johnson ignited a fire in me and reaffirmed my belief that choral music can change lives.

Likewise, my singing and studying with Kathy Saltzman Romey at the University of Minnesota were incredibly formative in my musical development. During the 2006–2007 academic year, I was privileged to apprentice with Romey and the Minnesota Chorale as they prepared repertoire for collaboration with the world-renowned Minnesota Orchestra, as well as for the Bridges outreach program. In her work with the Chorale, Romey skillfully balances her commitment to building relationships through music with her belief in music as a vehicle for social activism.

I was especially inspired by the success of the Chorale's Bridges program—specifically the breadth of its partnerships within the community and its thematic and socially conscious programming philosophy. I believe that this approach reflects an emerging paradigm in community arts-outreach programs, wherein relationship building and collaboration are prioritized over the dissemination of "culture" to the underserved.

At the close of my doctoral studies in conducting at the University of Minnesota, I struggled with how to shape my musical identity and give back to my community. Could I build on the ideological foundation established by my mentors in order to make something of my own? From this climate of possibility and creativity, The Alchemy Project was born. Here is its story:

Where does art end and real life begin? The Alchemy Project believes that the boundaries that separate art from life are meant to be crossed. Life without the arts is drab and meaningless, and without the human element, image, sound, movement, and language are just media. But add to image, sound, movement, and language the generosity of the human spirit, our shared experiences as a community, and our dreams for a better world, and suddenly art is empowered to be a tool for transformation.

The Alchemy Project is in the business of transformation. Our mission is to reach out into our community and to start conversation. To build relationships. To explore the world in which we live. To celebrate the human experience. And to reflect our humanity and our world with the voice, the body, the brush, and the pen. In short, the goal is to connect. Through this connection, the mystical process of alchemy begins—we are transformed. And we are empowered to transform the world in which we find ourselves living into the world in which we choose to live. No longer is our battle cry "Art for art's sake." Rather we call you to raise your voices with us as we sing "Art for the greater good!"

How do we do this? With pertinent and topical themes, our lecture series, interdisciplinary performances, and discussion events open a broad and inclusive dialogue that has never before had the chance to flourish in the Twin Cities community. Through this dialogue we hope to build relationships and discover what can grow when art is given the opportunity to be a vehicle for change.

In considering event themes, The Alchemy Project is drawn to the grey areas of life, near the boundaries that separate and divide us from one another, into the conflict zones. This emotional geography is full of risk; nonetheless, our aim is not to draw lines in the sand. By examining that which divides us, we hope to discover what truly unites us—the commonality of the human experience.

The Alchemy Project promotes community engagement through its innovative conversation events and high-quality, interdisciplinary arts programming. We develop program themes in partnership with a chosen humanitarian organization in order to explore the divisive issues facing our global community. As part of this unique partnership, we aim to raise awareness on behalf of the partner organization, and we donate the proceeds from each project to support the mission of that organization.

The Alchemy Project's inaugural program explored creativity and mental health at the intersection of text and music. We partnered with the Bloomington, Minnesota-based suicide-prevention non-profit Suicide Awareness Voices of Education (SAVE) by thematically linking the conversation events and concert program to the SAVE mission: to prevent suicide through public awareness and education, eliminate stigma, and serve as a resource to those touched by suicide. All of the proceeds from this project were contributed to SAVE to support their programs.

We held five extraordinary conversation events on the campus of the University of Minnesota in order to explore this topic in greater depth with a diverse group of scholars, artists, health-care professionals, and distinguished members of our community. During these events, we explored the relationship between text and music in the composer's creative process, the history of mental illness, society's relationship with the mentally ill, madness as metaphor, and the dynamic between healing and narrative.

As the culmination of the conversation series, The Alchemy Project launched its first interdisciplinary art event—a unique choral concert featuring the University of Minnesota Chamber Singers and the Alchemy Ensemble, performing remarkable settings of poetry and prose by authors who have struggled with mental-health issues. Poets included Sara Teasdale, Sylvia Plath, William Blake, Federico Garcia Lorca, Emily Dickinson, and Edgar Allen Poe. In addition to programming existing works of living composers, The Alchemy Project presented two world-premiere performances of commissioned works by Minnesota composers J. David Moore and Midge McCloy.

Subsequent programs will follow a similar model. Conversation and interdisciplinary arts events will be developed thematically around the mission of our partner non-profit organizations, and the proceeds from these events will be dedicated to supporting their mission. Future collaborations are envisioned with organizations such as Oxfam, Doctors without Borders, the Boys and Girls Clubs of Minnesota, and the American Red Cross.

The collaborative artistic philosophy of Conspirare and the legacy of community engagement and social activism embraced by the Minnesota Chorale's Bridges program connect The Alchemy Project to a national community of choral organizations committed to meaningful and artistic programming. Building on this foundation, The Alchemy Project's dynamic programming and community engagement practices come to life through our commitment to cultural dialogue and interdisciplinary exchange.

For more information about The Alchemy Project, visit our website: www.alchemyproject.org

Broadening our Vision: Choral Activism in the Twenty-First Century

Shekela M. Wanyama

The choral art form is uniquely suited to nurturing community life and inspiring social change. In societies around the world, song is one way to express sorrow, loss, and joy as well as to envision a new reality for the larger community. Choral organizations across the United States have long recognized the important role choral music can play in communities and, as a result, have developed outreach programs intended to expose wider audiences to their work.

Unfortunately, few outreach initiatives venture beyond short-term, surface-level interactions into sustained engagement with members of the broader community. The Minnesota Chorale's Bridges program and The Alchemy Project demonstrate the possibility for arts organizations to partner with community members in reflective and potentially transformational dialogue about contemporary issues. Through innovative collaborations and programming, these organizations move beyond traditional models of outreach to exemplify the power of choral singing in an increasingly fragmented society.

To better understand the cultural significance of the Bridges program and The Alchemy Project, it is helpful to examine theoretical and historical perspectives on arts in the context of social change. In particular, the Civil Rights Movement stands as an example of how song can be used to articulate a specific stance and sustain communities during times of political, economic, and social upheaval. Drawing on these lessons, choral conductors, administrators, and singers can begin to discern the components of effective community engagement practices and, in so doing, demonstrate the relevance of the choral art to our contemporary society.

Artists, activists, and scholars have long recognized the powerful role the arts can play in the functioning of a society. Whether or not we are aware, the arts are an integral part of our daily lives. From the music on the radio and the design of our clothing, to the books we read and the architecture of the buildings we live in, the arts have a subtle yet substantial impact on our understanding of the world around us. The arts assist us in defining and constructing our cultural existence.

Joost Smiers explores this concept further in *Arts Under Pressure: Promoting Cultural Diversity in the Age of Globalization.* He writes, "It is appropriate to describe the arts as being 'workshops' in which cultural meanings are crafted and created."[5] As Smiers explains, these cultural meanings are reflective of and contribute to the functioning of society: "Through the work of artists and the way their work is presented, social and cultural sentiments and convictions are produced, constructed, reproduced, and reconstructed."[6]

Artists serve as a prophetic eye for their surrounding community. They become creators of cultural legacy and offer visions for the future in their work. Through engagement initiatives, artists can use their work to reflect the experiences of community members and to stimulate constructive dialogue about the challenges present in broader society.

In his book, *Acting in Concert: Music, Community, and Political Action*, Mark Mattern writes, "The potential political significance of music extends well beyond . . . explicit uses [such as political rap or benefit concerts] to include . . . its impact on human identity and capacity, its role in defining or destroying communities, and its part in cultural revitalization and self-determination."[7] The political significance of music as identified by Mattern has been recognized by activists and artists alike. As a result, music has been used in a variety of social, political, and economic contexts to support change.

During the Civil Rights Movement of the 1950s and 1960s, participants used gospel songs, popular tunes, and African-American spirituals to negotiate difficult decisions, nourish weary spirits, and inspire courageous action. As the Movement spread throughout predominantly African-American communities in the southern United States, so did the songs, evolving as each community integrated them into local Movement activities and shared them with others. The result was a communication tool that was culturally oriented and relevant to Movement participants. The songs functioned as a collective documentation of individual and communal experiences. Singing the songs refreshed the spirits of those involved.

Bernice Johnson Reagon, a prominent scholar of African-American cultural history, was a songleader and member of the Student Non-Violent Coordinating Committee during the Civil Rights Movement. She has written and spoken extensively about the role song played in the Movement. In an interview with Bill Moyers, Reagon acknowledged the power of communal singing:

> When we sing, we announce our existence. . . . Song is a way you can extend the territory you affect. . . . People can walk into you before they can get close to your body. Communal singing is a way for a group of people to announce that we're here, this is real. The people who come into that space, as long as you are singing, cannot change the air in that space. The song will maintain the air as your territory.[8]

In contrast to traditional choral programming approaches that do not aim to assess or respond to specific circumstances, Reagon says songs from the Movement "have a lot more to do with stating a worldview, of positioning yourself in the world."[9] Movement participants shared in the formation of a new existence through the act of singing. In an essay entitled *Nurturing Resistance*, Reagon writes:

> I learned very early that I had to affect the space I sang in. The air that people breathed carried the sound of my voice as a songleader, joined by their own. I am now describing a feast of song, where that which is consumed is also created by the consumers, and what you take in is more than you can give out because when you put it out, it is enlarged by the sounds of others who commit themselves to participate in the creation.[10]

Much of the music from African-American culture and the Civil Rights Movement has discernable roots in specific geographic regions of the African continent. Because of the visionary, educational, and spiritual tradition of this repertoire, the preservation, sharing, and continued re-invention of these songs is linked to the survival of African-American cultural history and community. Without these songs, the strength of the community cannot be sustained.

The Civil Rights Movement presents just one example of how song and the activity of singing can support community development and social change. Choral musicians can use song to inspire transformative dialogue within rehearsal rooms and performance spaces. This dialogue may be complex and full of conflict or contradiction. At the same time, it can be affirming, nourishing, reflective, and productive, particularly when shared freely with the broader community.

Awareness of the potential for music and musicians to aid in the transformation of their communities is missing from engagement initiatives today. Without the communal creative process identified by Reagon, outreach activities between choral organizations and communities establish only surface-level connections. True engagement for choral organizations in the United States will take into account historical examples of song used in the context of social change and the lessons they provide.

I do not intend to suggest that the community engagement initiatives of choral organizations can be compared to the often life-threatening sacrifices of musicians engaged in resistance. Yet, I maintain that an acknowledgement of the power of communal singing will afford choral organizations the opportunity to reevaluate the potential impact of their work in the context of community needs.

Redefining community engagement activities comes with great risks. In our personal and professional lives, we operate within comfort zones that may not include economic, cultural, social, or political diversity. Community engagement requires moving beyond those comfort zones into unknown territory. Engagement is demanding and challenging, but can yield unexpected and surprising results. As Kathy Saltzman Romey says of the Minnesota Chorale's Bridges program, "It challenges our organization to assess, stretch, and push traditional boundaries—it is where the most growth occurs. Through Bridges, we are a healthier choral community."[11]

Successful community engagement will come from long-term relationships based on trust, open communication, and commitment to a goal that is meaningful to all who engage in the project. This is easier said than done. The establishment of productive relationships is often impeded by histories of cultural appropriation and misrepresentation, stereotypes, and the misinterpretation of deeply embedded cultural symbols, gestures, and language. No doubt these kinds of obstacles have hindered or completely thwarted efforts at collaboration in all areas of the arts as well as in other disciplines.

The adage "intent does not equal impact" approaches the root of these obstacles. One person's intent to be of assistance to another may not be truly helpful. The same concept applies to community engagement. In outreach programs, too often the organization doing the outreach is approaching the community partner from a perspective that does not fit the partner's needs. Engagement requires honest conversation among all parties involved in order to minimize confusion and maximize productivity. Community engagement may include the following directives:

1. *Understand cultural modes of communication and operate with a deeper level of cultural sensitivity.*

This requires dedicating more time for background research in areas such as music, language, cultural traditions, and mores. It is also necessary to acknowledge historical legacies of oppression and injustice, as well as to recognize the structures that support them. This learning process may require, in part, going to where community members gather, such as churches, schools, community centers, and homes. This may also include participating in social activities that are important to the community partner, rather than only those that serve the interests of the choral organization.

2. *Work closely* with *community members, and not* for *them.*

This may mean going so far as to invite community members into the project planning process from the very beginning, including them in every stage of the project's development, and ensuring that they have as much control over the outcome of the project as the organization initiating the engagement.

3. *Extend relationships and the goal of the partnership beyond the concert experience.*

The activities of the partnership cannot be limited to those that serve only the interests of the organization. The organization must also work to further the interests of the community partner, establishing a synergistic relationship that helps all partners reach their goals and fulfill their missions.

4. *Remove barriers to access.*

This may include making the concert experience more inclusive through creative programming that evokes the cultural world of the concert repertoire. Organizations should also explore utilizing media from other arts disciplines, performing in a variety of venues, hosting pre-concert workshops or open rehearsals, subsidizing tickets or offering free performances, and employing innovative marketing strategies to reach desired audiences.

5. *Create a more inclusive organization, from the inside out.*

This may require inviting community members to serve on the board of directors, hiring community members to be a part of the staff, and establishing internship or job-shadowing opportunities for interested individuals. This could also take the form of more accessible auditions and/or the implementation of an introductory choir that would assist singers in gaining the skills necessary for auditioning at a more advanced level. Choral ensembles can also develop innovative programs that enrich the performance experience with a diversity of voices. These actions—when taken in tandem with those listed above—may contribute to a more inclusive organization, both administratively and artistically.

Given the wide variety of choral organizations in the United States and the specific needs of the communities that surround them, it is difficult to suggest definitive models for community engagement. Community engagement will vary with each choral organization and the communities with which it hopes to partner. The Minnesota Chorale's Bridges program and The Alchemy Project present just two models among countless possibilities. The underlying assertion, however, is the same: that collaboration with community members can lead choral organizations to play a more proactive role in reflecting and supporting community development and positive social change.

Conclusions

This document is one attempt at articulating how choruses can play a more active and intentional role in twenty-first century society. We believe that through innovative programming practices and lateral approaches to collaboration, choruses can use music as a vehicle for deepening relationships and raising awareness of social issues in communities across the United States. However, the diversity of opinions, experiences, challenges, and successes in the areas of community engagement and programming are too numerous to be documented here. We hope that others will be inspired to contribute to this discussion. In so doing, we may begin to discern the common threads of practice and to implement changes that will lead to a more informed, connected, and culturally relevant choral art in the United States.

In the daily pursuits of fundraising, marketing, audience development, and other components of running successful choral organizations, it is easy to lose sight of why we work so passionately in service to the choral art. We are drawn to choral music because of its ability to renew and inspire. On a deeper level, we commit ourselves to the development of the choral art because we care about the condition of humanity. We must extend this generosity of spirit not only to our audiences, but also to our broader communities. As we work to support the health of the society around us, we may find—through the wealth of experience and knowledge contributed by community members—that we are also ensuring the continued enrichment of the choral field.

Choral ensembles can stand as models of collaborative effort in the face of increasingly fragmented communities. Moving from traditional outreach and programming practices into more inclusive community engagement and music-making activities is risky. It means asking tough questions about social conditions, personal and organizational identity, and access to resources. It requires a steadfast commitment to what is possible, even while indications of progress are faint or nonexistent. Finally, it requires a presence of mind that is visionary, coupled with the presence of spirit that is oriented toward the care and support of individual people as well as whole communities. This is a weighty endeavor, but one which we, as musicians, are charged to undertake.

Appendix: "Sing Me a Home" Resource Materials

Program Overview & Underwriting

In securing financial support for outreach initiatives like "Sing Me a Home," it is important that the social-service dimensions of the project are made clear to a corporation or foundation. The following is a possible program description emphasizing this aspect of the project:

> "Sing Me a Home" uses art as a vehicle to address a key social issue. The project aims to publicize and further the work of Habitat for Humanity, which directly addresses unmet human and social needs. Habitat builds houses not *for* families but *with* them, promoting self-sufficiency and strengthening families as nurturing and financially stable environments for children.

Grant proposals must address corporate/foundation guidelines, which may request the following information in their proposals: (1) challenge or need, (2) artistic medium, (3) partners and program activity, (4) civic engagement, (5) program goals and objectives, (6) community impact, (7) project promotion, and (8) assessment methods. The following program overview of "Sing Me a Home" treats each of these topics in brief:

1. *An Abiding Need*

For too many families throughout the United States, decent housing remains a distant goal. Of the many organizations dedicated to helping families achieve that goal, Habitat for Humanity is perhaps the most effective and best known. Habitat for Humanity builds homes in partnership with families, who join in the work of constructing their own dwelling. Habitat homeowners, no longer struggling just to shelter their families, are thereby empowered to be better parents, workers, and citizens.

2. *Our Voices Are Our Tools*

"Sing Me a Home" draws on music from around the globe to make vivid the meaning of home, refuge, and sanctuary. Much as Habitat's volunteers build with hammers and nails, singers build with their voices, helping to communicate the deeper emotional dimensions of Habitat's work. A home, after all, is not simply a box for the body but also a dwelling for the spirit—and music speaks of and to the spirit with unequalled immediacy.

3. *Partnering With Young People*

No aspect of the "Sing Me a Home" project is more important than the involvement of young people in creating and performing music. New songs with texts written by students from area high schools—as guided by a professional mentor/writer—will be sung at the final performance by choirs from those students' schools. The conductor and composer will visit the schools in advance of the culminating concert to rehearse the songs and offer insight into the creative process. In this way, students will contribute directly to the substance of the program, exhibiting a level of communal and artistic engagement not usually seen among their peers.

4. *Musicians: A Community Resource*

For adult musicians, "Sing Me a Home" provides an unusual opportunity to live their values and advance key social goals. Musicians—especially singers—are among our society's most underutilized resources. Possessing crucial communicative skills, they can shine a light on neglected issues and speak directly to the heart.

5. *Program Objectives*

Objectives of the project include: (1) calling attention to urgent community needs and to current efforts to meet those needs, (2) singing the stories of representative Habitat homeowners, (3) creating occasions for diverse Habitat constituencies to come together, celebrate, and reflect, (4) building a corps of singer-ambassadors who can carry this work forward, and (5) demonstrating the community-building power of partnerships between an arts-minded social service organization like Habitat for Humanity and a socially-minded choral organization like the Minnesota Chorale.

6. *Populations Served*

Target population(s) for the program are the many community constituencies of Habitat for Humanity, including current and prospective homeowners, volunteers, and supporters (together with members of area congregations that contribute to the organization's work); other groups concerned with affordable housing, urban poverty, and/or the social uses of the arts; and the chorus's concert audiences, both established and newly recruited.

7. *Publicity*

Projects are undertaken collaboratively with organizational partners and typically focus on niche and free media pertinent to the target audiences. "Sing Me a Home" may rely strongly on Habitat for Humanity's extensive networks and the many nonprofit affiliate organizations of affordable housing, together with their rosters of volunteers and supporters. In addition, public relations efforts can also involve television, radio, and press coverage, promoting the project as both an arts event and a story of social awareness and community service.

8. *Assessment*

The success of each year's Bridges project is measured against the objectives articulated for the project at the outset and with the larger organizational goals articulated in our strategic planning. Evaluative discussions involving all program partners are an integral part of each year's project. Student evaluations, solicited in the schools, and audience evaluations, solicited at the performances, enable the Chorale to obtain feedback from the broader community. A portion of the Minnesota Chorale Board meeting following each Bridges program is dedicated to discussing and evaluating the project.

Criteria employed for evaluating Bridges (in addition to the conventional measures of audience size and responsiveness) included:

- the depth and durability of relationships formed by the partners
- the long-term value of the experience as assessed by the participants
- the growth in community awareness (reflected partly by media coverage) of the Bridges partnership in particular and the Chorale in general
- the changes effected in the organizational culture of the Chorale (e.g., the acquisition of enhanced capacity for future projects) as a consequence of the program.

In the review of any Bridges program, the Chorale employs an outcomes-based assessment model using questionnaires and interviews to provide the needed data. Online questionnaires have proved to be particularly useful in this process and we are cultivating this medium energetically.

"Sing Me a Home" Timeline

To work effectively with the many program partners and achieve the project goals, the Minnesota Chorale organized a timeline consisting of six two-month stages, as outlined below. Partnering organizations and composers were selected six months prior to the beginning of the project, and the timeline was developed to work within one academic year.

1. September–October
   - Meetings are held with Habitat for Humanity, partnering school choir directors, administrators, mentor/writer, and student writers.
   - Interviews are conducted with Habitat families led by a Habitat volunteer, chorus conductor, and assigned student writer.
   - Letters of contract are sent to composers and writers.
2. November–December
   - Interviews are transcribed and sent to mentor-writer and student writers.
   - Habitat stories are distilled into short prose texts by student writers assisted by mentor/writer.
   - Composers visit assigned high schools to meet choirs, conductors, and student writers.
   - Chorale members visit partnering high school choirs to present choral music education sessions.
3. January–February
   - Student prose texts are completed and sent to composers.
   - Musical compositions are written with consultation among composers, high school conductors, mentor/writer, and student writers as needed.
4. March–April
   - Commissioned songs are completed and sent to choirs.
   - Choirs prepare works and composers attend rehearsals to offer musical insights.

5. May–June
    - Joint rehearsals are held with partnering choruses.
    - Final preparation for the performance program is completed with Twin Cities Habitat for Humanity and participating Habitat homeowners.
    - Concert program is presented featuring the entire consortium of project partners.
    - Thank-you letters are sent, final evaluations of project collected from the schools, and data compiled for the website.
6. July–August (and beyond)
    - "Sing Me a Home" materials are organized and posted on the website.
    - Singers perform commissioned songs at Habitat home dedications and/or related events.

"Sing Me a Home" Sample Interview Questions

The Chorale worked closely with a designated volunteer from Twin Cities Habitat for Humanity, who screened, identified, and contacted possible homeowners to participate in the project. The volunteer also helped to develop the interview questions (with additional input from the mentor/writer), organized and attended all of the family interviews, and assisted with the interview process. Below is a sampling of the questions included in each interview:

- Tell us about your family and its history. If you are not from this state, how did you come to the area?
- What do you remember most vividly about your earlier life? What things do you miss? What things have you tried to preserve or recreate in your Habitat home?
- In what ways do you feel that owning a Habitat home has changed your life and the life of your family? Has it changed the way you relate to each other and to the greater community?
- Please describe one of the hardest or most challenging experiences in your life so far, and how it affected you and your family.
- What hopes and dreams do you have for the future?

- If English is not your mother tongue, please teach us the words for sanctuary, community, home, family, friendship, love, and music in your native language.

Conclusion

Bridges is an ongoing, multi-year effort to channel and harness our art for the greater good. While we try to maximize the reach of each year's program, the real significance of Bridges has been felt over a much longer time span: the impact of the annual programs is additive. The cumulative results of more than a decade of Bridges programming include a deepened appreciation of the cultural diversity of the Twin Cities, a heightened awareness of the needs of the less fortunate groups among us, and a dense web of organizational and individual connections centered on music but extending far beyond it.

The long-term ambitions of Bridges make measuring its success a challenge. We know, more or less, how to evaluate each individual program; we have a much vaguer idea of how to assess the achievements of the series as a whole. We are working to develop better measures of effectiveness that will enable us to gauge the enduring consequences of Bridges in a more quantitative, less impressionistic way.

Biographies

Kathy Saltzman Romey is Director of Choral Activities at the University of Minnesota and Artistic Director of the Minnesota Chorale, the principal chorus of the Minnesota Orchestra. She completed an Artistic Degree in Choral Conducting under Helmuth Rilling from the Frankfurt Musikhochschule in 1984 and served as Director of Choral Activities at Macalester College from 1985–1992. A staff member of the Oregon Bach Festival since 1984, Romey is the principal chorus master of the Festival Choir, which she prepares for annual performances and recording projects. Romey also regularly serves as a chorus master to the Internationale Bachakademie Stuttgart for special programs and tours, and has prepared programs with the Westminster Symphonic Choir, Netherlands Radio Choir, and Carnegie Hall Festival Chorus.

Emilie Sweet is an Assistant Professor of Music at Lake Forest College in Chicago, Illinois. A native of Fort Wayne, Indiana, she holds degrees from Indiana University (B.S. in Music and Italian, 2001), the University of Arizona (M.M. in Choral Conducting, 2003), and the University of Minnesota (D.M.A. in Conducting, 2008). Ms. Sweet is the founding director of The Alchemy Project, a Minnesota non-profit organization that promotes community engagement through high-quality, interdisciplinary arts events. Also active as a professional choral singer, Emilie has performed with many of the finest choral ensembles around the country, including the 2006 Grammy-nominated Tiffany Consort and Holy Trinity Bach Choir (New York City), the Santa Fe Desert Chorale, VocalEssence (Minneapolis), Conspirare (Austin), and Cantique Early Music Ensemble (Tucson).

Shekela M. Wanyama is completing a Master's degree in Choral Conducting from Temple University, where she studies with Alan Harler. She holds a Bachelor's degree in music education from the University of Minnesota, where she was a student of Kathy Saltzman Romey. Wanyama served as an intern with VocalEssence's WITNESS School Program in Minneapolis, Minnesota from 2004–2005. In 2007, she worked in the Community Partnerships at the John F. Kennedy Center for the Performing Arts in Washington, D.C.

Bibliography

de Mille, Agnes. *Martha: The Life and Work of Martha Graham*. New York City, NY: Random House, 1991.

Leinsdorf, Erich. *The Composer's Advocate: A Radical Orthodoxy for Musicians*. New Haven, CT: Yale University Press, 1982.

Reagon, Bernice Johnson. "Nurturing Resistance." In *Reimaging America: The Arts of Social Change*, ed. Craig Little and Mark O'Brien, 1-8. Philadelphia, PA: New Society Publishers, 1990.

Reagon, Bernice Johnson. *The Songs Are Free*. VHS. Interview by Bill Moyers. New York City, NY: Public Affairs Television, 1991.

Singing City. "About Us." www.singingcity.org/AboutUs/About Us.html (accessed 16 September 2007).

Small, Christopher. *Musicking: the Meanings of Performing and Listening*. Hanover, NH: University Press of New England, 1998.

Smiers, Joost. *Arts Under Pressure: Promoting Cultural Diversity in the Age of Globalization*. New York City, NY: Zed Books, 2003.

Notes

[1] Christopher Small, *Musicking: The Meanings of Performing and Listening* (Hanover, NH: University of New England, 1998), 13.

[2] Agnes de Mille, *Martha: The Life and Work of Martha Graham* (New York: Random House, 1991), 264. Agnus de Mille's precedes this quotation with the following explanation: "The greatest thing she ever said to me was in 1943 after the opening of *Oklahoma!*, when I suddenly had unexpected, flamboyant success for a work I thought was only fairly good, after years of neglect for work I thought was fine. I was bewildered and worried that my entire scale of values was untrustworthy. I talked to Martha. I remember the conversation well. It was in a Schrafft's restaurant over a soda. I confessed that I had a burning desire to be excellent, but no faith that I could be. Martha said to me, very quietly . . ."

[3] Singing City, "About Us," http://www.singingcity.org/AboutUs/AboutUs.html (accessed 16 September 2007).

[4] Twin Cities Habitat for Humanity, "About Us," http://www.tchabitat.org/content/section/5/27/ (accessed 16 September 2007).

[5] Joost Smiers, *Arts Under Pressure: Promoting Cultural Diversity in the Age of Globalization* (New York: Zed Books, 2003), 81.

[6] Ibid.

[7] Mark Mattern, *Acting in Concert: Music, Community, and Political Action* (New Jersey: Rutgers University, 1998), 5.

[8] Bernice Johnson Reagon, *The Songs Are Free*, interview by Bill Moyers, VHS (New York City, NY: Public Affairs Television, 1991).

[9] Ibid.

[10] Bernice Johnson Reagon, "Nurturing Resistance," in *Reimaging America: The Arts of Social Change*, ed. Craig Little and Mark O'Brien (Philadelphia: New Society Publishers, 1990), 1-8.

[11] Kathy Saltzman Romey, interview by author on 16 June 2006, tape recording, University of Minnesota, Minneapolis, Minnesota.

Conducting the Choral-Orchestral Work

Beverly Taylor

Women are likely to face several challenges when they stand in front of an orchestra, but only one is of prime importance: the purely artistic one of interpreting a score and bringing it to life in sound. The other challenges that must be faced, although hardly negligible, are in the periphery. These concerns—personalities, professional unions, stick technique, and stereotypes—must not be allowed to obscure the basic job of the conductor, which is to make music, and in doing so to uplift the mind, heart, and spirit of both performers and listeners.

Before discussing this overarching concern of developing the skills needed to communicate through the orchestral and choral-orchestral media, these other challenges deserve mention. First, some orchestras will not be responsive to any person on the podium or to the choral ensemble with which they may be performing; second, if a choir is involved, the choir may not be responsive to the leadership or in musical sync with the orchestra; third, some orchestras, or choirs or cultures may not welcome the leadership of women, and fourth, some orchestras do not like choral conductors on the podium in any way, shape or form. We will return to these issues in an informal way after a look at the art of choral-orchestral conducting. Since the readers of this chapter are likely to be choral conductors themselves, we will begin with a look at conducting the choral-orchestral work.

Preparing the Choral-Orchestral Score

The main goals of conducting, whether for orchestra or chorus are the same—to be musical in bringing a masterwork to life, to give auditory expression to the written directions and stylistic considerations, to make artistic choices that reflect the values grasped in preparing the work.

The two chief differences between preparing the choral-orchestral work and straight choral works are dealing with the length of the work, with the explicit or implicit structure to it, and becoming knowledgeable about the color and workings of the orchestral parts. The conductor's preparation, in search of this knowledge, must include a phrase-length analysis based on a mixture of harmony, melody and texture, and which, while advisable to have when working with purely choral works, is of utmost necessity when working with orchestral sections that are free from text.

Conductors must mark choral-orchestral scores carefully. Each conductor has his or her own way of marking; some hate having any markings on the page and keep details in their head; others mark everything in colors, primarily by function (principal theme, countertheme). For me, the markings on the score are designed as a roadmap, an aide-memoire for the conducting. I want to find something quickly and accurately on the page when needed in rehearsal and conducting, and want to have clear indications in the margins at the end of each page indicating what lies on the next page. The score's function and design are studied ahead. Not all aspects of the structure, once learned, need to be indicated on the page.

I mark scores for three reasons: (1) the details of them stay in the mind longer when entered by hand, (2) easy-to-spot directions are most important when conducting in low light or with aging eyesight, and (3) when returning to a score after a number of years, or when asked to guest conduct or substitute conduct on short notice, a conductor more easily grasps the musical idea and formal plan to take the music to the next level when the score has been properly marked.

My Approach to Score Marking

Since red pencil markings are most clearly seen in low light, use them to indicate most cues (half a bracket for chief entries; half of a pair of parentheses for entrances without major structural importance), and to set off orchestral groupings. From top to bottom, on most conventional score lay-outs, mark woodwinds in red, but use green or another contrasting color for horns. Below the horns, red again for brass, then blue or another contrasting color for percussion. Below that, again, red, for strings or chorus. Horns should be marked with a contrasting color because their function is often independent of both brass and woodwind groupings. Further, horns can be less easily read than the woodwinds, which, with flute and oboe in treble clef at pitch and bassoon in bass clef at pitch, are fairly easily apprehended as a unit by choral conductors, despite transposing clarinets. Therefore, horns, which virtually always are in a transposing key, need to be notated in a way that doesn't mix them with the woodwinds, and which can make them easily located in a dense score. Similarly, the percussion's contrasting color not only delineates the brass from strings, but is easily spotted for the occasional and dramatic uses that are common for percussion: timpani rolls, cymbal crashes, chimes, triangles.

Many additional markings or special notations may be marked in red or other colors. *Pizzicato* chords should be noted carefully, such as a short red line through a stem, since these *pizzicati* need to be prepared and conducted as one would an accent or a chorus cut-off. Additional markings might be the indication of instruments that double voices—e.g., *col soprano*—or *rubato*, or *a tempo* markings.

The phrase numberings are placed in pencil at the top and/or bottom of the score. Unlike many ballet or dance pieces that are purely orchestral and repetitive, and which can be notated with shorthand signals such as "4 × 4" (four measures of 4/4), many choral-orchestral works are constructed with more asymmetry. In my system, I number each measure individually, circling the last measure in each phrase, so that as the eye picks the circle out, the body prepares the next downbeat in a phrase. Sub-groupings also exist, of course; the music may suggest an eight-bar phrase followed by a three-bar extension. Although this could be notated as an eleven-bar phrase, the function of the phrase is better understood by numbering eight bars followed by a plus sign and three more bars, for example numbered "+9 10 11" if very closely related or "+1 2 3" if less closely related. (See Example 1, Brahms *German Requiem* II, mm. 33–42.)

When phrases overlap, the new phrase takes predominance over the earlier one and starts the new set of numbers. This works well for music constructed in musical periods, but is not a good system for fugal works of uncertain phrase length and equal dominance between parts. A variety of systems of notation can be employed, but an understanding of phrase structure is the most important aspect of learning the structure of a long work, and of conveying it to the listener. Knowledge of phrase structure also is the basis for much of the work done when conducting by memory, although in choral-orchestral works, the text certainly is central to large portions of the structure and aids in memory. However, in knowing phrase structure, one is training the body of the conductor and muscle memory to respond to the music in patterns and gestures that will add to the listeners' and performers' grasp of the masterwork. While not representing the last word in expressive gesture, this phrasal underpinning, like choreography, needs to lie deep in the body and musical understanding for the long work to have organic flow. A study of the work by phrase length reveals where various sections of the work are alike and, more importantly, where they differ. When four bars are followed by four bars of similar material and then by six bars, there is a built-in energy

Example 1

Brahms *German Requiem* II, mm. 33–42

that can be generated by the two bars of extension and which should be reflected in the conductor's movements. (For example, see the Mozart Requiem "Hostias," mm. 3–21.)

Certainly, there is more to score preparation than the above, and good habits of reviewing each line of the orchestra horizontally (watching for changing transpositions and clefs, *pizzicati*, or long periods between entrances) as well as the individual choral parts horizontally (looking for suspensions, unisons, unprepared entrances) are a necessary addition to any analysis of harmony, color, or text meaning. One needs to decide on choral breaths, and on releases. For instance, the British normally put consonants *on* the eighth note tied over the barline, not *after* that eighth note. More efficient rehearsals are the result of making most of these decisions ahead of time, although changes may be necessary in the live rehearsal.

Before the first orchestral rehearsal, mark string parts. If the choral conductor is uncomfortable with doing the markings, then she or he should meet with the concertmaster to discuss tone and concepts; a helpful concertmaster is always willing to demonstrate tone and style. Similarly, decisions about figured bass, speed of recitative, ornamentation and *ad lib* accompaniments should be worked out with only the players and singers involved before the whole ensemble is present. If the work is without many dynamic markings or articulations (common in early music) or if the work is not well-balanced as written for the modern orchestra, the conductor can save much rehearsal time by writing the needed dynamics or articulations in the parts. Absolutely, one must make sure that the choral parts, orchestral parts, and full score have the same rehearsal numbers or letters and, if the distance between the rehearsal indications is large, then more should be added to facilitate the rehearsal.

For aid with bowing, one can find many instructional books and people who are willing to demonstrate styles. Many conductors will let you look at their bowed scores or parts in order to learn various approaches. Over the years I've received permission to do some score study in both the Cleveland Orchestra library and the Chicago Symphony library, copying down bowings used in past performances of works by Brahms or Verdi. Also, attending other choral, choral-orchestral, and orchestral rehearsals always increases one's ability to find good solutions for rehearsal problems.

Working out Balances Ahead-of-Time and During the Rehearsal

Chorus members have a huge advantage over the orchestral members in having the full score, or at least the full choral score, in front of them. As a result, conductors can easily make interior balance changes in the work, which will help project the chorus through or over the orchestra. Adding second sopranos to alto entrances, and baritones to tenor entrances often makes sense; having designated people to always do this saves time in rehearsal. Of course one must not change the vocal color too much; adding an entire alto section to a tenor section will project the melody, but perhaps do too much damage to the color. With experience, a conductor can more easily spot where the audibility of a critical line will be a problem. Often, the alto—the low, interior voice—does not project, particularly if it is an early work and the choir has no male altos. In this case, male altos may be the answer, or if it's an exposed middle range, sometimes a baritone in falsetto provides a strong support without introducing the tenor color. Add baritones, for instance, to support the sopranos in the Credo of the Bach B Minor Mass at the transition to "Et exspecto," to ensure consistent vocal quality and strength throughout that passage.

Another issue is that of small or solo groups; Verdi may ask for four solo voices from each choral part, such as in the "Libera me" of the Requiem. Typically this group is not big enough to be audible without the individual voices sounding pushed; the conductor should be free to change these numbers depending on the acoustical situation.

Many conductors have used a technique Robert Shaw may first have used, of having some singers tonguing melismas in the choral-orchestral setting. I call the singers the "dah-dah" singers, and they are instructed to add a "D" to the beginning of the prevailing vowel in runs such as in the *Messiah* "For unto us a child is born." I usually have ten to twenty percent of the singers do this, and more if needed. The tongued "D" sound is always soaked up by the orchestra, and what emerges for the audience is a cleaner run. The tongued part can be assigned to singers with heavier or less flexible voices; it helps give them a point to their sound.

Add these "D's" to other spots to clarify the texture as well, particularly loud entrances starting with "L," which are hard to launch cleanly, such as "Lord, our Creator," the final chorus of Mendelssohn's *Elijah*; several of our choir's singers are assigned to sing "Dord, our Creator."

In a discussion many years ago with Margaret Hillis when I was preparing to conduct the Verdi Requiem, she advised me to have every singer on stage sing the downbeat D♭ at the start of the "Tuba mirum" section, rather than merely the basses, in order to have anything cut through the massive brass chords of the orchestra.

In other works, balances can be worked out ahead by bolstering the vocal parts or deciding to cut down the forces or narrow them for certain sections of the piece—using solo strings with a soloist, for instance. The choral conductor needs to look through the score for sustained brass chords; often these can be re-notated as *forte-pianos*, or *forte-mezzo fortes*, so that the chorus isn't drowned out. When working with younger players, the choral conductor needs to be aware that the softest ensemble sound may be determined by the wind players' ability to play softly; the strings and chorus can be very quiet, but the overall balance may need to be adjusted to the winds, if they are unable to adjust their own volume to the desired soft level.

If the balance problem will be with an entire voice part throughout the work, the conductor may consider different standing arrangements that can strengthen the particular section, such as placing tenors in front of the basses or second sopranos in front of the first, since in normal acoustical situations the voices in front color those to the rear. If the work involves many imitative entrances, such as the Bach Magnificat, a standing order in sections is best since, both visually and aurally, this best projects the polyphonic music. In a work such as the Duruflé Requiem, however, which is more homophonic, modal, and which chronically goes flat, a mixed standing arrangement is best, for this nearly always improves intonation. One can always cue in an agreed-upon direction for a voice part, no matter where the chorister is standing, or one can cue in a generalized way, since the chorus is well prepared; after all, the orchestral conductor cannot cue every instrument that plays a line simultaneously, such as an oboe with the string section. Cuing musically and maintaining eye contact will ensure good entrances.

Other standing possibilities exist; for instance semi-mixed—basses mixed with sopranos, and tenors with altos—provides some measure of stereo sound, while allowing for more accurate intonation. Many Europeans favor placing high voices—soprano and tenor—behind the violins on the conductor's left, and low voices behind the violas and cellos on the conductor's right. This may be helpful for color and some doubling, but less good for overall intonation, and not all orchestras are seated with the low strings on the audience far right.

Have someone listen in the hall for at least several of the choral-orchestral rehearsals, to either take notes, or to provide feedback on balances during the course of the rehearsal. The alternative is to have an assistant conduct while one is out in the hall herself or himself. Frequently the conductor of choral-orchestral works may not be getting a clear picture of the overall sound from the stage. The proximity and volume of the instruments—since the stage tends to be much more crowded for choral-orchestral works—can make it almost impossible to gauge the effect of the voices on the audience, particularly if the hall is constructed in a way that propels the choral voices up and over the orchestra. A conductor needs to train an assistant to listen not only for balance between solo and orchestra, and orchestra and chorus, but also for interior balances and balances of cadential chords. I have found it typical for many halls to project a large amount of the sound of the fifth in the final chords of tonal pieces (frequently assigned to the horns) while often there is not enough third. The choral conductor may wish to tune the orchestra as if tuning a choir, by asking the members of the ensemble to sing/play the tonic, then fifth, then third.

When one refers to a specific note to be sung or played, use the term "concert pitch" to indicate the sound wanted; this means one does not have to tell each transposing instrument what to play, but may rely on the player to make the adjustment. To tell the orchestra to play a "concert D" might have the strings playing a notated D, the horns a notated A and the clarinets a notated E. Referring to concert pitch solves the problem.

Baton Technique Suggestions for Choral Conductors

Many conductors have been taught that the baton is an extension of the arm. That should be revised to say the baton is an *articulated* extension of the arm, not a splint. The energy goes through the elbow, wrist and hand to the *point* of the baton, not the handle. This will ensure that the beat is clear and not overly large, and that the wrist hasn't tightened, which would lock the arm and prevent expressivity of gesture. In general most choral directors have too large a beat when conducting an orchestra. If the choir is in front of you at all times, that may work, but with an orchestra wrapped around the conductor, a smaller, focused beat is easier for the players to follow and less wearing on the conductor for a long work. The hands should be able to work independently. Indeed, my coach at Aspen, Paul Vermel, suggested that on gentle cues to the violins on the left, it is less fussy, clearer and more graceful to use your left hand and scoop them up rather than turn your back on the cellos to use your baton hand.

Whereas many choral directors have been taught to never mirror their hands, because it is hard for two hands to beat precisely at the same instant, most orchestral conductors regularly do this, for emphasis, force, or to be more visible to more of the orchestra. However, all good conductors need to strive for hands that each work and complement various aspects of the music. A hand hanging by the side makes the conductor look uninvolved.

Gustav Meier suggests that the preparatory beats with the orchestra should mirror the group cued—brass and woodwinds need a clearer ictus for a clean entrance than do strings, who can start from almost no volume at all. This kind of conducting helps the performers and the audience apprehend the changes in texture and color for a richer reading of the music. Although some conductors feel that the job of the conductor is not to conduct for the audience's sake, but solely for the players, and to let the music speak for itself, there is another aspect to consider. While grandstanding at the expense of the music is ill-advised, the clear conducting of structure for the audience as well as the ensemble can only enhance the listening experience, especially at a time when many concert-goers have not learned how to listen.

Most choral-orchestral literature has a reliable rhythmic underpinning; the first subdivision is nearly always present in some part of the orchestral writing, and frequently the next smaller subdivision of the rhythm is present as well. The *basic* choral-orchestral beat comes from the elbow. A clear beat initiated below the elbow will activate the elbow in its natural hinge motion, providing a natural rebound that suggests the duple subdivision, without using an artificially imposed subdivision to do the work. This is the "bread and butter" beat of the classical style, including nearly every chorus of Haydn's *Creation*. A smaller beat can also convey underlying agitation. In the "Dies irae" of the Mozart Requiem, for example, a small, but powerful four-beat pattern, with a clear, sharp ictus, is more insistent and easier to follow than a flowing two, even if the tempo suggests it could be done in cut time. (See Example 2, Mozart Requiem, "Dies irae," mm. 1–4.)

Many conductors are taught that the principal beat (such as a quarter note in a 4/4 section) is represented by the whole arm, generated by the shoulder, while the subdivision is represented by the half arm, generated by the elbow, and the next subdivision governed by the wrist. I have found this to be largely true. In sections such as the final *Adagios* in Handel *Messiah* choruses, or the slow chorales of Mendelssohn's *Elijah*, the fully controlled legato gesture is generated by the shoulder and breath, and connected through the biceps and lower arm to the hand and/or baton, as it would be in conducting legato *a cappella* motets. But works like the Mozart Requiem or the Haydn *Creation*, or the fugues of the Brahms *German Requiem* have much more power if the ictus is strong, small and in the lower half of the arm, with power going *to* the beat, and not flicking away from it. For sections in sixteenths, or whatever the next lower subdivision is, the wrist comes into play; the beats have the strength of the upper arm behind them, but the beat is generated in the wrist and lower forearm. Putting the full energy into the wrist effectively focuses the orchestra and chorus, and prevents the conductor from getting worn out and flailing; more important, when the larger gesture is needed for dramatic climax, it looks fresh and not like all the preceding gestures.

Example 2

Mozart Requiem, "Dies irae," mm. 1–4

Even without the use of the left hand, and even without the subtlety of other gestures, one can save a great deal of time in rehearsal by using the appropriate part of the arm. For instance, if the rhythm of the piece is quarter-quarter-four eighth notes and then a measure of sixteenths, the arm may move in a connected fashion for two beats, ictus generated from the elbow for two, and then the ictus strong from the wrist (see Example 3).

Example 3

legato full arm *beat generated at elbow* *strong ictus generated at wrist*

This produces a much clearer response from the choral-orchestral forces than the generic metronome that many conductors display in their patterns, and it is easy to read peripherally, which is how many players may see the beat. The beat should generally take place at what I call the "power point," the ninety degree angle to the upper arm, where the full force of the beat can be felt. Below this angle, the force is dissipated, but above it, where many choral directors conduct, the beat is less easy to read and may have a pushed quality, rather than a full-bodied release of energy. Of course, individual phrases may call for raising the hands off this centered level, but the majority of beats should be in this "strike zone."

A word of caution: When being trained by a conducting teacher of a different body type, one must make sure to adjust the concept for one's own body. I am short and short-waisted but long-legged, and my orchestral conducting teacher, Gustav Meier, has a long torso. Most women's arms are proportionately longer in the upper arm than are men, and the elbow is at a slightly different angle from that of men (for a discussion one might read *Manwatching* by Desmond Morris, published by Jonathan Cape, 1977)—no detriment to making music, but one must watch for tension in the angle of the arm. When watching my teacher demonstrate a dramatically forte chord, I saw him hitting the beat at the middle of his torso; when I imitated him I looked like a crabby infant. His ninety-degree angle was mid-torso; I discovered mine was with my elbow resting on my hip. Once I discovered the ninety-degree principle, my beat too was powerful.

For all conductors, the strength of the body, and particularly the bicep, forearm near the elbow, and the middle of the back are important. For choral conductors who are used to substituting a large beat for a strong small one, much work will need to be done to grow in power in the small package of a controlled beat. For women conductors whose strength has not been in the biceps, there may be a tendency to overuse and over-rotate the shoulders. Using a mirror, and weights, and using isometric exercises or imagery can increase the strength throughout the whole arm. This takes practice, as at first the wrist will tend to stiffen as these connections are made. Sometimes an exercise such as making a fist to contract the bicep, and then willing the hands to open while the bicep remains contracted, can help in developing the strength and sensitivity of the arms.

A good example of how good physical conducting can communicate a passage more clearly occurs in the "Confutatis" of the Mozart Requiem. The opening powerful forte of the men's chorus is usually conducted in four—their prevailing rhythm—although the string writing contains thirty-second notes. By conducting a small but very forceful beat, articulated at the wrist, while thinking of the thirty-seconds, the conductor can convey the string articulation while preserving the larger beat for the men; to subdivide this section at the usual tempo of the piece would create a chaotic picture. The transition to the women's section is primarily in eighth-notes; as the primary beat moves more to the elbow and away from the wrist, the natural rebound of the arm will suggest the eighth-note subdivision, which can be elongated into a *ritardando* if desired. (See Example 4, Mozart Requiem, "Confutatis," mm. 4–10.)

The "Voca me" of the women can be conducted in more legato quarter notes, with a suggestion of the moving eighths of the strings. On the return to the men's music, the strong wrist comes into play again with the thirty-seconds in the strings.

This technique is especially important when working in tempos that lie irritatingly between the macro- and micrometers, and are frequently in a moderate to slow 6/8 or 6/4. These include well-known choral-orchestral sections such as the "Lacrymosa" of the Mozart Requiem, the outer portions of Brahms *Nänie*, and the middle of the Fauré Requiem "Libera me." One can maintain the flow of the large two-dotted half-note pattern, but hit the ictus in the speed of the quarter note subdivision, with the whole arm taking up the slack of the rest of the beat. (See Example 5.)

Example 4

Mozart Requiem, "Confutatis," mm. 4–10

Example 5

Normal four,
even speed to each ictus
(good for legato passges).

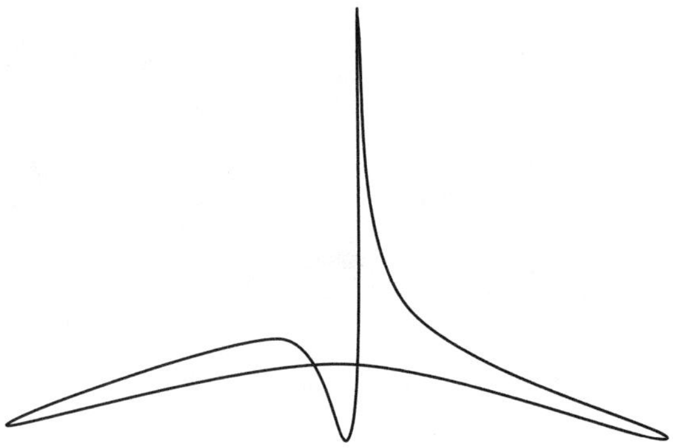

Four subdivided into eight
at the same tempo,
the speed to the ictus is
twice as fast.

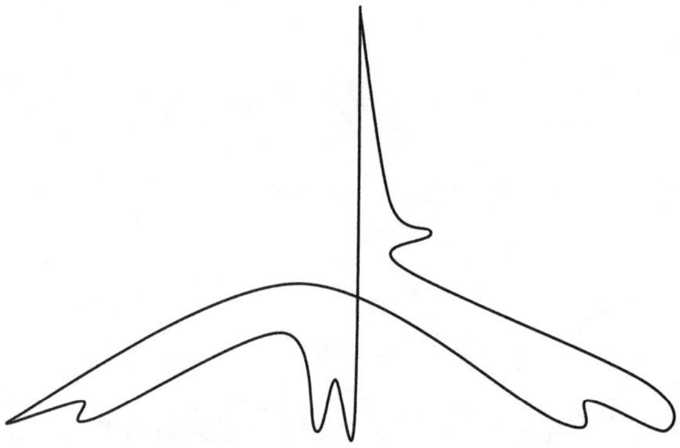

Hitting each beat
in the speed of
the subdivision,
but letting the arm
take up the slack
of what would be
the second half of
the subdivided beat.

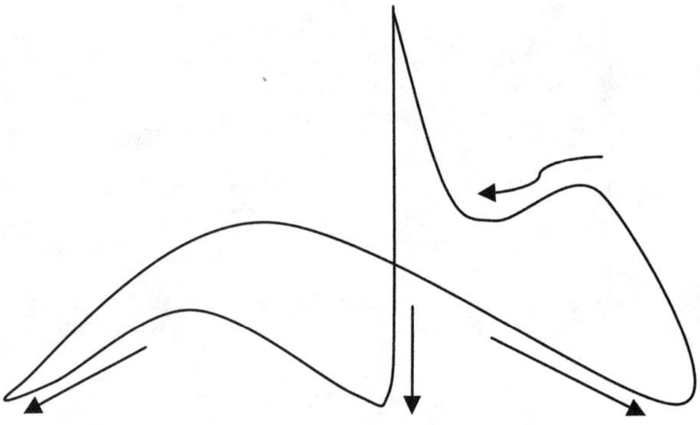

Alternately, the conductor might choose to conduct a hybrid meter such as quarter-eighth, quarter-eighth—something that choral conductors are sometimes taught is wrong when conducting orchestras. If it's clearer and more musical than conducting a whole movement in subdivision, then it should be by all means be used.

Compound meters (meters with beats triply subdivided, such as 6/8 or 12/4) generally are wider; orchestral players can catch the swing of these beats peripherally; when the conductor's general beat is a smaller, clear duple, without the swing, that too can be seen peripherally. This makes all the difference in conducting Stravinsky's *Symphony of Psalms*, where the players are watching their parts intently; meter changes can be apprehended peripherally simply by the height of the beat, the swing of the arm motion and the speed of the ictus.

These changes in emphasis are easy to manage as long as the body and mind have kept track of the tempo. For every shorter motion that the wrist makes, the body must have lag time to fill up the beat. For instance, in preparing the ensemble to come in on the last eighth note of a measure in common time, one might give a tiny third beat (for tempo information) and a fourth beat hit in the speed of the eighth note (which is twice as fast as the quarter note beat); the arm then picks up the slack by floating through the remaining eighth note, and the performers enter cleanly, since they've been able to envision the eighth note. These signals are clearest when the body behind it is stable—not in undue motion. When too much upper body motion follows the strong wrist beats, one can get an unwanted *accelerando*. Similarly, choral conductors facing orchestras and using in general too big a beat, or a beat which starts over the shoulder, will face problems of causing rushing in the ensemble; the conductor has caused this problem by the arm traveling farther, and therefore faster, from the previous beat to the new ictus, thereby skewing the general tempo.

In addition to making the beat smaller and clearer and stronger, the choral conductor must learn when to stop or suppress the *rebound* in favor of greater clarity for both choir and orchestra. Many choral conductors are trained in a buoyant, continuous rebound and high beat, which may encourage constant breath support and flow; however, this consistent beat actually is a component of a *lack* of clarity. Between phrases, a stop on the final beat of the first phrase and a lift of the arm, with breath, to start the next phrase, is clearer and more subtle in *rubato* or gentle sections and is particularly useful when the end of the first phrase is on an unstressed syllable of the choir; to use a full rebound or big preparatory beat for the next phrase would destroy the first phrase by putting an unwanted accent on the final syllable. (See Example 6, Beethoven Mass in C, Credo, mm. 95–104.)

Example 6

Beethoven Mass in C, Credo, mm. 95–104

Two further examples: in the sixth movement of the Brahms *German Requiem*, the repeated word "Wo" is used three times. The first two come to a dead stop. The hand should stop on one and not rebound, but lift for the next beat. This clarifies the music: one big beat, then a stop/silence, rather than beating through the rests. (See Example 7, Brahms *German Requeim*, VI, mm. 192–204.)

Example 7

Brahms *German Requeim*, VI, mm. 192–204

Another example: in the Verdi Requiem fourteen measures before the end of the "Rex tremendae" the chorus and orchestra finish a section with a forte "salva me." After two beats of rest, the basses echo "salva me" at a *pianissimo* volume. The conductor should stop the *forte* beat on beat three, without rebounding, wait for the two beats of rest, and gently breathe while lifting the baton gently for the *pianissimo* entrance. (See Example 8, Verdi Requiem, "Dies irae," mm. 367–375.)

Example 8

Verdi Requiem, "Dies irae," mm. 367–375

This is more dramatic, more true to the musical gesture, and is clearer. What it *does* require is that the conductor trust the orchestra and chorus to have established the rhythm enough to not require having the two beats of rest conducted. Yes, orchestras need nearly every downbeat, and clear cues, but once the rhythm is established, there can be some freedom in conducting musically, and the orchestra will respond to the conductor's musicality.

Following this thought are reminders that the choral conductor has the same freedom with the orchestra as with the chorus to change beat structure—for instance, to go in and out of conducting in four or two. One should simply relay to the orchestra at the start of the movement what pattern the start will be in, and make sure that the tempo is established before changing into a macrometer. Within these parameters, the conducting should *always* be different from measure to measure, growing smaller with unstressed syllables in the choral texture, and never *beating* hard through long held notes, but conducting *through* them, in an intense but legato fashion, avoiding the syndrome of simply beating time like a metronome. When the texture changes rhythmically, so should the hands and arms; bringing out offbeats by conducting the principal beats in the speed of the offbeat, but not letting a rebound slow the syncopation. This type of conducting is more aesthetically satisfying, saves rehearsal time by being clear, and reinforces phrasing already rehearsed. (See Example 12, Beethoven Mass in C, Gloria, mm. 318–325.)

Example 9

Beethoven, Mass in C, Gloria, mm. 318–325

beat legato half notes

beat one is in the speed of the quarter note with no rebound to bring out offbeat

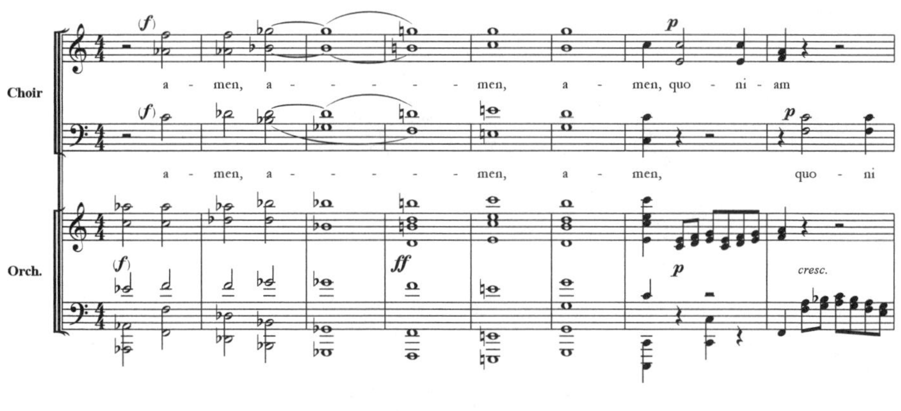

Cut-offs must be a follow-through of the preceding phrase, which might be loud and forceful or soft and tender. Cut-offs in orchestral conducting are almost always with the left hand, particularly if they are in the interior of the piece, that is, not a final chord. The left hand is raised (preparatory beat for the cut-off) and returns down to the beat point and *stops*. Circles to the outside, up, or fluffy waving motions do not help bring an orchestra to a clean cadence. However, for some final chords or cadences that end on a sustainable consonant for the chorus, such as "n" or "m," then, the conductor has the option of giving a double gesture at the end, one to close the consonant, the next for the final release. For these endings, I hold the chord with my left hand, use my right hand in what I call the "trowel" motion—a digging motion with a flexed wrist which prepares the consonant—and then use both hands to release the chord.

Example 10

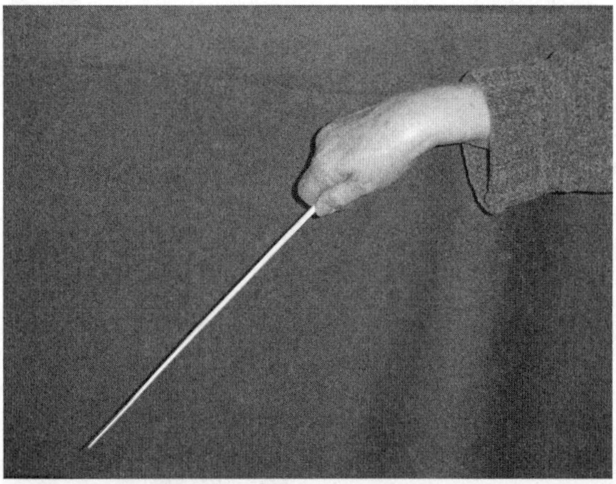

"trowel" motion

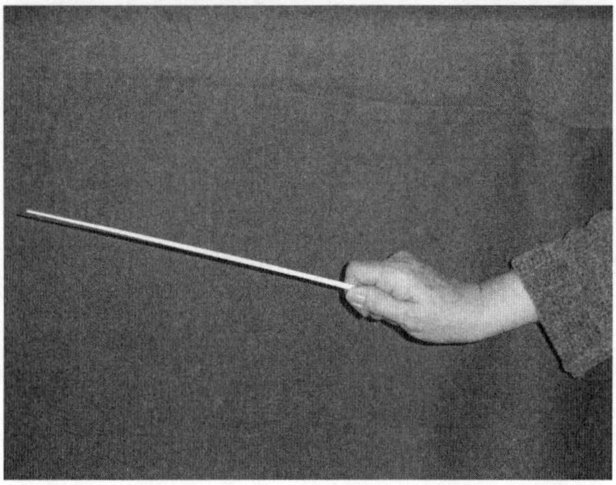

release

Another technique can be very useful to choral conductors working with orchestras, and that is the backhand swing, used for *rubatos* and delayed arrival chords; it spares the need for unmusical over-control and unnecessary subdivisions, when a gentle organic conclusion to the piece is desired. For example, in a slow six-beat pattern, beat five comes in, up and left, and beat six goes out and up, leading with the back of the hand, creating an upswing which gives room for the rubato before gently guiding the hands back to beat one. (See Example 11.)

Example 11

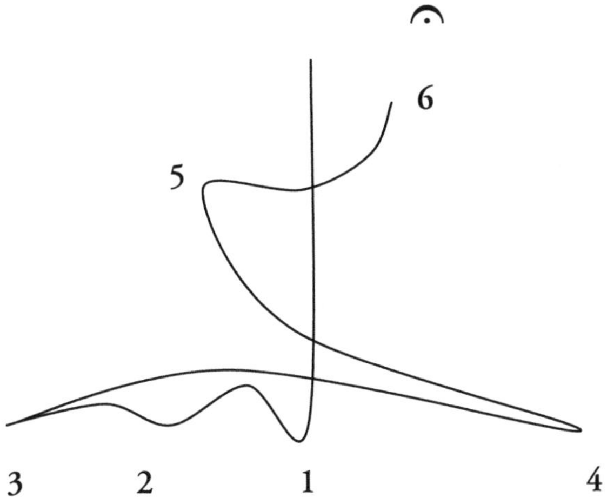

This allowance of space and time in which to have the music organically run its course can be practiced with the choral-orchestral ensemble; with very little time spent on the gesture, it can make for very musical phrasing.

Conducting the Major Choral-Orchestral Work in a Joint Rehearsal

The *first* problem to solve in a joint rehearsal (chorus and orchestra) is *ensemble rhythm.* The chief cause of the problem is that the chorus' vowels are not lined up with the conductor's baton. If the initial consonants of the chorus' words are lined up with the beat, the singers will sound late, because the major portion of the chorus sound is carried by the vowel, and the chorus is standing behind the orchestra. If the conductor on the podium has prepared the chorus, the problem should already have been solved by training the chorus to precede the downbeat by the consonant, and line up the vowel with the beat instead; the conductor on the podium can help the consonant attack by using the trowel-digging motion in the same way that one prepares a grace note which precedes a principal beat. If the podium conductor has not been the preparer, then this principle must be explained and demonstrated very early in the rehearsal, in front of the orchestra, so that both parts of the ensemble are committed to the same precise, and joint, attack.

The *ends* of choral-orchestral phrases need attention as well. For clarity's sake, final consonants may need to be released early, with a shorter articulation, particularly if the final consonant is voiced and would carry over to a new harmony on different pitches in the orchestra. (See Example 12, Haydn, *The Creation*, "The Heavens Are Telling," mm. 1–4.)

Example 12

Haydn, *The Creation*, "The Heavens Are Telling," mm. 1–4

Choral conductors need to accustom themselves to listening to the length of final notes with chorus and orchestra, and to increase the clarity by *dictating*—showing exactly the length desired on these chords or ends of phrases. For instance, many choral-orchestral works end with three unison quarter-note chords, perhaps with *tenuto* or *staccato* markings over them. How long is the *tenuto* or *staccato*? All the parts have it, but if the conductor does not show the length of each note, by an infinitesimal extention of its length, but simply beats in a generalized staccato with rebound, the chorus and orchestra might find these chords to be very messy. By avoiding the normal rebound and simply dictating the length of a note, clarity throughout the choral-orchestral ensemble is achieved. The choral conductor needs to look for where orchestral and choral articulations do not match and try to determine if changes should be made with one part to match another. If a change is made, the conductor reinforces the decision in the shortness or length of each beat. (See Example 13, Haydn *Nelson Mass*, Sanctus, mm. 13–16.)

Example 13

Haydn *Nelson Mass*, Sanctus, mm. 13–16

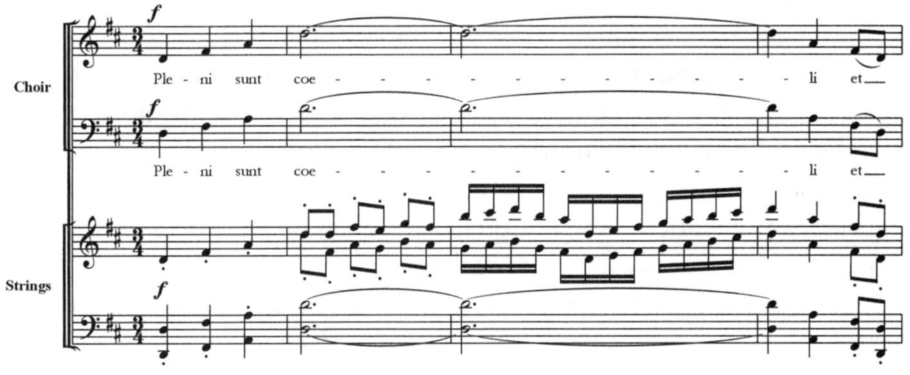

Much time can be saved in the rehearsal if the conductor periodically uses one group to demonstrate for the other. It should never be only in one direction; that is, both the chorus and orchestra should act as leaders. For instance, if a chorus is doubled by the orchestra, the conductor might have the orchestra play as the chorus speaks in rhythm, giving the singers both practice in placing their consonants and a chance for them to identify any parts in the orchestra that double theirs. In the major Bach choruses, having the chorus hear the constant sixteenth-note underpinning of the orchestra can only enhance their overall rhythm. On the other hand, if the phrasing in the orchestra is affected by the word inflection, particularly with lightened syllables, such as in the great choruses in Mendelssohn's *Elijah* or Handel's *Messiah* or any of the chorales in the Bach Passions, then the chorus can more quickly demonstrate the phrasing than the orchestra can learn by bowings and explanation alone. Of course the conductor should be reinforcing the phrasing with her hands at all times.

Needed drill and repetition become more interesting and musically deeper when rehearsing the chorus with various sections of the orchestra, thinning the texture so that conductor, chorus members and orchestra players can hear clearly. Give the strings a rest and work on inflection with the woodwinds and singers. Have the strings play with the singers. Repeat *tutti*. These actions give all the musicians a chance to "read the hall," that is, to get acquainted with the acoustics in this new format: the choral-orchestral entity. Both ensembles are used to rehearsing surrounded by quite a different sound. One must enable the players and singers to *hear*, if one wants quick growth in the music-making.

Both orchestral and choral directors use metaphors Sometimes orchestra conductors encourage their players to *sing*, and it is easy, while the choir is on hand, for the choir to demonstrate line, color, and drama for the orchestra. Sometimes choral conductors ask for singers to perform the kind of articulation of couplets, on-string or other bowings in a chorus rehearsal when seeking clarity or historical style, but the point comes home to singers when the strings can demonstrate the style for them on the spot.

Once the ensemble rhythm is established, the music-making can proceed faster. Rehearsals, as always, need to be carefully planned and timed, with particular attention given to starts, stops and transitions. If the joint rehearsals are few, then goals for each have to be established and perhaps set forth to the ensemble. For instance, when I performed the Verdi Requiem with two rehearsals with a union orchestra, the first was spent in running individual movements and rehearsing following each run-through. The second rehearsal was fixing each movement's problems first, followed by the run of that movement. When I performed the work with the university orchestra on six rehearsals, I had time as well as the need to work on style considerations, which good but young orchestra players clearly needed as much as they needed attention to technical aspects.

If at all possible, the choral conductor should meet with the orchestra alone first, to establish command and to introduce the work and text to the orchestra. Although the conductor must avoid excessive wordiness, she must give the orchestra a sense of the piece's text or purpose. As in opera, if the players are invited into the drama, it gives direction to their playing. In Stephen Paulus' *Voices*, the lumbering chords of the low strings became easier for the players to perform correctly when they knew that that particular movement was about weary lepers treading the streets. I introduced that concept saying, "I don't know how often you talk about text—" "We never talk about text," quipped the principal second violin. The players need the information as much as they need the story of a tone poem. Likewise the fast gestures of "Lasset uns" in the Bach *St. John Passion*—Helmuth Rilling describes it as the rolling of the dice as the Romans cast lots—are more successfully played when the players can envision the scene.

If there is more than one rehearsal, the rehearsal order usually is organized around the number of instruments involved, so that players or soloists are not sitting around longer than necessary. This is especially true in the opening rehearsals for most Baroque works, in which the ensemble size and content vary greatly from movement to movement. The conductor can organize these rehearsals from large to small or vice versa—flutes and continuo; strings and continuo; flutes, strings and continuo; *tutti* minus brass; full *tutti*, etc. But at the later rehearsals, the conductor should arrange the schedule to build dramatic scenes, so that players and singers can pace themselves. This is important also in works that require stamina throughout. For instance, always rehearsing the last movement of the Brahms *German Requiem* at the start of the rehearsal, when the singers are fresh, is a mistake. The singers need to learn to sing in tune and with beauty *after* they have given their vocal all in the sixth movement fugue.

The majority of the limited time a conductor has with the chorus and orchestra together should be spent on openings, transitions, *accelerandos*, *rubato*, endings, and balance. Run-throughs have their uses, but one must always have a backup plan if time runs short, particularly if a snowstorm, fire alarm, or accident changes your goals for your dress rehearsals. Security may precede artistry in importance in a rehearsal time crunch, but for the "magic moments" to occur in the work, these must be planned too, and experienced before the final performance. Has the chorus memorized the crucial junctures? Are the players aware of where page turns interfere with the drama? Even though every great performance grows in artistry and is unique in experience, a well-planned course of rehearsal with chorus and orchestra will set the stage for a memorable concert. The conductor needs also to plan details that may affect the very start of the concert, such as pitches for the chorus if the singers begin the piece on the downbeat of the first movement, as as the Mozart *Coronation Mass* or Beethoven Mass in C. The pitch can be given discreetly from a bassoon or cello, or the chorus can tune to the A of the oboe—especially good for dramatic openings such as the Bach B Minor Mass, which is most effective if not tied to a pedantic pause to give a pitch. These things must be practiced in the dress rehearsals and before, as there is a lag time between the tuning and the arrival onstage of soloists and conductor.

In preparation for these joint rehearsals, the choral conductor needs to spend as much time aurally envisioning the colors of the *orchestra* as the colors of the voices. If she can not find an appropriate musical term for what is wanted, then modeling with the voice, or using plain English can solve the problem. To a degree, the ensemble needs to play and sing through a section before detailed rehearsing. Many orchestral players will solve minor problems themselves after a first run. To stop every measure and evaluate is unnecessary, a waste of time, and occasionally rude. Still, players need as much guidance as singers for repeat offenses or intonation errors. A more common error among young but competent string players is that of playing upbeats with a strong accent produced by too much bow. By saving some bow on the way down, the upbeat can be a musical leading to the downbeat, something singers find much easier to do when directed. The singers can demonstrate this, and if the concertmaster needs to alter the bowing, it can be done fairly simply.

There is good news for the choral conductor who is afraid to use the equivalent of extraordinary and imaginative choral techniques with the orchestra. Some can be used. Imagination is not the property of singers alone, and an imaginative rehearsal approach is never a downfall; it's the execution that's in question. I first felt freed to express myself more "normally" with an orchestra after observing Colin Davis rehearse the Munich Radio Orchestra on the accompaniment part of a Mozart piano concerto. The musical figure was an eighth note followed by an eighth-note rest, another eighth-note and rest and a half-note; the rhythm was the same for the whole orchestra. He asked the players to come slightly off their chairs on the first eighth note, farther off their seats on the second, and to gently sit down on the half-note. Aside from their laughter as they tried to dance in their chairs while bowing their instruments, the notes received a gentle "up," "up" and deliberately and gently placed "down" that simply hadn't been there a few moments before. The effect was achieved quickly, with humor and goodwill. If the choral conductor has useful techniques, similes, modeling, or other demonstrations that will make the *musical* point, then they should be used! As always, conciseness is appreciated on the podium; the special technique must enhance the rehearsal, not allow it to get off track.

Pacing the Large Choral-Orchestral Structure

I've always been annoyed that my beloved Brahms apparently once said that women do not understand large structure. Nowadays, given methods of analysis, there certainly is no excuse for any musician not understanding large structure, but it is a different challenge if one doesn't have much practice in it. For the choral conductor who understands structure in a shorter piece, there is a leap to the larger canvas that must be made, even though the goals of shape and musicality remain the same.

A good structural composer will do much of the work for you, if you analyze correctly. For instance, since Brahms ends the *German Requiem* in a transformed version of the first movement, one can know to return to the opening tempo; and when starting the work the conclusion is already present in the mind of both conductor and performers. One needs to think about the weight of the ending, how much *rubato*, *ritardando*, and *fermata* is appropriate to bring to a conclusion the accumulation of seventy-five minutes of music. Brahms suggests tempos by his rhythms and texts and spices up the pacing with non-cadential hemiolas. In the second movement of the *German Requiem*, the flute writing clearly indicates the morning rain—"Morgenregen," and if one sings the correct word accent on "und Abendregen," taking the accent off the "und" and bringing out the hemiola, one can get a more interesting sense of Brahms' rhythmic play. Some recordings take this section so slowly that the "rain" is never heard at all. (See Example 14, Brahms *German Requiem*, II, mm. 109–119.)

Brahms sets up both fugues, in the second and sixth movements, with instructions for pacing that not everyone follows. In the second movement, the eighth-note motion in the strings in the section in 4/4 meter becomes the quarter note in the following section, now in 4/2 meter. For the fugue to sound as if it emerges organically from the preceding material, the eighth-notes in the introductory measures must flow at the same tempo as they become quarter notes in the fugue. This means that the conductor must practice and practice to "hit" this correct tempo right from the previous section. Most recordings do not do this cleanly. (See Example 15, Brahms *German Requiem*, II, mm. 203–208, orchestration reduced to show pertinent instruments.)

Example 14

Brahms *German Requiem*, II, mm. 109–119

(continues)

(continued)

und A - bend - re - - - - - - - - - - - - - gen. So
und A - bend - re - - - - - - - - - - - - - gen. So
und A - bend - re - - - - - - - - - - - - - gen. So
A - bend - re - - - - - - - - - - - - - gen. So

Example 15

Brahms *German Requiem*, II, mm. 203–208

(continues)

(continued)

- - wig - keit.
- - wig - keit.
- - wig - keit.
keit. Die Er - lö - se - ten des Herrn wer - den

Example 16

Brahms *German Requiem*, VI, mm. 204–209

The more difficult transition is in the sixth movement. There is such white heat generated by the "Wo, wo" section that many a conductor comes to the fugue at much too fast a tempo and makes an artificial pull back at the start of it. The correct transition is again governed by the string writing; the four measures preceding the fugue should be at the same tempo as the fugue. This means, again, that the conductor must train herself well in advance to hit the correct tempo so that this transition is strong, accurate and believable. (See Example 16, Brahms *German Requiem*, VI, mm. 204–209.)

Brahms does provide some guidance here. In his unpublished comment "*Breit*" (broad) for the final phrase "Wo ist dein Sieg" before the fugue, we see that the tempo can be dramatically slowed here, allowing the fugue tempo then to be set anew by the four measures following "Sieg," which precede the fugue. Of course if one hits the fugue too fast, one must live with it, or the structure is compromised.

If the structure of the choral-orchestral work is not as clearly constructed as the Brahms *German Requiem*, the text may guide the drama and the tempo. To conduct one of the Bach Passions well is to have thought out ahead the pacing of the recitatives and the segues into the choral parts so that an arc of consciousness runs through the whole scene. Then one can create an oasis with one of the quieter chorales before the next scene is animated. Climactic passages must be put in some kind of hierarchy in the conductor's mind: what is the relative difference between the four "Dies irae's" in the Verdi Requiem? With so many *fortes* and *fortissimos*, where is the true climax of a movement? Is it achieved through *rubato* or volume or both? Is it at the highest note or the harmonic chord of greatest tension? Is it on the final note? For the choral-orchestral conductor, study of individual movements must be arranged mentally with respect to the work as a whole.

Take for instance the seventh movement of the Verdi Requiem. In the last movement, m. 392, the soprano soloist works up to a thrilling high C, which lasts five beats, through the downbeat of m. 394. Where is the climax? On the first C, where many conducting students might place it? The last—my preference—as it is the place of greatest harmonic tension? But it doesn't stop there; momentum takes you to a powerful cadential 6/4 chord. These are all techniques Verdi uses to propel the performers and listeners forward and to increase the sense of tension and resolution. These awarenesses must become part of the conductor's action plan. (See Example 17, Verdi Requiem, "Libera me," mm. 390–400.)

Example 17

Verdi Requiem, "Libera me," mm. 390–400

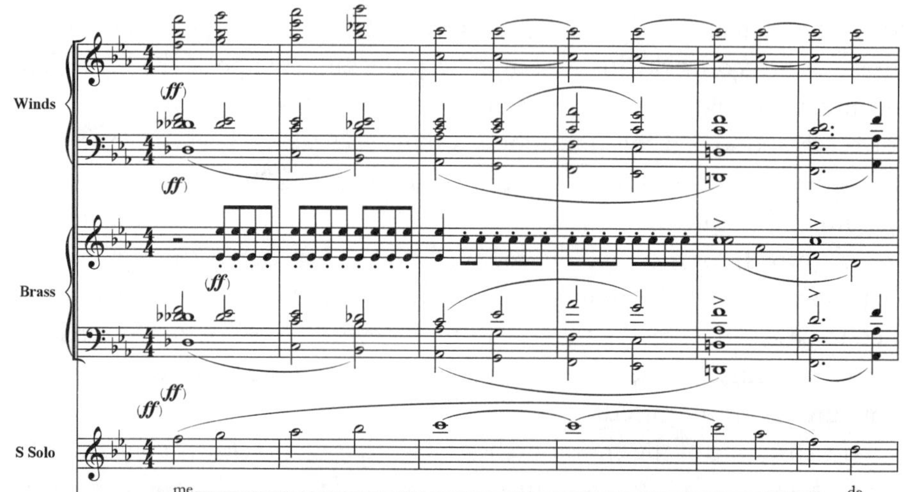

(continues)

CONDUCTING THE CHORAL-ORCHESTRAL WORK

(continued)

Women on the Podium: A Personal View

The question should be about leadership, not gender, and musicians who have had good experiences working with female musicians will be easy to work with; those who have not worked with female conductors, but whose minds remain open are also good to work with. Historical and cultural issues, however, may intrude where women are on the podium. An agent I know proposed my filling in for an ailing conductor in Venezuela; the word came back—no women conductors. In some places, particularly some years ago, one got more attention being female—which could be positive or negative. One would be easily remembered, but not automatically respected.

Competence is still the easiest way to earn respect, and a thorough preparation, and a genial personality, but it is no guarantee of long-term success. It has been my experience that anger from women on the podium is viewed with far less tolerance than from men, and that a woman may need to be faster, or funnier, more competent or livelier, or find another way to command. Many singers and players do not allow the full range of emotions from conductors—men as well as women today. We've become used to a general geniality, and in general it is a good thing in creating a working atmosphere; and yet to assume that the emotional energy required for performing a masterwork can be turned off and on like a switch is unrealistic. The conductor needs to encourage a full and appropriate range of emotional color from the performers and herself, yet the specter of overindulgence can cloud the purity of the music's interpretation. One must keep returning to the music for those checks and balances on how wide the emotional range is that may be shown by the conductor, and one needs always to humbly check her own technique and preparation before pointing the finger at other causes of downfall in a rehearsal. On the other hand, off days will occur from time to time with all conductors, and should be released into history with grace! If possible!

Depending on the players or singers' backgrounds, they may not consider women conductors as strong leaders until they work with them. One hears similar discussions about the quality of being "presidential." In our visual, advertising-saturated culture, we may expect presidents to be taller than average, male, white and Protestant. This has now changed, but public relations experts in politics, arts and entertainment weigh in continually on appearance. The same may hold true for women conductors: can they conduct all-state festivals or will high school boys not sing for them? Are they too small or "too feminine"? Are they too masculine? Where does this end? Organizations and individuals must check for open-mindedness when hiring festival and honor choir conductors, and all music teachers should encourage students to respond to qualities of leadership that go beyond surface attraction.

Onstage, the conductor who is a woman must remember to be the host, that she is in charge of the concert at that moment. This means that acknowledging the orchestra, orchestral soloists, chorus and chorus soloists, letting the soloists offstage first (and some male soloists will want to have the female precede him) and deciding whether to return for another bow is the province of the conductor.

Although these expectations and stereotypes about women conductors are adjusted yearly, there are echoes of old battles in the comments that women in the business have faced: when I first conducted in England in 1979, I was hosted by a woman in Horsham who exclaimed delightedly that she had never seen a woman conductor before, and that she had never thought women would make good conductors because they looked funny from behind—"not you dear, but don't you agree that women look funny from the rear?" She did not talk about the music much, and it was quite a good concert. . . . Or the man in Seattle who told me it must be hard for women conductors, because men in the choir would think it was like being scolded by their mothers. Or the woman who ran up to another conductor, Clara Longstreth, who was standing next to me and wearing a skirt—I had worn slacks for the public conducting workshop—who gurgled that she was glad to see a conductor who wasn't "afraid to be a woman." I didn't think my womanliness depended on my outfit; the fact is I tend to trip on skirts. But these comments, though far from earth-shattering, can contribute to a sense that the serious business of artistic decisions, of interpreting and communicating and bringing beauty and meaning to artwork and people can be diminished so easily in the minds of some concertgoers or performers. Any conductor must continually work to return the focus to the music and to the craft of working with musicians at all levels. Some teachers of women conductors feel that these negative comments should never be discussed with students, that women will be successful in the field if they don't expect criticism. This may be partly true, in encouraging those entering the field to take on the challenges of the work. But I have also come across women in shock at old attitudes occasionally thrown in their face; they don't know how to deal with these situations (being fired, demoted, passed over, behind-the-back campaigns) because they've never imagined them. I think students do not need to have their futures *predicted* for them, but that information about past histories is knowledge that is always valuable.

We come to the podium with our own skills, talents, and emotional baggage. The music demands an emotional truthfulness from us, but the podium is also a place where we must rally our gifts, spirit and courage. When facing an orchestra for the first time, I was well prepared musically, but had spent an inordinate amount of time in my mind reviewing my inadequacies; I assumed that I would not be respected, that I would be "found out." I did fairly well and grew in confidence, but could have proceeded much faster had I not mentally crippled myself fearing the judgment of the other performers. It took three things to change my attitude: one was irritation and anger when attending workshops, watching people less prepared or able do well because they didn't know their inadequacies well enough to be afraid; their charisma, their energy, woke up the players in a way that was elemental. I had to be angry at myself for not just getting up there and doing it! I realized how bound to other people's approval I had been all my life. The second motivator was a talk with a friend, a woman, who is an orchestral conductor and who also dealt with issues of needing approval. A friend of hers had counseled her to let the orchestra have their own opinions by all means; that way you were not *tied* to their opinions.

The third attitude-changer was conducting three movements of the Brahms *German Requiem* at the funeral of a minister/conductor friend who was well known in Boston, an experience I described in the religious/arts journal *Image*. I was conducting his chamber orchestra and chorus, and was grieving deeply. During the warm-up rehearsal, a clarinetist made a disparaging comment to me about how I was conducting the end of the seventh movement. I was shaken up by this, just before the service, and my self-doubts returned in full. In the service, I was alternately buoyed up and deflated by speakers, prayers, and hymns. As I was starting to conduct the seventh movement, someone behind me said softly, "love the orchestra," and instead of wondering what they thought of me, I realized that the players were people who were grieving Larry's loss, and my conducting changed; it became more intimate and loving, more curved and supportive. The music took on a life of its own. The movement ended so beautifully. I looked behind to see who had coached me. There was no one there.

Since that time I worry more about loving and projecting the music and "sending it out" to player, singer and audience; the time for worrying about what they think of me is largely, if not entirely, past. I worry more about knowing the score, as being unprepared can show immediately in one's conducting.

Conducting is a kind of dance, in which you invite the players, singers and audience to join you. Your body must be stable enough for clear cues, strong enough to support hundreds of people, yet malleable enough to be musical and expressive. The conductor must have energy to lead a group of people. How the energy is harnessed is an individual answer to a broad question of what makes a leader. A leader is not necessarily a ruler, and the amount of control a conductor has over the group is a mixture of talent, personality and choice. If I had to put it in just a few words, I would say:

"Be strong. Be yourself. Be a strong version of yourself."

Acknowledgements

For their insights and kind assistance with this chapter, I wish to thank Gustav Meier, David Rentz, Kimberly Dunn Adams, Joseph Huszti, Edward Maclary, and Jameson Marvin. For creating and formatting the musical examples, I wish to thank Kristin Kuster and Andrew Kuster.

Biography

Beverly Taylor is Director of Choral Activities and Professor at the University of Wisconsin-Madison, where she conducts the Concert Choir and the two-hundred-voice Choral Union, and also directs the graduate choral conducting program. Her ensembles have recently premiered two major works: John Harbison's *Emerson* for double a cappella chorus and Thea Musgrave's *Celebration Day* for chamber orchestra and chorus. Additionally, she has premiered and recorded works by Stephen Paulus, Robert Kyr, and Luna Woolf. Her recording of Robert Kyr's *Passion According to Four Evangelists* is available on the New Albion label. She conducts a wide variety of choral repertoire, but also has conducted more than one hundred performances of seventy choral-orchestral works.

Recognized by Boston Globe critic Richard Dyer as a conductor who "has the crucial gift of inspiring people to give their best and beyond," Beverly Taylor was Associate Director of Choral Activities at Harvard University for seventeen years before assuming her present post in 1995. While at Harvard, she directed both the Harvard-Radcliffe Chorus and the international prize-winning Radcliffe Choral Society. She led the groups on frequent domestic and international tours, directed a number of premieres of American music, and produced two recordings on the AFKA label. From 1989–1996 she was music director of the Back Bay Chorale of Boston, which performed under her direction with the Pro Arte Chamber Orchestra and other professional orchestras. As a guest conductor, Prof. Taylor has led the Artur Rubenstein Philharmonic Orchestra in Poland, the St. Louis Symphony Chorus, the Vermont Symphony, the Harvard Chamber Orchestra and Summer Chorus, the U. S. Air Force Band, the Harvard-Radcliffe Collegium Musicum and the Wellesley Chamber Singers, and has also worked with John Williams and the Boston Pops Esplanade Chorus. In Madison, Prof. Taylor is Assistant Conductor of the Madison Symphony and Director of the Symphony Chorus.

A graduate of the University of Delaware and Boston University School for the Arts, Ms. Taylor has studied with Gustav Meier, Paul Vermel, Andrew Davis, Helmuth Rilling, Robert Shaw, Margaret Hillis, and Herbert Blomstedt. She received an advanced conducting fellowship with Chorus America and an orchestral conducting fellowship at Aspen. Ms. Taylor is a frequent guest conductor and lecturer at festivals throughout the United States. Her choirs have toured internationally and been invited to perform at American Choral Directors Association conventions.

Passion and Authenticity: A Conversation with Marin Alsop

Melinda O'Neal

"A formidable musician and a powerful communicator, a conductor with a vision of what an American orchestra could be in the twenty-first century." —The New York Times

A Series of Firsts

Marin Alsop, a New York City native, violinist and daughter of professional string players, became the first female conductor of a major symphony orchestra in America when she was named conductor of the Baltimore Symphony Orchestra in 2007. Previously she had established an equally important precedent in England when she became the first female music director of the Bournemouth Symphony Orchestra. Further, she is the first and only conductor, male or female, to be awarded the prestigious MacArthur Fellowship, which she received in 2005.[1]

Alsop's attitudes, interests and plans are bold and innovative. She collaborates, builds programs to present music in new ways, maintains a research and development budget line to trial-run new ideas, and she is committed to performing contemporary music, often framing it in the context of standard repertory. She is intensely engaged, articulate, openly compassionate and ready for change ("One constant is I change often"). And Alsop is a tireless proponent and activist for the education of young conductors, children and audiences.

How has Alsop's relationship with the Baltimore Symphony's management and players grown, and how has their view of their roles changed since her appointment? In announcing a new education program for elementary school children, sponsored by the BSO in partnership with several city organizations and her own MacArthur Fellowship funds, Alsop said, "There has been a fundamental shift in how the BSO views itself. This is a societal shift. We see our role now as human beings in the world."[2] Further, Alsop has said, "The orchestra needs to be accessible, inclusive and create a culture of joy. The members of our orchestras do not reflect the diversity of our communities—we need to reach out."[3] The Baltimore Symphony Orchestra may indeed become the new model for symphony orchestras in the twenty-first century as she and her colleagues act with targeted funding and well-crafted concert series, performances and educational programs.

Our conversation was conducted by telephone and e-mail on 25 March 2008; topics ranged from the conductor and orchestra acting as agents for societal change to ideal traits of a conductor, score preparation, approaches to education, and working with choruses and chorus masters. Contextual information frames and is interspersed in the interview below; Alsop's responses to my questions are in italics.

◆◆◆

The Making of a Conductor

Every new conductor has experienced reticence and skepticism from orchestra players, soloists, choruses and audiences. Clearly issues of conductor competence and experience are involved, as well as player and audience expectations. Is there a different set of expectations for female conductors who are, by gender, already outside the traditional leadership model for orchestras? When Charlie Rose asked Alsop if she had ever not been hired because of her gender, she replied, "I just always said I must not be good enough yet . . . one learns more from rejection than success. I'm sure some rejection was gender based, but I never really felt that. Conducting is a challenging field for any gender."[4]

◆◆◆

Q: Certainly there have been important break-through moments where skepticism toward you has turned to trust. For example, I've noticed you often disarm your players and associates with your dry wit. In a way, this allows you to distract them from your unusual-for-a-woman position of "authority." Are there other approaches you use to bring the focus back to the music?

Music, music, music. If a young conductor shows passion and authenticity, the world is his or hers.

How do you separate the questioning of your authority from the questioning of your artistry?

As long as the conductor is two-hundred percent prepared, two-hundred percent sincere and the music comes first, there really should not be any issues. Generally that has been my experience.

◆◆◆

At the 2008 Conductors Guild Conference in Baltimore, Alsop enumerated traits and guiding principles she recommends for a conductor: "be an optimist-realist; seize each opportunity; look without pre-conception; maximize every opportunity; promote, engage and take chances; allocate ten percent of the budget to research and development as a permanent line item; develop a team that can actualize your vision; provide for access and inclusion; celebrate the community; develop partnerships and alternative technologies; let the audience know how integral they are; invest in yourself; be the best conductor you can be; be open rather than defensive; break the business formula."[5]

Clearly, this list amounts to more than mere abstract ideals, judging from the impact Alsop is having in Baltimore and from her success as a conductor internationally. Alsop is indeed "walking the walk."

Score Preparation

On training conductors, Alsop emphasizes the importance of getting the composer's message across. Conducting, she believes, is synonymous with bringing out the character of the music while at the same time maximizing everyone's potential as human beings. She challenges each conductor to be his or her own teacher; be self-aware so as to apply self-criticism in a dispassionate way; be authentic but do not take things too personally. A young conductor must base his or her confidence on continually improving competence and being aware of the broader context.[6] Alsop's deep commitment to conductor training is woven into nearly all her activities and programs.

◆◆◆

Q: How do you approach learning a choral-orchestral score?

The same way as any symphonic work, but the text is critical and an important starting point.

Do you have a particular philosophy or procedure for score marking in general and for choral-orchestral works in particular?

I mark my choral works the same as I mark my orchestra scores. I do a complete analysis—harmonic, all bar periods, dynamic, metric, all these analyses. I want to understand the history of the text; if there's a translation I write it in so I know what every word means. And then I often mark t's and s's, which for me are very important in terms of ensemble; I usually mark those just for myself. I try to show those in my conducting technique; that's my job.

You conducted a piece ten years ago. What sort of freshening process do you go through? Do you go back to the keyboard?

No, I'm not a pianist. One constant is I change often. Reading helps—a new biography on the composer, some new scholarship about the piece. Now with the internet there is so much more [information] available. There are a lot of ways to freshen up one's approach, such as listening to new recordings of major standard works. But I think it mostly happens naturally. As we grow and change, our vision and insights grow and change naturally.

I've noticed you often conduct from memory. Would you describe your process for memorization?

Yes, I do a lot of scores by memory. It's hard for me to explain because I'm one of those very fortunate people who don't have any problem memorizing. It's one of those things like [perfect] pitch, you either have it or you don't. (I don't have perfect pitch but I'm always envious of those who do.) I have sort of a photographic memory and then I supplement it. All these analyses and charts really help to get the piece into my memory bank. To sit down and memorize a score cold would be impossible. Once I've done a piece a couple of times, it's usually memorized. It's "do it like this," but I can't describe why. Choral-orchestral scores are like concerti for me, so I don't conduct them by memory.

From whom did you learn your process for score analysis?

A combination of people. My first conducting teacher was Carl Bamburger, who was head of conducting at Mannes, and then I studied with Harold Farberman. I developed my own system based on the input I got from a variety of people. But I'm not big on systems. I think it needs to work for the individual. Some have a very rigorous system of score marking, but I think what happens, with all the colors and all these things, is that people become dependent on the system rather than on the score. And even though I always thoroughly mark my scores for myself, because it's part of my preparation, I could easily do without. Most important is having insight into the piece.[7]

Chorus and Orchestra: Process to Product

Q: Would you discuss your preferred process for working with a chorus? Do you have a hierarchy of approaches in mind for particular rehearsals in the count down time-line?

It really depends so much upon the work. Generally I only have one piano rehearsal with the chorus due to scheduling challenges, regardless of the difficulty level. And then my rehearsal technique is completely dependent upon the level of the chorus and their preparation.

How do you engage the chorus master in the rehearsal process once you've taken over?

I usually have a discussion with the chorus master about tempi, pronunciation, etc., before the piano rehearsal. And then after I rehearse, I expect the chorus master to tweak things and improve any problem areas. I will often mention which areas I would like worked further.

What chorus seating dispositions have you found work best for you in various works?

Simple SATB [front to back, from left to right] seems best for me, but I can work with almost any configuration that the chorus master deems best.

What are the traits of the chorus or the procedures of the chorus master that you have found work best for you?

First of all, I like everything to be super prepared; that always impresses me. Generally if they e-mail or phone to ask me questions, I really do like it if they incorporate what I've said into what they are doing—often they ask me questions and then don't do what I've requested. If I'm really going to spend time going over it, I want them to do it that way. And then, to be responsive, especially in the piano rehearsal if I say, work on that a little bit more, take notes, etc.

I like to work in an atmosphere of respect. I don't like yelling. Some chorus masters I've worked with get a little bit exercised with their choir. Maybe they are frustrated, but I don't care for that type of atmosphere. I like it to be professional, enjoyable. If there is something that can't be worked out, I like it when they say, "don't worry, I'll fix it afterward." And jump in when I turn to them and say, "Can you help me with this?" In the piano rehearsal, I try to engage them, not just ignore them. I'll say, "where did you put the 't' on this? What are you doing on that, could you help me with this?" so they become a translator to the chorus and it feels like a collaborative atmosphere. I invite comments and seek feedback.

In a first rehearsal with chorus and orchestra, do you run the music in its entirety and then rehearse each section, or do you rehearse section-by-section and then run the work?

I rarely run through a work. This seems a poor use of what is usually limited rehearsal time anyway. But, again, it depends upon the number of rehearsals available and the level of the chorus.

What are some of the most memorable experiences you have had with chorus masters and choruses, and perhaps some unfortunate but repeatedly encountered experiences to be avoided?

Most memorable is Brahms' Requiem at St. Paul Cathedral in London with the Orchestra of the Age of Enlightenment. The chorus was excellent and about 100 singers (not huge, not the usual 180) . . . part of the City of London Festival but with original instruments. This was a different kind of aesthetic. I liked the streamlined quality of it; it felt leaner even though the acoustic was less than lean. I also performed Desert Music *by Steve Reich with BBC Singers and BBC Symphony, about forty singers, all professional. They were spectacular. Reich's piece is so challenging, and they were so completely on top of it.*

Do you prefer to work with amateur or student groups or professionals?

I've worked far more frequently with amateur and volunteer choruses than I have with professional choruses.

What are the most positive aspects of each of those experiences?

I find that it's always positive. Sometimes you don't know the quality of what you're going to get, however. When I went on tour to Spain with the Bournemouth Symphony and did Holst's The Planets, *we agreed to use the local women's choir wherever we went. This created some difficulties because the quality varied tremendously and the language barrier created some funny situations. So, you never know. Recently I did* Symphony of Psalms *and that was great. I find choral singers are very keen; that's what I like. They are really engaged, really interested; they laugh at my jokes, and they're very responsive. That's really what I like about it.*

So, the chorus is singing late. Do you give a particular verbal instruction or a different gesture? How do you fix late singing?

Usually I stop and tell them they are late. To start conducting ahead of the orchestra starts a vicious cycle and doesn't achieve much. I have my own little gestures, such as pointing to the middle of my forehead, the location for the Indian dot (tilaka). That gesture means "watch me," and I tell them, "If my forehead is bleeding, you know you're really way behind." So, I try to make a joke of it and move it along. You know, it's a matter of singers trusting the conductor. If they trust me after the first rehearsal or two, I can then say to them: you must not listen so much to yourselves; listen but don't listen. They seem to come along pretty well.

The Orchestra in Society and Education

Alsop distinguishes between the role of music as art and the role of the orchestra as an agent of societal change.

◆◆◆

Q: What change does music bring to society? As we become more informed about classical and other forms of music and we experience it more, what is the impact and net gain on society?

I don't know that art brings change. Art reflects change. It's a microcosm of the greater society. I think one is able to come into this space where you're protected and sit down and experience the world around us, if it's contemporary music or music from a hundred years ago. It's like a snap shot, a little time capsule, and music gets around us in ways words can't. So music is a reflection of changes in society.

Your programming, however, pushes the envelope of beliefs, styles and tastes. You do more than reflect the status quo.

Oh, I hope so.

So, in terms of choice of repertoire—what and where and in what context—you are indeed an agent for change.

That's probably just a reflection of what I am as a human being. You have to be true to yourself. That's my goal in life, to be true to who I am and not a poseur. Fortunately, I have lucked out in finding the perfect fit to be who I am. Oddly, it was such a rough start [with the Baltimore Symphony Orchestra]. It didn't feel like it was going to be perfect at all. Then it has ended up being perfect! I love Baltimore, it's great, and I love the orchestra.

One way of changing the status quo is to focus on research and development. What do you mean by allocating ten percent of the symphony's budget for research and development?

If you have a $10 million budget, then allocate $1 million for creative programming or to develop a new series or address important organizational issues. Have money designated, which the organization can afford to lose, and be bold with it.

Could you give some examples?

It depends on the organization. Try a new series. If you have a masterworks series maybe you want to try a discovery series. In Baltimore we started the series Composers in Conversation because we had invited in so many living composers. Every Wednesday night I (or another moderator) interviewed them. Next year we're going to do a series called Off the Cuff where I take the major piece of the week and dissect it and play examples, which takes about twenty minutes, and then we perform the piece. It's a shortened concert at an earlier time. So that's something new we'll try. Before I arrived they did a series called Symphony with a Twist and an Explorer series. The Twist series worked and that's staying in; the Explorer series did not. The BSO has had a good commitment to trying new ideas.

◆◆◆

Alsop has spoken often of how orchestras are not a reflection of the diversity of the communities they serve, and therefore, of the need for orchestras to educate: "In most cases, when you look at symphony members, they don't look like the communities we live in. We must reach out to various groups to gain diversity, so that communities feel engaged and reflected."[8] In addition to Conversations with Composers and the new BSO series, Off the Cuff, the following are some of the programs Alsop has initiated in recent years, effectively changing the role of orchestras and orchestra players and bringing focused educational programs to important components of society:

- In May 2008, Alsop announced a pilot effort in Baltimore whereby BSO staff and selected players will teach young people at the Harriet B. Tubman Elementary School, one-on-one and at no cost to the student, in a program modeled on El Sistema in Venezuela.

- Alsop initiated a BSO-Peabody Conducting Fellowship whereby a conductor is mentored by Alsop, has private lessons with her in addition to conducting classes at Peabody, and guest conducts the BSO in subscription concerts. Additionally, Alsop has inaugurated side-by-side concerts: Peabody students rehearse and perform alongside BSO players. Richard Strauss' expansive *Alpine Symphony* was performed in this manner in the BSO's Meyerhoff Hall in 2008.

- Alsop teaches conducting in Conductors Guild workshops, champions new music and conductor instruction at the Cabrillo Festival, and she is a driving force in the Taki-Concordia Conducting Fellowship, a national program to encourage women conductors.

Alsop's progressive efforts are meeting with significant success. In particular, the Composer in Conversation series has been especially effective in bringing new music into intellectual and emotional immediacy for listeners. Composer-conductor interactions not only framed new music in the context of standard repertory, but they allowed the audience to hear, first-hand and in an intimate setting, about a composer's perspectives and creative processes. Additionally, the free flow of ideas and information to and from the audience and those on stage succeeded in leveling the performer-audience landscape. Everyone was involved, engaged and on equal footing.

◆◆◆

Q: What is the net gain you seek, and who benefits most from the programs you have initiated?

It should be a win-win-win situation or there's something wrong—the orchestra, the greater community, the people receiving instruction or attending programs.

And in teaching conducting and cultivating the next generation of conductors, what is the most important concept you strive to get across?

Music, music, music. If a young conductor shows passion and authenticity, the world is his or hers.

Coda

Alsop's ability to see the orchestra within the broader context of more diverse modern-day communities and her focus on the needs of today's audiences reflect entirely different thinking from top-down approaches of the past. She is particularly cognizant of her primary responsibility in getting the composer's message across while at the same time maximizing each person's potential as a human being, whether orchestra player, audience member, student, or staff member. She is committed to learning deeply about a work and performing a panoply of musics and styles in new frameworks and with innovative approaches. She is an educator every step of the way. Alsop counsels holding oneself to an extremely high standard, being dispassionately self-critical and being true to oneself.

A role model for the twenty-first century orchestra and a twenty-first century conductor? Yes, indeed.

Biography

Conductor Melinda O'Neal is artistic director & conductor of the Handel Choir of Baltimore (Maryland) and professor of music at Dartmouth College (Hanover, New Hampshire). From 1979–2004 she was music director and conductor of the Handel Society of Dartmouth College, a student-community oratorio society performing choral and choral-orchestral works with guest vocal artists and the Hanover Chamber Orchestra.

The Handel Society of Dartmouth College under O'Neal's direction performed works including Berlioz's *Roméo et Juliette*, Vaughan Williams' *Dona Nobis Pacem*, Schubert's Mass in E♭ Major, Haydn's *Harmoniemesse*, and Bach's *St. Matthew Passion*, to name a few. The ensemble concertized in Austria and Germany, performed an excerpt from Berlioz's *L'enfance du Christ* in Carnegie Hall and toured to Toronto, Canada. Projects of special and recent interest include presentation of Berlioz's rarely heard individual songs and choruses such as Vox Populi in 2003, and in partnership with the Dartmouth Medical School, commission and premiere of *The Staff of Aesculapius* by Charles Dodge in 2001.

With the Handel Society, O'Neal prepared Mahler's Symphony No. 2, and conducted Poulenc's Gloria and Brahms' *Schicksalslied* in collaboration with the New Hampshire Symphony Orchestra in Manchester. As chorus master of the New Hampshire Symphony Chorus' performance of Verdi's Requiem, Richard Dyer of the Boston Globe wrote, "The chorus master Melinda O'Neal had trained them to sing everything musically—there was none of the fancy murmuring and false theatrics that disfigure so many performances of this genuinely dramatic music. Everything they did was clean and honest." Of Monadnock Music's performance of Gluck's *Orphée et Eurydice*, Richard Binder wrote, "The twelve-member chorus, prepared by Melinda O'Neal, was divine. Singing stylishly and with a superb balance both internally and in relation to the [solo] singers, they were one of the evening's highlights." As guest conductor in residence for the Seattle Symphony Orchestra Chorale in 1995, O'Neal prepared Berlioz's *La damnation de Faust* for Gerard Schwarz.

O'Neal founded two professional chamber ensembles: Boston Vocal Artists' Sonique (Massachusetts) and Group Vocale de St. Denis (Hanover, New Hampshire). Sonique's concerts included "Bon Anniversaire, Berlioz!" (solo and ensemble music by Poulenc, Duparc, Milhaud, Saint-Saëns and Berlioz), American and British twentith-century solo and ensemble repertoire, and music by North American composers Christian Wolff, Ileana Perez Velasquez, Charles Dodge, and John MacDonald.

For seventeen years O'Neal conducted the all-undergraduate Dartmouth College Chamber Singers. This thirty-two-voice ensemble presented an annual Feast of Song renaissance music-drama banquet and inaugurated a series of collaborations with the period instrument orchestra Arcadia Players (Amherst, Massachusetts), performing vocal-instrumental works by Purcell, Bach, Mozart, Haydn and Handel. Chamber Singers concertized on tour in England, Spain, Germany, and Austria as well as America's east coast and midwest Chamber Singers regularly premiered works by Dartmouth faculty and students as part of the music department's New Music Festival.

As a visiting professor in residence (1996–1997), O'Neal taught conducting at the doctoral, masters and undergraduate levels at University of Georgia (Athens) where she also conducted the Concert Choir, University Chorus and Camerata. As a visiting professor and conductor at Indiana University (1999), O'Neal conducted the Contemporary Vocal Ensemble and taught and advised graduate conducting students. Dartmouth College students she has taught or advised have continued their studies at Columbia University, Indiana University, University of Illinois, Temple University, Peabody Institute, and Boston University, to name a few.

With O'Neal's appointment in 2004, Handel Choir of Baltimore became a newly reconfigured community oratorio ensemble of forty-five voices, performing baroque, classical and early romantic style works with a period instrument orchestra. Collaborations have included engagements with Baltimore Symphony Orchestra, Baltimore Chamber Orchestra, Pro Musica Rara, Peabody Early Music, and American Opera Theatre. Recent projects include a recording of Handel's *Alexander's Feast* with the Bach Sinfonia (Dorian label) and commissioning and premiere of Jonathan Leshnoff's *Requiem for the Fallen*. A review in *The Baltimore Sun* cited that "Melinda O'Neal has steadily and rapidly honed this formerly uneven ensemble into quite a potent chorus . . . two Bach cantatas received dynamic performances from the choristers, who were backed stylishly by a period instrument orchestra. . . . It was a thoughtfully constructed, entertaining program delivered with an informed sense of historic style."

O'Neal holds masters and doctoral degrees in choral-orchestral conducting from Indiana University in Bloomington and a bachelors in music education from Florida State University in Tallahassee. She studied score preparation, choral literature and conducting with Julius Herford, Jan Harrington, Fiora Contino, Helmuth Rilling, Robert Shaw, Marcel Couraud, John Nelson, Thomas Dunn and Joseph Flummerfelt. O'Neal teaches conducting, studies in music and text, and music theory at Dartmouth College, and her continuing research and performance interests include the relationship of text and music, historical performance practices and the music of Hector Berlioz. Her articles on Mozart and Berlioz may be located in the *Choral Journal*, *Journal of the Conductors Guild*, and *Becoming the Complete Conductor* (ECS Publishing), and her performer's guide to the vocal music of Berlioz is in progress. O'Neal is a past board member of the Conductors Guild and serves on the research and publications committee of the American Choral Conductors Association.

Notes

[1] The MacArthur Fellows Program awards unrestricted fellowships to talented individuals who have shown extraordinary originality and dedication in their creative pursuits and a marked capacity for self-direction. There are three criteria for selection of Fellows: exceptional creativity, promise for important future advances based on a track record of significant accomplishment, and potential for the fellowship to facilitate subsequent creative work."
Source: http://www.macfound.org/site/c.lkLXJ8MQKrH/b.959463/

[2] Marin Alsop: lecture sponsored by Ballard Spahr Andres & Ingersoll, LLP. Baltimore, MD, 21 May 2008.

[3] Interview with Charlie Rose: "A Conversation with Music Director of the Baltimore Symphony Orchestra, Marin Alsop" on 15 January 2008, Public Broadcasting System (http://www.charlierose.com).

[4] Ibid.

[5] Notes from Marin Alsop comments as featured speaker for Conductors Guild Annual Conference luncheon, 11 January 2008, Radisson Plaza Lord Baltimore Hotel, Baltimore, MD.

[6] Notes from Marin Alsop comments as featured panelist "Training Young Conductors" for Conductors Guild Annual Conference, 11 January 2008, Radisson Plaza Lord Baltimore Hotel, Baltimore, MD.

[7] Also refer to chapters by Ann Howard Jones and Beverly Taylor on score preparation.

[8] Marin Alsop: lecture sponsored by Ballard Spahr Andres & Ingersoll, LLP. Baltimore, MD, 21 May 2008.

Our Teaching

Women Conductors as Leaders and Mentors

Hilary Apfelstadt

Introduction

In theory, my qualifications for addressing this topic are adequate: I have advised a doctoral dissertation on leadership in conducting; have published and presented papers on leadership; have been entrusted with the title of Director of Choral Activities at a large university; and been honored by election as ACDA national President. Yet, as the Scottish poet, Robert Burns (1786), said "Oh wad some Power the giftie gie us to see oursels as ithers see us!" In my mind, I am still the child from Nova Scotia who was among the last to be picked for the ball team at recess in elementary school; hid behind my father's trouser leg as a young child when being introduced to adults; was very soft-spoken and obedient in school; never served as class president or did anything that required me to be highly visible. I was shy, conservative, quiet, one of the high school music room crowd who "hung out" there after school, always part of the group but never leading it. I played second violin, took the basso part in piano duets, and preferred singing in ensembles to performing solos.

To this day, my initial reaction to the word "leader" is to think of someone naturally outgoing, assertive, somewhat crowd-pleasing, and even charismatic. None of those characteristics is mine by nature. If they bear any resemblance, it is through learned behavior.

What personal leadership qualities would I acknowledge? Organization, dependability, conscientiousness, motivation, the will to follow through and meet obligations, and a passion for "getting it right" are all characteristics I claim. These are the less flamboyant and more down-to-earth aspects of leadership that sometimes elude naturally charismatic personalities, but they are among the qualities that can serve leaders well.

Differences in people's leadership styles are intriguing. Surely you have noticed how some student conductors command respect from the outset seemingly through body language alone, while others struggle to get their students' attention; how some people exude style over substance; how "charisma" at its worst can lead followers to dangerous ends. Abuse of power is a misuse of leadership qualities. Leadership is not about having power over others; it is about getting a group of people to work together for the greater good. It is an essential element of our profession and worth consideration; in fact, I believe we should be teaching toward leadership and certainly developing our own leadership skills and style in order to provide effective models.

In this essay, I will outline generic characteristics of leadership as applied to conductors of either gender, and then describe research pertaining to leadership style among conductors. I will address gender issues specifically, along with suggesting practical ways women conductors especially can enhance their leadership skills. Included in this essay is a section on mentoring, including particular emphasis on women conductors.

Leadership Style and the Conductor

With the myriad musical concerns we have in our field, it may seem incongruous to focus on what could seem to be primarily a nonmusical one. Yet our roles as conductors are a combination of musical and nonmusical elements. The root word for conduct, *conducare*, means "to lead" and "to care," implying both. Even conductors of professional ensembles have "greater management responsibilities than (their) predecessors," according to research by Mintzberg (1998), quoted by Yu in his 1999 dissertation. Those of us who teach know that nonmusical tasks absorb much time. Whether it is writing hall passes, collecting tour money or permission slips, processing purchase orders for music and equipment, or tracking down incoming students by e-mail, we spend considerable time engaged in nonmusical tasks. Indeed, it is not enough these days to be good musicians: we have to be good managers, good amateur psychologists, good public relations experts, and more.

If we accept that leadership involves getting a group of people to work toward a common goal, then it behooves us to examine the characteristics of leaders that enable them to accomplish this task. Those involve both professional and personal attributes. Professional skills involve the leader's grasp of subject matter or content; an exemplary conductor knows the music thoroughly. Personal skills include presentational aspects; for a conductor, that translates into stance, posture, speech delivery, inflection, and articulateness. Fine conductors are able to express ideas effectively both gesturally (non-verbally) and verbally. Other personal skills include "self-awareness: self-regulation, motivation, empathy and social skills" (Goleman, 1998, cited in Yu, 1999, p. 44).

Much of the research on leadership has been done in the fields of business and in education. Studies in leadership among conductors are based on such models.

Yu (1999) outlines the history of leadership theories beginning with *trait theories vs. behavioral theories.* As implied, *trait theories* implied that leadership was an innate characteristic. (The statement that someone is a "born leader" typifies this theory.) While each of us has taught students whom we knew to be innately gifted as teachers or conductors, we have also observed students develop into strong leaders despite having less inborn ability. While some people exhibit leadership qualities naturally, others can develop those strengths. That was the thinking behind *behavioral theories* that suggest leadership is based on a set of behaviors. In other words, one can learn to lead by using appropriate behaviors. When we teach young conductors about posture and delivery, about rehearsal organization and implementation, we are teaching them leadership behaviors—behaviors that will enable them to function more effectively as conductor-teachers.

Situational leadership theories suggest that leaders function differently according to context. This leadership style requires flexibility on the part of the leader (or conductor). Think, for example, of a situation where all the singers are highly professional compared with a situation where all are amateurs. The professionals need and expect a different leadership style from the conductor than the amateurs do, as the former are less dependent for musical direction than the latter. For example, in the professional setting, the conductor may be able to focus on musical details immediately, in a highly intense environment. With amateurs, however, the pacing and tone will change, particularly if the participants are hesitant or very inexperienced. Treating them like professionals with the same high expectations for accurate reading, for example, would not be as effective as taking more time to teach the music, perhaps in a less intense manner.

Other leadership style models include *transactional* (process-oriented) and *transformational* (more emotional or charismatic) approaches. *Transactional* models "are based on social exchange and focus on the relational tie between leaders and followers," the result being "heightened responsiveness" on the part of the followers (Apfelstadt, 1997, p. 25). *Transformational* leaders appeal to the emotional response of their followers, although this characteristic is known to be risky if the leader "demonstrates too much approval seeking" (Apfelstadt, 1997, p. 26). Armstrong and Armstrong, cited in Apfelstadt (1997, p. 26) "suggest that the transformational (conductor) engages ensemble members in such a way that mutual benefits result" because of the leader's being "enthusiastic, having the ability to share a vision, working well with people, providing good modeling, and offering encouragement through praise."

Although there are many models of leadership in existence, Yu (1999) suggests that the most appropriate for conductors seem to be *situational* theories. Although good leaders may possess innate strengths, they can also learn leadership skills and adapt these to various situations.

The fundamental elements, regardless of the name of the theory or the terms used, seem to relate to *task* (productivity) and *relationship* (between leader and followers). The third element, particularly in *situational* leadership models, is *motivation* of the followers.

Hersey and Blanchard's (1982) Situational Leadership Theory, or SLT, was developed at the Ohio State University. Its main components are *task orientation* (high or low), *relationship orientation* (high or low) and the *motivation* of the followers to be led. SLT remains a good model because it is straightforward and clean. Is the leader behavior high task or low task? Is the leader relationship-oriented or task-oriented? Are the followers willing to be led or not?

Originally designed for the business context, SLT categorizes leadership in four quadrants: high task/low relationship ("telling"); high task/high relationship ("selling"); high relationship/low task ("participating") and low relationship/low task ("delegating"). Applied to a choral rehearsal, we could envision the following:

1. A high task/low relationship style might involve a conductor recording a CD for a publishing company demonstration. The choir would be well prepared, focused on getting the task accomplished, and with a minimum of social interaction. The conductor's focus would be on successful completion of the recording session with little need for interaction beyond the musical context. It would likely be a short-term situation with a very specific goal to be accomplished in a limited time.

2. A high task/high relationship style would involve a conductor and ensemble working together for musical excellence in an environment of mutual respect and enjoyment. Everyone would be part of the "team" working as one to accomplish the goal of music making. This is easy to envision in settings where highly motivated conductors and singers work together frequently and are comfortable in those relationships.

3. A high relationship/low task style could involve the conductor in a situation that is more social than musical. For example, if I had to teach a Girl Guide troop a song around the campfire, my purpose would be more to help them enjoy a social time through music than it would be to teach musical skills. Our relationship could be very congenial; the girls would have fun but not necessarily accomplish much musically.

4. A low relationship/low task setting is the most difficult to relate to a musical setting. Here, there would be neither musical nor relationship emphasis. In the business model, the term used is "delegating." One can imagine an officer manager turning over responsibilities to the other employees and not supervising or checking on them; there would be little interest in the goal itself or how it was accomplished.

There are rehearsal situations where a conductor might delegate tasks to student leaders who would run sectionals, for example, but the conscientious conductor would check on the students and hold them accountable for returning to the rehearsal with the notes learned. In that case, the task emphasis might seem to be delayed (for the conductor) but not for the students. This can actually be a good way of facilitating student leadership qualities, provided enough guidance is given and follow-through occurs. Otherwise, a conductor with a low relationship/low task style would be ineffective in rehearsal.

Several researchers besides Yu (1999) have examined leadership styles among conductors in choral and instrumental contexts. Their findings suggest that effective conductors favor the high task/high relationship leadership style. These conductors get the job done in a way that leads both to musical satisfaction (goal achievement) and enjoyment (relationship focus) of the musicians. Russell (1980) found that high school orchestra conductors favored a high-task, high-relationship style. Goodstein (1987) surveyed band directors at the high school level, noting that they, too, shared this outcome. Allen (1988) focused on collegiate and high school choral conductors whose ensembles had performed at regional and national ACDA conventions, and found that they acknowledged the high task/high relationship style as their primary one. Finally, Davidson (1995) found similar results despite gender.

Howard Swan wrote, "it takes a very great person, a Very Great Person (and notice that I don't say a very great musician) . . . to be an inspiring choral conductor . . . because the choral conductor has to be . . . the leader of his group" (Swan in Fowler, ed., 1987, p. 41). To some extent, this statement alludes to the fact that there are intangible characteristics among leaders that defy definition. Perhaps those are the things that we tend to think are there by nature, not nurture. We have all known people whose combination of musical skills and personal attributes draws people to them more than to others. It is not a matter of schooling necessarily or even of experience, but something that escapes labels. Perhaps it is the very combination of qualities that truly adds up to more than the sum of its parts.

Gender Issues in Conducting

Occasionally I receive e-mails asking for my thoughts on women conductors or some gender-related aspect of music education. The writers' questions usually relate to discrimination or perceived discrimination, to gender bias, and to general advice for young conductors, especially female.

Following is my response to a female graduate student who asked this question several years ago: "What are the disadvantages of being a female conductor?' [Note that "disadvantages" is a loaded term, implying that women are less fortunate than men in our profession. Personally, I have not always found that to be the case.]

> Fortunately, the world is changing and there are more of us in positions of some prominence. As that trend continues, we won't have to "prove" ourselves in a man's world so much anymore. Male-oriented people expect us to be "weaker," I think, perhaps more soft-spoken, less assertive, and faced with that expectation, we might have to become someone we aren't. I have not succumbed to that pressure although I have been told to "speak lower (in pitch)" and "be meaner," neither of which is in my nature, regardless of gender. So I have learned to be definitive through the confidence that comes with solid preparation; to be assertive without being aggressive in a threatening way; to pace rehearsals quickly so there is no lost time; to be gesturally clear and convincing to the best of my ability.
>
> If we women go into the business in defensive mode, we won't help our case. Good solid preparation and a sense of purpose will serve us well. In the end, it is the musical results we get that should make the difference, regardless of gender. I have encountered very weak conductors of both genders, and equally strong leaders of both genders. The potential for leadership skill is not gender-based in my opinion, although it may be gender-biased in some people's minds. (E-mail sent 27 November 2000.)

[Note: Personally, I think that women are sometimes expected to be more flowery or "weak" gesturally. Working with instrumentalists is often a challenge for choral conductors and may be worse for a woman than a man, who is apparently expected to be clear and definitive. A male colleague once complimented my conducting, telling me that it "didn't look one bit like a woman." I inferred that he had low expectations of women conductors.]

I know of no research that indicates superiority of either gender in conducting. My conviction is that the characteristics of good leadership can and do transcend gender.

Not everyone agrees with that last statement, however, noting that women and men seem to have some natural differences in the ways they lead. From a business perspective, Fisher (2005, p. 133) writes about "the natural leadership talents of women," citing a number of characteristics she believes that relate to "women's brain architecture and hormones, skills that leadership theorists now espouse as essential to leadership effectiveness." She suggests that both genders possess these abilities but that "women display them more regularly than men" (p. 134).

First is what Fisher calls "web thinking," which is a "broad, contextual, feminine way of reasoning" (p. 134). She believes that women approach issues differently than men, looking at them with a wider lens, gathering more information and considering more options (p. 134). Men compartmentalize more than women do. *Second* is the ability to "tolerate ambiguity" because they process information simultaneously more than linearly (p. 135). *Third*, women rely more on intuition and once the information is gathered, they store it in chunks. "Then when a single detail of a complex situation appears, the experienced person can instantly recognize the larger design and predict outcomes than another must deduce with plodding sequential thought" (p. 135). Fisher notes "women, on average, excel at this form of thought" (p. 135).

Fourth is long-term planning, in contrast to men's tendency to focus more on immediate issues. Fisher believes that this characteristic may be hormone-related, citing research that suggests that when men are injected with testosterone, "their thinking becomes more focused on the present" (p. 136). Women, on the other hand, tend to think ahead.

Fifth is mental flexibility and imagination, related to Fisher's concept of web thinking. Other skills include expert articulation (verbal skills) and social skills or social intelligence. According to Fisher, women "have evolved a keener ability to pick up the nuances of posture and gesture, read complex emotions in faces, and hear slight changes in tone of voice" (p. 137). Finally, Fisher suggests that women have:

> remarkable facilities for networking, collaboration, empathy, inclusion and

> sharing power. Men tend to cast themselves within hierarchies and view power as rank and status; women, on the other hand, form cliques and tend to regard power as an egalitarian network of supportive connections. These traits have also been linked with hormones" (p. 138).

Rather than assigning rank to these characteristics, however, Fisher affirms the interconnectedness of gender-based leadership characteristics. She says that "men and women are like two feet—they need each other to get ahead" (p. 139). She affirms the value of both types of leadership characteristics in today's workplace.

It could be beneficial for researchers to examine gender issues in conducting leadership. To this point, that topic has been largely unexplored. Davidson (1995) addressed it but found no significant differences. What mattered most to her subjects' leadership style, regardless of gender, was their experience level as conductors.

Examining women's attributes, as defined by Fisher (2005), might be very effective in the field of conducting. *Web thinking*, the ability to take a holistic view of the process of conducting and rehearsing; *mental flexibility* in terms of responding to what actually happens in rehearsal; *long-term planning*, always essential to our work both in developing curriculum and also in deciding how and when to teach repertoire; *creativity*, an asset in programming; *imagination*, in fueling artistic fires; and *verbal and social skills*, in terms of expressing oneself and detecting others' responses—all of these are essential to the conductor's process. Fortunately, many of these qualities are teachable. In my experience, not all women students use these latent abilities to advantage, but encouraging them to do so and providing a framework for development is essential if they are to reach their potential.

Leadership in Action

When I address the topic of leadership in conducting courses with my students, we focus both on contextual framework and practical applications. What good is it to know about leadership if you cannot demonstrate it? A few of the students appear to be *born leaders*. They have a natural ease with people; they carry themselves well; they command respect; they get things done. Most students however, have to be taught leadership behaviors, just as I was. In devising a model for rehearsal planning, we focus on *preparation*, *presentation* and *evaluation*.

1. *Preparation*: This begins at the moment of repertoire selection and is most intensive and time-consuming. Everything we teach and every gesture we make comes from the score itself. As conductors, we must "know our stuff." That involves the following considerations, once we select the music:

a. Score study: What musical elements comprise the composition? What is the context? What is the composer's intent? What is the form of the music? What is the source of the text? Do you know the translation, if applicable? Do you know how to pronounce the text, if it is not your native language?

b. Score marking: This stage imprints the musical details on the conductor's brain. Once the measures are numbered, breath markings, phrasing, form, dynamics, articulation, cues and other musical details need attention. Some conductors mark scores heavily; others like to work from a cleaner score, but regardless of how much actual marking goes on the page, this stage of the process involves meticulous decision making.

c. Rehearsal preparation: The better the conductor knows the score, the more smoothly the rehearsal planning process can proceed. While studying the score, the conductor should be learning to sing the parts; practicing the piano if one must assist from the keyboard; and practicing conducting.

While planning rehearsals, the conductor must focus on devising sequenced strategies for optimal learning, not only for a single rehearsal but also over time. How long will it take the chorus to learn the music? What preparation is needed in terms of warm-ups and aural skills exercises? What strategies will best lead to expressive understanding and performance of the music? Well-prepared conductors demonstrate good leadership skills by acknowledging the importance of being fully prepared, of knowing the content they are teaching, and of demonstrating that process of preparation in rehearsal.

2. The second phase of the leadership-in-action model is *presentation*, involving visual, aural and kinesthetic aspects. Hamann et al (2000, p. 104) write that "many researchers have found that effective teachers are identified as those who have highly developed teacher-delivery skills, including but not limited to eye contact, vocal inflection, facial expression, gesturing, proximity, or posture." In a study designed to determine "what effect, if any, music teacher classroom delivery skills or lesson content had on university music

students' perceptions of lesson or teacher appeal" (p. 102). Hamann et al found that "effective teacher-delivery skills enhanced students liking and interest levels in lessons, regardless of the quality of their content" (p. 111). This would seem to support the notion that *how* we present something can be less important that *what* we actually say or do.

A. *Presentation: Visual*

Some of the following points seem so basic as to be assumed at times, yet in some cases, they must be taught.

a. Posture/stance: I always tell student conductors to stand like a singer with shoulders back and down, allowing a free, open chest area. This facilitates good preparatory position. Arm placement is important: conductors must leave some space between their arms and ribcage as a visual reminder to the singers to take room to breathe. Just as in singing, if one keeps good head position with the chin parallel with the floor, there is no danger or looking haughty (chin up) or shy (head down). Working in front of a mirror or recording oneself in rehearsal are helpful self-monitoring strategies.

b. Eye contact: It is helpful to look directly at the singers, panning the group so as not to favor any one person over another. Avoid looking over the singers' heads or at the ceiling. Knowing the music well enough to stay out of the score as much as possible is a good visual leadership strategy. Cues can be given visually through eye contact, as well as gesturally. Good eye contact is a sign of confidence, something an effective leader demonstrates.

c. Dress: Conductors are in the public eye and must be conscious of that when choosing attire for rehearsal or performance. We should aim to *be appropriate and non-distracting*. Student conductors often favor t-shirts with text on them; depending on the words, such shirts may distract or even offend a singer in the ensemble. Thus a plain shirt is preferable to one with a logo or message.

For concert dress, men are at an advantage over women as they have fewer options. Formal dress codes for men dictate tuxedos, tails or dress suits. In a religious setting, robes may be used to cover street clothes. Women must be very careful not to let the whims of fashion dictate concert dress. That means showing no cleavage, no bare midriffs or shoulders, or having no long slits in skirts—all of those are distracting. For stage appearances, dark formal-length dresses (or dressy pants) are best. Women should wear tasteful jewelry and keep their hair off the face. It is wise to *check in a full-length mirror before going on stage.* Dressing appropriately removes the risk that the focus will be on the conductor and not on the music.

B. *Presentation: Auditory*

a. As a child, I was often reminded that *what* I said was sometimes less important than *how* I said it. The quality of one's speaking voice needs to be well modulated; projected, but not harsh; assertive, but not aggressive or arrogant. A sharp or impatient tone can sound rude, no matter how innocuous the content. If the conductor sounds disrespectful, for example, it will be hard to maintain collegiality with fellow musicians. No one wants to follow a leader who lacks respect. A conductor who mumbles or speaks too softly cannot be heard. Clear articulation at an appropriate volume for the size of the space is ideal. In festival situations with very large choruses, it is advisable for the conductor to use a microphone to avoid vocal strain.

b. *Inflection* is another aspect of speaking that makes an auditory impression. Natural variation in inflection, coupled with appropriate accents and emphasis on words, is the ideal. A statement should sound like one, not like a question. If one's voice trails up in pitch at the end of a sentence, the speaker sounds uncertain or lacking in confidence, thus undermining the content of the message.

c. Monitor *speech tempo* by listening to a tape of a rehearsal; clear articulation, at a reasonable tempo, is essential to comprehension. Speaking too fast in rehearsal can affect comprehension and concentration. Tannen (2003) says that people are speaking much faster now than they used to, and that examples abound in the media and in the classroom. On the other hand, speaking too slowly or deliberately may make the listener feel the speaker is condescending or simply boring and lose interest. It, too, can undermine confidence if the speaker sounds indecisive, as though searching for the next word. This is especially inappropriate in a rehearsal setting where effective pacing is vital to success.

d. Another quality noticeable in women more than men, in my experience, is the effect of *pitch range* on the listener. The younger or more childlike a woman sounds, the less she seems to command attention. Coupled with unassertive inflection or "cuteness," this can be a great drawback. Tannen (1994, p. 167) says "the very notion of authority is associated with maleness." She continues, "Anyone who is taller, more heftily built, with a lower-pitched, more sonorous voice, begins with culturally recognizable markers of authority, whereas anyone who is shorter, slighter, with a higher-pitched voice begins with a disadvantage in this respect." Personally, I deplore the sound of artificially lowered voices such as those affected by popular television anchorwomen sometimes. There is a balance point, however, between lowering the speech range too much to be healthy and not sounding authoritative enough because of too high a speech range. If you suspect your speaking voice is a detriment to your leadership in any way, consult a speech therapist.

C. *Presentation: Kinesthetic*

Actual *conducting gesture* is another way in which we convey leadership on the podium. Each of us has a unique gestural vocabulary that can either further our communication or lessen it. Body language is both kinesthetic and visual. Gestures must reflect the music and develop from study of the score. Conductors function as icons for the musical information and content. What we show is reflected in what we hear if the singers are truly responding to our gesture.

In teaching conductors, either male or female, I urge them to avoid weak gestures. Often these can be improved simply by adjusting posture, but sometimes it is related to a lack of conviction about the music or a lack of self-confidence. Continued score study and gestural practice are good remedies in either case. ("What you know is what you show.") Good conductors are clear and convincing. I recommend using a baton if it helps with clarity and is appropriate to the style. It may increase the conductor's authority particularly with instrumentalists for whom a baton is part of the conductor/ensemble culture.

Mentoring as an Essential Component of Leadership

One of the ways in which leaders can make a difference is by mentoring others. There is no question that leaders need and seek models, or that they provide these for others through mentoring activities.

Funk and Wagnalls Standard College Dictionary (1973, p. 847) defines "mentor" as "a wise and trusted teacher or guide." For those of us who hold university positions, mentoring may involve working both with graduate students and also with junior faculty. There is plenty of advice given on both topics, and while there are some differences, there are also similarities. I found considerable material on mentoring in both contexts. One can readily find documents on line that deal with mentoring graduating students, such as that from the University of Michigan, The Rackham Graduate School (2006). In fact, the Michigan model provided the prototype for the Graduate School at the University of Washington as faculty there sought to develop their own guidelines for mentoring graduate students (2006). Many universities describe junior faculty mentoring procedures in documents related to promotion and tenure, many of which are also available on line.

Mentoring Graduate Students

"A mentoring relationship is a close, individualized relationship that develops over time between a graduate student and a faculty member and that includes both caring and guidance" (University of Michigan document, 2006, p. 6).

In terms of graduate student mentoring, it is worth noting that there is a distinction between "advisor" and "mentor." Every graduate student must have an advisor but not every advisor is a true mentor. Advisors are charged with overseeing one's academic program, possibly including supervision of a thesis or dissertation. Penny Gold (2001, p. 46) says:

> A mentor, on the other hand, may have little to do with one's dissertation, but is someone ahead of you in academia . . . with whom you come to have more informal personal relationship. A mentor is someone you can go to for advice on all sorts of issues in academic life.

The Council of Graduate Schools (cited in the University of Washington document, 2006, p. 5) describes mentors' multiple roles as:

> Advisors, people with career experience willing to share their knowledge; supporters, people who give emotional and moral encouragement; tutors, people who give specific feedback on one's performance; masters, in the sense of employers to whom one is apprenticed; models of identity, of the kind of person one should be to be an academic (Zelditch, 1990).

Given the complexity of this definition, it is reassuring to read in the following paragraph the no one "should try to fulfill all the roles described for every student," and that, in fact, students need multiple mentors (University of Michigan document, 2006, p. 6).

Heard (2005, p. 468) says that "studies confirm what many of us intuitively know—the single most important influence in a young person's life is the relationship with a caring adult. This is the cornerstone of mentoring." A good mentor demonstrates several characteristics, among them being caring, empathic, nurturing, approachable, and respectful. In addition, mentors must be generous, as mentoring is time consuming and demanding. It is not a process that ends with the student's graduation.

Blake-Beard (2005, p. 108) says "leaders should be prepared to give the mentoring initiative the necessary time for results to be measured and for benefits to be gained." Speaking in a business context, she regards mentoring as "an integral part of (her) stewardship of the organization" (p. 109). I believe that we women conductors must mentor aspiring conductor-educators with great attention to providing exemplary role models. This monograph, with its focus on female conductors, will be a good resource in that regard. We must not, however, limit our efforts to working with female students even though there are indeed unique aspects of our gender that we are best equipped to address. Young men need mentoring as well. If nothing else, women can help male students understand what is and is not acceptable in dealing with their female counterparts.

Graduate students interviewed for the University of Michigan Graduate School document on mentoring (2006, pp. 7–12) cited eight characteristics as being basic to good mentorship. Each is listed below, followed by suggestions for implementation:

1. *Engage graduate students in ongoing conversations.* Being friendly and accessible to students, both during office hours, and also occasionally outside of class or school settings, makes students feel the mentor has genuine interest in them.

2. *Demystify graduate school.* A good mentor is well informed about academic rules and regulations, or can point the student in the right direction. Aspects of graduate school such as taking comprehensive exams or writing a dissertation may be unfamiliar and daunting to a new graduate student.

3. *Provide constructive and supportive feedback.* Tempering criticism with helpful suggestions, giving honest opinions in a tactful way, giving prompt feedback, and heading off potential problems with the student's progress—all these are responsibilities of good mentors.

4. *Provide encouragement and support.* Giving students a safe place in which to discuss their ideas, encouraging them to branch out and consider new ways of thinking or approaching problems, helping them submit papers and arti-

cles for presentations and publication are all important behaviors of a good mentor.

5. *Help foster networks.* Bringing together students with similar interests and encouraging them to pursue these through appropriate channels is helpful to developing graduate students' professional networks. Setting up discussion groups or, in our case as conductors, pairing students for recitals, for example, can be very appropriate.

6. *Look out for the student's interests.* An effective mentor is aware of students' strengths and academic needs, and is often well positioned to help students make valuable connections. Inviting a student to lead a seminar, a rehearsal or make a presentation helps make others aware of the students' abilities and can provide excellent professional development.

7. *Treat students with respect.* There is no place for demeaning treatment in a good mentoring relationship. Students appreciate knowing that their mentor listens to and respects them. Setting aside time devoted to that student alone, and keeping records of conversations and communications to and from that student enables the mentor to focus on the individual with full attention and accurate information, thus making the student feel valued.

8. *Provide a personal touch.* Graduate students are people, too. Many of them have families and responsibilities apart from school. An understanding mentor takes these things into account and shows interest in the student. If personal issues beyond the role of the mentoring relationship arise, the mentor should suggest additional resources such as counseling.

The University of Washington document on mentoring (2006, pp. 7–9) presents yet another view of mentors' roles, noting three: 1. Disciplinary guide; 2. Skills development consultant; and 3. Career consultant. The first relates to the academic discipline and its culture; the second to the need for students to hone their communication skills (both verbal and written), their team orientation, and their leadership skills. Given the potential of graduate students to become the "rising stars" of their generation of scholars, they need to acquire expertise that will serve them in the future, as well as the present. The third role, career consultant, involves the mentor's guiding the student through the job market with insights about "careers as an evolutionary process—one that requires planning, flexibility, and adaptation to change." In order to accomplish this, "an effective mentor finds ways to help students develop relationships with other potential mentors" (p. 9).

Palmer (1998, pp. 75–76) describes the various tasks she accomplished with young black women for whom she served as mentor: unofficial advising; editing papers; counseling them on academic discourse; and non-academic issues such as integrating into the community. She likens the process to mothering in a sense. Mark (1998, p. 81) affirms the similarity but distinguishes this kind of mothering from that she gives her son. She calls it "activist mothering," saying "it is political action in its most important manifestation. When I parent a young person, I am teaching them to parent themselves. I am reminding them of values and ways of acting that will benefit the whole community."

Mark distinguishes between mothering and "pampering," maintaining that this kind of mentoring comprises "strong guidance, respect, willingness to listen to and support a student through . . . any number of difficult life passages" (p. 81). Later, she points out that "responsible parenting actually moves toward disengagement and independence" (p. 83), hence encouraging the students' eventual autonomy.

Evan (2005, p. 147) believes that women have a responsibility to each other: "we need to show the younger generation the way so that it is not as hard for them as it has been for us" and believes that mentoring is "one way we take care of each other" (p. 147). Many women administrators credit mentors as essential to their success. Glazer-Raymo (1999, pp. 157–158) interviewed women academic leaders who mentioned the importance of finding a mentor and the role that mentors played in their success in reaching their administrative career goals.

It is vital to note that all mentoring relationships go through stages, from beginning to end. One model, proposed by Zachary (2000) includes four stages: 1. *preparing*; 2. *negotiating and developing a mentoring agreement*; 3. *enabling*; and 4. *coming to closure*. In the first, both mentor and mentee lay the groundwork for the relationship. In the academic settings, graduate advisors, potentially mentors, begin that process when we audition and evaluate students' readiness for graduate school.

The second stage is one in which the terms and expectations of the relationship are defined and clarified. At my own institution, we have a written guide for our choral conducting majors in order to delineate information about the program and expectations of our students. We discuss this together at the beginning of the school year and can refer to it throughout the year as situations arise that may require a reminder.

Stage three involves the advising, nurturing, guiding, overseeing and evaluating of the student as the mentor helps facilitate the student's progress through the program. This is the most intense and lengthy stage.

Stage four, closure, can be a difficult one. It occurs when goals have been met. Because mentoring is "goal oriented," it must come to an end when those goals are accomplished. "Once a new professional has attained his/her learning goals, or in cases where a relationship is counterproductive, it is time for the relationship to end" (p. 1). Zachary suggests that planning for closure is essential.

In my experience, closure is not necessarily abrupt; we may continue to serve as resources for our graduate students after they complete their degrees, advising about job possibilities, providing references, recommending repertoire, and perhaps visiting them in their workplace, at their invitation, of course. Some students enjoy maintaining contact, just as do some mentors; other students are in contact only occasionally, perhaps rarely seeing the former mentor at a conference or a performance.

Mentoring Junior Faculty

In many respects, the qualities of a good graduate student mentor are those of a good mentor for a junior faculty member. It is a time-consuming, but essential process, requiring a mentor who is genuinely interested in the new faculty member's advancement, helping him or her to negotiate the elements of the academic world. A faculty mentor must be available, communicative, encouraging, helpful, and must accept the importance of mentoring among his/her professional responsibilities.

An alert graduate student, or one with a good mentor already, should be somewhat acquainted with the variety of tasks required of a professor, having observed the graduate mentor engaged in them already. Research and creative activity, in the form of conducting, writing, and so on, coupled with teaching, and supplemented with service work on committees and for professional organizations, are elements of the academy that a conscientious mentor should share with graduate students, particularly those aspiring to university positions. Likewise, an apprentice conductor for a professional chorus or community choir needs the same consideration. Every position has its set of rules and regulations, its own culture, if you will, and it is that cultural understanding that enables organizations to continue and flourish.

Various resources exist for faculty mentors. Humboldt State University has a document entitled, "Best Practices for Mentoring Probationary Faculty," (retrieved 21 June 2007) that outlines suggestions for mentoring junior faculty, as well as establishing a "formal procedure for ensuring that probationary faculty members receive adequate support throughout their RPT (Retention, Tenure and Promotion) experience" (p. 1). The university also provides workshops on mentoring to supplement these suggestions. Each department on campus has a mentoring plan, and each incoming faculty member is assigned a mentor prior to the start of the first teaching term. There are regular meetings between the faculty member and his or her department chair and the Faculty Development Coordinator to discuss the effectiveness of the mentoring process. If a new mentor is needed, one is assigned.

In an addendum to the Humboldt State document, one finds a list of suggested activities. For example, before a new faculty member arrives on campus, the mentor can contact him or her to answer questions; to provide course catalogues, syllabi, and class schedules; to help order books for courses; and to assist the faculty member in making contacts to find housing, child care, and so on. Once the new hire arrives, the mentor introduces colleagues, gives a tour of the campus, provides resources pertaining to teaching and administration of the college or university, and makes the new colleague aware of research and grant opportunities, etc.

A list of ongoing mentoring activities is provided, including inviting the new hire to observe student advising sessions; helping with preparation of Professional Development Plans and annual review materials; providing support in relation for issues that arise concerning teaching or other professional matters; and "help in pursuing scholarship and/or creative activities specific to the candidate's areas of interest and expertise" (p. 3).

As conductors, we might collaborate with new colleagues, sharing performances, as well as introducing them to colleagues at other schools in the region and in professional organizations such as ACDA and the National Association for Music Education (MENC). The presence of an ongoing mentor would greatly enhance the new faculty member's experience by minimizing the stress that can arise in an unfamiliar setting. It is easy for us to get so busy in our own activities that we forget about new colleagues, but perhaps recalling our own challenging initiation into academia or the professional world in general is a good reminder not to do so.

A number of universities provide mentoring opportunities specifically for women faculty. For example, the Women's Studies Program at Syracuse University has a Faculty Mentoring Program through which new faculty can make connections with tenured professors who will meet monthly to discuss issues of concern. New faculty can either identify their own mentors by searching the list and making contact individually or the Women's Studies Program will help find mentors.

The University of Wisconsin-Madison established a Women Faculty Mentoring Program (WFMP) after a 1989 survey indicated that women were leaving the university prior to promotion, of their own accord. Senior women volunteer to mentor junior women from different academic disciplines. The program does not replace existing departmental mentoring structures but rather seeks to supplement these. Programs include an orientation workshop, and brownbag sessions on a variety of topics, as well as a banquet celebrating successful promotion and tenure.

In 2004, an evaluation of the program was published. More than half the women responding to the evaluation survey indicated they had participated in the program (p. 6). Of that number, nearly 70% felt the program was very or quite valuable (p. 10). Among the benefits cited were a decrease in feelings of isolation (p. 11), an "increase in knowledge about acceptable practices in the department" (p. 11), and a boost in confidence to "remedy negative situations that were potentially harmful. . . ." (p. 11). One respondent was especially positive about how her mentor helped her deal with family/work/balance issues and achieve a better balance herself (p. 15). Some women who were dissatisfied mentioned how long it took to be paired with mentors as a drawback, hence underscoring the need for connections to be made early on in the person's career at the new site.

[For additional mentoring resources found on-line, see the Reference list at the end of this chapter.]

Informal Mentoring

The mentoring models discussed thus far pertain to formal mentoring, whether of graduate students or junior faculty. A third, less formal type of mentoring, of which we are all a product, is environmental and familial mentoring. One of the most interesting books I read in preparation for writing this chapter was *How Jane Won* by Sylvia Rimm with Sara Rimm-Kaufman (2001). What struck me in reading the stories of these fifty-five successful women was how often they mentioned the influence of family members, teachers and coaches upon their lives. The authors note "girls who see themselves as smart are poised to succeed," (p. 8) and indicate "there were women in business, media, and science who deemed themselves failures before they receive guidance from mentors" (p. 10). Rimm and Rimm remind the reader that "good role models abound" and encourage us to seek out mentors, to the point that when considering a job, we should think about whether or not we will be well mentored there (p. 15).

The authors interviewed several artists who credit the influence of teachers as being greater than that of parents (p. 236). Artist Rodene Brchan tells of an art professor whose criticism and high standards she came to regard as his way of making her stronger (p. 253). Martha Aarons, a flutist with the Cleveland Orchestra, says "teachers took me under their wings," (p. 256), citing the case of a fifth-grade teacher who shared and encouraged her love of opera. Her flute teacher during high school groomed her for an orchestral career (p. 257). Pamela Frank, solo violinist, praises both her first teacher and her parents for "making music fun" and not pushing her too hard, but rather allowing her to enjoy playing (p. 262). Encouraged to enter a competition in high school by her violin teacher, she received advice that helped her acclimate to the professional world (p. 264). Frank credits a number of people with helping her develop her confidence along the way.

The influence we have, even when not intentionally mentoring, cannot be underestimated. Except for one woman who led the children's choirs in which I learned to sing, I had no female conducting mentors. Yet women teachers who modeled strength, competence, passion for music, and commitment to their profession, served as unknowing mentors for me as a prospective female conductor. It never occurred to me, singing in choirs conducted by men, that I could not do that myself, nor that I could not teach conducting eventually. In my case, supportive parents, excellent teachers of both genders, and a desire to succeed served me well. It is my professional goal to contribute now to the growing number of female choral conductors by serving as a model and mentor, just as are my colleagues who have also contributed to this monograph.

Conclusion—Leadership and Longevity

Good leadership requires tremendous energy, intensity and stamina. It is relentlessly demanding. Yet author Thomas Moore, in *The Re-Enchantment of Everyday Life* (1996, p. 357) , says "if we are indeed too busy, then it's obvious we need to relax, to learn how to do less and behold more, to become lazy in the soul instead of hyperactive in the spirit." No matter how ambitious, successful or simply busy we are, we must take time to refuel.

In practical terms, it is simply not possible to function at a highly intense level without time to rejuvenate. A simple but effective metaphor is that of financial resources, thinking in terms of deposits and withdrawals. Zero balances result from spending everything we have. If we spend more than we actually have, we become overdrawn. We can live on credit for a time, but not indefinitely; it has limits, just as our energy has limits. By making physical and emotional deposits to our personal banks, we can sustain our energy and fulfill our leadership roles. Common sense tells us to consider nutrition, sleep, exercise, spiritual growth and the importance of quiet time.

Most conductors I know are highly ambitious individuals with relentless schedules. Women in particular, having been raised to be nurturers, frequently expend energy on everyone else at their own expense. To be professionally effective in the long term, however, we must take time for ourselves and replenish our energy supply. Self-care is self-indulgent only if we become completely self-absorbed. One does not have to be narcissistic to be healthy. To say, "I can be the best conductor/teacher/leader when I am rested and healthy" is wise. To ensure it is a necessity. To be a good leader, mentor, conductor, spouse, parent or child, we must take care of our personal resources.

Biography

Dr. Hilary Apfelstadt is Associate Director of the School of Music, Professor of Choral Studies, and Director of Choral Activities at The Ohio State University. She conducts the OSU Chorale, the Women's Glee Club, teaches conducting and choral repertory, and coordinates the graduate conducting program. Her choirs have performed at regional and national conventions of the American Choral Directors Association (ACDA) and at state and regional conferences of the National Association of Music Education (MENC). She has conducted many honor choirs and all-state choruses in Canada, the United States, and in Cuba, and guest conducted in England. A prolific author, she has published over seventy articles on choral music in various refereed journals.

Currently national President of ACDA, Dr. Apfelstadt was a member of the Robert Shaw Festival Singers for several years and recorded two compact discs for Telarc with the Singers in France. Her degrees are from the University of Toronto, the University of Illinois and the University of Wisconsin—Madison. She also has a diploma in piano performance from the Royal Conservatory of Music in Toronto. In addition to her duties at the Ohio State University, Dr. Apfelstadt is Director of Music at Linworth United Methodist Church in Columbus.

References

Allen, S. G. (1988). *Leadership Styles of Successful Choral Conductors in the United States.* Ed.D. dissertation, The University of North Carolina at Greensboro. DA1-A 49/10, p. 2855, April 1989.

Apfelstadt, H. (1997). "Applying Leadership Models in Teaching Choral Conductors." *The Choral Journal,* 37 (8), 23–30.

Best Practices for Mentoring Probationary Faculty. Retrieved 21 June 2007 from www.humboldt.edu/~acaden/BestPracticesForMentoringProbationaryFacultyFinal05-04-12doc

Blake-Beard, S. (2005). "The Inextricable Link Between Mentoring and Leadership," in Coughlin, L,, Wingard, E., & Hollihan, K., eds., *Enlightened Power: How Women are Transforming the Practice of Leadership.* San Francisco, Jossey-Bass, 101–109.

Burns, R. (1786). "To a Louse." Retrieved 2 July 2007, from www.robertburns.org/works/97.shtml

Davidson, B. (1995). *Leadership Styles of Successful Male and Female College Choral Directors.* DMA dissertation, Arizona State University. DA1-A 56/12, p. 4692, June 1996.

Evans, G. (2005). "Are We Looking After Each Other? Women Leaders Winning the Game," in Coughlin, L,, Wingard, E., & Hollihan, K., eds., *Enlightened Power: How Women are Transforming the Practice of Leadership.* San Francisco, Jossey-Bass, 143–149.

Fisher, H. E. (2005). "The Natural Leadership Talents of Women," in Coughlin, L, Wingard, E., & Hollihan, K., eds., *Enlightened Power: How Women are Transforming the Practice of Leadership.* San Francisco, Jossey-Bass, 133–140.

Funk and Wagnalls College Dictionary (1973). New York: Funk and Wagnalls.

Glazer-Raymo, J. (1999). *Shattering the Myths: Women in Academe.* Baltimore, MD: The Johns Hopkins University Press, 1999.

Goldsmith, J., Komlos, J., and Gold, P. (2001). *The Chicago Guide to Your Academic Career: A Portable Mentor for Scholars from Graduate School through Tenure.* Chicago: The University of Chicago Press.

Goodstein, R. (1987). "An Investigation into Leadership Behaviors and Descriptive Characteristics of High School Band Directors in the United States." *Journal of Research in Music Education,* 35 (1), 13–25.

Hamann, D., Baker, D., McAllister, P., & Bauer, W. (2000). "Factors Affecting University Music Students' Perceptions of Lesson Quality and Teaching Effectiveness." *Journal of Research in Music Education,* 48 (2), 102–113.

Heard, M. (2005). "Being a leader of leaders," in Coughlin, L,, Wingard, E., & Hollihan, K., eds., *Enlightened Power: How Women are Transforming the Practice of Leadership*. San Francisco, Jossey-Bass, 463–471.

Hersey, P. and Blanchard, K. (1982). *Management of Organizational Behavior: Utilizing Human Resources*, 4th ed. Englewood Cliffs, NJ: Prentice-Hall, Inc.

How to Mentor Graduate Students: A Guide for Faculty at a Diverse University. (2006). The University of Michigan, The Rackham School of Graduate Studies. Retrieved 29 April 2006, from http://www.rackham.mich.edu/StudentInfo/Publications

How to mentor graduate students. (2006). The Graduate School, University of Washington. Retrieved 25 June 2007 from http://www.grad.washington.edu/mentoring/GradFacultyMentor.pdf

Mark, R. (1998). "Lavender Labors or Activist Mothering," in Coiner, C. and George, D. H., eds., *The Family Track*, 80–85.

Moore, T. (1996). *The Re-Enchantment of Everyday Life.* New York: HarperCollins.

Palmer, T. C. (1998). "Mentoring, Mothering, and Mayhem: Costs of the Super-Woman Syndrome," in Coiner, C. and George, D. H., eds., *The Family Track*, 75–79.

Rimm, S. with Rimm-Kaufman, S. (2001). *How Jane Won.* New York: Three Rivers Press.

Russell, T. (1980). *Leadership Styles of High School Orchestra Conductor-Educators.* Ph.D. dissertation, The Ohio State University. DA1-A 41/07, p. 2988, January 1981.

Swan, H. (1987). "The Lost Art of Inspiration," in Fowler, C., ed. *Conscience of a Profession: Howard Swan, Choral Director and Teacher.* Chapel Hill, NC: Hinshaw Music, 39–49.

Tannen, D. (1994). *Talking from 9 to 5: Women and Men at Work.* New York: Harper.

Tannen, D. (2003). "Fast talk." *The Diane Rehm Show*, 9 January 2003. Retrieved 25 June 2007 from http://www.wamu.org/programs/dr/03/01/09.php

Women in Science & Engineering Leadership Institute, University of Wisconsin-Madison, *Women Faculty Mentoring Program.* Retrieved 25 June 2007 from http://wiseli.engr.wisc.edu/iniatives/wfmp/wfmp_main.htm

Women's Studies Program Faculty Mentoring. Women's Studies @ Syracuse University. Retrieved 25 June 2007 from http://womens-studies.syr.edu/mentoring.htm

Yu, Sheng-Hwa (1999). *Conductor Leadership Style as a Force for Choral Ensemble Success.* Ph.D. dissertation, Temple University. DA1-A 60/07, p. 2423, January 2000.

Zachary, L. J. (2000). *The Mentor's Guide: Facilitating Effective Learning Relationships.* San Francisco, Jossey Bass. Cited in *The Stages of Mentoring.* Retrieved 30 June 2007, from http://www.coe.uga.edu/chds/mentoring/stages.htm

Zeldich, M. (1990). Address to the Western Association of Graduate Schools, cited in *A Conversation About Mentoring: Trends and Models*, published by the Council of Graduate Schools (www.cgsnet.org) and cited on the University of Iowa website. Retrieved 3 July 2007 from
http:// www.grad.uiowa.edu/Awards/MeritAward.asp

Additional Website Resources on Faculty Mentoring

http://www.artsandscience.utorontoca/info4faculty/mentoring.html

This provides a very concise outline of benefits to mentors and mentees, expectations, goals and a list of typical issues.

http://www.asu.edu/clubs/gwa/GWAmentorhandbook.pdf

This contains a Mentoring Handbook produced by the Graduate Women's Association at the University of Arizona in 2000–2001.

Recommended Reading

Toth, Emily. (1997). *Ms. Mentor's Impeccable Advice for Women in Academia.* Philadelphia: University of Pennsylvania Press.

Women, Conductors, and the Tenure Process: What's Up in the Academy?

Sharon A. Hansen

◆◆◆

*For as long as I can remember, singing in choir was an inspiring, uplifting experience for me. Because of my love for the choral art, I became a public school choral music teacher, and while teaching, received my Master's degree. I then found further inspiration in a role model with whom I studied during my doctoral program. This respected choral mentor told me that it shouldn't make any difference who was standing on a podium, male or female, and that what **would** matter is my ability—and wide-eyed and innocent, I believed him. I believed I would be evaluated in my university **teaching** according to my musical and academic skills, as I had been during my university **training**. It was actually very much more than just that.*[1]

◆◆◆

Introduction

Since the early 1990s, women have been entering into and graduating from colleges and universities in record numbers (see Table 1). These same women are also entering and leaving graduate school in record numbers. (Table 2 shows the percentage of women doctoral graduates in the humanities.) The 2006 Chronicle of Higher Education special report, "A Look at Minority and Female Doctorate Recipients," states:

> The proportion of Doctorates earned by women of all nationalities has grown steadily within all broad fields of study since 1974. Women earned a majority of Doctorates awarded in education, the social sciences, and the humanities in 2004.[2]

As an example, in 2003–2004 in the liberal arts and sciences, general studies, and humanities, 39 men and 56 women received Doctoral degrees. In all fields, *25,323 men* and *23,055 women* received Doctoral degrees that same year.[3] Clearly, the number of women poised to enter professional life has steadily increased in the last thirty-five years. But is the Academy ready for this?

Table 1. Number of Bachelor's Degrees Conferred, by Gender and Ethnicity, from 1990–1991 to 2003–2004[4]

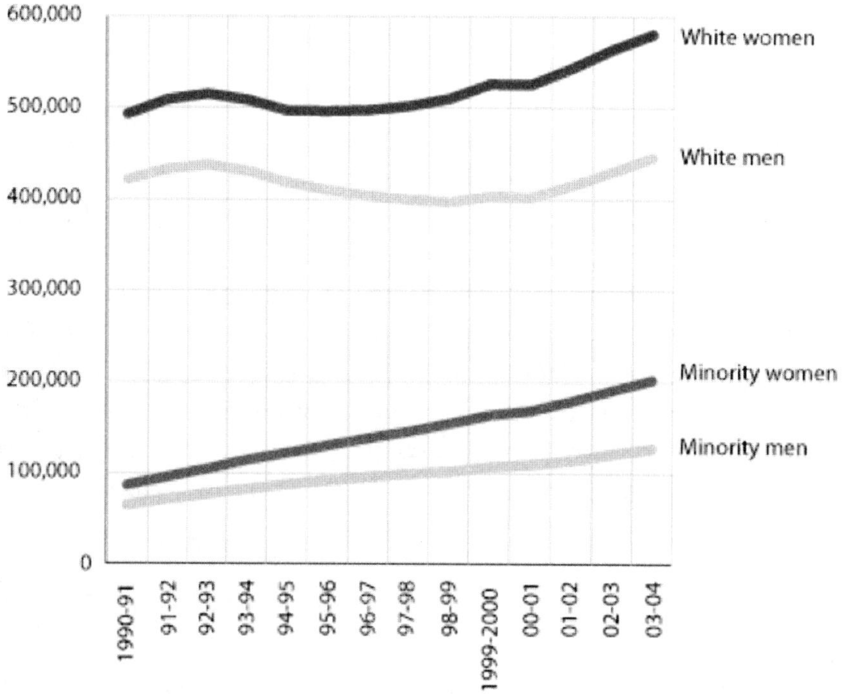

Table 2. Humanities Doctoral Graduates 1974–2004

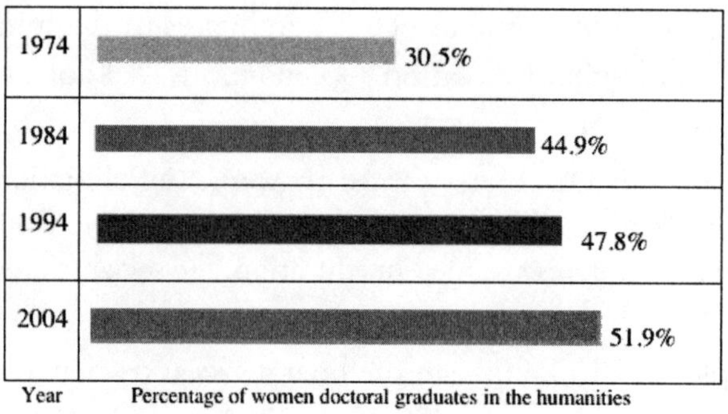

No researchers have published studies on the subject of female choral conductors and their academic route to tenure. Indeed, the last comprehensive report on the status of American female music faculty members in all fields was compiled between 1984 and 1986, and was published by the College Music Society in 1988.[5] To assist in establishing a context for the reader, the author will discuss in this chapter the following topics:

- the present state of women in the academy in general, including the discriminatory and sex-biased behaviors experienced by female faculty members on the tenure path, and the pitfalls that besiege female faculty members who find themselves in traditionally "male" positions;
- the current status of research concerning female faculty members in music (in general) and in the choral profession (specifically);
- what women can do to improve their chances for a successful tenure outcome.

The year 2007 marked the thirty-fifth anniversary of Title IX. The author cannot imagine a more fitting tribute to the women who have gone before than identifying the challenges that female choral conductors in the Academy have and are continuing to face. Although this chapter has considerable information within that, upon first reading, may seem somewhat disheartening, the author does not intend it to be read in that fashion. Rather, the author presents this material to serve as an informative reflection, not to induce an outcry of victimization. Most importantly, the information is provided so that women in the choral profession have access to material that may not otherwise be easily available to them, material that will allow them to "strive, survive, and thrive" in the Academy.

The author asked women who are tenured choral conductors in institutions across the country to describe their own path toward tenure. The reader will find a wide disparity in the tenure experience from one female faculty member to another. These women's voices and their stories appear throughout the chapter.

◆◆◆

The six years prior to my tenure decision were fulfilling and satisfying. Colleagues were supportive, and my administrators were as well. The year my paperwork was due we had an interim chair and he offered to help me prepare. We had several meetings in the fall and he offered many helpful suggestions (especially regarding writing style). He helped solicit letters of support from other choral professionals (as required by my university) and wrote me a strong letter.

My music department colleagues were equally affirming and my dean came in to my choir rehearsal the day the college committee voted to approve my tenure so that he could give me the good news himself.

All in all, my tenure process was a very positive one—not too demanding and very affirming.

I have never felt sexual bias in my position, which I have been in for eighteen years. Our university actively tries to recruit women and retain them.

◆◆◆

Title IX and Dr. Bernice R. Sandler

Women born after the mid-twentieth century have experienced a world relatively free from overt discriminatory practices in relation to their pursuit of higher education. This was not the case for women who were trying to attend college before 1970, as these stories attest:

- Virginia state law prohibited women from being admitted to the College of Arts and Sciences of the University of Virginia, the most highly rated public institution of higher education in the state. It was only under court order in 1970 that the first woman was admitted. *Kirstein v. Rector and Visitors of University of Virginia, 309 F. Supp. 184 (E.D. Va. 1970).*

- Luci Baines Johnson, the daughter of President Lyndon Johnson, was refused readmission to Georgetown University's school of nursing after her marriage: in 1966, the school did not permit married women to be students.[6]

In the last forty years, women have experienced an ever-increasing presence—as student or professor—in the American academy. The passage of Title VII of the Civil Rights Act of 1964 prohibited employment discrimination based on race, color, religion, sex, and national origin, and emerged as a result of a change in America's social consciousness. The passage of Title IX of the Education Amendments of 1972 (now known as the Patsy T. Mink Equal Opportunity in Education Act in honor of its principal author, but more commonly known simply as Title IX) placed women's equity in a high position in educational and social reform. Title IX was enacted on 23 June

1972, and states: "No person in the United States shall, on the basis of sex, be excluded from participation in, be denied the benefits of, or be subjected to discrimination under any education program or activity receiving Federal financial assistance."[7]

The history of Title IX is one that parallels the civil rights movement. At the time of its discussion, Americans were becoming more and more concerned about educational inequities facing women and girls. On both sides of the United States, synergistic threads were being woven that would lead to the creation of Title IX. On the west coast, Representative Edith Green of Oregon, a vocal advocate on behalf of women's rights, introduced a higher education bill that contained provisions regarding sex equity. Meanwhile, on the east coast, Dr. Bernice Sandler, currently Senior Scholar at the Women's Research and Education Institute in Washington, DC, had her own personal experience with sex bias in the Academy. Sandler, known to many as the "Godmother of Title IX," became extremely interested in law after she was not considered for a professorship at the University of Maryland despite a strong résumé. Dr. Sandler explains:

> They were expanding the department with seven new openings and they did not even consider me (and told me, when I asked why not, that I came on "too strong for a woman"). The date was probably in early 1969 although it could have been late in 1968, as it was during the academic year 1968–1969.[8]

A *Women's eNews* article continues the story:

> Sandler hit the books and found that there were no laws prohibiting sex discrimination in education. She noticed a little-known footnote prohibiting federal contractors from discriminating in employment. "I was alone in the house and I shrieked because I immediately made the connection that universities had contracts and couldn't discriminate," she says.
>
> She filed charges of sex discrimination against the University of Maryland, the first of about 250 complaints. In so doing, Sandler also took the first step in the legal journey to establish Title IX, legislation passed in 1972 that prohibits federally funded educational institutions from sex discrimination. It was championed by Rep. Edith Green, a Democrat from Oregon, and Sandler became known as the Godmother of Title IX, a law that has changed every aspect of education for all U.S. women and girls.[9]

Although the consensus was that sex discrimination in education should end, there was little agreement between lawmakers as to the best methods for reaching that goal. After a number of Congressional hearings, Title IX was eventually sent to the full Senate, which approved it on 22 May 1972. It then went to the House, and was passed on 8 June. President Nixon signed Title IX on 23 June, and on 1 July it went into effect. President Gerald Ford signed the Title IX final regulations on 27 May 1975.[10]

Were it not for the efforts of Sandler and Green in the early 1970s, this present essay on women and tenure would have had a very different tone. Vast numbers of women have been entering the workplace since Titles VII and IX were enacted. The early-to-mid twentieth-century model of the man as breadwinner and the woman as housekeeper was slowly unraveling as women were receiving record numbers of post-secondary degrees.

Former United States Secretary of Education Richard W. Riley (1992–2000) summarizes:

> The great, untold story of success that resulted from the passage of Title IX is surely the progress that has been achieved in education. In 1971, only 18 percent of all women, compared to 26 percent of all men, had completed four or more years of college. This education gap no longer exists. Women now make up the majority of students in America's colleges and universities in addition to making up the majority of recipients of Master's degrees. Indeed, the United States has become a world leader in giving women the opportunity to receive a higher education.
>
> Accompanying this untold story of success is the too frequently told story of the barriers that women continue to encounter—despite their history of accomplishments and despite the history of the legislation that protects them from such barriers. Too many women still confront the problem of sexual harassment, women still lag behind men in gaining a decent wage, and only one-third of all intercollegiate athletic scholarships are granted to women. Clearly, much more remains to be done to ensure that every American is given an equal opportunity to achieve success without encountering the obstacle of gender bias.[11]

◆◆◆

"Stay out of trouble," was my generation's approach to getting tenure. Presumably, that meant not raising a fuss when an older Full Professor patted my Assistant Professor bottom at an orientation for incoming graduate students. Since he was the older brother of a high school contemporary, I always had regarded him in an avuncular role, so I was quite surprised at his gesture. He would have known that my husband was in the room at the time, so the gesture was furtive and unseen by any others. Rather than feeling anger or revulsion at the time, however, I thought the gesture

by this single, older man was really quite pathetic. In true womanly fashion, I felt sorry for ***him!*** *This was, of course, long before days of workshops and university rulings on sexual harassment.*

Presumably, "staying out of trouble" generally meant agreeing to all assignments and responsibilities piled on by the administration and by senior colleagues. In my case, serving as Graduate Advisor as an Assistant Professor, a role frequently assigned to a senior professor, meant that I was busy processing application materials—without secretarial assistance, in my case. Prepare a dossier for promotion? Didn't have a lot of time for such things. Besides, how did one do that? This, too, was before the days of faculty mentors.

Why agree to endless assignments? Because refusing would not accord with the "Stay out of trouble" rule. Did senior colleagues, male and female, believe that since their own Assistant Professor years were marked by overwork, they should pass on the suffering to those beneath them on the tenure ladder? To see what the younger colleague could do? To discover whether or not the younger colleague was up to it?

Further, did I agree to the seemingly endless assignments, independent studies, and committees because I felt I had to prove that I could do it? That I could do whatever was dished out? "Stay out of trouble" and show your stuff! Why didn't I say, "If I do this, what would you like me to give up?"

◆◆◆

The "Chilly" General State of Women in the Academy

Over the last twenty-five years, there has been an outpouring of research on the status of women in the Academy—the sheer quantity of which is daunting to the serious researcher.[12] Spearheading the work was, and continues to be, Dr. Bernice R. Sandler, the previously-mentioned "Godmother" of title IX. In 1982, Sandler and Roberta M. Hall originated the term "chilly climate" to describe an environment of discriminatory and often hostile behaviors in which women often found themselves working. Sandler and Hall wrote that these "many small behaviors . . . together make up an inhospitable situation for women in academe."[13] Their three reports, *The Classroom Climate: a Chilly One for Women?* (1982), *Out of the Classroom: a Chilly Campus Climate for Women?* (1984), and *The Campus Climate Revisited: Chilly for Women Faculty, Administrators, and Graduate Students* (1986), are hallmarks of early work that identify biased behaviors often found in the Academy. These significant reports offered numerous suggestions for improving conditions for the female professoriate.[14]

Sandler and Hall described the culture of women in academia thusly. Young professors who enter the Academy generally expect to be evaluated on the basis of the work they do. Having recently left graduate school, these new professors still function with their recent student experience fresh in their minds: that is, they do their work, and they are evaluated on the basis of that work. Naively, perhaps, young professors believe this to be the reality even more so *inside* the Academy than it is outside. They are surprised, shocked, and sometimes incapacitated when, instead of the quality of their work as a basis for evaluation, they are met with chilly and biased evaluative conditions. Bernice Sandler explains:

> Colleges and universities ideally provide an environment that differentiates . . . *only* on the basis of merit. However, faculty and students are not automatically immune from the limiting preconceptions held by the larger society or from the everyday behaviors by which different perceptions of men and women are reinforced and expressed. To the contrary, despite increased enrollment of women students in recent years, college is still often considered a "masculine" environment.[15]

> When men and women behave according to our expectations we are comfortable and approving. But when someone violates these deeply held expectations, men and women alike often become uncomfortable, disapproving, or defensive.[16]

What might be some of the chilly conditions that female professors of myriad disciplines experience along their tenure journey? Why do these conditions exist? Especially for the young female choral conductor, negotiating the tenure path as a woman in a traditionally male profession, what are some of the pitfalls she may encounter? Sandler described a number of ingrained, societal, sex-biased behaviors confronting female professors:[17]

- Gender affects how we view competence, and how we evaluate competence.
- If a woman has success, it often is attributed to luck or affirmative action.

- Women are expected to be more warm and motherly.
- Women are supposed to make people feel good, to be emotional soothers.
- Women are expected to smile, be friendly, and not look serious.
- Women are not supposed to challenge students and make them feel uncomfortable.
- Women are not expected to be strong, dynamic, intellectual teachers.
- At the same time that students may expect more caring and warm behavior from a woman faculty member, they may nevertheless interpret such behavior as weakness, perhaps seeing it as "too feminine." However, should a woman faculty member act in a strong and assertive member—like her male colleagues—she may be viewed as "too masculine." Thus, women faculty are often caught in a double bind: no matter how they act, their behavior is "not quite right." *(Author's note: This observation parallels the notion that female conductors who lead with strength and assertiveness are "bitches," but men who lead in such a manner are ably powerful and bold.)*
- To the extent that students expect a woman to make them "feel good," "not cause trouble," and to soothe the emotions of others, they may well be uncomfortable with a faculty member's responsibility to challenge students, to stir them up intellectually, and to have authority over them. *(Author's note: This observation is especially true for female conductors, who, by the very nature of the position, "challenge students, stir them up intellectually, and have authority over them.")*
- Men can be said to have good judgment, but if a woman should exhibit the same quality, it is simply intuition.
- Men are more likely to be idealized, receiving more attention, eye contact and direct praise from students. Students may be more forgiving of demanding male teachers ("He has very high standards") and more critical of the same behavior in female teachers ("She has unrealistic standards; she is such a bitch.")
- Female teachers are more likely to be scrutinized more and held to a much higher standard than a male teacher.

- Our society tends to value men more than women, and to assume men's words and work are important, women's less so.
- Women in general get poorer student evaluations than men.
- Student ratings are affected by whether the female teacher is sociable and likeable.
- If you are "feminine," your student ratings are lower.
- If a professor is a strong female, she is rigid and controlling; if a professor is a strong male, he is intellectual and rigorous.
- Men can be described as assertive or aggressive and that can be a good thing, but if a woman should exhibit the same qualities, she is said to be abrasive or a bitch.
- Men can be called forceful if they have a strong opinion, but women are called aggressive or hostile under the same conditions.
- If a male professor is a careless dresser, he is eccentric; if a female professor is a careless dresser, she is sloppy.
- Women are expected to talk with "woman speech": that is, speaking softly, asking questions at the ends of statements, using a lot of qualifiers, apologizing often, exhibiting excessive politeness (deferential speech.) However, male professors use "Academy speech"—strong, assertive speech. If a woman does not use "Academy speech," she is perceived as less qualified than a man, but if she should use "Academy speech," she is perceived as abrasive and rigid.
- Male faculty who act dispassionately may be viewed as "objective," but female faculty who exhibit the same manner are called "cold."
- A female professor by her very nature causes dissonance: she is a woman in a position of authority, a place that she isn't supposed to be.
- Female faculty are far more likely to be called by their first name by students than men.
- Students are much more skeptical of remarks made by a woman than a man, and will more often challenge the source of knowledge with anger.
- Female faculty report more grade appeals than male faculty.

- Female faculty represent a disconnect between female societal and professional roles. Male students or colleagues often respond to female faculty according to the norms of society: for example, in a sexual way, or as if she were a mother figure. Since many male students or faculty are not comfortable with women as professionals, they use a societal role with which they are comfortable in communication: flirting with the female faculty, calling her by her first name, calling her "honey," saying such things as "You have such a pretty face, I hate to see you frown just because I am late to class."

- Some male students or faculty may touch a female faculty member, or invade her personal space by standing closer to her than they would to male faculty.

- Some female faculty report being sexually harassed by male students.

In a number of situations in the Academy, women are simply "damned if they do and damned if they don't." In her 1995 book *Lifting a Ton of Feathers: A Woman's Guide to Surviving in the Academic World*, Paula Caplan calls these the "Catch 22's in the Academy." The following are a few of these provocative scenarios.[18]

- If a woman fails, it "proves" that women are inferior; but if she succeeds, she becomes "proof" that nothing stands between women and success in academia and so women have no right to complain.

- If a woman makes her preferences known, she is demanding, selfish, and non-collegial; but if she asks her department chair or other boss what *they* want her to do, and she does it, she is considered spineless or lacking in focus.

- If you do any nurturing or caretaking—of colleagues, other staff, or students—that work may be invisible or unappreciated, but it can even be used as "proof" of your lack of professionalism; but if you *don't* nurture, your lack of nurturing behavior becomes highly visible, and you are considered a "cold bitch."

- Women academics are not considered real women if they don't have children and devote a great deal of time to them; but women academics who devote much time to their children are said not to take their careers seriously. Even if you do not have children, you may be taken less seriously because some day you might have them.

- When women academics band together, they are perceived as threatening; but when they do not band together, many remain isolated and powerless or begin to think of themselves as crazy.
- If you try to improve the climate for women—including yourself—on campus, you are considered a troublemaker, but if your don't make such an attempt, you go on suffering and are considered a masochist.
- A woman who speaks up is aggressive and doesn't know when to quit; but a woman who remains silent is passive and incompetent and has nothing worth saying.
- If you do well in your academic work, you are not "truly feminine," if you do badly, you will fail for sure.
- Writing for publication requires concentration; but if you refuse to become overloaded with work other people ask you to take on, you are considered uncollegial and even "bitchy."
- In academia, there are many unwritten rules; but if you break one, you are condemned for that, and if from time to time you ask what the rules are, you are considered ridiculous, overanxious, or paranoid.
- Women who socialize with male faculty may be considered loose or predatory; but women who do not socialize with male faculty will be out of the mainstream network and can miss out on information and support.
- Women who join the old boys' network thereby help to isolate and exclude other women and members of marginalized groups (both sexes); but women who don't join are less likely to move up the career ladder.

Sandler (2006) and Caplan (1995) both provide pages of practical strategies that female faculty can employ in a number of specific situations. That knowledge is power is an overwhelming thread in the literature this author examined.

◆◆◆

I have come to the conclusion that it would be best for me not to make a contribution. Sadly, it would mean that I would have to unearth a lot of the past that I would simply like not to revisit. In fact, even thinking over your request has meant dragging up a certain amount of very painful memories and concomitant anger that is surprisingly close to the surface, even after more than a decade.

◆◆◆

In the mere thirty-five years since the passage of Title IX, the Academy has found itself in shifting sands. An entire generation of predominately white, male professors hired after World War II, during the burgeoning of college campuses nationally, began to retire in the late 1970s and through the 1980s. The "chilly climate" Sandler and Caplan have so vividly described was—and continues to be—entirely dependent upon on the prevailing faculty attitude that comprised any one given department, school, or university. Each tenure-track female faculty member had her own unique experience, based on the climate in her department, and that paralleled the sea change of norms and standards in the Academy—and in society. Because each female faculty member's experience is so individual, it is difficult to make a generalization about a "female experience" in the Academy. Sandler, however, makes one point clear:

> Do these behaviors happen all the time to every woman? Of course not. But they happen often enough to communicate to women faculty (as well as women students and men) that woman are not welcome in academe or elsewhere. They are outsiders. Their very presence is a threat to some men. Add to this a curriculum that may ignore women or treat them badly, the small number of women on most faculties, the smaller number at the rank of full professor, the even smaller number of women administrators at the higher reaches, and the subtle inequities of daily life with some colleagues, and the climate for women faculty members is indeed chilly.[19]

◆◆◆

I never expected to be told that I couldn't do something, the more advanced the education I obtained. I had conducted choirs ever since I was in grade school. I was praised for my leadership and musicianship skills. I taught all levels of public school successfully, and worked in church music for decades. It was only when I started in my very first academic position that I experienced discrimination and harassment on the basis of my gender. For the entire duration of my path to tenure, I experienced male faculty and administrators coming on to me, demeaning my intelligence, usurping my authority with my students, not supporting me as a faculty colleague, undermining the program I was building, undercutting my musical decisions, and interfering with my personal life. I was constantly on guard, thinking I wasn't good enough, always wondering when the next trap would be laid. Most of my faculty colleagues—male **and** *female—simply looked the other way.*

In spite of all of this, I went up for tenure in my sixth year (the norm at the time.) Tenure and Promotion were not linked when I went up. I was refused tenure on the basis that "next year the University was making a change, campus-wide, to link tenure and promotion." After all I had been through in those six years, and all the work I did to prepare my tenure dossier, to have tenure denied, forcing me to return to that hostile work environment once again as a junior faculty member, was a harsh blow. (The tenure denial was indeed only a postponement—I did receive tenure and promotion the following year.)

I learned a difficult lesson during those years, that the Academy does not look after its own. Only **you** *can look after you.*

◆◆◆

Since women now represent more than fifty percent of all Doctoral degrees, how are women faring in the Academy today? A report released by the American Association of University Professors, the *AAUP Faculty Gender Equity Indicators 2006*, provides a detailed list of how 1,445 colleges and universities measure up. The report underscores the persistent issue of equity: "Women still represent a distinct minority of tenured and tenure-track faculty members, despite the fact that among American citizens, women are earning more than half of all Ph.D.'s conferred."[20] The authors maintain that, regardless of the record numbers of female students on college campuses, including record numbers of females graduating with Master's and Doctoral degrees, women only hold *twenty-four percent* of full professor positions across the United States.

> Women's integration into the faculty ranks . . . has occurred much more slowly. In 1972, women made up 27 percent of all faculty in higher education. By 2003, women comprised 43 percent of all faculty, 39 percent of full-time and 48 percent of part-time faculty. Women occupied about 9 percent of full professor positions at four-year colleges and universities in 1972, and still only 24 percent of all full professors in 2003.[21]

The report provides the following additional statistics:

- *The proportion of full-time faculty members who are female:* Nationally, women constituted just 39 percent of full-time professors in the 2005–2006 academic year, while making up 48 percent of the part-timers. The situation represents an inequity, the report says, because part-time positions typically pay less and have little job security. (The AAUP's 2006 "Annual Report on the Economic Status of the Profession" states that the proportion of full-time appointments among all faculty positions has been declining over the last thirty years.)[22]

- *The percentage of women within the tenured and tenure-track ranks:* Women held 44.8 percent of tenure-track positions in 2005–2006, and only 31 percent of the tenured positions. (According to Schuster and Finkelstein, the majority of new full-time faculty hires since 1990 have been off the tenure track.)[23]

- *The proportion of women who are full professors:* At all types of institutions in 2005–2006, women held on average just 24 percent of full professorships. (In traditionally male-dominated fields, the percentage of female full professors may be minute or non-existent, a pattern that is even more pronounced for minority women.)[24]

- *The average salary of female faculty members compared with males:* In 2005–2006 female professors earned on average just 81 percent of what men earned. (This comparison has remained virtually unchanged since the AAUP began collecting separate salary data for women and men faculty in the late 1970s.)[25]

◆◆◆

Maybe it's because I teach at a women's college, but I had a "normal" tenure experience here, receiving tenure and promotion to Associate Professor after six years. At that time it was not standard procedure to receive a promotion with tenure, so I applied for a promotion the year before I was up for tenure, thinking that if they turned me down, they probably wouldn't turn me down twice, so it would help ensure a promotion with tenure the following year. And that is exactly what happened...the early promotion was denied (the reason given was that I hadn't developed enough of a "national reputation.") Apparently one year later they felt I had, as I did receive the promotion along with tenure.

I never felt gender was an issue during the entire process. In fact rarely have I felt at all constrained by the gender issue in this field, and instead have felt it to be an asset at times.

◆◆◆

When gender discrimination exists, it is often subtle and systemic.
—Nancy Hensel[26]

Although women are indeed making progress in the Academy, the progress is slow, especially in those fields traditionally male (the hard sciences, mathematics—and in music, conducting). The female conductors who navigated their way through tenure processes in the 1970s and 1980s, before the tide of affirmative action offices, faculty mentoring programs, and departmental assessment committees, managed somehow—and if they ended up on the other side, it was often with scars they carried for life.

Young female tenure track faculty members today are at times better prepared to meet the challenges of the countless unique and difficult situations they will encounter on the road to tenure. However, it cannot be assumed that female faculty now have it somehow "easier" than before. Misbeliefs, assumptions, and myths pepper young faculty's perceptions of what life will be like in the Academy. One thing is sure: the tenure pathway is not always paved, nor is it always in a straight line.

◆◆◆

When I was being reviewed during the tenure process, one of the music department's Emeritus Faculty members came up to me at a party and told me that I needed to add a little "feminine charm" to my demeanor, that I needed to take full advantage of the power of being "charming." When my mouth finally came up off the floor, he continued that women conductors shouldn't try to be strong like the men conductors. He instructed me that women, instead, should be nurturing and sweet, and "charming." This was a faculty member who still had considerable influence on my tenure decision, since he was a previous faculty member at the university, whose wife was still a full sitting member of the music department's voting professoriate. Indeed, time and time again from one faculty member or another during those six years leading to tenure, I was told that a women conductor needed to be different than her male counterpart—inferring that women shouldn't be strong, assertive, commanding, or any number of the other adjectives used to describe strong male leaders.

◆◆◆

In the aforementioned book *Lifting a Ton of Feathers: A Woman's Guide to Surviving in the Academic World*, author Paula J. Caplan identifies twelve myths about academia concerning the bumpy and crooked tenure path (see Table 3).

Table 3. Twelve Myths About Academia from *Lifting a Ton of Feathers* by Paula Caplan[27]

1. The myth of meritocracy: the belief that in academia, people are formally rewarded simply according to the quantity and quality of the work they do.
2. The myth of objective standards and neutrality in the classroom and in hiring, promotion, and tenure.
3. The myth of non-discrimination and fairness.
4. The myth of democracy.
5. The myth of collegiality.
6. The myth of liberalism and openness.
7. The myth that, in academia, the primary goal is the search for knowledge.
8. The myth that, in academia, people's search for knowledge is done cooperatively, not competitively, and that this cooperation is rewarded.
9. The myth that "they" really want you to do service, teaching, and research in equal amounts and that, when it comes time for tenure and promotion, they will count all three as equally valuable.
10. The myth of individualism.
11. The myth that all teaching and scholarly work, regardless of its content and methods, will be regarded as equally important and valuable, as long as they are of good quality.
12. The myth that partial acceptance in academia means full acceptance.

A *myth* of collegiality . . . a *myth* of objectivity . . . a *myth* of non-discrimination and fairness? Should the young female faculty member really expect more in the Academy than society as a whole exhibits? There seems to be the mistaken notion somehow that the Academy is held to higher standards of behavior than elsewhere in the workplace. In this author's view, women who serve the Academy are high achievers for whom these myths have had little or no bearing on their professional training. It is only when these strong and intelligent women find themselves surrounded by faculty colleagues who believe *otherwise* that these myths become realities.

In addition to these rather generalized misperceptions about the Academy, female professors sometime have difficulty navigating the set of precepts that society imposes on them in terms of what is considered "correct behavior" for their gender. This difficulty has a direct bearing on women's capacity for job satisfaction. As female professors begin their procession toward tenure, how satisfied are they with their experience in the tenure track? In "The Study of New Scholars," a report by Cathy Trower, Senior Researcher in the Harvard Graduate School of Education, Trower writes:

> When it comes to the academic workplace at major research universities, women are far more dissatisfied than men and far less likely to become full professors. . . . As more women earn Ph.D.'s and enter the academic workforce, we should be seeing a much greater number of women on the tenure track. Unfortunately, while many other institutions in our society have changed, major research universities still adhere to a "Father Knows Best" model of climbing the academic success ladder.[28]

The report studied 983 assistant professors at six major research universities. On a satisfaction scale, they found that young female professors were less satisfied than young male professors on 19 of 28 measures. What were some of the items that contributed to this lack of satisfaction? These young female academicians were unclear about expectations for tenure, they lacked time and money for research, and they lacked support from their department heads.[29]

The University of California, under a Sloan Foundation Grant, recently implemented the *UC Family Friendly Edge Initiative*. This study examined gender imbalances throughout the UC System, and made policy recommendations to invoke a friendlier environment for all professors, especially women.

> Some of the program's initial recommendations include part-time options for tenure-track faculty, and university-sponsored infant and child care. Another recommendation is that the university discount gaps in applicants' résumés if they're related to family responsibilities. This means that women who take time off after getting a Doctorate would not be penalized in the hiring process. . . . Some women, however, feel pressure not to take advantage of such programs. Last September, the journal *Science* reported on a study that described what the authors (Lisa Wolfwendel of the University of

> Kansas and Kelly Ward of Washington State University) call a "culture of fear" among tenure-track women. Essentially, many women are afraid (with good reason) that slowing or stopping the tenure clock will have a negative career impact.[30]

With newly minted female faculty entering the halls of academe every day, the presence or absence of a culture of fear in which they work is inextricably linked to the success they will have in negotiating the rough road of tenure. Achieving tenure in choral music is an arduous task in and of itself, where the choral conductor proves her worth through extensive and focused research and performance. When biases interfere with these already grueling six years of amassing a superb research record, not to mention honing one's teaching and extending one's service reach, the young female conductor may be so disadvantaged that she may not find success in achieving tenure. To throw further fuel on the fire, in some revered halls, teaching and service may have very little to do with tenure: as one faculty colleague once told me, "We just assume *everyone* can teach, so we don't really *need* to evaluate it. We place the *real* importance on research." Young female conductors need to have full awareness of the sorts of biases that plague the professoriate. Through reading and research that develop ones' awareness of potential pitfalls, female faculty can work to cultivate strategies that will counteract the possible derailment of their path to tenure.

◆◆◆

> *I believe I was forty years old before I first heard those all-important words, "teaching load." Since I had been a student at the same institution, many on the faculty had been my professors, and they regarded me with great familiarity, more as former student than colleague. Nevertheless, they all seemed to be working hard, so my assumption was that I also should work hard. Especially since I was a woman and most of them were men. In fact, the mentality of women of my generation was not unlike the gerbil in the cage. Work to show you are working. Work to prove you really are worth something. Be all things to all people. Especially important—be supportive and nurturing to all people. Because I was a woman, especially an untenured woman!*

◆◆◆

Burning with idealistic passion, the young, female, D.M.A. or Ph.D. choral conductor typically enters a new position fresh out of doctoral studies. Even with previous teaching experience, the first year in the Academy can be a difficult time. The new professor is perceived as the "new kid on the block" as alliances are formed, faculty cliques jostle, and students of the former choral director moan and groan that everything is different now. The new faculty member may come into contact with difficult situations in the departmental or with campus administration, may suffer with the first realization of the amount of rebuilding she needs to do, may sense faculty political games being played (if she is perceptive), and may hear firsthand from a number of faculty their concern about whether she is up to the job of conducting, "since they never had a woman before."

In addition to these new challenges, as well as to the many aforementioned societal biases, entering female faculty may have additional hurdles that their male colleagues do not share. Traditionally, men have been able to juggle home and career, since their wives navigated the home front as they navigated the expectations of their job. With the women's rights movement, however, a new workforce burst onto the employment stage. The traditional definition of "family" was being rewritten daily. How has the female professoriate fared in terms of balancing work and family?[31]

> Women in the Academy often share certain realities that are not experienced by their male colleagues. Many of these women are courageously yet precariously navigating the tenure track while simultaneously juggling the roles of mentor, wife, caregiver, and maturing scholar. The loud ticking of these different clocks can become almost deafening for women scholars on the tenure quest.[32]

The female choral professor can find it daunting to fathom—in the midst of concerts, tours, programs, guest conducting, guest clinicing, guest adjudicating, sectionals, choir retreats, articles to be written for professional journals, lectures to be presented nationally, and all the regular daily matters that concern one's station of being a professor—that she might have time for a family. Research shows that for many female professors across disciplines, the harsh reality of academic life presupposes family decisions.

> A successful tenure outcome requires much more than publications, teaching, and service. It requires that you, the candidate, make it very *easy* for everyone deciding your professional fate to say, "She deserves to remain a part of us and what we do here. She is OK. She *fits.*" But the cold reality is that women who succeed in academe often do not have children or limit their family to one child. . . . Even though few female faculty will eagerly enter into a conversation that espouses this point of view, they either believe or have been told that it can be more difficult to "get there" when you

> have children traveling with you. Why? Because that other lifelong relationship—motherhood—is also time-sensitive and time-consuming. . . . Many women faculty strongly believe or suspect that it is risky to start a family when you are a newly minted Ph.D., a woman scholar, tenure-track and junior faculty. It is a decision (or pathway) that carries the real potential to affect you quite differently than it will your male counterpart who is also beginning a family. Some colleagues will place you on the "mommy track"; others will question your commitment to the department.[33]

In September 2005, officials of 27 major research universities met to discuss ways to make the tenure process more flexible. Robin Wilson reported on the meeting in his 7 October 2005 *Chronicle of Higher Education* article:

> Officials of 27 major research universities who met here in late September . . . said the lock-step, up-or-out nature of academic careers not only leaves no room for young professors to enjoy their family lives, but also hampers women's efforts to advance in the profession.
>
> When tenure policies were established on campuses, in the late 1930s and early 1940s, "the work force really had a single focus—on work," said Kathleen E. Christensen, director of workplace programs at the Alfred P. Sloan Foundation. "Now we have a work force with a dual focus—on work and family."
>
> That shift has created a "profound mismatch," she said, between how young professors want to live their lives and how the academic workplace is structured.[34]

The researchers found considerable data that describes how women, the Academy, and babies simply do not mix. Tenured women are much less likely to become parents than tenured men, and female faculty who do have children may advance more slowly than either female faculty with no children, or male faculty with children. The researchers conclude that unless faculty positions become more flexible and family-friendly, women faculty members *(author's note: especially those in time-intensive fields such as conducting)* will continue to search for part time, lower paying, less secure, off-the-tenure-track positions, "so they will somehow be able to put together a life and a career."[35] Author Virginia Valian takes it one step further. In her book, *Why So Slow? The Advancement of Women*, she purports that "the accumulation of small disadvantages over the course of an entire career may limit women's ability to progress at the same rate as men."[36]

◆◆◆

Perhaps it is naive of me, but only rarely have I been aware of gender issues in my own quest for tenure and promotion. (There are other instances, like the time a male conductor told me that I had done a good job in a master class with Sir David Willcocks: "That was really good. You don't conduct like a woman at all!") Apart from that instance, not related to tenure, I have been remarkably fortunate. There are rare occasions now when I feel invisible in my area meetings at school because I am the only female conductor at my institution, and notice that ideas I present are not always heard as readily as the same ones presented by my male counterparts, but again, in relation to tenure, I more or less sailed through.

At my first university, I was judged in two areas, conducting and music education, and was told by a senior faculty member afterwards that he felt I was tenurable in either area by itself, so there should be "no question" about my successful application because I had done twice as much as needed. At that point, there were lots of articles, two ACDA conference performances and a regional MENC performance, along with various guest conducting gigs. Other senior faculty told me the same thing afterwards.

I was actually hired with tenure at the Associate Professor level at my second position, and five years later, went up for full professor. A handful of people voted against me, including (I suspect) another female who felt I was too outspoken about vocal/choral issues. There was, and is, a bit of a tug-of-war sometimes with voice faculty and I had apparently held my ground about choral expectations for singers once too often. The vote, however, was overwhelmingly in my favor; my Director and Dean supported me and all the external letters were strongly positive, so again, I survived the process successfully.

All this makes me feel very fortunate. I knew what was expected; the criteria were clear, and I did my best to meet them. My upbringing was such that gender was never a detriment; I was not sensitized to look for trouble, but rather to do my best and compete with myself primarily. My parents taught me that gender should not hold anyone back from striving for their goals. Sometimes I have probably overlooked subtle putdowns from men and simply chosen to persist on the career path as I saw fit. If anyone insults my daughter or my female students, however, they can expect to hear from me about it!

◆◆◆

Female Faculty in the Music Profession: Data Collection

The College Music Society. As stated in the introduction, there has been little to no research about how female *choral* music faculty members have been and are presently faring in the Academy. Attempts at gathering data specific to choral conductors in general, and female choral conductors specifically, is difficult at best. Indeed, the last such data collection occurred between 1984 and 1986, when the College Music Society's (CMS) Committee on the Status of Women authored *CMS Report Number 5: Women's Studies/Women's Status*.[37] In that report, one lone statistical table shows choral conductors by rank and gender, comparing 1977 to 1986. An examination of the data from those two years reveals that women choral conductors in the tenure track numbered 201 in 1977 and 260 in 1986. Males during the same time period numbered 1,037 in 1977 and 1,267 in 1986. Female choral conducting faculty held just a little more than sixteen percent of all tenure track choral faculty positions in 1977, and just at seventeen percent in 1986.[38] The author contacted CMS to see if there was a more recent report, but was told than none existed.

The College Music Society, a consortium of college, conservatory, university, and independent musicians and scholars interested in all fields in music, sends a yearly survey ("Directory of Music Faculties") to music departments in order to update its database. The CMS database comprises music faculty and institutions that serve higher education in the United States and Canada, and includes over 30,000 music faculty at over 1,800 music schools, departments, and conservatories.[39] The author contacted CMS to gather specific data about female choral faculty members, but a database sort is not available except for those faculty who are actual *members* of CMS. In addition, CMS emphatically asserted that gender differentiation is not completely accurate in their database, since they do not specifically request gender when they ask each institution to update their information. The results of this author's inquiry, based on the best practices of CMS to ascertain gender identification, are in Table 4.[40]

Table 4. College Music Society Data: Choral Directors by Gender and Rank, 26 February to 8 March 2006

2,579 American and Canadian choral directors listed in the CMS database
Source: *CMS List 24 (Directors of Performance Organizations—Choral)*

Gender of all choral directors listed in the database

Male	1,689	(273 of whom are CMS members)
Female	850	(132 of whom are CMS members)
Undisclosed Gender	40	(1 of whom is a CMS member)
Total	2,579	(406 of whom are CMS members)

Rank and gender of the CMS members listed in the database

Professor, male	83
Professor, female	31
Professor Total	114
Associate Professor, male	54
Associtae Professor, female	34
Associate Professor Total	88
Assistant Professor, male	96
Assistant Professor, female	35
Assistant Professor Total	131
Adjunct/Lecturer, male	24
Adjunct/Lecturer, female	23
Adjunct/Lecturer Total	47
Undisclosed Rank and Gender	26
Total, All Ranks	406

(The author also requested information relating to rank, gender, and size of institution, [e.g., Research I, Research II, etc.], but the data was not available from the CMS database.)

◆◆◆

I felt like I was treated fairly throughout the entire tenure process, which went very smoothly. At my university, soon after arriving I was contacted by a group of tenured female faculty who offered themselves as mentors to all of the new women faculty. They threw us a lunch soon after our arrival on campus and spoke to us in detail about the tenure process. They made themselves available to all of us who were junior faculty as we made our way through pre-tenure evaluations and the tenure process. Although I never availed myself of their assistance, it was good to know that their support was behind all of us.

◆◆◆

NASM. The National Association of Schools of Music annually compiles data gleaned from degree-granting music programs throughout the United States through its *Higher Education Arts Data Services* survey, known as the HEADS Survey. The data summaries provide statistics on enrollment, faculty numbers and salaries, administrative processes, budget, presentation information, and a series of ratios providing comparisons in two or more of these areas. Most data are reported by size and type of institution.[41]

The numerous charts in the *2007–2008 HEADS Music Data Summaries* reports results from more than 600 private and public institutions in the United States. Tables 5–11 illustrate various aspects about the status of female music faculty in the Academy during the 2007–2008 academic year. Table 5 shows the general breakdown of total numbers of music faculty by rank and gender.

Table 5. Music Faculty by Rank and Gender[42]

Females: 556 institutions reported 3,133 female music faculty		
Professor	720	(22.98% of all ranks)
Associate Professor	908	(28.98%)
Assistant Professor	899	(28.69%)
Instructor	223	(7.17%)
Lecturer	177	(5.64%)
Unranked	150	(4.78%)
Visiting Faculty	56	(1.78%)
Total	3,133	(30% of total music faculty)
Males: 576 institutions reported 6,914 male music faculty		
Professor	2,198	(31.79% of all ranks)
Associate Professor	1,927	(27.87%)
Assistant Professor	1,633	(23.61%)
Instructor	434	(6.27%)
Lecturer	276	(4.03%)
Unranked	320	(4.62%)
Visiting Faculty	126	(1.82%)
Total	6,914	(67% of total music faculty)

Table 6 shows the percentages of music faculty who are male and female, categorized by the type of support the institution receives (public or private).

Table 6. Music Faculty by Gender, Institutions Categorized by Type of Support[43]

Private institutions	Females comprise ≈ 31% of the total music faculty
	Males comprise ≈ 65% of the total music faculty
Public institutions	Females comprise ≈ 30% of the total music faculty
	Males comprise ≈ 68% of the total music faculty

Table 7 shows the number of music faculty by gender and length of service, categorized by the type of support the institution receives (public or private).

Table 7. Music Faculty by Gender and Length of Service, Institutions Categorized by Type of Support[44]

Private institutions	Females	Males	Total	
1–4 years of service	313	578	917	(26.29%)
5–9 years of service	241	549	824	(23.63%)
10+ years of service	532	1,153	1,746	(50.07%)
Total	1,086	2,280	3,487	(100%)
Public institutions	**Females**	**Males**	**Total**	
1–4 years of service	664	1,339	2,051	(30.03%)
5–9 years of service	508	1,087	1,635	(23.94%)
10+ years of service	875	2,208	3,142	(46.01%)
Total	2,047	4,634	6,828	(100%)

Table 8 shows the numbers of music faculty who are tenured or not tenured by gender, categorized by the type of support the institution receives (public or private).

Table 8. Music Faculty by Gender and Tenure Status, Institutions Categorized by Type of Support[45]

Private institutions	Tenured	Non-Tenured	Total	
Females	419	667	1,086	(≈31%)
Males	1,058	1,222	2,280	(≈65%)
Public institutions	**Tenured**	**Non-Tenured**	**Total**	
Females	1,090	957	2,047	(≈30%)
Males	2,777	1,857	4,634	(≈68%)

Female music faculty do not fare particularly well in comparisons with their male faculty members' salaries. There is a wide disparity between private and public institutions, and within individual ranks. Table 9 shows female and male music faculty salaries at institutions with 201–400 music majors (other sizes of institutions are listed in the full report), categorized by the type of support the institution receives (public or private).

Table 9. Full-Time Music Faculty Individual Salaries Institutions with 201–400 Music Majors[46]

Private institutions				
Female music faculty	lowest	median	highest	average
Professor	$49,720	$82,410	$159,091	$84,665
Associate Professor	$33,447	$60,860	$104,656	$63,643
Assistant Professor	$24,150	$51,667	$75,500	$53,547
Instructor	$16,000	$35,830	$54,989	$34,336
Lecturer	$29,020	$49,674	$75,000	$46,901
Unranked	$21,940	$56,559	$141,000	$60,161
Visiting Faculty	$33,258	$41,873	$46,350	$42,211
Male music faculty	lowest	median	highest	average
Professor	$43,750	$85,260	$187,000	$87,268
Associate Professor	$40,500	$63,629	$120,000	$64,708
Assistant Professor	$38,000	$52,850	$102,000	$54,212
Instructor	$12,000	$23,256	$76,577	$29,957
Lecturer	$30,500	$46,143	$86,250	$47,239
Unranked	$20,592	$63,323	$162,180	$66,821
Visiting Faculty	$21,600	$47,500	$84,175	$49,714
Public institutions				
Female music faculty	lowest	median	highest	average
Professor	$38,900	$74,403	$119,800	$74,816
Associate Professor	$27,591	$59,667	$89.873	$59,718
Assistant Professor	$26,673	$48,323	$75,000	$49,180
Instructor	$25,509	$36,000	$60,000	$37,030
Lecturer	$23,962	$42,334	$60,000	$38,942
Unranked	$15,500	$30,574	$60,750	$37,489
Visiting Faculty	$30,000	$40,000	$75,000	$44,450
Male music faculty	lowest	median	highest	average
Professor	$35,940	$80,002	$169,182	$80,109
Associate Professor	$27,310	$60,056	$101,057	$60,957
Assistant Professor	$21,006	$48,533	$79,512	$49,940
Instructor	$21,250	$39,674	$89,090	$38,262
Lecturer	$19,884	$41,277	$83,647	$40,723
Unranked	$10,000	$32,016	$121,900	$38,687
Visiting Faculty	$22,000	$39,333	$58,240	$40,511

Last, two interesting tables (Tables 10–11) detail the results of a demographic survey of doctoral students by degree program. Students were identified as either graduating or still enrolled in 2006–2007. Unfortunately, conducting as a degree program is not specifically broken down into choral or instrumental track. Table 10 shows the number of conducting majors who graduated with Doctoral degrees in 2006–2007 (25 universities reporting).[47]

Table 10. Doctoral Students in Conducting Who Graduated in 2006–2007

	Male	Female	Total
Black or African American, non-Hispanic	2	0	2
American Indian/Native Alaskan	0	0	0
Pacific Islander	1	0	1
Hispanic	0	2	2
White, non-Hispanic	37	15	52
Asian	3	3	6
Other	3	3	6
Total	46	23	69

Table 11 shows conducting students who were still enrolled in doctoral programs in conducting but did not graduate in 2006–2007 (42 universities reporting).[48]

Table 11. Doctoral Students in Conducting Who Were Enrolled But Did Not Graduate in 2006–2007

	Male	Female	Total
Black or African American, non-Hispanic	12	6	18
American Indian/Native Alaskan	2	0	2
Pacific Islander	0	0	0
Hispanic	20	2	22
White, non-Hispanic	220	69	289
Asian	24	8	32
Other	25	12	37
Total	303	97	400

The HEADS reports, and to a lesser degree the CMS data, clearly show disparity in the status of women music faculty—and women choral faculty in particular. According to the HEADS report, male doctoral conducting graduates and students currently outnumber females by a ratio of 3 to 1. Male music faculty in general outnumber female faculty by a ratio of 2 to 1. Much depends on where you teach, what sort of funding the institution receives, and what sort of degrees the particular institution grants (i.e., whether an institution is a four-year institution only, whether it offers the Master's, or whether it offers both Master's and Doctoral degrees). What is particularly unsettling about this data is that it is not easy to come by, and therefore, not in the normal "field of vision" of a female faculty member on the tenure track. CMS and NASM reports are not necessarily materials that are made available to young, tenure-track faculty. The information contained in these reports is invaluable to all entering and tenure-track faculty, so that each faculty member understands clearly where the current research places her institution—and her profession. Such knowledge is very useful in salary, rank, or promotion negotiations.

But this assumes everyone who is a full time ensemble director is also tenure track—or are they?

◆◆◆

When I was hired at my university, there were no tenure track faculty in music. (At the time, my university did not have a music major. We now only have a MS in Music Technology, but we have more than six hundred students participating in my area's ensembles.) I was hired in 1992 as a Visiting Professor (the common practice at the time: after a couple of years, if all went well, they would open up the faculty line and you could apply for the position.) I had a lot of success, and saw the real potential of the ensembles here, so after three years at the Visiting Professor level, the line was opened, and I won the position—as an Assistant Professor of Music and an Associate ensemble director (the second position), non-tenure track. All of my colleagues at the time, including the department chair, were in similar positions—all non-tenure track.

Eight years later, the principal ensemble director, who was also the music department chair, retired, and a search was opened for the chair position. Since then, I have been the principal ensemble director for four years. When my predecessor retired, the incoming chair was given a few "new hires" as an incentive to build our small department. What is really interesting to me is that all the new hires in our department—including the new department chair position—are tenure track. I have been here for fifteen years, have my Doctoral degree—and I have had fifteen, one-year contracts. Our music department now numbers nine faculty members, and the entire senior faculty who have been here the longest are non-tenure track. I am not able to have my line converted to tenure track, unless I risk losing my job in a national search. I am not even allowed to seek promotion, because there is nothing to "promote," since I am not on tenure track. I go to faculty meetings, but cannot vote, even though I am a senior faculty member in the department with a long history of commitment to the school.

Before our new department chair came four years ago, we were evaluated on a regular basis. I always had positive evaluations, and had no fear about not being renewed year to year. In the last four years under the new chair, however, we have not had regular evaluations.

Since I am the only woman in the department, I suppose I could play the "woman" card that would enable me to have my non-tenure track line converted to tenure track, but I am choosing not to play that card for fear it would backfire and I would be terminated.

I don't believe my situation is necessarily related to gender—it's just "how it was when I came," and things haven't changed for me or several other of my male colleagues (also senior members of the faculty but holding Assistant Professor rank, non-tenure track) who were hired under the same conditions I was in the 1990s. That being said, I work with wonderful students and have built a very successful career here.

◆◆◆

My tenure story does not hold much interest for aspiring female conductors. Briefly, a prestigious liberal arts institution had the agenda to make the choral conducting position in the music department a non-tenured position, before I went through the strenuous tenure application process. The entire music department voted to recommend that I be granted tenure. The PTR committee did not contain a single faculty member from the arts. The documented justification for not granting me tenure was "inadequate quantity and quality" of publication. Of course, I fought the decision (without litigation), but without success.

Today, the choral conductor at that institution is, indeed, in a non-tenured position, following the example of many small liberal arts schools.

◆◆◆

Women as Professor/Conductors

So what about the conducting profession specifically offers challenges to females? Clearly, women have entered all aspects of musical life, from playing in professional orchestras to having solo careers to teaching in the Academy. What is it about conducting?

> The orchestral conductor stands elevated on a podium commanding the most prestigious musical organization in Western culture. As Elias Canetti observed, "there is no more obvious expression of power than the performance of a conductor." This display of power conflicts with traditional views of women and may explain why conducting remains "the last male bastion" in musical life.[49]

◆◆◆

I was visiting guest professor of conducting one year at a European university. Upon the conclusion of the concert season, my ensemble had a picnic, to which all their family members were invited. My husband (also a professional musician) and I had the occasion to sit across the table from the father of one of my students. This man, who was an esteemed science professor with two Doctorates, asked me what could have possibly led me to become a conductor. I explained that, much like he in the sciences, I had ability in conducting, an analytical mind, and a passion for my subject. He looked at me blankly and said, "Yes, of course, but there are men in your ensemble, and men don't want to be told what to do by a woman!" For me, it was just one more in a long line of sex-biased statements that I had experienced over the years, but it was something quite different for my husband. I will never forget the look on his face!

◆◆◆

Whether in the professional realm or in the Academy, women have had a difficult time getting to the podium. Among the fields of orchestral, choral, and wind band conducting, choral music has been the most friendly to female conductors. Even still, according to data provided by Chorus America, although there are 202 Professional Choirs registered in Chorus America's database (including members and non-members), women conducting those choirs number only 29, with male conductors outnumbering female conductors by a ratio of 6 to 1.[50] Historically, women have been visible and well accepted as choral conductors primarily only within the realm of elementary, middle school, small high school, small college, or sectarian institutions. In the choral profession, female choral conductors are generally whole-heartedly accepted as children's choir directors (although not typically as boy choir directors), as junior high and middle school choir directors, as women's chorus directors, as training choir directors (a training choir to the top choir, usually conducted by the woman's male colleague), as high school directors in small schools, as church choir directors (but not typically in the largest, most prestigious church positions), as community choir directors (again, not typically in the most prestigious of positions), and as two-year and small four-year college choir directors, among others. As mentioned earlier, female choral conductors number some 850 according to the CMS 2006 directory. Are female choral conductors likely to inhabit the top choral positions in US and Canada?

In 1991, Lori R. Hetzel completed a M.M. thesis titled "The Current Status of Women Choral Conductors at the Collegiate Level."[51] Two years later, Kay Norton collaborated with her for a 1993–1994 article titled "Women Choral Conductors at the Collegiate Level: Status and Perspectives."[52] The pair set out to discover which doctoral choral conducting institutions employed at least one female conductor on the faculty, as well as to collect additional data regarding the backgrounds of the conductors. They sent out 601 surveys to women collegiate choral directors, whose names were obtained from CMS List 24 ("Directors of Performance Organizations—Choral." Returned to them were 290 surveys, and 276 of those were used to obtain data.

Of the 276 surveys, seven women responded that they held the Baccalaureate, 148 the Master's, and 120 the Doctoral degree.[53] The average length of service was 8.6 years.[54] It was where the women taught that was most telling.[55]

- 61 (22.8%) taught at a community college
- 104 (38.9%) taught at a private institution with fewer than 100 majors
- 21 (7.8%) taught at a private institution with more than 100 majors
- 58 (21.7%) taught at a state institution with fewer than 200 majors
- 18 (6.7%) taught at a state institution with 200–400 majors
- 5 (2.6%) taught at a state institution with more than 400 majors

Female conductors who taught at community colleges and private institutions comprised *69.5%* of all the respondents. Female conductors who taught at large state institutions with more than 200 majors comprised only 9.3% of the respondents. The median consisted of 21.7 of the respondents. Women conductors who reported teaching at graduate programs numbered 28, comprising only 10.1% of the total respondents.

This author was curious about the present state of the female choral conducting professoriate. She set out, with the help of the CMS Directory, a network of professional colleagues, and college and university websites, to discover where women were teaching across the United States and Canada. She was most interested in the status of women who were teaching in graduate choral conducting programs, programs where women choral conducting faculty were in a position to mentor young women seeking a professional degree. A survey of 140 graduate choral degree-granting institutions in the United States and Canada reveals quite interesting data. Female choral conductors in the top or co-leadership position are currently teaching in ten research universities of the forty-six (21.73%) that offer the Doctorate in Performance: Conducting as the terminal degree (see Table 12). *(Note: In the Academy, there is wide variance as to names of degrees. For the purposes of this survey, "Doctorate in Performance: Conducting" means D.M.A., D.M., or D.A.)*

Table 12. Universities That Offer the Doctoral and Master's Degrees in Choral Conducting with a Female Choral Director in the Top or Co-Leadership Position

Boston University	Ann Howard Jones
North Dakota State University	Jo Ann Miller
Ohio State University	Hilary Apfelstadt
University of Alberta—Canada	Debra Cairns
University of Colorado—Boulder	Joan Catoni Conlon
University of Minnesota	Kathy Romey
University of Oregon	Sharon Paul
University of Toronto—Canada	Doreen Rao
University of Wisconsin—Madison	Beverly Taylor
Yale University	Marguerite Brooks

Female choral conductors in the top leadership position currently are teaching in only *fifteen* research universities of the ninety-four (15.94%) that offer the Master's in Performance: Conducting as the terminal degree (see Table

13). *(Note: Again, for the purposes of this survey, "Master's in Performance: Conducting" means M.M., M.A., or M.F.A.)*[56]

Table 13. Universities That Offer the Master's Degree in Choral Conducting with a Female Choral Director in the Top or Co-Leadership Position

Austin Peay State University	Karen Kenaston-French
Central Michigan State University	Nina Nash Robertson
Juilliard	Judith Clurman
New England Conservatory	Amy Lieberman
New Mexico State University	Jerry Ann Alt
Northern Arizona University	Edith Copley
Pennsylvania State	Lynn Drafall
Pittsburg State University	Susan Marchant
University of Denver	Catherine Sailer
University of Louisiana—Monroe	Deborah Chandler
University of New Orleans	Caroline Carson
University of Wisconsin—Milwaukee	Sharon A. Hansen
Washington State University—Pullman	Lori Wiest
Western Washington University	Leslie Guelker-Cone
Winthrop University—South Carolina	Katherine S. Kinsey

Combined, these twenty-five female professors chair only 17.85% of all 140 surveyed graduate choral conducting programs in the US and Canada. (This translates into a more than 5.5 to 1 ratio of male choral conductors leading graduate institutions than females.) Assuming for a moment that the number of female conductors in the CMS list (850) is relatively accurate, and taking into account the twenty-five women mentioned above, a deafening question arises for the profession: where are the remaining 827 collegiate female choral conductors working? If the author were to make an educated guess, she would propose that her sister colleagues are working primarily in community colleges and private institutions (where women, usually better multi-taskers than men, "do it all" in their small departments), and then, to a lesser extent, working in smaller public institutions, much as the previously mentioned 1993 Hetzel-Norton study reported.

But there is yet another piece to this puzzle. Because women conductors historically have found acceptance in the public schools and churches, many female choral conductors in the professoriate hold academic positions in Choral Music Education and in Church Music. These positions often have significant conducting duties as part of their job descriptions. It was beyond the scope of this chapter to survey all major institutions to discover where *all* female choral conductors are currently working, for even coming to an accurate listing of female choral conductors and their institutions has proved quite problematic. Although CMS has a list of choral conductors in the US and Canada, they explained that they do not regularly screen for gender, and as such, their lists may not be completely accurate. Attempts at accessing accurate data from American Choral Directors Associateion was likewise futile: the ACDA listing of 801 "Women University Directors" from 30 May 2007 included women who were children's choir, elementary, middle school, high school, youth, and church choir directors; additionally, most of the women's names had no affiliated institutions, so the list was not accurate or useful. The author has made a polite but strong appeal to CMS that perhaps it is time again for them to issue another "Report on the Status of Women," now that it is more than twenty years after their initial investigation.

◆◆◆

Concerning overwork, one revelation occurred when I discovered, to my great surprise, that the head of my department actually was unaware that, all at the same time, I was on three search committees, that I also served on university committees, and that I was teaching an overload. He had no idea, as I had not complained. This was before the days of faculty activity analyses.

I did conduct two ensembles, which were my lifeline to sanity. Conducting allowed space and time to not be a departmental underling. Yet, there, too, were opportunities to "Stay out of trouble." Don't make a fuss when one senior male professor, a generation older than I, jokingly said, after at least two of my concerts, "Pretty good for a girl." He really thought he was being funny.

When I did come up for tenure in my department, the vote was unanimously positive. I always wondered why. Was it the quality of my work, or the quantity?

While women of my generation still may be inclined to "Stay out of trouble," getting tenure does allow one to tell someone to "Go stuff it" when you think it necessary. And you still can be supportive and nurturing!

What is a Woman to Do? or "You Can't Make a Difference in the Academy without Tenure!"

The average American female choral director on the road to tenure will conduct her home school's ensemble(s); teach methods or conducting classes; serve as a business manager for her choral department, planning budgets and other fiscal materials; serve as tour manager, hotel planner, and church stay recruiter; serve as secretarial staff, producing her own programs, course materials, and more; schedule and hear all choral auditions; schedule all outside rehearsals, sectionals, and make up classes; and in her spare time, guest conduct across the country, write scholarly articles, and make numerous local and regional high school visits for recruitment purposes—and more. With this enormous burden of work on the tenure-track choral faculty's shoulders, is it any wonder that learning to negotiate the politics of the academic environment is low to non-existent on her radar screen? But it is exactly learning to dance that subtle dance called "collegiality" that may win the young professor what it is that she wants: tenure.

There is an enormous wealth of literature presenting advice to female tenure-track faculty, how to negotiate the years leading to the tenure decision, how to avoid "getting in trouble," how to deflect inequitable treatment.[57] Literature in Women's and Gender Studies is profuse; reading anything by Drs. Bernice Sandler or Paula Caplan would be extremely beneficial to the young female conductor just starting out, simply to level the playing field. But the author also highly recommends that every young female professor read "Ms. Mentor's" advice columns and books.

Dr. Emily Toth, otherwise known as "Ms. Mentor," is Professor of English and Women's Studies at Louisiana State University. She is author of *Ms. Mentor's Impeccable Advice for Women in Academia* (Philadelphia: University of Pennsylvania Press, 1997), *Ms. Mentor's New and Ever More Impeccable Advice for Women and Men in Academia* (Philadelphia: University of Pennsylvania Press, 2008), and is a regular contributor to the "Careers" section of the *Chronicle of Higher Education* with her column titled "Ms. Mentor: Words of Wisdom about Academic Culture."[58] She is an outspoken feminist and critic of the inequities of the tenure system, but understands that women will only have the power to change the inequities in the Academy if they have tenure. Ms. Mentor uses humor, honesty, and exaggeration to get her point across: at the core, she believes that it is not just the "Big Three"—Teaching, Research, and Service—that will get you tenure. Ms. Mentor writes, "Collegiality" (whether they like you) often outweighs the three official criteria—teaching, research, and service—when academics decide on tenure. Your department colleagues are really asking themselves: Do we want to see Cora in the mail room for the next 30 years?"[59]

On 26 September 2006, Ms. Mentor presented a faculty workshop at Marquette University in Milwaukee, Wisconsin. The following are excerpts from her presentation as well as from several of her advice columns and book.

- Charming gets you a long way in Academia!

- Getting tenure is not as hard as getting hired. There are rules, and you must follow them to the rule!

- Keep a Tenure Diary at home. Put everything related to your teaching career in that diary:
    - print out all emails that are job related, that refer to what people think of you (pro or con)
    - keep copies of your contract and contractual agreements
    - keep copies of student and peer evaluations and reports
    - keep all notes of praise
    - keep all memos to department chairs and other administration
    - keep copies of your students' best work *(author's note: keep copies of all CD's and programs of your students' concerts)*

  Keep all these materials in a box at home—you will need them as documentation when preparing your tenure file.

- Besides your tenure diary, devote yourself to two things your first year: establishing a productive research routine—and being well liked.

- Become familiar with the University's Policy Statement on Tenure and Promotion. Quietly, non-confrontationally, keep track of whether the rules are being followed. If things go awry, you'll need proof.[60]

- Make sure your colleagues know that your research is well underway *(author's note: articles, guest conducting, special concerts, invitations to lecture)*

- The Route to Tenure: Don't take a stand, don't take sides. Claim ignorance. Assistant Professors should just ask for lots of advice from everyone and not take sides. Be charming. Smile a lot.

- In academia, there are officially three criteria for tenure: excellence in research, teaching, and service. But the biggest thing to have, especially for a woman, is—*charm*. Virtually all tenure policies say a candidate needs some kind of excellence in all three areas . . . but what matters most is "collegiality," a minefield for women.[61]
- If you work your butt off, you aren't collegial!
- Women should learn to use their skills of persuasion and manipulation to productive end.
- Assistant Professors should learn to work well with the office staff. This is very important. Without them, nothing gets done, and work gets "lost."
- Women have this savior complex. They believe they're going to save the world, that they are going to save and help everyone! Women have to stop being responsibility magnets. It's the "Women Who Love Too Much" syndrome.
- A woman's prime career years coincide exactly with her prime fertility years. So do you wait until you are tenured to have your children (average age 40!), or do you have your children in graduate school?
- No one talks about moving after grad school. Think about whether you can be mobile with your family, and if you can't, it may be necessary to rethink the doctoral program.
- Women tend to be perfectionists in many things—but adequate is often OK and enough. Do many things adequately—but do a few things with your full attention (publishing, for example).
- Academic women tend to have impossibly high standards for everything. We were the good girls who always got straight A's in school! We need to learn how to lower our standards on non-essentials.
- Your "In-Box" will never be emptied. . . . Don't sweat the small stuff (and it's all small stuff).
- Your role, especially in your first year, is to be a sponge, a grateful guest, and a visiting anthropologist studying the lore and habits of the natives.[62]
- Choose your battles carefully.

- Within five years, [the young faculty member] has to get great teaching evaluations (or at least passable ones, if he's at a large research university). He has to do sufficient publication and research to impress his colleagues as well as peers at other universities who'll write tenure support letters. He has to do enough service (committee work) to seem energetic and committed to his department's "mission" (which may or may not be evident). And he has to be viewed as "collegial"—bright, cheerful, easy to get along with.[63]

- Young professors need to up their appearance of authority. Look older!

- Your size, your age, and your experience will all allow you to exude more self-confidence.

- Realize that tenure is the most important piece of property you own.

- Realize that older female faculty know their voices. It takes a lifetime to know your voice.[64]

Ms. Mentor's advice on "charm" may ring contrary to the leadership style required of the conductor. Some may ask how one can be at once charming and assertive? How far does charm have to go before it becomes vacuous? Doesn't conducting require rigor, great organizational prowess, and the ability to assert one's authority? And aren't these characteristics, generally discouraged in women, in opposition to "charm"? As opposed to the definition used by the Emeritus Professor in one of the aforementioned stories, Ms. Mentor explains that charm is simply a matter of showing that you "fit in," that you are liked and respected. Passing for "charm" in the Academy means that the young faculty member should:

- meet everyone and be seen at every faculty occasion, including visitor's talks (for choral conductors, that means attending faculty recitals, visiting guest artists' performances, and all of her conducting faculty colleagues' performances);

- "do lunch," have dinner parties, go to all social occasions;

- exchange chitchat, be considerate and friendly, listen carefully, look alert, and smile.

Ms. Mentor explains that these behaviors are not difficult for most women to manage, since they tend to be raised learning the basics of social hypocrisy, or what is generally referred to as "good manners."[65]

◆◆◆

The situation at this institution is uncommon: tenure is only offered to those in the fields of musicology and music theory. It is speculation on my part, but I think this is a situation that is more common in this region of the country than it is elsewhere. In this region, performance and pedagogy are not viewed in the same way as music theory and musicology for purposes of tenure.

When I came, it was made very clear to me that I would not be eligible for tenure and that I would not be employed in a tenure-track position. When I inquired about that, I was told in no uncertain terms that the institution was able to "do more for me with term appointments" under any circumstances. Tenure was simply not a consideration, even for a full professor, which I was to be.

It does not seem to me that this has affected my ability to function effectively at this institution. It has not altered my status in any way, I don't think, especially since so few people in the college have tenure-track positions. Once one ventures outside of the college, there are different perceptions, of course, but within the college, the majority of us are in the same boat. It is a large faculty with very few tenured faculty members.

One's bargaining position could be affected adversely if one were to try to negotiate with another institution for a faculty appointment. Coming from this institution without tenure and trying to enter another institution where tenure is granted routinely could be problematic until accomplishments and recommendations are taken into consideration. Presumably the question would then be moot.

So, I have had a series of long-term appointments with reviews every five years.

◆◆◆

Conclusion

Female choral conductors have both shared and uniquely personal experiences along that long and winding road toward tenure. Perhaps at this juncture, some words about the nature of tenure would be helpful.

> Tenure is a promise of lifetime employment awarded to scholars who demonstrate excellence in scholarship, teaching, and service. According to the landmark *Statement of Principles on Academic Freedom and Tenure* made in 1940 by the American Association of University Professors and the Association of American Colleges, tenured faculty can be fired "only for adequate cause, except in the case of retirement for age, or under extraordinary circumstances because of financial exigencies." . . . Tenure conveys the approval of the academic community as a whole, and ushers the fortunate candidate into a job with extraordinary job security and prestige. . . .
>
> A negative tenure decision is always painful. . . .While universities and colleges stress the permanent nature of the tenure contract, they often gloss over the fact that a negative tenure decision terminates the candidate's job and, sometimes, her or his career.[66]

As one examines the research on the status of female faculty in the Academy, and of female music and choral faculty in particular, the numbers speak loudly to the professoriate. Female choral conductors are outnumbered by their male choral colleagues by a ratio of 2 to 1, according to the 2006 CMS statistics. But the ten women who lead U.S. and Canadian choral conducting doctoral programs (out of the forty-six universities surveyed in 2007) are outnumbered by their male colleagues by a ratio of 3.6 to 1. And the fifteen women who lead U.S. and Canadian choral conducting Masters' degree programs (out of the ninety-four surveyed in 2007) are outnumbered by their male colleagues by a ratio of more than 5 to 1. With more than 850 women listed as choral conductors in CMS, only 25 were leading graduate programs in the US and Canada. Who is mentoring our upcoming female choral conductors? Is part of the problem that there are so *few role models* for young female choral conductors, especially female role models who serve in prominent graduate institutions and who have high, national visibility? If there is no model, how will an entering choral conductor know what to do, how to do it, or even know if she *has* done it? Further research is also needed to buoy up this author's assertion that the majority of women presently working in choral conducting have positions in community colleges and private institutions, perhaps not all by design.

Women in the humanities are graduating in higher percentages now than ever before. However, ingrained societal and academic biases continue to plague female faculty. Unlike some, this author does not believe women need to lose their sense of humor in the academy: however, that bias and discrimination exists today is irrefutable. The career trajectory of a female choral conductor may be one of continual compromise until such time as society, our profession, and the Academy have enough tenured female faculty members that the rules can change for good.

And so the author asks,

> What really counts for tenure, Ms. Mentor?
>
> Service, in fact, is usually unimportant, except in small liberal arts colleges—or if Sophia is well liked but without a distinguished record in anything else. One assistant professor with mediocre teaching and publications was given a "service award" at a Far West university because her colleagues wanted to tenure her anyway. That happens.
>
> Teaching is often not counted very heavily, except sometimes in small liberal arts colleges. But if Sophia's teaching is horrendous, with terrible evaluations and constant student complaints, those will be used against her, if her colleagues want to get rid of her.
>
> Research and publication are important: they are measurable, public achievements. If Sophia gets major grants, or publishes in a university press book, plus articles in the best refereed journals in her field, usually her tenure will be assured. . . . If she doesn't piss someone off. . . .
>
> Ms. Mentor wishes she could say that merit will always be rewarded in academia, but such is not the case. What is rewarded is likeability, followed by publication. And then teaching.
>
> Ms. Mentor exhorts her readers to Make Nice. It saves time.[67]

Ms. Mentor explains:

> Would that it were so—that the untenured were always welcomed warmly, treated with respect and dignity, mentored ably, and encouraged to be the superb teachers, researchers, writers, and colleagues that most are capable of being.
>
> Ms. Mentor would delight in being a member of such a department. Indeed, she would love to live in such a world. (Perhaps she might even step down from her ivory tower to share the wonder.) However, Ms. Mentor knows that in these deplorable days of downsizing, de-tracking, and disap-

pearance of positions, collegiality is often tossed aside. . . .

[The] best revenge is to get tenure, for that is the only way she can begin improving the manners of her colleagues. Her silence now, and her quietly cleaning her silk blouse herself, are but a means to a greater end.[68]

Ms. Mentor, ever the pragmatist, recommends that women do what they must to get tenure, and then change the recipe. Only the permanent chefs, after all, ever get to tinker with the sauce.[69]

Biogrpahy

Sharon A. Hansen

Employment: 1994–present: Professor and Director of Choral Activities, University of Wisconsin—Milwaukee; 1986–1994: Assistant/Associate Professor of Music Education and Choral Conducting, University of Northern Iowa; 1975–1986: public school teaching and graduate work.

Degrees: B.M.E., University of Nebraska—Omaha; M.M., University of Nebraska—Lincoln; post-graduate work, University of Illinois at Urbana-Champaign; D.M.A., Conservatory of Music, University of Missouri—Kansas City.

Professional Service: Member, editorial board, ACDA *Choral Journal* 1995–present; Editor, *Choral Journal* column "On the Voice," 1999–present; Wisconsin State R&S Chair for Youth and Student Activities, Chair, WCDA Collegiate Choral Symposium, 2001–2008; Founding Board Member (2006–present;) and Founding Treasurer, *Southeastern Wisconsin Chapter of the Voice Foundation* (its first local chapter); prior community board membership, *Milwaukee Children's Chorus* and *Early Music Now*.

Performance and Publications: Founder (1998–present) and Music Director, the Milwaukee Choral Artists, one of three professional female choral ensembles in the U.S.; Numerous performances and premieres with MCA (ACDA Regional and State Conventions, guest performances with the Boston Camerata, KITKA, and contemporary music ensemble Present Music, and other national performances); Articles on choral conducting and choral music education in the *Choral Journal* and the *Music Educators' Journal*; editor of numerous articles in ACDA *Choral Journal* "On the Voice," and guest editor of the first *Choral Journal* Focus Issue on the Voice, November 2008.

Professional Interests: Conducting and movement pedagogies; repertoire for women's ensembles; foreign language and world music; French choral music; contemporary music; repertoire for mixed chamber choirs; music of Eastern Europe (Romania.)

Acknowledgements

I would like to take the opportunity to thank the many people who gave generously of their time, and who served as an inspiration to me in the preparation of this chapter. I honor each of them for their contributions, and list them alphabetically as follows:

- Dr. Joan Catoni Conlon, University of Colorado—Boulder, for her initial guidance in this project, and for her subsequent feedback and editing expertise;

- Ms. Catherine Davies, Director of Membership Services, Chorus America, and Ms. Julie Johnson, Director of Data Resources, the College Music Society, for their invaluable and always friendly assistance in data collection and interpretation;

- Dr. Eph Ehly, Professor Emeritus, Conservatory of Music, University of Missouri—Kansas City, whose continued support and encouragement have enriched my career and my life;

- Dr. Timothy Noonan, University of Wisconsin—Milwaukee, for his careful eye and attention to detail in the reading of my bibliography and notes;

- Dr. David Rachor, University of Northern Iowa, whose love, support, and critical review has enlivened me all our married life;

- Dr. Gillian Rodger, University of Wisconsin—Milwaukee, for her cogent comments upon reading my initial draft;

- Dr. Bernice Sandler, Senior Scholar, Women's Research and Education Institute, Washington, D.C., for setting the wheels in motion in 1968, and for her gracious sharing of information throughout this project;

- Dr. Emily Toth, Louisiana State University, for her wit, wisdom, and supreme inspiration in teaching women to navigate the tenure path.

And finally, to all my colleagues, the many women conductors who so selflessly shared their stories so that all could benefit—thank you. It is to you—and to those women who will come after us—that I dedicate this chapter. May you find your path smooth, and your joy boundless.

NOTES

[1] The italicized paragraphs in this chapter are the personal reflections and stories of women conductors. Their identities are being withheld out of respect for each woman's privacy and candor.

[2] N.a., "A Look at Minority and Female Doctorate Recipients," *The Chronicle of Higher Education*, Volume 53, Issue 6 (29 September 2006): p. B16–17. http://chronicle.com/weekly/v53/i06/06b01601.htm

[3] N.a., "Earned Degrees Conferred, 2003-4," *The Chronicle of Higher Education*, The 2006–7 Almanac, Volume 53, Issue 1 (29 September 2006): 22. http://chronicle.com/weekly/almanac/2006/nation/0102201.htm

[4] Robin Wilson, "The New Gender Divide," *The Chronicle of Higher Education*, Volume 53, Issue 21 (26 January 2007): p. A36. http://chronicle.com/weekly/v53/i21/21a03601.htm.

[5] N.a., "Women's Studies/Women's Status," College Music Society, CMS Report Number 5. (Boulder: College Music Society, 1988.)

[6] Richard W. Riley, "Title IX: 25 Years of Progress—June 1997." http://www.ed.gov/pubs/TitleIX/part1.html.

[7] *Title IX, Education Amendments of 1972, Title 20 of the United States Code, Sections 1681–1688.* http://www.dol.gov/oasam/regs/statutes/titleix.htm.

[8] Dr. Bernice Sandler, personal e-mail communication with author, 31 May 2008.

[9] N.a., "Seven Who Stake Our Claim to the Future: Hannah Rosenthal, Bernice Sandler, Elizabeth Saylor, Susan Weidman Schneider, Charlene Ventura, Sheila White, Marie Wilson," *Women's eNews*, 3 January 2007. http://www.womensenews.org/article.cfm/dyn/aid/3006.

[10] Riley, "Title IX."

[11] Ibid.

[12] See Bibliography for a selected list of readings.

[13] Bernice Resnick Sandler, "Women Faculty at Work in the Classroom, or, Why it Still Hurts to be a Woman in Labor." http://www.bernicesandler.com/id29.htm.

[14] Roberta M. Hall and Bernice R. Sandler, "The Classroom Climate: a Chilly One for Women?", Washington: Project on the Status and Education of Women, Association of American Colleges and Universities, 1982; Roberta M. Hall and Bernice R. Sandler, "Out of the Classroom: a Chilly Campus Climate for Women?", Washington: Project on the Status and Education of Women, Association of American Colleges and Universities, 1984; and Roberta M. Hall and Bernice R. Sandler, "The Campus Climate Revisited: Chilly for Women Faculty, Administrators, and Graduate Students," Washington: Project on the

Status and Education of Women, Association of American Colleges and Universities, 1986.

[15] Hall and Sandler, "The Classroom Climate: A Chilly One for Women?", 4.

[16] Sandler, "Women Faculty at Work in the Classroom."

[17] *Improving the Climate for Women Faculty,* Workshop series sponsored by the Office of the Provost, the Committee on Faculty, and the Women's Studies program, Marquette University, Milwaukee, 28 February to 1 March 2006. (Material can be found in Sandler, "Women Faculty at Work in the Classroom.")

[18] Paula J. Caplan, *Lifting a Ton of Feathers* (Toronto: University of Toronto Press, 1995), 65–73.

[19] Sandler, "Women Faculty at Work in the Classroom."

[20] Robin Wilson, "AAUP Report Blames Colleges for Gender Inequity Among Professors," *The Chronicle of Higher Education*, Volume 53, Issue 11 (3 November 2006), p. A11. http://chronicle.com/weekly/v53/i11/11a01101.htm.

[21] Martha S. West and John W. Curtis, "Organizing Around Gender Equity." Publication of the American Association of University Professors, 5. http://www.aaup.org/AAUP/pubsres/research/geneq2006toc.htm.

[22] Ibid.

[23] Jack H. Schuster and Martin J. Finkelstein, *The American Faculty: The Restructuring of Academic Work and Careers*. Baltimore: The Johns Hopkins University Press, 2006. In: Martha S. West and John W. Curtis, "Organizing Around Gender Equity." Publication of the American Association of University Professors, 5. http://www.aaup.org/AAUP/pubsres/research/geneq2006toc.htm.

[24] Caplan, *Lifting a Ton of Feathers*, 22.

[25] Wilson, "AAUP Report Blames Colleges for Gender Inequity Among Professors."

[26] Nancy Hensel, "Realizing Gender Equality in Higher Education: The Need To Integrate Work/Family Issues." Publication of Education Resources Information Center (ERIC). http://findarticles.com/p/articles/mi_pric/is_199110/ai_2332580643.

[27] Caplan, *Lifting a Ton of Feathers*, 48-55.

[28] Cathy A. Trower and Jared L. Bleak, "The Study of New Scholars." In "Major Universities Discourage Women Seeking Tenure," a press release from the Harvard Graduate School of Education, 12 April 2004. http://www.gse.harvard.edu/news/features/trower04122004.html.

[29] Robin Wilson, "Where the Elite Teach, It's Still a Man's World," *The Chronicle*

of Higher Education, Volume 51, Issue 15 (3 December 2004): p. A8. http://chronicle.com/weekly/v51/i15/15a00801.htm.

[30] Catherine Hess, "The Ivory Tower's Glass Ceiling: Female Academics Seeking Tenure are Falling Below the Curve," *San Francisco Bay Guardian Online*. http://www.sfbg.com/39/28/careers_education_women.html.

[31] See chapter titled "Juggler or Gymnast?" by Hilary Apfelstadt in the present volume.

[32] Deborah Brunson and Michelle Howard-Vital, "Happy Mother's Day: Women Scholars, Tenure, and Parenthood," p. 1. Paper to accompany Round Table Presentation: "Structuring a Supportive Environment for Women in Higher Education," Mid-Atlantic Conference on Scholarship of Diversity, 18–19 March 2004. http://www.multicultural.vt.edu/MACSD/proceedings/Article_Mothers-Day_VATech_Proce.pdf

[33] Ibid., 3.

[34] Robin Wilson, "Rigid Tenure System Hurts Young Professors and Women, University Officials Say," *The Chronicle of Higher Education*, Volume 52, Issue 7 (7 October 2005): p. A12. http://chronicle.com/weekly/v52/i07/07a01202.htm.

[35] Ibid.

[36] Virginia Valian, "Why So Slow? The Advancement of Women," (Cambridge, MA: MIT Press, 1998), in Martha S. West and John W. Curtis, "Organizing Around Gender Equity," publication of the American Association of University Professors, p. 15. http://www.aaup.org/NR/rdonlyres/356548BE-AF67-4D79-928C-03DDC73C8EEF/0/OrganizingAroundGenderEquity.pdf

[37] "Women's Studies/Women's Status," CMS Report.

[38] Ibid., 141.

[39] For information on this database, see The College Music Society, http://www.music.org/cgi-bin/showpage.pl?tmpl=/infoserv/facdir/facdirhome&h=63.

[40] Personal e-mail communication with author: original inquiry, 26 February 2006 to cmsmembership@music.org and response on 6 March 2006 from data@music.org.

[41] Higher Education Arts Data Services (HEADS) Project. http://heads.arts-accredit.org/index.jsp?page=Home.

[42] MUSIC Data Summaries 2007–2008, National Association of Schools of Music Higher Education Arts Data Services (HEADS). (Reston, Virginia: 2007). Music Chart 10.

[43] Ibid., Music Chart 7.

[44] Ibid., Music Chart 10.

[45] Ibid., Music Chart 12–1.

[46] Ibid., Music Charts 14–1, 14–2, 15–1 and 15–2.

[47] Ibid., Music Chart 27.

[48] Ibid., Music Chart 28.

[49] J. Michele Edwards, "Are Women Moving from Success to Significance?", paper presented at The International Festival for Women in Music Today. Seoul, Korea, 9 April 2003.

[50] Catherine Davies (Director of Membership Services, Chorus America), personal e-mail correspondence with author, 13 July 2007.

[51] Lori R. Hetzel, "The Current Status of Women Choral Conductors at the Collegiate Level," (M.M. thesis, University of Missouri-Kansas City, 1992.)

[52] Lori R. Hetzel and Kay Norton, "Women Choral Conductors at the Collegiate Level: Status and Perspectives," *College Music Symposium* 33/34 (1993/1994): 23–40.

[53] Ibid., 29.

[54] Ibid., 30.

[55] Ibid., 31.

[56] Julie Johnson at CMS, who graciously provided the data, emphasized the challenges of keeping accurate their database of some 1800 institutions. The CMS data are updated once a year, but are only as accurate as the individuals inputting the information from each institution. The above lists were based on information gathered 27–31 May 2007. The author would gratefully receive additions and corrections to the list.

[57] For voluminous bibliographies, see the works by Sandler, Caplan, and Toth cited above.

[58] For a listing of Ms. Mentor's columns in *The Chronicle of Higher Education*, see: http://chronicle.com/jobs/news/archives/columns/ms._mentor/.

[59] Emily Toth ("Ms. Mentor"), "The Tenure Gloat," *The Chronicle of Higher Education*, Volume 50, Issue 19 (16 January 2004), p. C3. http://chronicle.com/jobs/news/2004/01/2004011201c.htm.

[60] Emily Toth ("Ms. Mentor"), "Your First Month In A New Job," *The Chronicle of Higher Education*, n.v., 27 August 1999. http://chronicle.com/jobs/news/1999/08/99082701c.htm.

[61] Emily Toth, *Ms. Mentor's Impeccable Advice for Women in Academia* (Philadelphia: University of Pennsylvania Press, 1997), 160–161.

[62] Toth, "Your First Month In A New Job."

[63] Emily Toth ("Ms. Mentor"), "Academic Failure?", *The Chronicle of Higher Education*, Volume 50, Issue 39 (4 June 2004), p. C3. http://chronicle.com/weekly/v50/i39/39c00301.htm.

[64] If not otherwise noted, material stems from Emily Toth's lecture, "What Women Academics Need to Know–But Often Aren't Told," in the Workshop series sponsored by the Women's Studies program, Marquette University, Milwaukee, 26 September 2006.

[65] Toth, *Ms. Mentor's Impeccable Advice*, 164.

[66] Susan K. Dyer, ed., *Tenure Denied: Cases of Sex Discrimination in Academia* (2004), publication of the American Association of University Women Educational Foundation and American Association of University Women Legal Advocacy Fund, Washington, 2–3.

[67] Toth, *Ms. Mentor's Impeccable Advice*, 163–164.

[68] Ibid., 158–159.

[69] Ibid., 96.

Feminine Perspectives on Conducting and Teaching Choral Music

Doreen Rao

dedicated to the spirit of change, the nature of hope, and listening hearts

Introduction

Some things never change—or do they?

Some feminist scholars insist that the European classical-music tradition perpetuates the stereotypes in our male-dominated culture. If this is so, and it may be, how can enlightened conductors and teachers today conduct and teach the European classics in a way that honors this history and redefines musical performance and rehearsal pedagogy from a feminine perspective?

Should we dismantle these treasured traditions? Should women boycott classical-music concerts? Or should we transform our relationship with these works and consider the benefits these efforts might bring to our increasingly diverse and socially conscious society? Transforming or re-conceptualizing our conducting and teaching relationships in the classical music tradition is an elusive and complex task that calls for change—change in our profession's ability to *recognize* the feminine, to *listen* to what the feminine voice has to say, and to *assimilate* those qualities that are different from the "malestream."

Strangely, some feminist critiques on performance show a resistance to change, suggesting that we must first confront the "dynamics of male domination" that are the root causes for the exclusion of women.[1] Being both a radical optimist and an impatient pragmatist, however, I believe that the potential for transformation and renewal exists right now in the hearts and minds of a growing number of gifted and articulate conductors—both women and men! To say that things won't change until we "confront male domination" is an academic indulgence that duplicates the oppositional and dualistic thinking of the past. This feminist prescription mimics patriarchal tendencies and ignores the present generation of conductors and teachers who are successfully pioneering the future in their own voices.

The danger associated with avoiding this opportunity for change is captured in the story of the lamplighter in Antoine de Saint-Exupéry's *The Little Prince.*[2] Having landed on the fifth planet, the little prince met the lamplighter, whose occupation it was to light and put out the street lamp.

> "Good morning. Why have you just put out your lamp?"
>
> "Those are the orders," replied the lamplighter. "Good morning."
>
> "What are the orders?"
>
> "The orders are that I put out my lamp. Good evening." And he lighted the lamp again.
>
> "But why have you just lighted it again?"
>
> "Those are the orders," replied the lamplighter.
>
> "I do not understand," said the little prince.
>
> "There is nothing to understand," said the lamplighter.
>
> "Orders are orders. Good morning." And he put out his lamp.
>
> Then he mopped his forehead with a handkerchief decorated with red squares. "I follow a terrible profession. In the old days it was reasonable. I put the lamp out in the morning and in the evening lighted it again. I had the rest of the day for relaxation and the rest of the night for sleep."
>
> "And the orders have been changed since that time?"
>
> "The orders have not been changed," said the lamplighter. "That is the tragedy. From year to year the planet has turned more rapidly and the orders have not been changed!"

The "orders have not been changed," and that accounts for the tragedy of women behaving like the mostly white, male, conducting teachers who taught them. The question of *how women can conduct and teach as women* is central to the intent of this essay. Equally pertinent is the opportunity to examine *what constitutes a feminine design for conducting and teaching choral music*—a design that recognizes the feminine voice, but extends beyond gender differentiation toward an inclusive human practice defined by the unique cultural conditions of the twenty-first century, and not by blind obedience to 19th-century Eurocentric romantic ideals.

In what follows below, I will propose what could constitute a feminine design for conducting and teaching choral music, based on a retrospective on curricular trends and instructional innovations in performance teaching. This is followed by a discussion of the characteristics of feminine wisdom, enhanced by the gender-inclusive perspectives rooted in Zen. Lastly I will "re-dream" a conducting curriculum that reflects the social realities of the twenty-first century, guided by the principles of diversity and inclusion, the ethics of empathy, the voice of feminine wisdom, and the principles of peacemaking—for all of these qualities seem to be intertwined.

Part I: Retrospective

I have learned reluctantly that in the world today, there is no escaping the catastrophes that are synonymous with our time. Millions of people around the world suffer from everyday violence that comes with corruption, oppression, and injustice. Racism, sexism, and homophobia continue to flourish; violence is the daily fare of our media and popular culture; historical wounds continue to fester; and the gap between rich and poor grows ever larger. Heartbroken by the terror of 9/11 and the cycles of violence that have followed, I started questioning the philosophical constructs that had informed my conducting and teaching practices, particularly those practices related to teaching the next generation of choral conductors. The need for change has never seemed greater.

Given the dramatic changes in our cultural and political landscape, I embarked on a research project with my University of Toronto graduate students.[3] We sought to investigate the curricular trends and instructional innovations in performance teaching since 1975, and to identify emerging themes that distinguished this literature after 9/11. We asked the question, "To what extent have our professional practices changed in the years since the terrorist attacks on the World Trade Center?"

Reviewing and cross-referencing a wide range of literature, we collected large quantities of data that coalesced into what we agreed took on the qualities of a comprehensive retrospective in performance teaching. A sketch of this study is presented next, showing a broad spectrum of distinguishable trends followed by an exploration of four themes underlying and related to conducting and teaching choral music.

Overall, our retrospective revealed repeated themes and significant shifts in theory and practice that led chronologically from the earlier, perception-influenced aesthetic-education theories and general-music trends of the 1970s and 1980s (with a focus on musical *knowing*), to the production-based, praxial philosophies and performance approaches that demanded our attention in the middle of the 1990s (with a focus on musical *doing*), toward the ethics-related phronesis theories that emerged in the late 1990s (with a focus on a musical way of *being*—following a moral course of action that is "right" and "just" in a given situation).[4]

Aesthetic-education theory championed by Bennett Reimer[5] separated musical performance and ensemble singing from what was considered at the time to be a more "democratic" model of classroom general music. The emphasis on developing an understanding of music through listening charts and analysis of recorded music was challenged by those of us who believed that musical understanding or musical perception was embodied in music-making.[6] We called singing and playing forms of knowledge, or thinking-in-action.[7] These opposing theories of aesthetic versus praxial music education began to relax as our profession discovered that the complex mysteries of musical experience and the diverse human practice of "musicking" could not be reduced into a single belief or philosophy. Wayne Bowman's seminal work on educating musically[8] discussed contemporary pluralist perspectives and distinguished training and indoctrination from education. This scholarship posited the thesis that educating students musically in choirs is concerned ultimately with the development of character and identity, or what Professor Bowman calls an ethical *way of being*.

In the literature just following the new millennium, we noted the emergence and subsequent influence of the concept of *pluralism* followed by a multiplicity of philosophical trends and teaching methods that define our practices today. The values of diversity and multiculturalism particularly were seen in repertoire listings, reviews, concert programs, and textbooks. It was noted that an apparent integration of instructional methods and teaching styles was being recommended to accommodate the growing diversity of choral literature and the increasing ethnic diversity of students singing in choirs. Clearly, in addition to a growing openness to world musics in choral classes, the scholarship, repertoire, and program content developed post-9/11 included the prevalence of social and spiritual themes concerned with commemoration, remembrance, social action, and world peace.

Gradually, a multidimensional view of music education emerged beyond the limitations of oppositional, dualistic thinking that has dominated professional practice for too many years. Philosophical argument and lively criticism aside, it seemed clear that the movement from socially and culturally de-contextualized methodologies generated by nineteenth-century aesthetic thought and reflected by twentieth-century Eurocentric repertoire and prescriptive rehearsal pedagogies, was being replaced by socially and culturally responsive programming as reflected by an expanding multicultural repertoire and a movement toward reflective rehearsal methods.

Notable Findings

The statement and question: "Some things never change—or do they?" is explored in further detail through the following discussion of what I consider to be our research project's most notable findings. I introduce these next as an example of the kind of change that reflects what I view as *the emergence of feminine wisdom* in the field of conducting and teaching choral music—a central notion that I develop later in this essay. The following four themes appeared prominently and repeatedly in the literature after 11 September 2001. I will briefly introduce each of these themes, followed next by short elaborations taken from the class discussions on our retrospective.

Our findings suggested that the conventional performance values of *uniformity* are slowly being replaced by a growing consciousness of *diversity*. Diversity was clearly evident in concert programs and repertoire lists that included a broad range of cross-cultural choral music performed stylistically by choirs demonstrating sensitivity to cultural traditions and authenticity. We found that the hierarchical values of *exclusivity* were being replaced by a growing sensitivity to *inclusion*,[9] as demonstrated by a growing number of choirs coming on stage with physically challenged and special-needs students. Taken as a whole, it would seem that the patriarchal drive for *perfection* is slowly being replaced by the values of *reflection* and a *concern for the quality of human experience*. Could these important changes have been motivated by the feminine values held by the growing number of female conducting teachers leading university conducting programs around North America?

Conducting Choral Music Is an Innately Personal and Politically Important Practice

The prevailing wisdom of the past did not appear to recognize what is often called "personal voice"—cultural context or lived experience as a valid part of what has historically been defined by aesthetic education as the *musical experience*.[10] Political realities or personal references were, and still are in some cases, considered extra-musical (non musical) and aesthetically impure. Even today, the concept of the "personal I" or "lived experience" is held suspect in the university world of performance education and research.

Working from "a personal and politically informed voice" requires conductors to look carefully at the relationship between choral singing and everyday life. Social identity, physical health, psychological well-being, and awareness are just a few of the many personal considerations relevant to every student. Although there seems to be a growing enthusiasm for learning new ways of approaching the podium, there is still an obvious resistance from many conductors—as observed at local concerts and national conferences—to work outside the safety zone of familiar patriarchal traditions and Eurocentric practices. It is too easy to hold on to the same set of beliefs that informed us as children and students and that continue to protect us from taking on the difficult task of experimentation and professional risk.

On the brighter side, growing numbers of choral conductors and music teachers recognize that diverse musical traditions and practices offer an opportunity for students to explore, affirm, and celebrate diverse cultural heritages. Christopher Small addresses this matter, suggesting that music is culture and that it is inextricably social.[11] Small suggests that in music teaching and learning we bring into existence a set of relationships between the sounds and between the participants that reflects "ideal relationships." In *exploring* we learn from the sounds and from one another the nature of the relationships; in *affirming* we teach one another about the relationships; and in *celebrating*, we bring together the teaching and the learning in an act of social solidarity.[12]

Conducting Choral Music as an Act of Social Conscience

The notion of conducting as a form of social conscience is related to matters of social action. Socially driven choices related to repertoire, pedagogy, and performance objectives are starting to reflect a growing understanding of the ancient history of singing as a healing practice that extends beyond the traditional goals of aesthetic experience and the development of musicianship, toward the inclusion of social and political imperatives for sustainability.

The relationship between conducting a choir and social conscience can be understood from a variety of cultural perspectives. Among indigenous people including the Sami of Scandinavia, the Aborigines of Australia, and the First Nations of Canada, singing is used therapeutically as a form of medicine and healing to affect human consciousness and improve health—to sustain life.[13] In the Baltic nations choral singing is a matter of personal and cultural conscience related to and inseparable from their nations' political and social agenda. In many African cultures including the Ewe of Ghana, the Shona of Zimbabwe, and the Zulu of South Africa, singing forms the basis for family and community ritual and ceremony.[14]

Like Christopher Small's thesis of music as relationship-making,[15] German scholar Heidi Gottner-Abendroth's observations on the nature of musical performance point to the need to resituate performance within a social context, to recognize its role in shaping and reinforcing social structures. Abendroth urges us to view performance as a collective, collaborative activity. In contrast to the conventional conception of performance as contemplation, Abendroth conceives performance as a mode of social action with the power to interact with and change the world.[16]

It seems more important than ever that today's conductors view their work as *service*—service to traditional aesthetic and educational values. Conducting a choir as a form of service or as *an act of social conscience* is closely related to the theme of conducting as *an innately personal and political practice*. This kind of thinking takes us beyond traditional aesthetic values of music for its own sake. As a growing number of universities around the world undertake studies in peace, peace education, and conflict resolution,[17] it seems timely that the performing arts also consider concrete and creative ways to study the relationship between music and service.

Of the many ways to approach the subject of conducting as service in secular terms, the Zen perspective on *mindfulness* (the development of awareness) comes closest historically to forming a solid foundation for peace education and service to others. Mindfulness is a life skill based on the practice of breathing meditation, the simple, non-sectarian act of breathing in and out consciously. The practice of breathing meditation can be found in those educational programs throughout North America that value service and the development of social conscience as an important part of their program goals.

Conducting as social conscience related to service begins with the ability to be fully present in the here and the now. Mindfulness is a form of listening to self and others, a skill of receiving or "bearing witness" to the choir, to the audience, to the community. The skill of mindfulness encourages deep listening—the first step toward expanding an awareness of the music, the students, and the world—a foundation for social conscience.

Conducting Choral Music Is a Moral Responsibility

When we speak about moral responsibility in the performing arts, we are suggesting a moral course of action that is "right" and "just" in a given situation. It is a matter of doing the right thing at the right time. Arts philosopher David Best argues that education in the arts has an utterly inescapable moral dimension: "No teacher can avoid the moral responsibility of deciding what to teach and how to teach it."[18]

Choral conducting as moral responsibility is based on the emerging concept of *phronesis*. In his ground-breaking discussions of phronesis, Canadian scholar and music educator Wayne Bowman posits that "we are what we do."[19] The theory of "right action" or *phronesis* is connected to *the way we practice conducting and teaching choral music*. As mentioned earlier, *phronesis* signifies discerning a moral course of action that is "right" and "just" in a given situation.

Unlike the praxial view of conducting and singing as a form of knowledge, phronesis is a concept that extends beyond knowing or knowing-how. It is related to knowing where, knowing when, and knowing who! Phronesis is a form of action that is experience or character driven rather than knowledge or formula driven. The practice of conducting choral music as a matter of doing the right thing at the right time is closely related to the conductor's ability to survey a wide range of factors in each ensemble situation—her ability to identify what is important to attend to and her ability to make the right choice from among unlimited possibilities for action.

If we agree that musical performance in education is distinctly ethical in character, we have to agree with David Best that the conductor's work has an inescapable moral dimension and with Wayne Bowman, who tells *us we are what we do*. Zen teacher and peace activist Thich Nhat Hanh says that our actions are our signature. What does the development of moral responsibility have to do with conducting choirs? Maybe, everything.

Choral Conducting Is a Way of Life

The phenomenal and social facts of choral-music experience cannot be reduced to the conditions of its sounds. Neither can the significance of the choral-music experience be considered mere sonorous pattern. Choral singing is not a stimulus to which we respond, but a way of being that each singer constructs.[20] Wayne Bowman tells us that musical feeling is not something that music *causes*, but rather something that, as music, *is*. At the core of musical experience lies a "body in a state of music."[21] From this perspective we understand that choral singing lets us experience mind-body unity as does no other experience. Choral singing connects us to ourselves in a way that is utterly unique.

Choral singing is a powerfully therapeutic corrective to the disembodied knowledge that dominates our societies and educational institutions; it connects perception with conception; it situates us at the nexus of knowing, doing, and being; and it engages the whole human organism.[22]

Choral singing delivers us from the dualisms so destructive of our human experiences of wholeness, unity, and freedom. It resides in the place we understand as vocal resonance. It links our insides with our outsides and links ourselves with others. The essence of shared humanity, choral singing is an essential *way of being* that is both unique and profoundly important to our individual and collective lives.

In summary, I'd like to think that we conduct and teach choral music the way we aspire to live. This may be understood by some scholars as a "soft" theoretical construct, but it seems logical, direct, and socially responsible, and is encoded in my DNA. We care for our families and friends. Our lives are about relationships and relationship-making. We are culturally situated, living in communities where we connect in acts of affirmation and celebration. We are, by and large, character-driven professionals who care about the quality of our students' musical experiences, who celebrate and affirm our cultural heritages, and who have entered our professional communities with the intention of doing *good works*.[23]

Part II: The Sacred Feminine

If there is to be a future, it will wear
the crown of feminine design.
—Aurobindo, Indian Mystic

Like me, the majority of professional women today developed under the influence of the so-called "wisdom" of scientific thinking camouflaged as empirical truth. Divorced from the mysteries of our own feminine qualities and taken in by patriarchal projections of what constitutes the professional practice in music performance and education, many women in music missed the revolutionary potential of a more feminine design. Most women on the podium have been taught to behave like men. In this patriarchal, perfection-seeking milieu, we have been taught to conduct free of emotion or personal expression; how to rehearse efficiently for maximum productivity; how to execute a public performance without personal attachment. For some of us, this is solid ground. For others, this is a form paralytic imprisonment.

In a series of lectures on the historical basis and current resurgence of the *sacred feminine*, Andrew Harvey tells us that unless we awaken to the mysteries of the sacred feminine, we will not survive the next stage of humanity.[24] Understanding the sacred feminine is also central to imagining a new, more diverse, and inclusive model for conducting education. Before we begin to conceptualize a gender-inclusive conducting and teaching curriculum built to include feminine nature and feminine values, we should first explore the characteristics of what we call the *sacred feminine*.

Any discussion of the sacred feminine, the feminine spirit and her characteristic qualities, must necessarily recognize the non-Western, ancient origins of mystical traditions in which God or Ultimate Reality is encountered as the Divine Mother. As we learn from the remarkable scholarship of the late poet, philosopher, and religious scholar Lex Hixon, in Western, Judeo-Christian cultures our root metaphor for the Divine is masculine. Not so in India, where the Divine-Mother tradition centers upon the Goddess Wisdom, sometimes recognized as the dark, sword-bearing Kali.[25] This feminine metaphor of "Mother" stands outside existing philosophical frameworks in most Western endeavors, yet it is recognized across traditions and cultures and can be found in the mythology of all the greatest tribal cultures.

Unlike the masculine metaphors for Divinity and the masculine attitudes toward reality, I see the Goddess-Wisdom tradition as an important and neglected resource for rethinking our programs and practices in the secular, modern world, particularly the world of the performing arts and education. The "Mother" metaphor provides us with an open space beyond narrow, sectarian, religious thought. Some might call this *awareness*.

Our profession has no image, no language, and no guidelines for this unitive form of thought and practice. Our models of creativity and power are male—everyone from the great artists and writers and composers, to God. This thinking is supported by Lex Hixon, who tells us that there is no image in Western imagination of the strong women whose contact with her primal power of wisdom is welcomed. Yet it is somewhat reassuring to know that this form of revolutionary spirit and long overdue balance of energy has been changing as a result of the women's movement[26] and continues to change today as a result of feminist scholarship and political reform.

In the world today, feminine wisdom can be seen in operation at the deepest levels of our culture. Wherever humans need celebrating, protecting, nurturing, and empowering, feminine wisdom is at the forefront of change. The voice of feminine wisdom is present in social and political movements; in science and medicine, where research is now finding the values of nonlinear, holistic, and intuitive modes of thinking more closely associated with Eastern wisdom; and in areas of ecology, psychology, and health care. This voice tells us that we are not caring for one another and the planet in the way a mother cares for her child.

Feminist and educational theorist Nel Noddings believes that mother caring, rooted in receptivity, relatedness, and responsiveness is basic to education. Prioritizing her concern for relationship, Noddings's feminine approach to ethics and moral education was a seminal work on the ethics of care based on mother care and family relationships. Noddings suggests that the primary aim of education must be the maintenance and enhancement of caring. "The one caring has one great aim: to preserve and enhance caring in herself and in those with whom she comes in contact. To receive and to be received, to care and be cared for."[27]

While there is a growing consciousness of the feminine values of nurturing, intuition, and unity, and while comprehending the feminine is crucial to the maturing of our profession, it is important to realize that these feminine values are manifest in males and females alike (the "gender-free" feminine). Both men and women can benefit from this form of consciousness and use it as a guide, particularly those who are not bound by the biologically and culturally conditioned abstractions we know as "masculine" and "feminine."

Characteristics of the Sacred Feminine

A number of characteristics that could be identified as the sacred feminine are found in every tradition and across cultures. These are drawn partly from the Divine-Mother tradition of India, particularly nineteenth-century Bengal, where God or Ultimate Reality is experienced as Mother. Feminine metaphors for Divinity are rooted in Hinduism and Buddhism. For the purpose of examining what constitutes "the feminine art of conducting and teaching choral music," I will discuss three characteristics of the sacred feminine.

The first feminine characteristic is *unity*. A feminine design for conducting and teaching choral music would encourage knowledge of unity—the unity behind all multiplicity including religions, human traditions and practices, cultures, historical periods, and styles. This feminine vision of *unity* recognizes the interconnectedness and relatedness of all things from musical form to audience participation.

From a Zen Buddhist perspective, this kind of unity is described as *inter-being*. In his first talk on *dharma*, the Buddha is to have said, "I have seen deeply that nothing can be by itself alone, that everything has to inter-be with everything else."[28] Zen teacher Thich Nhat Hanh tells us that we *inter-are.*[29] In the wisdom of the sacred feminine, life is One, all paths lead to One. Nothing is separate. This unitive form of awareness reaches beyond the polarity and closely guarded conventions that continue to dominate our profession and our university curricula.

The second characteristic of the sacred feminine involves *the ability to recognize reality*—the natural laws of the universe, its movement, and its rhythm. Learning to honor the laws of nature and of life, the rhythm of the body and the seasons, requires developing the feminine powers of reverence, attention, and the ability to listen. A feminine design for conducting and teaching choral music would include opportunities to practice *deep listening*, not just listening to tonal accuracy or rhythmic precision, but listening *for* the quality of the singer's relationship with the music and with other members of the ensemble. The feminine powers of intuition, receptivity, and flexibility of approach are not as accessible to the masculine powers of reason and will. The feminine part of the psyche naturally and spontaneously receives, accepts, and interprets these laws and rhythms.

Listening, or the ability to receive without judgment, is a foundation of Zen practice and a step towards understanding the feminine power of receptivity. One of three tenets or precepts concerned with the ability to listen and receive is the precept of "bearing witness." In the language of the Zen Peacemaker Order founded by spiritual teacher and social activist Bernie Glassman, people need to "bear witness" to the joy and suffering of the world. They need to listen deeply, be inclusive, and connect without fixing their position.[30] When we *bear witness* to the unfolding of our daily lives, not shrinking from any situation that arises, we learn. We open ourselves to *what is.*[31]

Brother David Steindl-Rast, a Benedictine monk, calls this kind of listening the "listening heart."[32] He tells us that the world deserves attention—the music of beauty, the lamentation of grief. All of it deserves our listening. What makes an authentic monk? Listening with our ears, listening with our hearts, listening to the rhythms of life with reverence and compassion hold equal promise for discussions on what makes an authentic conductor. Brother

David's description of the "listening heart" fits the profile of the sacred feminine characteristics of reverence and attention.

The third quality of the sacred feminine is a *healthy, exuberant and sensual vision of life*, one that does not separate mind, body and spirit; one that accepts the conditions and challenges of life without fear. Unlike patriarchal wisdom, feminine wisdom does not aim for an unnatural perfection but works toward a wholeness in which the transcendent is not separate from the practical. In this vision of life, life itself is seen and known and felt and lived as completely sacred.[33] This is a fundamentally healthy and joyful vision, one that does not split off body from mind and spirit, one that accepts life's conditions, its ordeals, and wonders.

From this sacred feminine vision of non-separation comes the Buddhist ideal of the *bodhisattva*, one who listens and hears the cries of the world in order to come and help. A bodhisattva, which means *awakened being*, is one who gives up nirvana to stay in the world to help all beings cross over from suffering to understanding and enlightenment. Bodhisattvas commit themselves to lifetime after lifetime of service.[34] In Indian, Chinese, and Japanese cultures, the bodhisattva Avalokiteshvara often takes the female form and represents what the Prajnaparamita Heart Sutra calls "perfect understanding." In this Zen tradition, knowledge (views and ideas) can block the way of understanding or wisdom.[35]

Ancient and mystical embodiments of the sacred feminine include Kali, the beautiful, black Hindu Warrior Goddess of unitive wisdom. While her mode of appearing is dramatically different, the Virgin Mary appears in the Eastern Orthodox tradition as the victorious leader of triumphant hosts and in the West through figures such as Saint Joan of Arc. Fatima, daughter of the Prophet of Islam, Shekhinah, and the Sabbath Queen in Jewish tradition join Kali and the Virgin Mary as embodiments of feminine form representing indivisible wholeness, which is woman's essential nature.

We can find examples of the sacred feminine throughout ancient and modern life, mostly in women, but also in men. The feminine characteristics of nurturing, intuiting, and unifying, as well as the powers of receptivity, responsiveness, and the *listening heart* can be identified in contemporary movements in society. Efforts exist to establish a consciousness of the sacred feminine and to celebrate its virtues in feminism, ecology, theology, and especially in traditional, native circles. Today's conductors and teachers of choral music need to be receptive and responsive to the many potential benefits of a feminine design for conducting and teaching choral music. This is the first step toward a gender-inclusive curriculum.

The Need for Feminine Design in Conducting and Teaching Choral Music: More Research and a Personal Narrative

The task of defining a *feminine design for conducting and teaching choral music* may not be an easy one, and the reader might ask why imagining such a design is necessary at all. Aren't things fine just as they are? The work presented here is based on the premise that things are not fine just as they are, at least not for me and not for many of my colleagues. Recent research supports this concern.

In a doctoral study completed at Michigan State University, author Janet Brenneman asks the same question. "Is there a problem?"[36] Brenneman's narrative-style research reminds us that Western society should not ignore the gender issues that still play a role in the personal and professional lives of women in music, the fact that gender issues are prevalent in women's experiences today, and that there is a lack of recognition of these matters across the profession. While Brenneman's study examines the problems of women choral conductors and how these problems impact their careers, it also asks the important questions closely related to this essay. "Whose knowledge is being represented and deemed worthy of attention? Who is represented, and who and what are the subjects that are being ignored?"

I suggested earlier that the feminine values described in this essay as *feminine wisdom* or the *feminine voice* are far from being recognized across our choral-music profession, much less assimilated into our conducting and teaching curricula. As Brenneman points out, gender is an influencing factor in shaping institutions, ideologies, and interactions among individuals in a given cultural context.[37] Her narratives and analyses of emergent themes help her to support the theory that our practices as choral conductors and choral teachers are most certainly influenced and encompassed by gender.

The use of a brief personal narrative may further illustrate the need to imagine a feminine design for conducting and teaching choral music. While personal narrative is often useful in developing an empathic understanding of current practices and developing a professional recognition of the importance of change, it is also an honest and authentic way to develop a relationship with readers. This particular endeavor seems to require the kind of involvement that goes beyond the "arms-length" distance of so-called "objective," more abstract writing methods passed down to us by patriarchal generation after patriarchal generation. In the spirit of personal narrative, I offer the following description of my own experiences. These might be used to frame the task of "re-dreaming" a curriculum for conducting and teaching choral music in a feminine voice.

My story has been told in print on more than one occasion, so I will spare readers any redundancy in that realm.[38] Instead, I will relate here a few stories from the time Margaret Hillis appointed me assistant conductor to the Chicago Symphony Chorus in 1984–1985. The first woman to be appointed to this post, I was scared but thrilled to take on the responsibilities Miss Hillis assigned. I was not so thrilled with what happened next.

Virtually no one spoke to me, much less congratulated me on this historical appointment. All the support and enthusiasm that characterized my professional relationships with male and female colleagues alike when I conducted the Glen Ellyn Children's Chorus turned instantly from celebration and acceptance to dismissal and withdrawal. Disappointed, I tried to imagine why my colleagues withdrew. Perhaps they withdrew because they thought of me as a "children's-choir conductor" who couldn't possibly qualify to conduct an adult professional chorus. But later, when I left Chicago to become a full-time university conductor and teacher in Toronto, I had the same kind of experience in different forms. Looking back, I suspect that the privileges of enjoying an active and successful career were assured as long as I continued to work with children doing what most men were not doing at the time.

Working with children is where women are historically and culturally accepted, even in choral music. I could innovate and pioneer with the full support of my colleagues until I crossed the conventional boundaries from education and children's choirs to the university and professional-choir podium. When I made these changes in the eighties, I felt like there was a "keep out" sign posted on almost every door, both in the United States and Canada. This was no place for a charismatic female, even one with years of conducting experience and a Ph.D. Clearly, there was an implied segregation between education and performance, children's choirs and professional choirs, and to some degree, I think there still is.

After more than twenty years conducting university and professional choirs and teaching conducting at the graduate and post-graduate levels, the majority of my colleagues still think of me as a children's choir director! They frequently confuse me with Jean Ashworth Bartle, and I continue to ponder why being the first female assistant conductor of the Chicago Symphony Chorus, one of the first women to assume a university appointment as director of choral programs at a major university, and the first woman in North America to hold an endowed chair in conducting could be so visibly invisible. It is difficult to imagine the feminine design for conducting and teaching choral music much less a gender-inclusive design when in fact such a wide gender gap and gender imbalance exists between men and women holding choral-conducting positions in post-secondary institutions.[39]

It is equally perplexing to me that after many years of performing and teaching, I have noticed that my female conducting students continue to struggle with some of the same challenges that I faced twenty years before them. While these women are now accomplished conductors and professors of choral music and choral-music education in universities throughout North America, they continue to struggle with issues of professional values, curriculum goals, instructional methodologies, and assessment techniques as they have been passed down to us through time. Some of these young women accept the prescribed way of doing things based on generations of patriarchal values mandated before them, some get angry and spend the rest of their careers being wounded, while some leave the profession to save their souls (not to mention their family lives).

I stayed. Throughout marriage, parenting, graduate school and a fast-paced career living in two countries and working around the world; despite discrimination, inequities, and too many stories to tell, I did not accept the prescribed way of doing things. One of my former university Deans said to me that I was "unusual," "a controversial figure!" Another Dean objected to my performance commitment to the works of living composers; he thought I should do "more German Romantic" repertoire and less new music. One year at the University of Toronto I was verbally assaulted by a male voice student for not selecting him as a soloist. The Dean called this terrorizing incident a "personality conflict!"

I have always had a clear vision and a personal passion for doing the work that I wanted to do, the way I wanted to do it.[40] For me, the price of embracing the conventional way of doing things that resided outside the naturally feminine framework of my moral and ethical "comfort zone" was too high. Dismissed by colleagues who did not recognize, much less embrace the feminine values embodied in my conducting and teaching style, I learned long ago that in spite of many challenges, living out my authentic voice as a conductor and teacher was more productive and satisfying for me than following the more conventional, patriarchal sector that separated all things, including performance and education, children's choirs and professional choirs, gay choirs and black choirs, and anything else that could be separated out and controlled.

For example, I have conducting colleagues who still think that "teaching" in choir has something to do exclusively with children. There are music teachers who still think that "performing" in classrooms has nothing to do with the goals of music education. I have often thought that these kinds of perceptions have less to do with the distinctions between the nature and values associated with musical performance and music education and more to do with the lack of understanding for the feminine characteristics of non separation, intuition, receptivity, and flexibility of approach described earlier.

Innovation, creativity, and visionary thinking are often suspect, especially if you are a female working intuitively and crossing long-established boundaries on the podium and in the classroom. If this description resonates for you, expect your career to be rich in adventures, satisfactions, and challenges. Men are rewarded for ambition, productivity, and innovation. Women are often considered "driven" and "demanding" if they are ambitious, "high-strung" if they are productive, and "suspect" if they are innovative. Unfortunately, this probably sounds familiar. It is to me.

These stories could go on, but what of a *feminine design for conducting and teaching choral music*? A feminine design would likely draw on the post-9/11 literature in performance and music education, feminist research, and ancient mystical traditions—perhaps even the study of matriarchal cultures. While there are no clear images or examples of such a conducting program today, it is essential to start imagining what a feminine design might look like. Perhaps imagining such a design would support both men and women down the long path toward a gender-inclusive conducting curriculum, a curriculum that reflects the values of diversity over uniformity, reflection over perfection—and ultimately, humanity over gender.

PART III: CONDUCTING AND TEACHING CHORAL MUSIC: A FEMININE PERSPECTIVE

> *We can re-dream this world and make the dream real. All roads lead to death, but some roads lead to things which can never be finished. Wonderful things.* —Ben Okri, *The Famished Road*

As a woman mentored by two extraordinary female musicians—three including my talented mother—I have struggled to help my students find their *feminine voice*: a singing voice that reflects soul, a conducting gesture that reflects musical understanding, and a rehearsal language that is intuitive, compassionate, and authentic to each conductor. I have encouraged my students to develop their powers of attention, their receptivity, and their ability to listen with an *informed ear* and a *listening heart.*

This short summation of what constitutes a feminine design for conducting and teaching choral music is informed by contemporary pluralist perspectives, post-9/11 research, and a growing public interest in mystical and spiritually inspired traditions mentioned throughout this essay. The material is intended as a basis for reflection. It is not prioritized, ranked, or formally organized into a ready-made, one-size-fits-all prescription. Rather, it is one feminine perspective motivated by the principles of diversity, inclusion, and social justice. It is dedicated to the spirit of change, the nature of hope, and the listening hearts of socially conscious conductors and choral teachers.

I will offer the following design elements intended to reflect (1) social realities of the twenty-first century, (2) characteristics of the feminine voice including the qualities of receptivity, relatedness, intuition, and unity, as well as (3) Zen perspectives and peacemaking initiatives suggested earlier in this essay. This look at what constitutes a feminine design for conducting and teaching choral music is completed by a related list of curricular recommendations that may be used as a basis for "right action," a spiritually inspired theoretical construct this writer views as fundamental to the way we practice conducting and teaching choral music in our post-9/11 world.

THE WHERE? WHAT? WHO? OUR CONNECTION TO REALITY— LEARNING TO PAY ATTENTION

A curriculum design that embodies feminine wisdom starts with the conductor's understanding of the dramatic changes in our cultural and political landscape. Similarly, recognizing the social and cultural realities of each rehearsal and performance context, this conductor dwells in awareness by beginning her work with three questions: *Where am I? What am I doing?* and *With whom am I doing it?* The answers to these fundamental questions are situated and varied for every conductor in every setting. The *where am I* question is relative to our sense of place, our geography, institution, and the quality of the physical spaces in which we work. *Am I conducting a church choir in a beautiful and resonant suburban sanctuary? Am I conducting an amateur choir in a dry and dreary city-center office building or church basement? Am I conducting a children's choir in a wealthy school district?*

The *what am I doing* question relates to our choice of musical materials, rehearsal pedagogies, and concert programming for each ensemble. Our answers to this question reflect the conductor's social, educational, and artistic values. They also reflect the conductor's sensitivity to the abilities and potential of her choir members in relation to the quality of the repertoire and the level of challenge it provides the ensemble. The question, *who am I teaching* is crucial in terms of repertoire and pedagogy in the broadest sense. For example, if the enlightened conductor is working with a freshman-level high school choir, she is unlikely to choose an avant-garde repertoire she sang with her accomplished university choir. If she conducts a professional choir, she is unlikely to use rehearsal pedagogies dedicated to the vocal development of young singers. If she conducts a children's choir, her selection of repertoire and rehearsal pedagogy will reflect her commitment to the musical education of her singers. If she conducts an undergraduate-university chamber choir, her concerts may often link the performance of distinguished choral literature with social-action programs relative to pertinent issues impacting student's lives on campus.

In summary, this conductor practices awareness by considering the *where, what,* and *who* questions through her choices in repertoire, rehearsal pedagogy, and concert program planning. This conductor is connected to reality. She has abandoned the illusions, dreams, and ideologies of her past. She understands that we are at a critical juncture of life on the planet and people are fearful and uncertain. She mindfully acknowledges the realities of her teaching environment, the educational promise of her repertoire choices, and her singer's humanity.

The Personal and Political: Culturally Sensitive and Socially Responsive Choices—Learning to Recognize and Remember

A curriculum that recognizes feminine wisdom encourages the innately personal and political meanings logically inherent in distinguished repertoire and ensemble singing. This conductor's choice of repertoire, rehearsal pedagogy, and concert program planning reflect her social conscience, commitment to *diversity* over uniformity, *inclusion* over exclusivity, and *reflection* over perfection. Her culturally sensitive and socially responsive choices are distinctly ethical in character and concerned with the musical growth, social identity, and psychological well-being of her singers.

This conductor programs a repertoire that reflects the diverse traditions and practices of the world today—local and global. She embraces the central importance and exceptional beauty of the European classics and she carefully balances this body of repertoire with her commitment to world musics and the compositions of living composers. This conductor regularly commissions, premieres, and performs new music, often engaging her singers as co-creators. She consciously explores the cultural, social, and spiritual relationships that link ancient and modern life in each musical context.

Distrustful and wary of autocratic instruction and prescriptive rehearsal methods with limited ethical or educational value, this conductor's reflective rehearsal pedagogy[41] is shaped by her studied understanding of the composer's life and work and by her knowledge of the music's cultural and historical context. In an effort to encourage her ensemble's personal connection with the music and empower her singers' musicianship, she skillfully engages the choir in the sound and meaning of the text, working from an understanding of text to the musical mastery of pitch and time through considerations of phrasing and articulation. She knows that when the ensemble is meaningfully engaged in matters of musical interpretation, their interests and achievements will grow in direct proportion to the quality of that engagement.

In summary, this conductor's interest in educating musically exercises her moral responsibility in deciding *what to teach* and *how to teach it*. This conductor knows that what constitutes the meaning and value of choral singing today may differ from what has been valued historically. She knows that her musical and pedagogical mission extends beyond the conventional goals of beautiful tone and perfect intonation to the development of her students' cultural sensitivity and social responsiveness—personal and political imperatives for the twenty-first century.

The Choir as Community: Choral Community-Making—Learning to Respect and Show Regard for Others

This conductor values the educational potential of collective, collaborative activity and creates frequent opportunities for musical collaboration and relationship-making. Bringing the community into the choir and bringing the choir into the community on a regular basis increases her students' awareness of self and others. She likes to promote the kind of collaborative performance opportunities that invite deep, cross-cultural explorations of a diverse and distinguished repertoire. She recognizes that honoring each musical tradition and practice with respect may sometimes go beyond her individual skill set, requiring her to reach out and collaborate with culturally qualified culturally qualified friends, neighbors, colleagues, and members of her community. She realizes that these "tradition bearers" can bring the requisite language skills and the cultural understanding required to create a more authentic and informed performance collaboration.

Imagine for example, the conductor who invites a German Bach scholar to lead her university choirs in rehearsals and performances of Bach cantatas, Passions or oratorios. Imagine the conductor who invites a Black gospel choir to lead her all-white suburban choir in the tradition of contemporary gospel singing. Imagine the conductor who invites a Russian scholar to coach text in Stravinsky's *Les Noces* then serves borscht and pierogi by a local Russian chef after the concert. Imagine a choral concert in collaboration with an Argentine percussion ensemble (and tango dancers!) who also lead a dance party at intermission. Such dynamic collaborations create societies of purpose and communities of mutual regard, not to mention happiness. Cross-cultural collaboration inspires connectedness and celebrates the unifying potential of musical diversity and social inclusion.

In times of natural disasters, local or global, this conductor organizes benefit concerts that engage her singers in the practice of recognizing and imagining the suffering of others. She chooses a repertoire that is pertinent musically and culturally—a repertoire that will require commitment and that will evoke the empathy of the singers and their public.

This conductor's rehearsal pedagogy pays attention to those musical and textual qualities that relate to the social specifics of current events—the relationship of intervallic dissonance to suffering, the understanding of a harmonic progression as a manifestation of conflict and resolution, the symbolic qualities of compositional word-painting devices. Her educationally appropriate and socially sensitive pedagogy leads to what I call a twenty-first-century form of musicianship: guiding her students beyond the basics of notation into the realm of personal meaning and toward the opportunity for service.

In summary, this conductor recognizes the value of choral singing as community-making. She invites cross-cultural collaborations in her rehearsals and concerts through her choice of a balanced repertoire taught with respect for the social traditions and unique musical practices embodied in and surrounding those particular choices. This conductor's rehearsal pedagogy is always engaging—enhanced and enriched by the unique expertise of the members of her local community. She invites scholars and artists, friends and neighbors with whom she shares the responsibility to induct her students into the diverse human practice called choral music. She conducts and teaches with enthusiasm and with attention to how the experience of making music together represents the collective values of community and the power to change lives.

The Singing Space: a Place to Listen—Learning to Be Quiet

The recognition and assimilation of feminine qualities is an important first step in moving toward a gender-inclusive practice for any educational curriculum related to musical performance. A summary of what constitutes feminine qualities as these relate to conducting and teaching choral music begins naturally with the valuing of openness, space, and awareness. This conductor demonstrates an open attitude toward new projects and new experiences; she provides interactive opportunities for her students in a psychological and physical space that encourages creativity and imagination.

The feminine nature of nurturing, intuition, and receptivity is demonstrated by this conductor's promotion of *music education* as the central mission and purpose of performance. In this choral program the conductor develops a curriculum of rehearsals and concert experiences that place the student's musical development, social identity, and psychological well-being front and center. Supported by a balanced repertoire as well as culturally and socially inspired performance projects undertaken collaboratively, this performance curriculum thrives as an interactive, mutually respectful, and reciprocal interchange of ideas between the students, teachers, and communities.

This conductor approaches the podium in the spirit of *not-knowing*,[42] starting her rehearsals with the courage to practice *non-doing*.[43] In her *stillness* she begins quietly breathing in and breathing out to stop, calm, and concentrate before she starts to conduct and rehearse. Given the gift of *stillness* or quiet space, the students reflect the conductor's calm, replicate the quiet, and prepare themselves to sing. In just three conscious breaths, everyone is fully present.

As the rehearsal begins, this conductor's neutral and purposefully understated conducting gesture allows her to create an open space for listening. She knows that if she is too energetic or physically active during the introductory reading, she will be unable to actually hear what the choir *can do* and what the choir *cannot do*. This conductor's ability to keep a steady pulse and skillfully negotiate the musical transitions without stopping nurtures the choir's confidence and empowers the singers to exercise their intuitive knowledge. In this kind of environment, the choristers bring themselves fully to the task.

This conductor's ability to practice *conducting as listening* demonstrates her receptivity: to the ability to *receive* both the right notes and the wrong notes, *survey* a wide range of possible teaching opportunities, and to *identify* what is important to attend to, and make what she views as the right pedagogical choices from among many possibilities for action. *Conducting as listening* allows this conductor to smile at the "wrong" notes and meet the choir's musical inaccuracies with humor and compassion. Her rehearsal environment empowers and affirms the students' musical intuition, celebrates their success, and provides them with safe place where they are encouraged to listen to one another. This kind of rehearsal environment establishes an open and unmediated space in which neither the conductor nor the singers are afraid to take creative risks and make "mistakes."

During rehearsal this conductor works intuitively in an improvisatory fashion, prepared at every stage to help her singers meet the musical challenges successfully through her skillful conducting gestures, her creative pedagogies, and her deep musical understanding. She empowers the singers through reflective practice and collaborative problem-solving, using each teaching opportunity to develop the singers' musicianship and support their growing self-awareness and musical understanding.

Instructing her choir, this conductor practices *conducting as teaching*, using active and supportive conducting gestures that show the music nonverbally and teach the singers how to solve the musical problems *in-the-action* of singing. Her choristers *sing* their understanding. This specialized non-verbal form of reflective rehearsal pedagogy teaches the choir to *think-in-action*, a dynamic form of self-awareness that requires a wide range of refined conducting and rehearsal techniques.

During the course of regular rehearsals, and as the choir learns to meet the choral challenges with musical know-how, this conductor celebrates her choir's accomplishments and increases the level of challenge to further explore alternative vocal sounds and musical interpretations. In an environment of exploration and affirmation, she teaches *singing as listening*, varying her choir's seating and standing configurations to include *listening circles* and *listening partnerships*—alternative rehearsal pedagogies that encourage caring and receptivity. In both *listening circles* and *listening partnerships*, the singers "bear witness" to one another and to the sound of the choir by using unmediated eye-contact across the room (the *listening circle*) and from singer to singer (the *listening partnerships*). These varied configurations encourage self-awareness, personal contact, and emotional interactions that help transform the singer's *listening ears* into the singer's *listening heart*.

In summary, in a performance environment or singing space that does not separate the transcendent experience of music from the practical realities of time and place, this conductor's vision embraces the integration of mind, body, and spirit in each rehearsal interaction and at every performance opportunity. She invites an open, non-judgmental space for deep listening, the kind of listening that transcends the ear and drops down into the heart. With *listening hearts*, rehearsals are like performances and performances are a relaxed, natural celebration of rehearsal relationships.

The Therapeutic Corrective: We Are What We Sing!—Learning Self-Awareness and Understanding

This conductor knows that choral singing engages the body more comprehensively, more directly, and more deeply than do most other sensory experiences. She knows that the singer's body constitutes the core of the musical experience and that in artistic matters like singing in tune and singing with beautiful tone quality, the singer's body, personal experiences, and the music itself are inextricably intertwined—the singers becomes the song!

This conductor knows that the mind-body unity and the healing power of choral singing offer the students important and therapeutic periods of being fully present, being conscious in and through the musical experience. Through her choice of spiritually and poetically inspired repertoire she seeks to create and sustain an experiential space where concerns like *meaning*, *value*, and *quality* are central.

This conductor establishes a purposeful atmosphere of calm and concentration in which verbal interactions with and among the students are limited to thoughtful questions or comments with the intention of making a mutually respectful human connection. This conductor favors non-verbal, action-oriented connectedness over verbally directed rehearsal interactions. The quality of the understanding in this rehearsal contributes to the contemplative nature of this spiritually charged and musically concentrated exchange, in which conductor and students share a common commitment.

This conductor recognizes the natural rhythms of her choir's energy levels and their individual and collective levels of musicianship. Because she recognizes reality, she knows that her rehearsals are likely scheduled as part of a very busy day and are wedged between many other commitments. This conductor knows that her singers will benefit from breathing meditation, *tai-chi* movement, or yoga practices adapted by the conductor to calm the body and the mind at the beginning of each rehearsal. She knows that the experience of calm leads to deep concentration and she knows that rehearsing with this quality of concentration will enhance learning and increase the potential for musical understanding and enjoyment.

This conductor challenges her choir in carefully timed increments, rehearsing targeted segments of the musical form that allow the choir to meet the musical challenges with a growing musicianship in short periods of time. She knows that the cumulative effect of meeting musical challenges with musical know-how empowers the singers and affords optimal experiences of enjoyment, what psychologist Mihaly Csikszentmihalyi calls "flow."[44] This conductor knows that happiness counts!

Because this conductor knows that *we are what we do*, she finds ways to combine her teaching goals and concert plans with social-action initiatives. This form of socially responsive action extends beyond the conventional goals of teaching *musicianship as musical literacy* towards a more broadly based and socially infused definition of teaching *musicianship as service* to others. Such performance initiatives link our insides with our outsides and ourselves with others. They teach the connectedness of receiving with giving. Singing for AIDS prevention, singing for Amnesty International, singing for UNICEF, singing against violence and political oppression: these clearly illustrate and embody the nonviolent political power of choral singing. Planting the seeds of *a singing nation* that recognizes the power of choral music to change the world may be a dream for us in North America, but looking cross-culturally to the *singing revolution* of our Baltic neighbors,[45] we find a model with great promise and a history to prove it.

This conductor's historical and cultural sensitivity allows her to appreciate the ancient ways of indigenous cultures and shamanic societies that practice *singing as a form of healing*. Closely linked to the ideal of choral singing as social action, this conductor easily embraces the knowledge that her work with young singers can profoundly impact their health and well-being. While this notion may be too abstract for modern musicians in urban cultures, it is still a reality central to life in many tribal and devotional cultures and the subject of a growing body of contemporary research around the world.[46]

This conductor knows the proverb *we are what we do*. Choral music is *who* she is when she conducts it and teaches it. She knows that what her choir sings and the way they sing it benefit each individual, the community, and all beings. She knows that conducting and teaching choral music is distinctly ethical in character and she remembers that her work has an inescapable moral direction. Her actions are her signature.

In the feminine spirit of unity and non-separation, this conductor recognizes the unity behind all multiplicity. This form of feminine wisdom is manifest in the conductor's informed choice of repertoire (concert programs representing a wide range of styles organized around a unified theme), the conductor's diversified and situated rehearsal pedagogies (honoring culture and style variation in the way each work is conducted and rehearsed), the careful preparation of her performance spaces (contemplative, concentrated environments with varying configurations for deep listening), and her ability to create *community-in-concert*. This conductor finds ways of engaging the audience in each concert, bringing them into the music from the *performers' perspective*. Through podium dialogue, group singing, and interactive performance opportunities like the use of popular hymns or ostinato patterns composed for audience participation, this conductor goes beyond polarity and convention by practicing non-separation and unifying the choir and the public into a community of music-makers.

In summary, a curriculum design that recognizes feminine wisdom recognizes choral singing as a therapeutic corrective for disembodied experience. This conductor considers the quality of her student's self-awareness and understanding of others as a teaching and performing imperative that reflects a twenty-first-century definition of *musicianship* as a form of commemoration, remembrance, and social action. Aware of the historical and cultural traditions relative to the role of singing in society, this conductor recognizes the transformative, healing potential inherent in conducting and teaching choral music.

Conclusion and Recommendations

When will choral conductors and choral-music educators find the courage to fully recognize and assimilate a gender-inclusive choral curriculum that reflects the feminine nature and feminine values detailed in this essay? The realization of such a curriculum is an aspiration to which we can all aspire. As an integrated, inclusive, non-compartmentalized way of working that flies in the face of life in our busy and consumer-oriented Western culture and its patriarchal institutions, it may be a lot like swimming upstream! We have to change our view of choral singing into something that is not separate from being in the world as it is today, from twenty-first century social reality and from the dramatic changes that characterize our global landscape.

I wish I could tell each reader how to realize this aspiration, but I can only intuit such a gender-inclusive, feminine perspective. These are the kinds of changes that come from within each conductor and teacher seeking release from the closed-throated, tight-fistedness of fear and anxiety that surrounds getting the notes learned and the choir on stage. These are the kinds of personal revelations that occur when the music and the "musicker" become one—where the composer, composition, conductor, and choir are no longer separate from the public. This is where we meet, where we really meet, in a field beyond the technical requirements, the course grade, and the fear of failure.

The practice of equanimity—of *letting go* into the music so that we *are* the music—can only be achieved with a collective realization that comes from collaboration, cooperation, community-making, and commitment. It happens when young singers work in a relaxed, concentrated atmosphere and when they are not forced or coerced autocratically or prescriptively into some unrealistic ideal of tonal perfection or mechanical precision. The "miracle of the moment" comes with non-fear—it unfolds with trust and shared intentions. It comes when the teacher listens deeply, bearing witness to the singers and the sounds they sing. It comes when the conductor speaks honestly, working instructively and constructively with a listening heart. The feminine quality of receptive attention is strangely involuntary. It happens when the conditions of trust and connectedness are present, when transparency and spontaneity are alive and well.

The quality of the repertoire, its structure, and its content build the foundation for deeply meaningful musical moments. And the quality of an interactive and reflective rehearsal pedagogy provides the conditions necessary for problem-solving, cooperation, and enjoyment. But we can't *make* it happen. We can only prepare skillfully for these transformative moments by being still within, by being fully present in each rehearsal and performance, by listening with a quiet mind and an understanding heart, by functioning with a spacious awareness, by focusing our attention, and by taking responsibility for what arises. Listening to our singers with presence and awareness is an expression of our skill and our confidence. Doing this for our students is doing so for ourselves and for others.

By not filling the teaching and learning space with too much talking or with busy and overactive conducting gestures, we offer the music and our students an unqualified respect that nourishes the deep listening required to transform an ordinary rehearsal into an extraordinary, life-changing event. This kind of collective realization cannot be forced by you or others. It must be mutual. It won't work if the singers feel oppressed. It doesn't happen because the conductor orders it to happen. As Rumi says, "I [stand] in front of him in silence and set up a ladder made of patience."

Ultimately, our ability to "re-dream" a conducting curriculum that reflects the social realities of the twenty-first century—guided by the principles of diversity and inclusion, the ethics of empathy, and the voice of feminine wisdom—is intimately linked with the principles of peacemaking. The conductor who embraces her responsibility as a peacemaker is one who practices compassion and loving-kindness. She practices compassion for her own limitations and for the limitations of others. She practices joy and equanimity, the ability to *let go*. This conductor is committed to conducting and teaching choral music as peacemaking.

The conductor as peacemaker is one who is *fully present and aware*, she is one who *honors diversity*, one who *empowers* her students through instruction, one who encourages the choir's commitment to *service and community building*, one who *celebrates the differences* among people and ideas, one who practices *learning partnerships* and *co-creativity*, one who *engages in honest connection* in each rehearsal, one who *helps her students help her*. This conductor is one who encourages the joy and transformative musical moments that *constitute an ethical way of being musical.*

This conductor recognizes and assimilates the virtues of conducting and teaching choral music as the opportunity to practice the unity behind multiplicity; the interconnectedness of things historical and cultural; the sensitivity and social responsibility related to personal and political realities; and the reverence and respect for one's self, others, and the Divine. This conductor is a peacemaker, one who climbs the roof of life, sings loud, and invites her students to do the same.

Go up on the roof at night
in this city of the soul.
Let ***everyone*** *climb on their roofs*
and sing their notes!
Sing loud!
—from "Each Note" by Jalal al-Din Rumi (1207–1273)
in *The Essential Rumi* translated by Coleman Barks, 1995

Biography

Doreen Rao's distinguished career as conductor and master teacher links the standards of professional performance with the goals of music education. Celebrated for her spirited and moving concerts, Rao's commitment to choral music in education is recognized in her innovative programming, teaching initiatives, worldwide conducting appearances, and her award-winning publications with Boosey and Hawkes.

Doreen Rao holds the University of Toronto's Elmer Iseler Chair in Conducting. As the Director of Choral Programs, Dr. Rao founded the Faculty of Music's Centre for Advanced Studies in Choral Music that supports and enriches the Faculty's ensemble and conducting programs, hosts the artists-in-residence program and sponsors the Toronto Bach Festival with Helmuth Rilling.

Rao conducts the award-winning University of Toronto MacMillan Singers and Chamber Choirs. Her young ensembles collaborate regularly with the Toronto Symphony Orchestra and a roster of internationally celebrated artists and educators. She leads the University's graduate program in conducting performance and teaches graduate research and philosophy courses related to music performance in education.

Recognized as one of the world's leading experts on children and youth choirs, Doreen Rao founded and chaired the ACDA National Committee for Children's Choirs. This pioneering work inspired the children's choir movement in America. In a national tribute presented to her by the American Choral Director's Association, eminent American conductor Robert Shaw wrote: "The world of choral music owes her special thanks. She is preparing our future."

Following her undergraduate education at the University of Illinois, Rao spent the first years of her career in Chicago singing professionally and teaching choral music in schools. She served as Music Director and Conductor of the Glen Ellyn Children's Chorus, an ensemble that performed and recorded regularly with the Chicago Symphony Orchestra and Chorus.

During Rao's long association with the Chicago Symphony Orchestra Chorus, she served as assistant conductor to her mentor Margaret Hillis and prepared choruses for concerts and Grammy award-winning recordings with Sir Georg Solti, Claudio Abbado, and James Levine. Her choirs also performed on numerous occasions with Leonard Slatkin and the St. Louis Symphony Orchestra, and with Helmuth Rilling at the Oregon Bach Festival.

After graduate studies at Northwestern University, she joined the Voice Faculty at Roosevelt University's Chicago Musical College. There, Rao performed and taught voice and choral music before accepting an invitation to conduct the Northwestern University Chorus and complete her doctoral studies in philosophy and aesthetics.

Rao's innovative "Sing with the Symphony" school and family concerts were first introduced by the Toronto Symphony Orchestra to actively involve audiences in listening as performers. In a pioneering career of "firsts," Rao has conducted honor choirs, all-state choirs and festival choirs for numerous national and international conferences, associations and performance organizations around the world. Most recently she enjoyed conducting the inspired young Texas All-State Chorus with Orchestra for the Texas Music Educators Association.

In a recent article, music critic Robert Everett-Green wrote, "for her, every note has an urgent meaning, not just within the composition, but within the wider world." Journalist Bronwyn Drainie described Doreen Rao as "a brilliant artist and teacher . . . whose methods and materials could re-energize the art of choral singing." The Phi Mu Alpha Sinfonia awarded her with their

National Citation for her significant and lasting contribution to the cause of American music. The American Choral Director's Association has honored her for her commitment to choral excellence. A CBS television documentary called her musical achievements "extraordinary."

Doreen Rao is the Founding Director of the CME Institute for Choral Teacher Education, an internationally acclaimed professional development program for conductors, composers, choirs and teachers. She is also the Artistic Director and Conductor of the New Millennium Festival Concerts, an innovative peacemaking initiative with concert series in New York, Toronto, and London.

Bibliography

Best, David. *The Rationality of Feeling: Understanding the Arts in Education*. London: Falmer Press, 1992.

Bowman, Wayne. "Educating Musically." In *The New Handbook of Research on Music Teaching and Learning*. New York: Oxford University Press, 2002.

_____. *Philosophical Perspectives on Music*. New York: Oxford University Press, 1998.

Brenneman, Janet Sue. *Footsteps of My Own: Gender Issues that Influence the Formative Experiences of Exemplary Women Choral Conductors*. Michigan State University Press, 2007.

Csikszentmihalyi, Mihaly. *Flow: The Psychology of Optimal Experience*. New York: Harper and Row Publishers Inc., 1990.

Damon, William, et al. *Good Work: When Excellence and Ethics Meet*. New York: Basic Books, 2001.

Elliott, David. *Music Matters: A New Philosophy of Music Education*. New York: Oxford University Press, 1995.

Glassman, Bernie. *Bearing Witness*. New York: Bell Tower, 1998.

Gottner-Abendroth, Heidi. *The Dancing Goddess: Principles of a Matriarchal Aesthetic*. trans. Maureen T. Krause (Boston: Beacon Press, 1991). Cited by Wayne Bowman, *Philosophical Perspectives on Music*. New York: Oxford University Press, 1998.

Hanh, Thich Nhat. *The Heart of the Buddha's Teaching*. Berkeley: Parallax Press, 1988.

Harvey, Andrew. *The Return of the Mother*. Berkeley: Frog, Ltd., 1995.

Hixon, Lex. *Mother of the Universe*. Wheaton: Theosophical Publishing House, 1994.

Jon Kabat-Zinn. *Wherever You Go, There You Are*. New York: Hyperion, 1994.

Noddings, Nel. *Caring: A Feminine Approach to Ethics and Moral Education*. Berkeley: University of California Press, 1984.

Rao, Doreen. *Circle of Sound Voice Education*. New York: Boosey and Hawkes, 2005.

_____. *We Will Sing*. New York: Boosey and Hawkes, 1993.

_____. *Craft, Singing Craft and Musical Experience: a Philosophical Study with Implications for Vocal Music Education as Aesthetic Education*. Ph.D. dissertation, Northwestern University. Ann Arbor: UMI Dissertation Services, 1988.

Reimer, Bennett. *A Philosophy of Music Education*. Englewood Cliffs: Prentice-Hall, 1970.

Saint-Exupéry, Antoine de. *The Little Prince*. trans. Richard Howard. China: South China Printing Company, 2000.

Small, Christopher. *Musicking: the Meanings of Performing and Listening*. Hanover: Wesleyan University Press, 1998.

Steindl-Rast, David. *A Listening Heart*. New York: The Crossroad Publishing Company, 1983.

"The Singing Revolution." www.singingrevolution.com

"Zen Peacemaker Path." Sweetwater Zen Centre. www.swzc.org

NOTES

[1] Roberta Lamb, cited by Wayne Bowman in *Philosophical Perspectives on Music* (New York: Oxford University Press, 1998), 378.

[2] Antoine de Saint-Exupéry, *The Little Prince.*

[3] University of Toronto graduate course, *Music Performance in Education*, 2003.

[4] The concept of *musical knowing* is closely associated with the 1970s work of Bennett Reimer in "music education as aesthetic education." The concept of *musical doing* derives from the Greek *techne*, defined as "music as making and doing with skill and understanding," a thesis introduced in Doreen Rao's 1988 dissertation *Craft, Singing Craft and Musical Experience: A Philosophical Study with Implications for Vocal Music Education as Aesthetic Education* (Ann Arbor: UMI Dissertation Services, 1988), and later developed by David J. Elliott as "a praxial philosophy of music education" in *Music Matters: a New Philosophy of Music Education* (New York: Oxford University Press, 1995). The concept of *musical being* is closely associated with Wayne Bowman's work "Educating Musically" in *The New Handbook of Research on Music Teaching and Learning* (New York: Oxford University Press, 2002).

[5] Bennett Reimer. *A Philosophy of Music Education* (Englewood Cliffs: Prentice-Hall, 1970).

[6] Rao, 1988; David Elliott, 1995.

[7] Doreen Rao, *We Will Sing* (New York: Boosey and Hawkes, 1993), 3.

[8] Bowman, 2002.

[9] This research can be found in the work of University of Wisconsin Professor Deborah Bradley, *The Sounds of Silence: Talking Race in Music Education* (electronic article in *Action, Criticism and Theory for Music Education*, 132).

[10] Rao, 1988.

[11] Christopher Small, *Musicking: The Meanings of Performing and Listening* (Hanover: Wesleyan University Press, 1998).

[12] Small, 1998.

[13] Doreen Rao, *Circle of Sound Voice Education* (New York: Boosey and Hawkes, 2005).

[14] Ibid.

[15] Small, 1998.

[16] Heidi Gottner-Abendroth, "The Dancing Goddess: Principles of a Matriarchal Aesthetic," trans. Maureen T. Krause (Boston: Beacon Press, 1991), cited in Bowman, 1998, 378–379.

[17] Such as the University of Toronto's Trudeau Centre for Peace and Conflict Resolution, Costa Rica's Peace University, and a growing number of university-affiliated peace centers around the world.

[18] David Best, *The Rationality of Feeling: Understanding the Arts in Education* (London: Falmer Press, 1992).

[19] Bowman, 2002.

[20] Rao, 2005.

[21] Philosopher Roland Barthes, cited by Rao, 1988.

[22] Bowman, 2002.

[23] William Damon, et al., *Good Work: When Excellence and Ethics Meet* (New York: Basic Books, 2001). In this text, the term *good work* is used in a dual sense: first, work that is deemed to be of high quality and second, work that is socially responsible. This study led to several other related lines of investigation that include a look at how contemplative practices or meditation influence how professionals carry out work.

[24] Andrew Harvey, *The Return of the Mother* (Berkeley: Frog Ltd., 1995), 1.

[25] Lex Hixon, *Mother of the Universe* (Wheaton: Theosophical Publishing House, 1994), 6. The Hindu goddess Kali, whose name means "she who is death," has been worshipped for over 1400 years and is traditionally associated "with death, sexuality, violence, and, paradoxically in some later traditions, with motherly love." ("Kali." 2008 *Encyclopædia Britannica Online*. Accessed 8 November 2008 at http://search.eb.com.lib-proxy.fullerton.edu/eb/article-271769.)

[26] Ibid., 2.

[27] Nel Noddings, *Caring: A Feminine Approach to Ethics and Moral Education* (Berkeley: University of California Press, 1984).

[28] Thich Nhat Hanh, *The Heart of the Buddha's Teaching* (Berkeley: Parallax Press, 1988), 6.

[29] Hanh, 1988.

[30] Sweetwater Zen Centre, "Zen Peacemaker Path"; *Zen Buddhism—Sweetwater Zen Centre*. www.swzc.org

[31] Bernie Glassman, *Bearing Witness* (New York: Bell Tower, 1998), 37.

[32] David Steindl-Rast, *A Listening Heart* (New York: The Crossroad Publishing Company), xi.

[33] Andrew Harvey, *IU*, 160.

[34] In Tibetan Buddhism, singing is considered one of the signs of enlightenment!

[35] Thich Nhat Hanh, *The Heart of Understanding*, 8.

[36] Janet Sue Brenneman. *Footsteps of My Own: Gender Issues that Influence the Formative Experiences of Exemplary Women Choral Conductors* (Michigan State University Press, 2007), 12.

[37] Ibid., 45.

[38] Rao, 2005.

[39] VanWeeldon's demographic profile, cited in Brenneman, 2007, 39.

[40] Eileen M. Hower, *A Vision for Choral Music Education: the Imagination and Influence of Master Teacher and Conductor Doreen Rao*, The Pennsylvania State University.

[41] "Reflective practice" engages the students collaboratively in musical problem-solving opportunities arising from the rehearsal of pitch, time, and text in relation to the desired performance outcomes. This form of pedagogy encourages the kind of personal insights and thoughtful interactions associated with performance knowledge, or thinking-in-action.

[42] "Not-knowing" is the first of three precepts (steps to peace) in the Zen Peacemaker Path founded by Roshi Bernie Glassman. *Not-knowing* is giving up "fixed ideas" about ourselves and the universe, letting go of your knowing.

[43] "Non-doing" is explained succinctly by Jon Kabat-Zinn in *Wherever You Go, There You Are* (New York: Hyperion, 1994).

[44] Mihaly Csikszentmihalyi, *Flow: The Psychology of Optimal Experience* (New York: Harper and Row, 1990).

[45] "The Singing Revolution," www.singingrevolution.com

[46] Mind and Life Institute: Dedicated to fostering dialogue and research at the highest possible level between modern science and the great living contemplative traditions, especially Buddhism. It builds on a deep commitment to the power and value of both of these ways of advancing knowledge and their potential to alleviate suffering.

Teaching Graduate Conductors

Marguerite Brooks

Introduction

To paraphrase C. S. Lewis, people and music are amphibious, part spiritual and part animal, belonging to the eternal world while inhabiting time and physical space. This dichotomy plays itself out in the study of conducting: the work that we require in time and physical space must be applied to the intangible substance of the music, the love of which is, after all, what brought us to the study of conducting in the first place. Instruction in musicianship, languages, diction, repertoire, analysis, performance practice, gesture, voice, orchestration, rehearsal management, score reading, and more must be balanced with the application of those skills to the service of the music. Taught and learned well, these studies allow us to become conduits for the transformational power of music, not just for ourselves, but also for the audience and for the singers and players with whom we work.

Since conductors do not, as a rule, speak in performance, we teach the vocabulary of our nonverbal communication to our performers. We all have taught conducting gestures to ensembles we have worked with—to children and adults—in order that we all speak the same language. Having done that, we know we can teach just about anyone the basics of keeping time. We also know that time-beating does not a conductor make.

We remember strong performances led by aspiring conductors with only rudimentary gestural skills but total knowledge of, commitment to, imagination about, and passion for the score combined with a strength of will which impels an ensemble to outdo itself. We then envision those same people with a conducting technique as sophisticated as the rest of their talents, and the performance such a combination would generate. This vision motivates us as we teach.

How exciting it is to work with a student who comes into a lesson having found the right gesture for a phrase of Shostakovich that contains harsh, accented chords played with a series of string downbows. She has combined her analysis of the piece with the needs of the ensemble to arrive at a clear and expressive motion. How challenging it is to work with a student who resists analyzing even superficial phrase structure and then has difficulty doing more than routinely beating time. How humbling it is when we conduct, both in those places where just the right gesture propels the music off the page and in the moments when our involvement can be minimal, our conducting is virtually unnecessary, and we can disappear into the music.

Those of us who teach have had outstanding students from whom we have learned much and who have challenged us to evolve as educators. Effective teaching requires us to individualize our instruction, to formulate a specific syllabus for each student based on the student's knowledge and experience. In other words, we teach the person, not just the subject matter.

How Much Can We Realistically Hope to Teach?

At the graduate level we teach conductors; our colleagues teach singers, violinists, pianists, composers, and so on. Our conducting students already are employable at some level in their chosen field, and most have worked or are currently working as conductors. They have chosen, however, to come to school, and for their years in residence we expect that they will put their education first. We expect them willingly to devour new music; to plumb the riches of the university's libraries, faculty, and course offerings; to expand and refine their gestural vocabulary; to try our suggestions at least once; to meet all of our exit requirements; and to succeed in their applications for further graduate study or employment. We expect them to leave us knowing more than when they first arrived, and to show us that they are equipped to continue their education without us.

Our students trust that we will teach them. Our responsibilities include guiding each aspiring conductor toward completion of degree requirements and preparing each for fruitful pursuit of a professional life. Because there is simply too much to teach in a two- or three-year time frame, and because ultimately the responsibility for assimilating the material lies with the individual student, in reality we are in the business of training conductors to learn on their own, to be independent, to be self-starting. One could argue that self-motivation is a personality trait no conductor can do without. So we toss students into the deep end of the pool, ropes and preservers at the ready, expecting conductors to emerge who aren't afraid to ask questions and who know where to find as many answers as possible.

I would never relinquish individual instruction tailored to each student, in spite of the amount of preparation it requires of the faculty. The need for individual attention is no less essential for a conductor than for a violinist. Nor would I relinquish having a critical mass of students, knowing that their collaborative learning and the creation of lifelong colleagues are indispensable ingredients of any curriculum. I would not relinquish ensembles that exist solely for the students to rehearse and conduct, whose members recognize their purpose and revel in it. And lastly, I would not relinquish an institutional educational philosophy that insists that students study outside of their specific disciplines.

Graduate conducting teachers face both temporal and psychological challenges. Students are with us for a short time, during which they are champing at the bit to conduct, as they should be. Master's degree candidates are required to study voice and must pass a piano proficiency test and a foreign language test. All graduate conducting students are required to sing in one large and one small ensemble during their residency. They are expected to take courses outside of the choral department. Our task as teachers is to provide as much material and podium time as we can in a very few months, and to remind students often that time spent in the library, classroom, or practice room is as valuable a part of their education as the performances they conduct.

The first weeks in a new school are typically daunting, as each conductor realizes that the entire class is talented, that there is a lot to learn, and that time is already flying. Students find it difficult to be challenged by a new teacher on gestures that have worked in the past, to have gaps exposed in their preparation, to have musicianship skills pushed to their limits, and to remember that study is indeed hard work. We often spend the first weeks of the fall term restoring students' self-confidence, reminding them that perfectionism is overrated, and segmenting the learning process so they feel less overwhelmed.

Working with More Than One Teacher toward Similar Goals

What my faculty colleagues and I try to cover in two years' worth of lessons is enormous. Each of us presents material in our own way, each of us teaches all the candidates at some point in their residency, and, remarkably, the end results are the same. Absent turf wars and animosity among faculty members, which ultimately hurt only the students, a variety of approaches enriches a student's experience. What a student can't seem to hear from one teacher often is heard loudly and clearly from another source. Even though students have individual lessons with only one faculty member at a time, ensemble conducting is observed by all three instructors, which ensures conversation among faculty members and awareness of how each student is being taught. Visiting conductors enrich the mix.

Individualizing Graduate Conducting Instruction

The student and I formulate a syllabus each term, some of which is covered in detail during the lesson and some of which I take on faith from the student's report. Students are generally honest about what they have and haven't accomplished. Depending on the student's progress, any given lesson might include topics in orchestration, score reading, musicianship, study of basic orchestral literature, or conducting and rehearsal technique.

A centerpiece of the syllabus is repertoire study, with selection of choral literature based on the student's previous experience. Each student prepares a repertory list of pieces conducted and works sung. Some students come with an encyclopedic knowledge of the English Cathedral tradition but know no repertoire from eastern Europe or South America. Some students have conducted the *St. John Passion* but no smaller unaccompanied pieces. And some are early music buffs with no experience with music of the twentieth or twenty-first centuries. The ideal student has done a bit of everything. The syllabus, tailored to the individual's strengths and weaknesses, aims for a balance of chronology, geography, and genre, taking into consideration the works to be performed during a student's years with us, as well as the rotation of musicology courses.

One of my colleagues keeps a list of one hundred or so choral pieces with which every conductor should be familiar. The odds are good that every syllabus will include the composers on this list, if not the specific works. The repertoire study also includes standard symphonic literature, opera, and chamber music, categories that rely the most on self-reporting during lessons.

Preparation for the Conducting Lesson

For a lesson, students are expected to learn one piece well, complete as much of a written analysis as possible, and be able to conduct at least sections of the piece from memory, preferably sections with conducting challenges. Students are also expected to listen broadly throughout the composer's *oeuvre*, read about the composer and know where to go for current scholarship, read in the composer's writings, if any, and be able to contextualize the piece.

Students work through texts in orchestration, score reading, and musicianship if their skills are not already strong in those areas. Score study is balanced with acquisition of the gestures that form our nonverbal vocabulary and with development of varied rehearsal techniques.

Conducting

Instructors observe students as they conduct a group, then work in lessons on the observed gestures. Ideally, in advance of any public conducting, the student and teacher have reviewed the student's analysis, discussed the composer, placed the piece in context, and reviewed long- and short-term rehearsal plans. The student will have conducted from memory in front of a large mirror and, if studying with one of my colleagues, made a video recording of that conducting session. After the student conducts in public, watches a recording of his or her conducting session, and reads my notes, we review what actually happened and work from there. We take the conducting technique apart for clarity and expression, try new gestures (perhaps realize that a gesture the student thought was exaggerated was barely noticeable), assess the effectiveness of the rehearsal plan, and discuss what the student heard or didn't hear.

The conducting repertoire is selected together by student and instructor. The first piece rehearsed in public with a laboratory chorus must be five minutes or shorter, in English, suitable for an ensemble of twenty-four voices, and in our libraries. This first piece is chosen by the student, with limited input from me. We negotiate on all ensuing choices of repertoire, whether for a master class or for a degree recital, based on the student's educational needs. Everyone at some time conducts, even if only in rehearsal, representative works from the sixteenth century through the twenty-first, pieces in languages other than English, sacred and secular music, and music using (or perhaps scored only for) instruments. Those candidates without instrumental experience are expected to expand on their orchestral conducting study, particularly during the summer, when they have the time to immerse themselves in instrumental sound. As we discuss choices of repertoire, we spend time learning how to put together an effective concert program.

Repertoire for recent degree recitals has included Stravinsky *L'histoire du soldat*, Barber *Prayers of Kierkegaard*, Harbison *Mirabai Songs*, Beethoven Mass in C, Purcell *Dido and Aeneas*, J. S. Bach *Komm, Jesu, komm* and *Nun komm, der Heiden Heiland*, Kreek *Taaveti laulud*, Brahms *Vier Gesänge*, Vittoria *Tene-*

brae, Pärt *Summa*, David *Deutsche Messe*, Finzi *Requiem da camera*, Duruflé Requiem, and Rheinberger *Cantus Missae.*

DIRECTING THE LESSON: "WHERE IS YOUR ANALYSIS?"

I am reasonably sure that my students tire of my persistent questions: Where is your analysis? Where does this phrase lead? What are the micro and macro levels of this part of the piece? Where is the climax of the piece? Are there tempo relationships? What vocal sounds are called for? What are the vocal demands? What is the text? What does this word mean? How will this vowel affect the ensemble sound? What are the balance issues? What are the dynamics, whether notated or implied? What articulation works here? What is the hardest part of the piece? What size vocal and instrumental ensembles does the piece require? How will you rehearse and teach? Have you marked the parts? Are you sure of this bowing? How is the memorization coming? Can you conduct this three different ways? What adjectives or adverbs can you use to describe this line? And finally, what gestures will you use to show all this?

Students frequently resist analysis, which is time-consuming, frustrating, and solitary. Analysis is largely invisible to the ensembles and the audience, and until it is finished it doesn't seem to have anything to do with making the perfect gesture or developing a cogent rehearsal plan. The results, however, are revelatory: conducting motions suggest themselves, rehearsal strategies fall into place, memorization becomes easier, and the pacing of the work unfolds. Whatever method of analysis is used, the study is critical to understanding, rehearsing, and conducting a piece of music.

TECHNIQUE OF CONDUCTING

Students tend to be more fascinated with gesture than with any other aspect of conducting. There are many wonderful authors and teachers from whom to learn what to do with arms, hands, fingers, face, and body position. We as instructors can suggest our favorite books and videos. We can invite guest conductors, speakers, and teachers to our campuses. We can send students to seminars and master classes, to rehearsals and concerts. We can refer students to our own colleagues. But ultimately we are responsible for the day-to-day observation and nurturing of our students.

We begin with the conductor's awareness of the body. How do we stand, what is our relationship with gravity, is the body aligned, where are our feet, and how do we maintain the sense of being grounded without feeling stuck? How do we keep this balance when we raise our arms to conduct, and then concentrate on listening at the same time? How do we use gravity to make natural motions?

In a foundational exercise we ask students to conduct an ellipse, without a click, increasing and then decreasing height and width. The next step is to conduct the ellipse with clicks. We add increasing and decreasing partials, making the shape proportionally larger and smaller. From this exercise, we can move easily to compound irregular meters. We try to do this while maintaining consistent speed of motion. We gradually add conducting patterns, dynamics, and articulation.

Conductors must learn to place the locus of each beat so as to differentiate the beats in a measure. All beats should occur on a horizontal axis, at varying distances from a vertical axis. The downbeat is clearest if it coincides exactly with the intersection of the two axes, and if it is the only beat placed there. All other beats should occur to the left or right of that intersection. If all beats occur at the same place, regardless of how the hand is turned or the direction from which each beat is approached, they all look like downbeats to the last stand of instrumentalists or to singers on the ends of the rows. Many choral conductors have been taught to place all beats in the same place, and this is a difficult habit to break. The epiphany usually comes, though, when a student is rehearsing the instruments in a piece with mixed, irregular meters in which the players are counting and miss entrances because the conducting is unpredictable and unreadable.

Once clarity is achieved in placement of the beat, all of the rules can and should be broken in the service of the music. The horizontal axis can be abruptly raised (for a *subito piano*, for instance) or lowered (to follow an expressive bass line).

We use all available hinges: shoulder, elbow, wrist, and knuckles. We use one hand, first without and then with a stick. We turn the hands so they face up, down, and sideways, and the fingers many ways.

We discuss common metrical practice and vary each beat according to its relative stress in a measure. We consider each beat as preparation for the next. We conduct mixed and irregular meters, using both right and left hand. We practice rhythmic dictation, whereby the student conducts and I speak the rhythms I think the student is conducting. This last exercise is designed to practice the difference, for example, between a measure containing a whole note and one containing a dotted half note followed by a quarter note. Once a conductor can provoke an event on the desired beat, with its dynamic level and articulation, it is a short jump to conducting recitatives, both *secco* and accompanied.

We endeavor to create an independent left hand, often beginning with polyrhythms. We might, for example, conduct in three with the left hand and in two with the right hand. Occasionally, we use no patterns at all. We might conduct expressive cheironomy, or chant, or simply phrase direction. We then show the same shape within the context of patterns. We ask questions about a phrase: Can you tell me in words what the music is doing? Can you show this with hands and face and no pattern? Can you put that expression into a pattern?

We identify a set of clear and expressive gestures to fit a phrase. Then we weigh those choices with the needs of the music—perhaps an accompanying figure in the string section needs the conductor's attention more than the beautifully expressive solo line. Perhaps absolute clarity is paramount. Perhaps the ensemble doesn't need to be shown more than the shape of the music. Perhaps an instrument or voice needs a cue for a seemingly unimportant entrance, change of register, or change of rhythmic pattern. Usually all downbeats must be unfailingly recognizable, but sometimes a beat pattern is just a pattern and is irrelevant. What should be done with the fermata or the hemiola? What gesture, helpful in rehearsal, is ultimately unnecessary in performance? What emergency gestures might be handy in performance?

Most of this is a nonlinear approach to teaching, based on the needs of the student grappling with the requirements of a given piece. Often we work laboriously on one phrase at a time, hoping that the student can extrapolate what we learn to the whole piece. The moment the student discovers that this is actually fun is an exciting one, although the tendency to want to micromanage the piece is often a sign of this stage of development. But now the real conducting has begun.

CONCLUSIONS

The music is the genesis of all gesture. All conducting teaching is complemented by and, in turn, complements the study of the music, whether in the classroom, the library, ensemble rehearsals, or other venues.

Judging whether a student is a relative novice or an experienced conductor is less important than addressing his or her individual needs. Some doctoral candidates need to reexamine their technique, and some master's degree candidates need to develop beyond basic time-beating. If I notice that I need to correct the same flaw in more than one student, I look to my own conducting first; the odds are that my bad habits also are my legacy to my students.

As professional conductors, we are indebted to our own teachers and to the students who continue to teach us. Although I cannot possibly catalogue all of the lessons I received, I can single out three mentors. My first teacher, Tamara Brooks, helped me develop a conscience about preparation. The first assignment in her basic conducting class was to compose eight measures, which we then conducted. The lesson: never conduct something you don't know inside and out. My second instructor, John Nelson, spent a summer with me memorizing and conducting recitatives from the *St. John Passion*, passages which I remember to this day. With Robert Page I developed a philosophy of teaching. A simple question from one of Page's students inevitably elicited an exhaustive list of possible solutions as well as the names of the people who suggested those solutions. In order to help my students begin to collect a stockpile of strategies, I present them with as many options as possible and endeavor to stay up-to-date myself with new repertoire, scholarship, and conducting techniques.

As we work to strengthen our students' weaknesses, we must also confront our own. I memorize laboriously, musical analyses notwithstanding. To overcome this aversion I conduct a bit of every rehearsal from memory, knowing that my mistakes are obvious. When I make a mistake, I apologize rather than blame the ensemble for my error.

I recently read a university catalogue that stated the following: "_____ University makes no claim that enrolling in a particular class or following the course curriculum will produce a specific achievement, employment, qualification for employment, admission to postgraduate degree programs or licensure." This language clearly puts the onus on the student. Elsewhere, though, the same bulletin states that the mission of the faculty is to teach. For a teacher of conducting, instruction includes so much more than appears in any bulletin. We also prepare students for auditions and competitions, give interview and employment advice, provide honest, positive criticism, and model, to the best of our abilities, the characteristics we encourage in our students. We try to treat students as individuals and to remember that we are about them first, not ourselves and our own careers.

At the same time, we need to conduct our own ensembles, search aggressively for new music, and go to concerts. We must read both in music and recreationally, since we are involved with the written word as text. We have to study scores; to make music as instrumentalists or singers; and to practice, rehearse, and perform in the service of the music and its composer. The challenge is to find a personal balance that works.

Most conductors can agree that music has pride of place, and is itself the source of everything we do as conductors. I try to teach my students that making music in our field is by definition collaborative, that the study of conducting and music are lifelong endeavors, and that the final authority is the music itself.

Biography

Marguerite L. Brooks was named to the faculty of Yale University in 1985 to direct the Choral Conducting program at the Music School and choral music at the Institute of Sacred Music. She came to Yale from the State University of New York at Stony Brook, where she served as director of choral music and was tenured in 1984.

Brooks studied with Tamara Brooks (not a relative, alas) at Mount Holyoke College, Robert Page at Temple University, and John Nelson at the Aspen Music Festival. She began her musical journey as a pianist, singer, and sometime organist; she credits her early teacher William Penfield and the a cappella group the Mount Holyoke V-8s (in which she sang and served as pitch) for her eclectic musical interests.

As founding conductor of the Yale Camerata and its chamber chorus, the Pro Musica, Brooks has championed music of the twentieth and twenty-first centuries, giving first performances of several student compositions each year as well as premieres of works by established composers including Kathryn Alexander, Martin Bresnick, Daniel Kellogg, Tawnie Olsen, Stephen Paulus, Daniel Pinkham, Francine Trester, Gwyneth Walker, and Ellen Taaffe Zwilich, among others.

The Camerata's most recent project was a performance of the J. S. Bach *Weihnachts Oratorium*, undertaken as part of a conference about the changing traditions of Christmas and as an opportunity to explore the overall structure of the work.

In addition to her work at Yale, Brooks is Director of Music at the Church of the Redeemer (UCC) in New Haven.

Artistry through Improvisation in the Choral Rehearsal

Sue Williamson

The National Standards for music education (2000) consists of nine content standards for implementation in K–12 music classrooms:

1. Singing, along and with others, a varied repertoire of music
2. Performing on instruments, alone and with others, a varied repertoire of music.
3. Improvising melodies, variations, and accompaniments.
4. Composing and arranging music within specified guidelines.
5. Reading and notating music.
6. Listening to, analyzing, and describing music.
7. Evaluating music and music performances.
8. Understanding relationships between music, the other arts, and disciplines outside the arts.
9. Understanding music in relation to history and culture.

Historically, American choral programs have based curricula on three standards: Standard 1, singing along and with others, Standard 5, reading and notating music and Standard 7, evaluating music and music performances. While emphasis on these standards has resulted in decades of rewarding and artistic choral performances, choral teachers and their students may also find value in exploring the remaining standards: Improvisation, composition, and cultural knowledge. Since current research in musical participation suggests that less than ten percent of high school students are involved in music performance programs, including improvisation and composition standards may increase musical participation in our school programs and enhance the range and quality of choral experiences for directors and students.

In particular, teaching improvisation (Standard 3) is viewed by many choral directors as a daunting task. Recently, I spoke with secondary choral directors regarding their views on teaching improvisation. Most expressed concerns and frustrations. One director felt "it's not a part of my job." Another stated "Well, I'm interested, but I don't have any idea how to do it!" Many directors believe that jazz is the only genre that facilitates teaching improvisation. For those who have no jazz experience, approaching improvisation in the choral setting is frightening. But, if we are committed to the advancement of choral artistry, we must also venture into lesser known artistic territories, including improvisation.

However, with escalating pressure for core subjects and standardized tests in secondary schools, and mounting academic pressures in higher education, how can we possibly allocate more time to incorporate improvisation ideas? And, what benefits would we receive from its inclusion in our traditional choral ensembles?

The purpose of this essay is help answer those questions by describing effective strategies for teaching choral improvisation in middle school, high school and collegiate contexts. Examples of improvisation are provided which can be easily incorporated into busy teaching schedules and yet are aesthetically satisfying. In relaying these examples, I draw from the perspectives of four choral musicians who teach choral improvisation. I share reflections from my teaching followed by sections describing the experiences of three gifted choral teachers: Karen Keeler, Stephen Ross and Matthew Potterton. In each case, the essay presents the teacher's personal background regarding improvisation, their views of the benefits and challenges of teaching improvisation, and examples of age-appropriate methods are presented.

But, first, in order to accurately explore this aspect of choral artistry, I present definitions regarding the term *improvisation.*

What is Improvisation?

Researchers define improvisation in numerous ways. Azzara (2002) states "in much of the research, the definition of improvisation involves an ability to make music spontaneously within specified musical parameters." (p. 171) Briggs (1987) refers to improvisation as "musical dialogue" and notes the importance of non-musical factors such as environment and context in contributing to the experience. Others, including Sarath (1996), Nardone (1997) and Werner, stress the importance of "inner directedness" and being present in the moment.

While vocal improvisation was prevalent in the Renaissance, Baroque and Classical periods, and is a salient musical characteristic of many world music choral traditions, research on vocal improvisation has centered on vocal jazz. One of the purposes of this essay is to provide introductory improvisation experiences that are not genre-specific. Improvisation is not exclusive to jazz. Nor does it is have to be the domain of soloists, rather than ensembles.

Choral improvisation, as practiced by the teachers in this essay and by me, consists of two types of structure: First, choral improvisation occurs when all singers improvise simultaneously. Second, choral improvisation is experienced when a portion of the choir sings a repeated pattern, such as a scale or short melodic fragment, while the other portion improvises. Because choral improvisation involves all singers and provides a thick texture of choral sound, students feel much less nervous than in solo improvisation. Since singers vocally improvise in a safe musical environment, choral improvisation provides an easy context with which to explore improvisation.

Personal Perspective

My interest in vocal improvisation developed in the early years of my teaching when I became enthralled with the South African singing group, Ladysmith Black Mambazo. I was teaching middle school during the apartheid movement in South Africa and was excited to share several freedom songs with my choirs. We began our cultural exploration with the piece "Freedom is Coming" and had some success recreating the cultural sound and style. However, we found difficult to emulate the element of improvisation, so naturally expressed in the South African recordings.

Several years later, I traveled to South Africa for a month to study black African choirs. I was housed with African families in the township of Mamelodi and in the cities of Johannesburg and Durban. The families graciously drove me to rehearsals and performances of community, school and church choirs. In all, I observed over twenty choirs. In each instance, regardless of the singers' age or skill level, I was overwhelmed by both the beauty of the sound and each choir's ability to extend pieces through improvisation. Improvisation was central to the traditional South African choral experience.

The African trip profoundly shifted my choral perspective and provided me with a new series of questions to guide my teaching:

- How can we create transformative choral experiences that feature improvisation?
- What methods and techniques are most successful?

In the decade since my travels, I have passionately explored transforming experiences through choral improvisation. I must confess that my intent is clear: I do not merely want to introduce singers to improvisation, or teach it because the National Standards suggest I should. I want choirs to experience a deep level of soulfulness. What I have found is that while the level varies, each choir experiences something uniquely wonderful through improvisation. And lest you think that this success is due to my improvisational prowess, I assure you that I am no more capable than any of you! I am, however, less scared. And, lessening vulnerability is crucial to a successful improvisation experience.

The exercises that follow are the result of my improvisation exploration with choirs of all ages and experience levels. While these experiences may be executed in any portion of the rehearsal, I have found them highly effective in warm-ups. Because relaxation and focus are key concepts during warm-ups, it is an ideal time to encourage new experiences. And, just as we teach carefully sequenced exercises during warm-ups, the following improvisation exercises are presented in steps that help the singers to sequentially build their skills and confidence. Most frequently, with high school and college students, singers can easily achieve accomplishment in one rehearsal or less. With middle school students, the exercises are best begun with the descending scale exploration, then moving to the second step at their point of readiness.

Descending Scales

An easy way to begin teaching improvisation during warm-ups includes choral improvisation on a descending scale. This type of choral improvisation features one half of the choir improvising, while the other half repeats a descending scale. Since the scale, particular in major keys, is usually keenly embedded in singers' ears, improvisation with a major scale is an easy way to experience creative success. As with all vocal warm-ups, the director should choose a key that is appropriate for the range and skill of her singers.

Begin by having the choir sing a D Major descending scale, concentrating on relaxing the voice and body and singing the scale tones with beautiful phrasing. Repeat this numerous times to help the singers relax and to unconsciously anchor the scale in their aural memory. This exercise is most effective at a tempo of ♩ = 60–90. Singers hold each note of the scale for a half note and focus on creating long beautiful sustained sounds. Directors of younger singers may want to have the singers do this as a part of warm-ups for several weeks before moving to the improvisation step. Importantly, the singers must feel very comfortable singing the scale before moving into improvisation.

When the director and singers feel comfortable and relaxed with the descending scale, divide the choir in half, asking half to sing the descending scale and half to make up something that fits with the scale pattern. Singers will naturally be a bit timid the first several times they experiment with improvising.

So, encourage the choir to sing with confidence and praise each vocal idea that emerges, regardless of its complexity or accuracy. The verbal praise of the director helps the singers to continue to vocally relax, which stimulates vocal creativity. Continue this version of the exercise without stopping at the end of the scale. After numerous repetitions of the descending scale and improvisation, when the director has heard a notable increase in improvisatory sound and musical ideas, ask the choir to switch parts.

When first teaching this exercise, I will accompany the choir with light arpeggios on the piano, so that even though they know the melodic pattern, they aurally perceive a fuller sound. A more harmonically advanced version of this exercise is practiced by the Collegiate Choir Singers of the University of Colorado. After using the scale as a warm-up, the director, Matthew Potterton, will have the accompanist play a series of changing chords underneath the scale. Then, singers improvise based on the harmonic structures provided by the pianist.

Conducted Chord Clusters

Unlike the previous example, where half of the choir is sings a scale ostinato and the other half is improvising, the experience of improvisatory chord clusters features each choir member improvising something different simultaneously. This experience creates a rich choral texture where each singer must truly listen to the others and respond to one another, and attempt to have his or her improvisations fit within the changing harmonic texture. This exercise is particularly effective after choirs have experienced success in scale improvisation.

After singers feel comfortable with the descending scale exercise, the director may suggest an extension of the exercise for further development. This exercise is best when singers stand in a circle formation. The circle shape allows the singers to more clearly hear each other and to form an energetic and kinesthetic bond.

After the singers are in a circle formation (or circles within circles for large choirs), all singers sing the lower "do" pitch upon your direction. Then, ask the singers to move to any pitch of the scale when you indicate that the chord should change. Frequently, singers will reduce their volume if their note does not harmonically fit with others. I recommend that singers try to keep their pitch and volume stable, even if it clashes with the notes of others. This exercise also strengthens the individual's ability to create and maintain his or her own part. I also encourage students to conduct this exercise, as a means of furthering the relaxation of the singers and building a positive group dynamic.

Free-Exploration Chord Clusters

The final step of the warm-up choral improvisation sequences is frequently the most enriching for the singers. After students feel comfortable with the first two exercises, the choir is ready to explore free improvisation through widely-ranging chordal clusters.

In teaching this exercise, have the choir sing four or five chords of the conducted chordal clusters exercise. Then, ask the singers to shut their eyes and continue to explore vocally. Stress that they may move to any note of the scale, including above and below the octave, and they should try to make their individual exploration fit with the voices around them. Frequently, choirs will ask to sit in group clusters for this exercise. The group cluster formation allows close physical proximity for singers to listen to each other and vocally interact. In addition, many singers report that when they feel they are really listening and vocally creating with others, they feel an "energy" or "deep feeling" present in the group. My last instructions to the group center on the need to be feel and listen deeply, so that they will know, without opening their eyes, when the improvisation ends.

This connection present in this experience is profoundly aesthetic experience. Older singers have also noted they appreciate improvisatory warm-ups because they can choose the range in which they vocalize.

Improvisation Using Ostinati and Movement

A fourth excellent source of material for choral improvisation involves the use of ostinati. A short repeated pattern provides a stable aural framework against which portions of the choir may improvise. Most ostinati work if they outline a typical harmonic structure and are easily learned. Bass ostinati from

American doo-wop songs, as well as ostinati from selected world music repertoire all are useful. One particularly effective ostinato is drawn from the bass part of the South African freedom song, "Freedom is Coming." Because the piece comes from Black South African folk traditions, it is culturally appropriate to be accompanied by dance, especially the rocking march-type step, a common movement with South African freedom songs. Have the singers begin in normal standing position, then move the right foot forward (beat one), shifting the body's weight to the right foot, then step back on the left foot (beat two) as the right foot moves to the side, then step on right foot (beat three), ending with transferring the weight to the left food (beat four), back in standing placement. This step looks like a rocking motion, with the left foot anchoring the body's movement while the right foot moves forward and sideways.

Teach the dance first because movement is embedded in this genre of singing and because concentrating on the dance will help singers not to overthink the improvisation. Have the choir stand in circle formation because the circle shape allows the singers to see the dance step across the circle and also to hear the singing more clearly. After the singers are moving comfortably with the step, have singers repeat the text in rhythm, concentrating on expressing the phrase "freedom is coming" in a convincing manner and coordinating the voice with the body.

American singers tend to lose energy after several repetitions, but the element of repetition is key for choral improvisation. I encourage the choirs to keep their energy moving and to infuse each repetition with more energy and confidence. When they are vocalizing with intensity, and seem to be physically engaged in the dance, I will teach the first four measures of the bass part as the ostinato (see Example 1).

Example 1

While choir sings the ostinato, I improvise a solo line, perhaps another ostinato, on the word "freedom," and quickly select others to join me. As I scan the choir, I will frequently choose singers who look most physically and emotionally comfortable to join in improvisation. Many singers will choose to sing the ostinato sung by the director. Others may feel free to create their own. Ideally, each member creates a new vocal line that adds to a rich thick wall of choral sound. See Example 2 for a transcription of a portion of a university choir's choral improvisation on this piece.

Example 2

(continues)

(continued)

CONTINUING THE OSTINATO IMPROVISATION

When five or six singers have created their ostinati, add more improvising singers to increase energy and textures. The use of multiple ostinati create a rich choral texture against which singers may choose to move from singing the original ostinato to creating their own. While you may be tempted to choose the best vocalists as improvisers, select some singers who seem ready to try, regardless of their improvisation skill.

Using ostinati are particularly effective when the director provides verbal instruction while the choir is singing. Rather than stopping to fix, to suggest or to add ostinati, the most effective improvisation occurs when the singers repeat the ostinato until it takes on the quality of a groove. This quality requires numerous repetitions and will be restricted if the choir is interrupted.

MIDDLE SCHOOL CHORAL IMPROVISATION: KAREN KEELER

Karen Keeler, a successful, enthusiastic teacher currently at Platt Middle School in Boulder, Colorado, began teaching choral improvisation three years ago. While initially hesitant to explore improvisation, Karen has found teaching choral improvisation to be a rewarding experience for herself and for her students. She remarks that she still feels a bit uncomfortable and views improvisation as a "yearly challenge," but that teaching improvisation develops her choral artistry by reducing her perfectionist tendencies. She states:

> The improvisation has given me more permission to make mistakes. Because I have perfectionist tendencies and tend to see things as black and white, or good and bad, it has been freeing for me as a choral artist. Basically, I knew I feared it (improvisation) and I refused to be the kind of teacher that avoids through fear.

Paramount to Karen's successful teaching is the positive and safe environment she creates for her students. She accomplishes this through her consistently positive encouragement and praise for her students' efforts rather than perfect accomplishments. She stresses trying new things and experiencing joy in the process. This nurturing attitude, which pervades Karen's teaching, is essential when introducing improvisation to middle school students. Madura (1999) notes "because risk-taking is essential to musical creativity, the teacher must be sure that students feel safe to express themselves without fear of ridicule from other students. . . . Fear is the enemy of improvisation." (p. 5) The importance of singers feeling safe in the choral environment cannot be emphasized enough.

In introducing choral improvisation to her beginning choirs, Karen focuses on vocal exploration and confidence building. She does not introduce improvisation until the students have created a positive and safe environment and are capable of exploring musical risk taking. Each choir begins at its own point of readiness.

A Structured Beginning

When the group has established a culture of artistic freedom, Karen begins to teach improvisation by writing a brief rhythmic pattern on the board and having students create words that match the rhythm. Providing the notated rhythm creates a comfort zone for the students who enjoy thinking up matching words, but who may be overwhelmed by improvising a text, melody and rhythmic pattern simultaneously.

Following word improvisation, Karen creates short body percussion ostinatos and has her students keep the pattern going while individual singers engage with her in spoken call and response. As in the introductory activities, a rhythmic structure is provided for the students so that the young singers do not freeze when called upon to improvise or become overwhelmed at the task of creating all elements of a vocal improvisation.

Vocal Maps

A second idea Karen uses is a student-created improvisation map. Modeled on the idea of drawing their own game boards, students create a one page map or maze, then mark places in their map where they should sing a particular scale degree, eventually singing each solfege syllable. To simplify the tonality with her sixth grade choirs, students are asked to begin and end their maps on the lower "do" and to include every solfege syllable in their game board in ascending order.

After all students have finished their improvisation game board drawing, they all sing a unison beginning pitch and then progress through their game board at their own tempos. The effect is a busying schemata of improvised vocal sound, through which students can begin to exercise the skill of singing by themselves and changing their improvisation by varying the tempo of their map progression. As students progress in their aural recall and improvisation skills, they create new maps through the year where the order of pitches is altered.

Small Group Solos with Chordal Accompaniment

After several months of introductory exploration and confidence building, the beginning choirs are usually ready to explore chordal improvisation. This was accomplished by having the singers hold a three-part chord, which was emphasized over the course of many months without improvisation, and then having small groups of singers improvise on a major scale while the choir was holding the chord.

I was present at a recording session with the combined sixth grade choirs as they shared this improvisation and I was amazed at the skill of their improvisation, and also the choir members' abilities to hold their pitch for long periods of time. The choir sang the chord initially on an "oo" vowel to open their sounds, then switched to a hum.

In summary, Karen has found success by including choral improvisation in her curriculum. She has enhanced her students' musicianship, their self-confidence, and their commitment to the choral ensemble by carefully sequencing their improvisational experiences. After beginning with rhythm, she added melodic improvisation only when students are ready. In so doing, the singers always experienced success and felt encouraged by their progress.

High School: Stephen Ross and the Valentine Project

Stephen Ross, who currently teaches at Skyline High School in Longmont, Colorado, is known for having a choral program that excells in traditional and progressive choral repertoire. Stephen became fascinated with improvisation in college. After starting his own a cappella vocal group, he discovered that improvisation was beneficial for ear training. He expressed "I had to really actively listen to what was going on in a song. Because of that, now I hear patterns and chord progressions, which I can teach my students."

Due in part to his successful previous experiences in improvisation, Stephen's curriculum includes not only improvisation, but more of the other eight areas of the National Standards than do the curricula of many of his choral colleagues. Like Karen, Stephen is committed to finding ways to incorporate all the standards in his teaching. "I'm in my fifth year of exploring with improvisation projects," he notes, "and I really want to continue to deepen my teaching and conducting skills in this area. I see so many tremendous possibilities for this to be broadened into choral repertoire and artistry."

Because of his choral program's intensely busy schedule, as well as Stephen's personal performance schedule, he has found success in teaching improvisation in short projects. Several times a year, including Valentine's Day and final exam, students create short pieces of improvisation or create their own arrangements of popular songs. These experiences are used in a variety of ways, both to provide improvisatory experiences, to connect students with popular repertoire, and to raise money for the choral department. The project featured in this section, "Valentine's Day Improv," has become such a popular school event that the choral department raises several thousand dollars each year.

Marketing for the project begins just one week before, when the students sell the telegrams during the lunch hour. Students, staff and faculty who desire to purchase a Singing Valentine fill out a short form such as in Example 3.

Example 3

Singing Valentine Order Form

To: (full name)
From:
Special Request:

These forms are collected by the choral department and distributed to the singing student groups one week prior to the Valentine's Day improvisation telegrams. Each singing valentine cost three dollars and is performed by a small ensemble the day before and on Valentine's Day. Each group of students has approximately five to six school days to prepare a Valentine arrangement. The schedule is as follows:

Day 1: Choose song.
Map out performance strategy and (who sings what).
Experiment and improvise.

Day 2: Start putting ideas together.
Make sure to add harmonies.
Begin to memorize.

Day 3: Plan choreography.
Rehearse entire piece.

Day 4: Work on problem areas.
Have a final format for the performance.
(How will you walk in? What costumes will you wear?
How will you determine pitch?)

Day 5: Practice, practice, practice!
Have your songs ready to perform by the end of class.

Day 6: Perform for a grade!

Day 7: Singing Valentine Performances.

Stephen has found it helpful to have the singers choose their groups. Peer selection was added to the project when he noticed that students were scared to improvise without their friends. He stated that "they're most successful with each other's support." Groups of three to eight members seem to work well for the project.

Students receive thirty-five points for the project and are assessed in the areas listed in Example 4.

Example 4

Singing Valentines Grade Sheet

Names:

Appropriate Song	___ / 3
Choreography	___ / 3
Lyrics Memorized	___ / 3
In Tune	___ / 4
Two-Part Section	___ / 4
Rehearsal Work Ethic	___ / 8
Performance (Effort)	___ / 10
Total	___ / 35

Although all choral students participate in the project for a grade, group participation in the school telegram project is voluntary. Stephen expressed:

> It's the most challenging thing for teenagers to perform for their peers and it's also incredibly positive and rewarding for the singers. But, singers need to have a certain level of confidence before they're ready. Having their friends in the group helps them, but occasionally, particularly with freshmen, I may have a student or group who don't feel ready to put themselves out there for public performance. I don't push it. I encourage them because they've accomplished a new experience and say they'll probably be more ready next year.

Like Karen, Stephen gives extensive attention in his teaching to creating a safe atmosphere for teaching improvisation. Although the students are formally assessed on the project, they are not graded on the quality of their improvisation. The assessment is oriented toward whether or not students have completed the tasks and used their time wisely, rather than the quality of the final product. Also, Stephen encourages the students to be highly encouraging of other groups' efforts. He notes:

> Especially in the jazz choir setting, where everyone is a top singer, we have made a huge deal of being a supportive choir member. Students have to clap after every solo, even when people fail, crash and burn, we note their at-

> tempts and good tries. Some kids are really taking musical risks and will go crazy in a positive way after their peers support them.

Stephen noted that the Improvisation Valentine's Project has provided his students with a fun introduction to improvisation. And, because the words and melody are provided for them, students are free to improvise within a somewhat fixed structure. While he finds that improvisation can be stressful for students with no experience, he has discovered that the combination of self-selected groups, of fun Valentine's songs, and the light-hearted nature of the project frequently helps students to explore improvisation in a fun, productive and safe way.

Collegiate: Matthew Potterton

Like many choral conductors, Matthew grew up in a musical family, where relatives sang in harmony. When Matthew began teaching, he was surprised that the singers in his secondary school had difficulty harmonizing a simple melody. So, early on in his teaching, he began to experiment with improvisation as a means of helping students learn harmonization.

Through the process of exploration with improvisation and creativity, Matthew's philosophy regarding teaching and artistry has broadened. He states:

> As music educators, much of our rehearsal focuses on non-creative issues such as technique, learning notes, or discussing the historical significance of the piece. And, this is of critical importance. But, this is not musical creativity. Because I value creativity and play in the musical process, I've grown increasingly interested in improvisation.

Currently, Matthew is pursuing his doctorate in choral conducting at the University of Colorado and is the director of Collegiate Choir, an auditioned mixed voice ensemble of undergraduate singers. The choir consists mostly of vocal majors, but includes non-music majors. Collegiate Choir rehearses four times a week for fifty minute rehearsals. Matthew began incorporating improvisation into the choral curriculum last academic year.

While many of the singers were initially hesitant, most of them have come to appreciate and enjoy the improvisation. Several students note that the improvisation training is transferring to their voice studio work. Because they had not had any improvisation experience other than jazz, they did not know how to create improvisatory passages in classical repertoire, especially in music of the Baroque. One noted:

> In performance, it's not ever acceptable to sing a wrong note, but with these exercises and Matt's help to step out from our normal roles as singers, I'm discovering that it's flowing into my classical work. I'm becoming able to come up with ornamentations for my Baroque pieces and it's so much easier. I'm just not as paralyzed about it sounding right.

Another student spoke to the emotional power he experiences during improvisation:

> You can do this and totally express yourself—you can express so much emotion. And it's great because everyone is singing and there's this big ocean of sound. You can't sing these like this and not feel . . . you have to be totally involved in the process . . . it's such a powerful emotional experience.

And one student, who experienced some anxiety regarding improvisation, felt her extreme tendencies towards perfectionism were lessening due to the improvisation experiences. She notes:

> I'm a very shy and very structured person . . . you know my room is always the most organized and cleanest. . . . I like to be in control. So when we started doing improv, I felt really uncomfortable, but it's helping me to open up and be more accepting of different types of music and be ok singing a wrong note and feeling like I'm not messing up.

Using Improvisation as an Introductory Teaching Tool

While Matthew has incorporated improvisation in his conducting in numerous ways, two examples may be highly effective in other teaching settings. The examples presented here are drawn from Matthew's recent lecture demonstration on choral improvisation.

First, he encourages improvisation during warm-up, and he encourages harmonization of a given melody, such as a simple song. Second, he might introduce a piece of repertoire via the improvisation process. In this exercise, students are to improvise a response that fits the melody, style and text sung by the director.

This strategy is particularly effective means to engage the singers aural attention as well as to develop their abilities to reflect on the composer's choices. Matthew begins by singing the melody line to a piece he is introducing and has the choir improvise a choral accompaniment. The students listen keenly to the melody and create vocally appropriate harmonies. After a several attempts, when the students' curiosity is heightened, Matthew distributes the printed score and the choir sight reads the piece. Instead of sight-reading for the purpose of note-gathering, this strategy motivates students to want to know how the composer set the melody.

One piece introduced in this manner was "Sing We and Chant It" by Thomas Morley. In introducing the piece, the choir experimented with having the full choir improvise their "fa la la" response and having quartets and octets improvise as well. Example 5 is a notation of some of the improvisations of the quartets.

Example 5

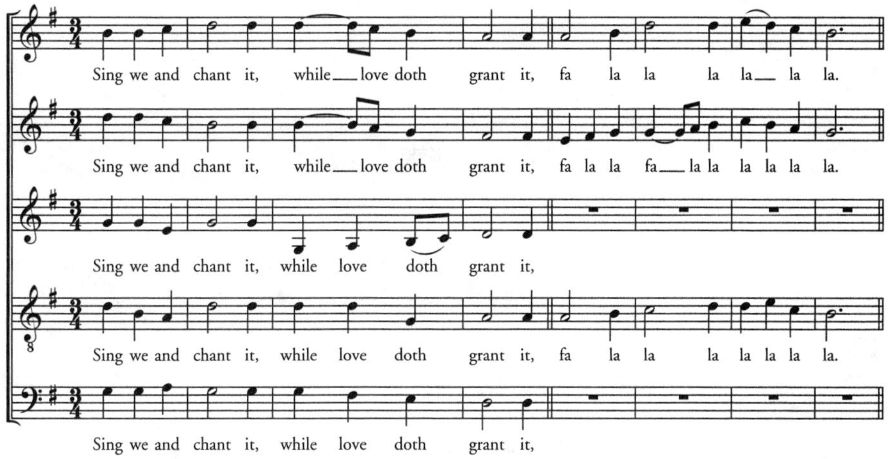

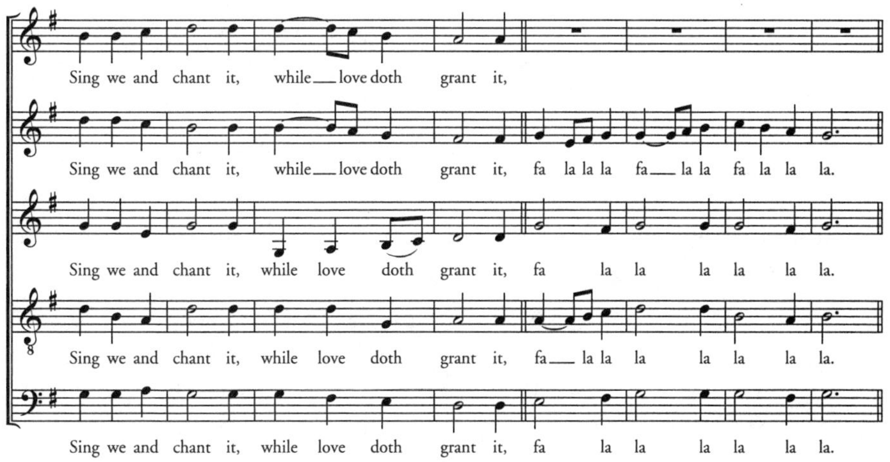

(continues)

(continued)

In summary, Matthew has discovered personal and collective benefits from his exploration of choral improvisation. He notes:

> I'm a structured person and it was scary to put myself on the line. You know you can't really have reservations when you have to put it out there. But I saw immediate success and the students were really intrigued by it, so it has become easier and easier. I believe that the process of improvisation immediately creates a strong bond within the choir—both musically and socially.

And that's what we want!

Conclusion: Suggestions for Implementation

Approaching choral improvisation may seem daunting to many conductors. However, there are key points, demonstrated by each teacher in this essay that can provide guidance. First, be aware of obstacles to success. Too much correction or critique from either the singers or the conductor inhibits and may stop creativity. The teacher should model a relaxed and positive attitude and encourage every effort at improvisation. Also, collegiate and community conductors should be aware that the more training the singers have, the more they will attempt to formulate and think through their improvisations prior to sharing. While this amount of intellectual thought is helpful in the preparation of notated music, it is likely to inhibit the spontaneous nature of improvisation. Encourage your singers to stay in the moment, and allow the sound to come without judgment.

Lastly, each teacher must present a non-authoritative teaching manner when working with improvisation. Since our singers are keenly aware of our body language and intentions, it is critical that we proceed with an attitude of exploration and fun, leaving the inner choral critic at the rehearsal door. It is very likely that many of our students already have improvisation experience, even if it is not in the context of a formal choral rehearsal or performance. Knowing that we do not have to be an expert to explore choral improvisation helps free directors of our fear of failure.

Following the examples provided in this essay is a mere beginning for the artistry and creativity that lies within each musician and each choral ensemble. When you experience the profound musical and personal connection present in choral improvisation, you will begin to trust the process of group improvisation and trust the creativity present within you and your singers.

Biography

Dr. Susan Williamson is an Assistant Professor and the Director of Choral Music Education at the University of Colorado—Boulder. Dr. Williamson has interests in the choral music of South Africa, where she conducted fieldwork in the summer of 1996. During her work there, she began to develop the topic of her chapter here, i.e., improvisation. In addition to the musical traditions of South Africa, Dr. Williamson's research interests also include informal learning in adolescence, teacher development, and renewal. She has presented her research at conferences of the American Educational Research Association, the Society of Ethnomusicology, the International Society for Music Education, and the Conference of Qualitative Research at the University of Illinois.

Dr. Williamson taught choral music in elementary, middle, and high schools in Indiana, Ohio, Colorado, and Washington. In addition, she conducted "Vivace" of the Northwest Girlchoir, an eighty-two voice auditioned choir in Seattle, Washington.

Dr. Williamson has presented choral clinics at MENC Conferences and the regional conference of the American Choral Directors Association. She is a frequent choral adjudicator and is a popular honor-choir conductor. She has been the featured honor choir conductor in festivals in Washington, Oregon, and British Colombia, Canada.

She received her Bachelor of Music Education from Ball State University, her Master of Music Education from the University of Colorado, and her Ph.D. in Music Education from the University of Washington.

BIBLIOGRAPHY

Azzara, C. D. (1992). *The Effect of Audition-Based Improvisation Techniques on the Music Achievement of Elementary Instrumental Students.* (Doctoral dissertation, Eastman School of Music, University of Rochester). *Dissertation Abstracts International,* 53 (4), 1088A.

Briggs, N.L. (1987). *Creative Improvisation: A Musical Dialogue.* (Doctoral dissertation, University of San Diego). *Dissertation Abstracts International,* 47 (8), 2787A.

Madura. P. (1995). "An Exploratory Investigation of the Assessment of Vocal Jazz Improvisation." *Psychology of Music,* 1995, 23, pp. 48–62.

Madura, P. (1999). *TIPS: Getting started with vocal improvisation.* Reston, VA: MENC Publications.

Sarath, E. (2002). "Improvisation and Curriculum Reform," in *The Handbook of Research on Music Teaching and Learning,* pp. 188–198. Oxford, England: Oxford University Press.

Nardone, P. (1997). *The Experience of Improvisation in Music: A Phenomenological Psychological Analysis.* (Doctoral dissertation, Saybrook Institute). *Dissertation Abstracts International,* 57 (11), 7246B.

Werner, K. (1996). *Effortless Mastery: Liberating the Master Musician Within.* New Albany, IN: Jamey Abersold Jazz, Inc.

Our Lives

Finding Balance: Professional and Personal

Hilary Apfelstadt

Prologue

This is more of an essay than a scholarly paper. In preparing it, I read many books from business and education circles, combed articles in a variety of magazines, and talked to friends and colleagues. In addition, I reflected on my own path as a conductor, an educator, and a mother. It is a path that is familiar to many of you, and seems a likely one for conductors of a younger generation to consider.

There are themes that arise in the readings and the conversations, regardless of the sources. Women are busy; they are stressed; they are overworked; they want to achieve; they see no barriers internally, but they recognize external hurdles and are frustrated by them. They do not find themselves restricted because they are women; indeed they know they are capable of accomplishments equal to men's. Whether or not they always have the opportunities to meet their potential is another matter.

There are women who choose to have children and not go on to graduate school, or to earn a master's degree but not consider a doctorate because they cannot imagine balancing study with raising children. On the other hand, there are women who return to get their doctorates when their children are nearly grown, because they have long harbored the dream of reaching that academic goal. Some women manage to do that with younger children. In all cases, a very supportive spouse, partner and/or extended family seems to be a common thread. These women cannot commute, study, serve as teaching assistants, and be present for their children all at the same time. If, however, they have a strong support system, they can and do succeed with that help. Single mothers may not have the spouse, but have some kind of network of family and friends. To me, their strength is amazing and admirable.

There are, of course, women who choose to be single or to be without children. Yet, they, too, may have responsibilities for parents, siblings or other relatives giving them dual roles as well.

Do men juggle academic or work demands with family responsibilities? Yes, of course they do, but in my observation, it often seems they have a spouse or partner who is taking on a great deal of the "mothering," the typical kinds of tasks that society has long expected women to do. Men can do those things, too, but traditionally, have not done so as much as women. Fortunately, society is changing and there seems to be greater equality than in the past. What men cannot do is give birth, however, and that fundamental difference is but one of several things that separate the genders. According to what I read and observe, many women continue to take care of domestic things almost instinctively, in addition to managing their professional lives. It takes a toll but there are ways to minimize that, some of which are suggested here.

Introduction

Do you remember the Superwoman era? It was the time when She had a career, a happy marriage and children who made her proud, while She contributed to her community through volunteer work at her children's school or in her church or a civic organization. Many of us aspired to that model, as impossible as it was to attain. Perhaps it was we who finally declared her "dead," along with the need to live up to impossible standards.

Right after my second child was born, when I was heading to the University of North Carolina at Greensboro to begin a tenure-track appointment as Assistant Professor, I talked to my mother about the conflicts I felt in taking this position while my children were infants. At the time, they were one year and a newborn, and their father had agreed to stay at home with them for at least the first year we lived in North Carolina. My mother, whose life-long work had been as a homemaker and helpmate to my father, a minister, said, "You didn't get a doctorate to stay home. You need to use your education." I was both relieved and surprised, half-expecting her to say that I should reconsider and take some time out from the workforce. The fact that she did not say that, however, showed not only her parental support of me (because she knew I really wanted to do both) but also her open-mindedness to the way the world was working at that time (1983). She herself had attended teachers' college but after marrying my father, had devoted her life to raising her family and working with him in his congregations. That was the way of her world, the world of a clergy spouse, but she recognized that it was not the way of my world, a generation younger.

During the next few years, my children grew, attended preschool and then began elementary school, and I attained tenure, but not without sacrifices, however. Every summer, they would attend daycare, both to save their spot for winter and also to permit me, and later, their father, to work on all the things we had to do to get tenure: researching, writing articles for publication, planning for the next school year. We always took a family vacation at the beach and usually went to visit grandparents for another few days. The children seemed happy to have structured activities most of the summer; many of their friends did the same thing. I was relieved to know they were cared for while I was meeting the university's year-round expectations, which, by this time, had become my own. It was the only life we knew and it worked fairly well, but I wondered if I would have been a better mother or a better professor/conductor if I had been able to focus on only one of my roles. Would I have been as happy or fulfilled? That is a moot point. When I spend time with these two young adults who are now in their mid-twenties, and see how they have developed into responsible and likeable people, making their way in the world with careers, friends and the potential for having families of their own someday, I am grateful beyond words for the privilege of having them.

Now past middle age, I sometimes wonder how things might have been different had I made other choices. Still, I love my work and my children tell me they are proud of me. Why, then, does that question still nag sometimes? I remember people being surprised when they found out I had a family. It was as though they did not expect me to be a mother if I were busy professionally. At school, I learned not to use the children as a reason for being absent, and remember many times scrambling to juggle schedules on snow days or sick days so that professional life would not be interrupted. Fortunately, attitudes have changed. We have not only maternity leave, but also paternity leave; we can take time to care for sick parents as well as sick children. Those are excellent gains for all of us, regardless of gender. In the mid-eighties, however, in my workplace, that was not the case.

The marriage did not survive. In the mid-seventies, it was expected that one married shortly after college graduation and that is exactly what we did. As we matured, we changed, more than the marriage could withstand. Do I blame that on my pursuit of a career? Not entirely, but I know that my professional intensity was great, and also that because our time with the children was very precious, we focused on them as the center of the marriage to the detriment of our own relationship. In the long run, things have turned out well, however. Both my children's father and I are happily remarried and the children tell us they believe we are each better for it. Still, the fact that they have to deal with blended families and for a time, faced the stigma of a "broken home," does not make me proud. And the question still nags sometimes: how would things have been different had I pursued either a career or a family? Now it is most often raised within the context of mentoring, when young women ask me how to balance professional aspirations with family issues. My own daughter wants her career established before she marries and has children; she seems typical of many of her generation in that regard. At the same time, she tells me I am a role model for her of someone who did "have it all." Perhaps she will attain that status in sequence rather than simultaneously, however.

Background: Women and Dual Responsibilities

As nurturers, women often take responsibility for managing the household and for making medical and dental appointments, getting children's schedules organized to include sports and play dates and rehearsals and trips to the mall, and whatever else fills their days and evenings. No matter how supportive our partners are, we are still the ones who birth the babies. That alone, without regard for how much help we have otherwise, is a unique demand. It takes time for our bodies to recover, for example, and we cannot necessarily do two things well at the same time. So for even a short while, we must be out of the work world. How many times have you heard a woman colleague say, "I need a wife?" What we really need is someone to manage the household and gender doesn't matter. Whoever would take that role would relieve us of some responsibility. That becomes more than ever apparent when we return to work after we bear or adopt children.

As conductors, we are already juggling a multitude of responsibilities: score study, gestural practice, rehearsal preparation, as well as non-musical, organizational tasks associated with our profession, such as overseeing budgets, fundraising, and preparing for tours. We can either do these things concurrently, a bit at a time, or we can approach them in sequence. The latter plan almost never lasts very long, however, because we actually need to keep track of everything at once and it is rare to be able to set aside any aspect of our work life. Score study is a constant; rehearsals occur daily or at least at regular intervals; tour planning takes frequent attention over a period of time, sometimes as much as a year or more. In addition, some things are beyond our control and yet we must be flexible in responding to them: school schedules change with little warning; our best soloist falls ill; personal issues can arise in an instant. Add to this already complex work the challenges of one's personal life, and you have myriad elements to consider.

Matthew Sigman (2005), in "Choral Conductors: A Balancing Act," interviewed several conductors, including Kathy Romey:

> The real balancing act, she says, is the "constant struggle" to maintain a professional career and a family at the same time. Romey has not stepped out of the field for any period of time while raising her children. "I made a conscious decision to do this," she says. "If I had stepped out, it would have been difficult to step back in" (p. 17).

Elizabeth Perle McKenna (1997, p. 122) supports this viewpoint in writing that one of the biggest penalties for dropping out is re-entry. For that reason, many women opt for the "mommy track" or for job-sharing models or for working from home, but even these alternate arrangements can be problematic because they "result in a loss of control" (p. 120). Since conductors cannot conduct from home, some of these alternate job models do not work for us, however!

Unlike Romey, who chose not to step out of her career temporarily to raise her children, some women do "opt out." A recent trend, labeled the "opt-out revolution" is the subject of an article by Brenda Cosman (2006). She says that in the U.S., the number of working mothers actually decreased in 2006 to 55% from 59% in 2000. In Canada, only Alberta appears to have followed suit. Still there is some evidence that women are choosing to stay home when the workplace is not family friendly. Author Cosman points out that women need to be aware of the risks, especially financial ones, and like Kathy Romey, suggests that it might not be easy to opt back in when the time comes.

Romey (Sigman, 2005, p. 18) "acknowledges that the personal choices she has made are similar to those professionals in all fields struggle with, and for which there are no easy answers. Both she and Patrick, her husband of twenty-five years, have made concessions to support the other's career. After the birth of their second child, Patrick was a stay-at-home dad for two years."

Indeed, McKenna (1997, p. 223) says "family issues are not the sole domain of women." Judith Warner (2005, book jacket) writes that "all of us—men, women, society at large—need to demand more support for our families from our government, from our workplaces, and from one another" (book jacket). If we want or need change, we need to ask for it.

McKenna (1997, p. 226) notes that more men are valuing family and work equally. At the same time, she warns women that it is impossible to "do it all," even though many of us "still expect it." (p. 62). She tell us that women "define ourselves through our careers," by what we do rather then who we are, and the result is that who we are becomes what we do. She says, "there is a price for this work-based identity, a price for success that we pay for with our lives" (p. 62). Among the worst prices for some women, she notes, is depression (p. 80). Mitigating factors are the delay of family; the stress of keeping family life, once it happens, from affecting work life; taking jobs that are more routine and involve less authority in exchange for more time with family (p.85); decreased income in exchange for diminished work responsibilities or less time on the job. For some people, money equates with success (p. 153) and diminished income means diminished success and value.

Although McKenna (1997, pp. 184–185) is writing primarily about women in business, she offers a number of suggestions relevant to women conductors struggling to find balance. She suggests that women must change "the way we value success and the way we judge our progress toward it," recognizing that one's career is "only one tile of a mosaic of life's meaning." She recommends the following:

1. Avoid being the "good girl," and accept that you cannot please everyone (p. 189).

2. Stand up for yourself in the workplace (p. 189).

3. Learn to fail; accept that perfection is not realistic (p. 190). [Note: I try to distinguish between "excellence" and "perfection," knowing that many of us musicians are profoundly Type A personalities and perfectionists, but it is not an easy task.]

4. Stop trying to be so "successful" (p. 193). [Note: Again, McKenna means this in the typical societal terms of success, where money, recognition and power equate with success. Most classically trained musicians do not have to worry about having too much money but we can easily thrive on recognition.]

5. Take your personal life to the office with you (p. 194).

6. Recognize the importance of community and colleagues (p. 195). [Note: how many of us are the only choral conductor in our school or community, or perhaps one of a small number? We must make connections with our colleagues, no matter where they are.]

7. Live by what you treasure (p. 200).

8. Recognize that there is no such thing as "women's work" (p. 202).

9. Work "outside the box" (p. 203).

McKenna suggests that balance between personal and professional demands is attainable: "The answer to making work and life enjoyable and fulfilling lies in using the two separate forces in a balanced way so that they combine to form a whole" (p. 171). She says that if women rely on the male model for success (accomplishment, power and money, all external factors), they are overlooking the internal sources: family, friends, and time. If one's inner life balances the outer, it enables us to "value ourselves for who we are, not what we do" (pp. 171–172). The image of a potter shaping clay with two hands, one inside and one outside the pot, is a good visual symbol for this balance.

Women in Academia

Women in academia have particular requirements, one of the most obvious being their potential need for time off for childbirth and subsequent accommodations to support their parental responsibilities. Jean Milew (2005, p. 13) writes poignantly of her first-hand experiences as a young graduate student weighing the demands of pregnancy, motherhood and academic work. She speaks of timing her pregnancy to coincide with the academic calendar so she would have the summer with her baby, and of her single-minded dedication to her "two passions," her daughter and her music, while completing her Ph.D. in composition. Just after graduation, she happened on an article by Mary Ann Mason and Marc Goulden, "Do Babies Matter?" (2002) and found that her instinct that babies do matter to female academics and their quest for tenure was indeed correct. According to Milew, Mason and Goulden "cite two leading theories that attempt to explain" the fact that "since 1975 consistent gender gaps in tenure and salary have not improved":

> The first is the familiar metaphor of the "glass ceiling," where discrimination excludes the majority of women from advancing past a certain rank. The second theory, "work versus family," reflects the nature of most of the American workplace, with its inflexible minimum forty-hour, five-day workweek that forces women to choose one or the other.

Milew goes on to summarize Mason and Goulden's findings that "the timing of having children matters significantly." The earlier the baby's arrival in the woman's tenure quest, the more likely the woman is not to achieve tenure.

"Women who do attain tenure, according to Mason and Goulden, are unlikely to have children and are also more likely to remain single." On the other hand, if the arrival of babies is delayed, women with children may advance just as well as those single women. Often, however, these women have only one child, presumably because of "age-related fertility factors" (p. 13).

Milew acknowledges that this issue is not related only to academic careers, as we have earlier noted in this article. She recommends that women must become more supportive of each other, setting aside notions of judgment about whose choices are better, stay-at-home mothers or working mothers. No matter what the lifestyle one chooses, "raising children takes time, and only an acknowledgement of that basic fact can ultimately allow women to achieve their career goals, and more importantly, raise their children better" (p. 15).

Universities have responded to this issue in various ways. "Stopping the tenure clock" is a familiar one that allows parents (not just women) to take time for the birth or adoption of a child and not have it count toward tenure. In 2005, the Ohio State University prepared a Status Report on Women at the university, under the auspices of the President's Council on Women's Issues. Kate Haller, Chair of the Council, cites the Mason and Goulden study as compatible with findings at the Ohio State University. She notes that data compiled for the Status Report "illustrate the slow growth, in both hiring and retention, highlighted by Mason and Golden [*sic*]" (2005, Message from the Chair).

Various initiatives to address the situation include proposing flexible work loads for tenure-track faculty, improving university child care services, and establishment of the President's and Provost's Leadership Institute, a program designed to prepare more women for leadership positions in the university. A number of "Family Friendly Rules and Polices" are described on the Human Resources website: extending the probationary period/tolling the tenure clock; paid parental leave; dual career hiring policy and spousal placement services. All of these are designed to make the university community more accommodating of its employees' need to balance personal and professional issues (http://hr.osu.edu/worklife/children.aspx).

In recognition of National Work and Family Month in October 2006, the OSU *onCampus* newspaper contained an article entitled, "Feeling balanced" (19 October 2006). Author Adam King reports that Elena Irwin, an associate professor in the Department of Agricultural, Environmental and Developmental Economics, "followed a part-time tenure track because she felt overwhelmed four years ago while raising her first son (she now has two) and working sixty-hour weeks." He also cites a case of job-sharing by two young mothers in the University Honors and Scholars Center. All three women, whether faculty or staff members, are highly positive about their experiences. These situations are examples of the Family Friendly Rules in practice.

Joan K. Peters (1997, p. 5) notes that "a mother's self-development is an asset to the development of her children" and policies such as those above allow mothers (and fathers) to develop themselves through sustaining their careers at a compatible level. Peters points out that customizing parental arrangements is a good solution; whatever suits the family is acceptable (p. 87). She also says that mother-reared children have one and a quarter nurturers, but that father-reared children actually have two because the mother steps in when she gets home (p. 113).

WOMEN IN PERFORMANCE

Not all musician mothers are in academia. Performers outside academic circles face similar challenges. The June 2004 issue of *Classical Singer* focuses on this topic in articles entitled: "My Mom's a Diva! Can Motherhood and Divahood Co-Exist?" and "Balancing Career and Family in All Stages of Life." A third feature article is about Suzanna Guzman, a professional opera singer who "considers singing the perfect part-time job for a single parent" (Riberdy, 2004, p. 39).

Opera singer Mary Jane Johnson says the most difficult part of balancing a family and career was "separation" (Clarke, 2004, p. 25). She had two adopted children from whom she had to be apart sometimes while studying or coaching. She solved the issue to some degree through frequent phone calls, especially after the children were too old to travel with her. Johnson tells of the highs and lows of balancing a career and family: it enabled the family to travel to exciting places, but it also meant that she was away when both her parents died and had to fly home from England and Australia respectively. Pacing her performing engagements was another solution that assured her time at home between major performances.

In response to a question about whether putting family first held back Johnson's career, and whether it was worthwhile, she said,

> Yes, and yes. In the end, you have to look back and be happy with what you did. I could have taken a different route, but I just chose to balance it this way. And I think that decision is the reason my life is still balanced today (p. 26).

She goes on to say "the secret of my success is my fabulous husband!" (p. 27) a statement that reinforces the value of a support system. Johnson says that her secure relationship and personal happiness enabled her to have a career, and make things work for herself and her family, and advises young people to "be happy first" (p. 29).

Kathryn Swenson (2004, p. 19), who became a faculty member at the Eastman School of Music after a career as a professional singer, reiterates the need for a supportive partner or spouse as she describes the challenges of balancing one's personal and work lives. Like Mary Jane Johnson, Swenson married young before her career expanded, but the fact that her husband is a singer presented its own issues. Juggling performance obligations that have one person out of the country at times is not easy, according to Swenson. She is firm in her belief that family comes first, however, and says that she regrets the fact that young singers tell her "they don't audition wearing wedding rings or reveal they have children." She advises them to "create a family," whether one's own or comprising a group of chorus singers, students or friends. Swenson attributes part of her success to her husband's willingness to share childcare equally and the existence of good hired caregivers, when necessary. Reading her testimony gives one confidence that here is a professional singer who has happily made a conscious decision to teach in order to mentor aspiring professionals, and whose life is in balance as best it can be.

A single parent, singer Suzanne Guzman (2004, p. 39) had to rely on hired help rather than family to help her raise her son, but found opera companies helpful and experienced in assisting with making arrangements. She admits that being a mezzo is an asset in that her roles are often less demanding than soprano roles and she is able to conserve her energy for her son. Finding that "opera companies have become far more friendly" about family issues, Guzman notes, "many, many opera singers are realizing that a secret to a happy life is to have those that you love with you as much as you can." For her, "singing is the best part-time job a single parent could ever have."

Women in the Middle

Women (and men) often find themselves caught in a bind between their professional responsibilities and their obligations as children of aging parents. In addition to being parents, many baby-boomers are themselves the children of elderly people who need help. The so-called "sandwich generation" is caught between needs of their parents and their children, all the while trying to maintain their careers. For years, I managed my mother's business from a distance of more than a thousand miles, relying on the phone, e-mail, and trips that increased in number as my mother's health deteriorated. Those trips included meetings with bankers and lawyers, interviews with potential caregivers, moving Mother out of her home, preparing the house for sale, organizing and selling many of the contents, selecting a nursing home, and spending many days at the hospital trying to navigate a challenging healthcare system with overworked nurses and other medical staff. My sister, who lived in the same city as our mother, visited her almost daily and our phone calls increased in number as time passed. In the last year, I was constantly at the ready to be with my mother should her condition worsen. Always one to support my career, my mother did not expect me to be with her constantly so my absence plagued me more than it did her, I think. In retrospect, I can say I did my best but there is always the nagging sense that it was not enough.

Mary Lou Quinlan (2006, p. 53) writes about "The Daughter Track," describing the challenges of being "caught between two competing priorities: sustaining a hard-won career and tending to parents who are living longer and needing more of our help." She gives examples of several women who cared for their parents in a variety of ways, some by leaving their jobs, some by sharing their homes with their parents, and all at emotional expense, sometimes financial as well. Quinlan says "discovering at midlife that you have a second career as caregiver comes with its own set of silent setbacks: Some of us miss out on promotions and forgo relocation offers. The underlying stress erodes our productivity. And our savings suffer, thanks to the escalating cost of care" (p. 54).

One issue raised in the article is that it is more often the female offspring than the male who care for their parents and suggests that is why it is not called the "son track," quoting Gina Petruccelli: "I believe that men are solution seekers and women are more patient" (p. 54). On the other hand, Barbara Kantrowitz and Karen Springen, writing in the June 18, 2007 issue of *Newsweek,* cite the case of Tim Kidwell, 56, who recently left his position as creative director for an ad agency in order to care for his mother, 78, who has Alzheimer's, and his father, 80, who has leukemia. Mr. Kidwell, who is now freelancing, says "you do what you feel is most important" (p. 56). The article contains additional examples of people giving up jobs to care for aging parents or even ill spouses and tells of the toll it takes, emotionally, physically and financially.

One of the most serious outcomes of the "daughter (or son) track" is stress, both on the individual caretaker and on the family. Kantrowitz and Springer (2007, p. 56) say:

> The strain of nursing an ailing parent often exacerbates long-simmering family tensions. Sons or daughters who never got along with their parents are the most likely to feel trapped by their obligations . . . Sibling relationships can also fray—especially when one son or daughter lives nearby and others are far away.

When the parent is accustomed to having control, giving it to a child can be a difficult thing. Power struggles can arise as the child feels the effects of role reversal, having to serve as the parent to one's own parent.

Finally, Quinlan (2006, p. 56) says "there's one daughter-track issue that never seems to get resolved: the guilt of never doing quite enough." She tells of her own conflicts between her professional side ("rational, calm and precise") and her personal side ("vigilant, loving and ready to protect") but says that the latter is more likely to outweigh the former. "No matter how successful I become, I am their daughter, first, last and always."

Georgia Witkin (2000, p. 280) discusses the effects of the "sandwich generation" on women, specifically noting the effects of caring for aging parents whether close by or at a distance. She also addresses divorce, remarriage and stepfamilies, and widowhood as having unique effects on women. Among her suggestions for reducing stress are relying on friendships, especially with other females; self-help in terms of exercise, rest, and nutrition; relaxation and meditation. She suggests that women must learn to say "no" without guilt or excuses and to learn to separate what we can control from what we cannot: "Being in control is not a goal for all times and all situations. To hold onto our sense of control, we must learn how to let ourselves go." In other words, "we have to stop pursuing control when circumstances are beyond our control" (p. 68).

Musicians exist in a world where the pursuit of excellence, even perfection, is key, and to accomplish that, we often seek control. We teach classes and conduct rehearsals, controlling (or so we think) both the process and the product. Conductors lead ensembles, controlling tempo, articulation, style, dynamics, and myriad other musical elements. We are conditioned to be in control. We are often inordinately busy, working well beyond the "nine to five" parameters. In addition to our primary jobs, we may have part-time ones as well, conducting a church choir in addition to teaching in a school or university, for example. Many of us travel to guest conduct or to attend conferences.

Singer Michelle Kunz (2006, pp. 49–53) offers many practical suggestions for performers who spend considerable time "on the road." Many of these are applicable to women conductors in similar circumstances, both at home and while away.

Witkin (2000, p. 95) suggests that although we may sense that we are overcommitted, we habituate or cope, thus appearing to handle huge workloads successfully. Unfortunately, over-crowded schedules do not accommodate emergencies. She says that although occasional overload is manageable, chronic overload is not, citing the following as some of the causes of chronic overload: disabled children, infertility issues, single parenting and acting as caregivers for aging relatives.

Conditioned by our upbringing to "to take care of everyone else and everything else first," we tend to give ourselves only whatever "leftover time" remaining (Witkin, 2000, pp. 97–98). Witkin suggests we need to put ourselves first and give ourselves permission to rest and relax. "Women who give themselves the gift of time give themselves an important stress management tool" (p. 99). She suggests that working mothers continue to try to do a lot at home and develop a conflict between their roles as a professional and as a homemaker. She notes that women in happy relationships and with low job stress are the least likely to suffer from depression (p. 102).

Knowing that the life of a musician, a conductor/teacher, a performer does not qualify as "low job stress," I offer the following suggestions, gleaned from readings, observation and self-knowledge, albeit gained in later life.

Commonsense Advice

1. *Be prepared: control what you can.* Devote premium time for score study, even if it means getting to work before anyone else does; score study is basic to everything we do as conductors. Restrict e-mail response to a couple of times a day. If you start the day with e-mail, you can sacrifice your most productive study/preparation time. If you check near the end of your day, you can dispense with a lot of things that might otherwise hold you back the next day. The same applies to returning phone calls: do it at specific times. Allocate a few minutes to this task rather than letting it absorb bits of time throughout the day.

2. *Be flexible so you can better cope with what you cannot control.* Plan a bit of "dead time" in each workday so you can deal with emergencies while still knowing you haven't used every minute of your workday. The downtime allows for overflow from the times you can't control.

3. *Be proactive about guarding your time:* Screen calls; prioritize e-mail; discourage idle chatter (learn to stand up when it's time to usher someone out); close your door when you need to concentrate without interruptions. Plan for exercise; plan for breaks; write in self-appointments. If the latter is the only way to get personal time, do it. I read about a woman who had a weekly appointment with a phantom visitor; during that weekly appointment, she took no calls and allowed no interruptions. As though she had a client, she gave herself fully to that time. It was hers to use as she wished and she knew she could count on that freedom regularly.

4. *Be present to the moment:* When you are involved in something, focus on it one-hundred percent. One big time-waster is multi-tasking to the extent that nothing gets full attention while a lot of things get a little attention. I tell choir members that for the forty-eight minutes they are in rehearsal, they can do nothing about their physics test or personal issues, but they can improve their singing and contribute to the ensemble. Likewise, when we conductors are engaged in rehearsal or score study or even a meeting of some sort, we can focus on that event and give it full attention. Uni-tasking may be more productive in the long run than multi-tasking. Women have long prided themselves on that ability but it may not do our needs justice.

5. *Believe that "no" is a complete sentence.* Women are notorious for being "pleasers," and trying to keep everyone happy. We cannot say "yes" to everything and must learn early on that in our profession, some "yes's" are more valuable than others. There are "yes" activities that are expected of us on the tenure track, for example. We need to perform, to write, and to participate in professional organizations. To do all of this well, however, we need the time to devote to each. If we allow too many service requests to crowd our schedules, for example, we do not have time to do the kind of performing and research that might make us better conductors. Knowing what "counts" or does not is part of the professional world that we must attend to with great intensity.

For me, the expression, "Don't do it if it doesn't count," is one fraught with frustration. We can become so pragmatic that we don't do anything unless it "counts." That is unfortunate. On the other hand, if service is a component of your employer's expectations, there are certain opportunities in professional organizations that one must take. For example, when you choose to be involved with schools in your local area, visiting choral groups prior to contest and giving the teachers and students some constructive comments, is a good thing. If you do so much of this, however, that your absences affect your own classes and ensembles, then perhaps it is time to re-think your priorities. A good mentor will help you know what is important to do; your conscience will tell you the rest.

There are non-professional demands on us for service as well. Extra tasks like sending out letters to neighbors for a community organization may have to go by the wayside. For years, I did that for various health organizations' annual campaigns. It was important to me not to say no to these good agencies, but the time came when I had so much going on that to agree to doing that one more time became a burden and I simply had to say "no."

6. *Be willing to put yourself first when necessary.* The hardest thing for many of us is learning to allocate personal time. In Number 3 above, I mention guarding your time, especially relative to your workday. This present section is about taking time to nurture yourself.

Author Stephen Covey (1989, 2004, p. 287), in *Seven Habits of Highly Effective People*, talks about the need to "sharpen the saw" and presents an image of a woodcutter who is so busy cutting wood that he doesn't take time to sharpen the saw. The duller the blade gets, the slower his progress. Taking a few minutes to remedy the situation would save him a lot of time in the long run. For me, sharpening the saw can take several forms: it may be taking time to read something for spiritual renewal every day; it may be about getting on the treadmill or taking a walk outdoors; it may be about listening to music for sheer enjoyment. For others, it may be about scheduling family time or a regular "date night" with a spouse or partner; it may be about visiting an elderly relative regularly; it may be about volunteering at a hospital or taking a shut-in a meal or bulletin from your church. Each of these things is time consuming but valuable in that it makes us feel better physically or mentally or both. Then, refreshed and feeling that we have made a difference, we can return to our routine.

We are people first, musicians and conductors second. As choral conductors, the instruments we conduct most often are human instruments. Nurturing our own humanity makes us better models.

7. *Recognize that "doing it all" may not happen all at once.* Perspective is a humbling and leveling thing. After more than three decades of teaching, I now see that over that time, I have accomplished some overall balance in my

life. Having a career and a family, taking the steps to do both, has sometimes been a huge challenge. At times, one took precedence over the other. Several years ago, emergency surgery literally stopped me in my tracks. For the first time in nearly thirty years, I did not return to teaching in the fall quarter; it was a sobering time. The need to recuperate provided a time to reflect and was, in retrospect, a gift. It taught me to consider priorities, as I had never done before.

Over the years, I have held various offices in ACDA, have conducted my choirs at ACDA and MENC conventions, and have done a good deal of guest conducting in various places. When my children were small, I lacked the experience to lead ACDA, and would have been foolish to try; I simply did not have the know-how to do that. Being a parent as well as a conductor/educator, however, taught me many skills that serve me well today in a national leadership position. Over the span of my life then, I have come closer to "doing it all" than I did at age forty.

As personal and professional responsibilities ebb and flow, so, too, does our response and involvement. As an empty nester, I now have the time to travel and to be involved with ACDA at the national level. When my children were in high school, I served as Central Division ACDA President. It was a busy time, but the task less demanding than serving as national president. With clear conscience, I can devote myself to those responsibilities knowing that my children no longer need me on a day-to-day basis.

CODA

For me, it has been a matter of juggling and balancing, taking opportunities as they came, weighing possible output and demands with potential results. There is no point in living with regret or dwelling on what might have been; each person's life develops its own path. At this point, it is enough to say that this life has had variety and good intent. Relatively late I have learned that it is all right, even wise, to let personal decisions override professional ones sometimes. Doing one's best is the best one can do. My parents' two mantras were "mind over matter," and "grace under pressure." Learning to work hard, to push oneself, to keep goals in mind is part of the first; learning to be flexible and make the best of things is part of the second.

Morgenstern (2004, p. 21) notes that "the top-tier performers are deeply committed to their work/life balance. In her experience, "the most successful workers create a balance that ensures they are energized, refreshed and renewed every day." Is that too idealistic for us in our stress-laden profession? I sometimes think if we could allow our music to have the same almost-therapeutic effect it has on some of our audiences, we would benefit greatly.

All around me are women who have made wonderful contributions to their professions, who have had children (or not), who have contributed to their communities and enriched the lives of many other people. As society continues to grow in appreciation of women's multiple roles, it enables us to face a better future than our mothers and grandmothers did. We have the ability to soar both professionally and personally, albeit not without a lot of hard work to achieve balance between the two dimensions. We will attain equality in our profession as choral conductors if we choose to make decisions that will allow that. The best education, the best opportunities, the best outcomes—those are ours for the seeking.

Biography

A biography for Hillary Apfelstadt appears earlier in this book after the chapter "Women Conductors as Leaders and Mentors."

References

Clarke, D. M. (2004). "My Mom's a Diva! Can Motherhood and Divahood Co-Exist?" *Classical Singer*, 17 (6), 20–23, 39.

Cossman, B. (24 July 2006). "The Opt-Out Revolution: The Changing Narratives of Motherhood Must be Closely Examined." *News@UofT*. Retrieved 17 August 2006 from http://www.news.utoronto.ca/bin6/thoughts/060724-2461.asp

Covey, Stephen. *Seven Habits of Highly Effective People.* New York: Free Press, 1989, 2004.

Kantrowitz, B. and Springen, K. (18 June 2007). "Confronting Alzheimer's." *Newsweek*, CXLIX (25), 55–56, 59–61.

King, A. (19 October 2006). "Feeling Balanced." *OnCampus*, 36 (6), 1, 10.

Kunz, M. (2006). "Take Your Family to Work—Every Day!" *Classical Singer* 19 (2), 46–47, 49–54.

Mason, M. A. and Goulden, M. (2002). "Do Babies Matter?" *Academe* 88 (6), 21–27.

McKenna, E. P. (1997). *When Work Doesn't Work Anymore: Women, Work and Identity.* New York: Delacorte Press.

Milew, J. (2005). "The Voiceless Who Need to Shout: Issues Confronting Women and Children in Academia." *Journal of the IAWM (International Alliance for Women in Music)*, 11 (1), 12–15.

Morgenstern, J. (2004). *Making Work Work.* New York: Fireside.

Peters, J.K. (1997). *When Mothers Work.* Reading, MA: Addison-Wesley.

Quinlan, M. L. (July/August 2006). "The Daughter Track." *More*, 9 (6), 53–54, 56.

Riberdy, A. (2004). "Suzanna Guzman: Why Singing is the Best Part Time Job." *Classical Singer*, 17 (6), 20–23, 39.

Sigman, M. (2005). "Choral Conductors: A Balancing Act." *The Voice of Chorus America*, 28 (4), 17–21, 24.

Swenson, K. C. (2004). "Balancing Career and Family in All Stages of Life." *Classical Singer*, 17 (6), 18–19, 30–31.

Warner, J. (2005). *Perfect Madness: Motherhood in the Age of Anxiety.* New York: Riverhead Books.

Witkin, G. (2000). *The Female Stress Syndrome Survival Guide.* New York: Newmarket Press.

Websites

Office of Academic Affairs website, The Ohio State University http://oaa.osu.edu/faculty_staff.php

Office of Human Resources website, The Ohio State University http://hr.osu.edu/worklife/children.aspx

Status Report on Women at the Ohio State University (2005). Brochure. Electronic access: www.womensplace.osu.edu or ballam.1@osu.edu

Nadia and Me

Harriet Simons

In July 1959, Europe was experiencing a searing heat wave. I was spending my first and only summer at the Conservatoire Americaine in Fontainebleau, France. One wing of the beautiful summer palace of Napoleon served as our school. Even without air-conditioning, our wing was nice and cool, and a pleasant place to be during the heat of the day. The carp pond beyond the palace also beckoned us on rare unscheduled afternoons.

We music students from America were in Fontainebleau expecting to extend our previous education via study with the French masters. I was a twenty-three year old music teacher from Iowa with a Bachelor's degree from a fine university. Having graduated with honors two years previously, I had begun a career in my chosen field of choral conducting. The high school choirs and small vocal ensembles that I conducted had received consistently superior ratings in Iowa music festivals. My career was blossoming; I felt as if I was on the brink of a successful career, but in the back of my mind I suspected that there was yet more that I could learn.

I asked Margaret Hillis, the well-known conductor of the Chicago Symphony Chorus, what steps she might recommend I take to further my education in choral conducting. She suggested that I consider studying in France with world-famous Nadia Boulanger. Boulanger had been the mentor of numerous American composers, but she also had been recognized as a conductor. Since I had enormous regard for Ms. Hillis, I decided to apply to the Conservatoire Americaine's Conducting program at Fontainebleau and was accepted. I embarked eagerly on my first European voyage and after several days at sea and a week's introductory tour of the continent, found myself in Fontainebleau on 1 July at a garden cocktail party hosted by Mlle Boulanger.

Running late, the Fontainebleau-bound tour group joined the party-in-progress. Those already there informed us that we had missed the ear-training exam that determined one's placement in the solfège classes taught by Annette Dieudonné. Concerned, I approached Mlle, introduced myself, and apologized for having missed the exam. Mlle was very kind and suggested that I just enroll myself in any one of the five sections until I discovered if that section was too easy or too difficult. After that, I could determine which section was most appropriate for me. I chose Section Three (neither the best nor the worst). Thus began my summer of self-discovery.

Hot as that summer was, the female students soon learned that wearing shorts was not an option. At Fontainebleau in July 1959, we were expected to be properly dressed at all times. Another rule was that we were to stand when Mlle entered the classroom. Sometimes it seemed that Boulanger took on the role of mother as well as teacher. Whatever the circumstance, it was immediately clear that everything counted. We learned discipline even before we had received our first class assignments.

On 1 July, we had been at the garden party. On 2 July, I had my first lesson in conducting. By 3 July, I was very angry at all former teachers and professors for somehow failing to teach me as much as I needed to know in order to prepare me for life as a professional musician. My education in music had finally begun!

My first lesson began with a question from Mlle Boulanger. "Miss Simons, what kind of a sight-reader (at keyboard) are you?" Under normal circumstances, I was considered to be a pretty good sight-reader. After all, I had earned some spending money as an undergraduate by sight-reading song literature accompaniments in the studio of a voice professor. On my first day alone with Boulanger, however, I was intimidated into modesty and mumbled to her that I was "fairly decent" as a sight-reader. To which Mlle demanded, "Well, don't you know for sure? Are you a good or a bad sight-reader?" I gulped and took a big chance by replying, "Good." To which she replied, "Fine! Come here and sight-read this!"

I sat down at the piano. She sat next to me. On the rack was the full score of Stravinsky's *Dumbarton Oaks Concerto*. Boulanger had conducted its first performance, although I was unaware of that fact at the time. I had never before played an orchestral score on the piano. Although I was familiar with transpositions and had conducted from instrumental scores in my undergraduate conducting class, it had never occurred to me that conductors were expected to *play* them at the keyboard! Luckily, this work on the rack was for chamber orchestra, and only the clarinet and horn demanded transposition. There was a long pause as I calculated what I was about to attempt. Finally, Mlle said, "I'll play the parts you miss." Naïvely, I asked, "Shall I play it up to tempo?" "Naturally!" she replied. And we were off! I believe I played only the flute and violin and maybe some double bass, but up to tempo! She played the rest.

I don't remember how far we got into the work, but Mlle eventually called a halt to the procedure and said I should play as much as I could with the left hand and—conduct with my right! Tears welled up in my eyes. What was I to do about the measure of 5/16 followed by 2/8 and 2/4? She taught me many things in that first encounter. At one point I failed to notice a clef change in the bassoon part. The memory of that minor slip still haunts me today.

Nadia Boulanger's incredibly high expectations became painfully clear for her new students in the first lesson she taught them. One sensed immediately that the student's confidence, even if feigned, was preferable to indecision. I wasn't exactly fabricating when I said I was a good sight-reader. But it was instantly clear to me that I had darn well *better* become a good sight-reader, starting right now! By the end of that first lesson, I was determined to master score-reading at the keyboard and anything else this incredible teacher might ask of me.

I had gone to France to study conducting, but I soon discovered that all of us, regardless of intended focus of study, spent most of our time in classes of harmony and solfège. We also participated in choral rehearsals that summer of Bach's Cantata 4 and Fauré's Requiem, works we also studied in conducting class. I thought, of course, that my days studying music theory were long behind me. I was not anxious to resume that study or to do the exercises in Dubois' 1921 *Traité d'Harmonie*. I much preferred singing the exercises in Hindemith's 1946 *Elementary Training for Musicians*, even though we had to use the system of "fixed do." We were expected to sing, play harmonic progressions, conduct and do music theory every day. All elements seemed to be considered equally important. Each student was to check the bulletin board to see what the next assignment would be. Many years passed before I learned that there was more than one meaning for the initials "N.B." at the bottom of a posting.

Boulanger stressed physical and mental independence in the conducting class, and gave us exercises to work on these important principles. Our very first class consisted of playing dictated rhythms at the keyboard—such as duple in the left hand and triple in the right. For example, she would speak something like, "one and two and," while we played a single note on the keyboard. Once a steady tempo was established, we were to simultaneously play a duple rhythm with the left hand and a triple rhythm with the right and vice versa. Exercises taught by Nadia Boulanger on that first day served me well over the years in the many conducting classes that I taught. Two of them were:

1. Place one hand on a table with the second and fourth fingers immobilized. Then, to work on mental and physical independence, we were to "play" an imagined arpeggio (1–3–5–3–1) keeping fingers two and four stationary.

2. Conduct a sequence of 2/4, 3/4, 4/4 and reverse until the tempo was absolutely steady. Then, while listening to her speaking instructions or asking questions, we were to continue conducting, in order to maintain patterns and tempo without being distracted by other things.

Students that summer each day also had to memorize Bach chorales and play a series of cadences. Indeed, most of my practice time as a conducting student was spent on those cadences. One was expected to play the series in any key, starting on major chords, minor chords, augmented chords and diminished chords. The cadences were studied in a particular order, beginning with the most basic one: I–IV–V–I in a major key, and becoming more complex.

On one of the two most memorable days for me that summer, I was called upon in harmony class to demonstrate my proficiency in playing the cadences. I had practiced a great deal, and was not particularly nervous as I approached the piano. "What key do you wish?" I asked. "Oh!" said Mlle to the class. "She can play in any key! Well, then, please play in F# Major." My heart sunk. But I *had* practiced in every key. I had to remain calm. I was pretty sure I could play the cadences in F# Major if I concentrated. I took a deep breath and played the first two chords, slowly and correctly. She stopped me. They weren't legato enough. I began again, played the two chords and was stopped. The four notes in the chord were not equally balanced. We started again. This time I got through four chords. She then told me to play the bass with the right hand and the other parts with the left. I did that successfully. Then, she had me play only the soprano, tenor and bass while singing the alto (in "fixed do" solfège, of course!) And on and on it went for thirty-five minutes. The class was deathly silent. I was concentrating as hard as I have ever concentrated in my life. I did not make a mistake as she kept adding things for me to do. The last thing I remember about that experience is that she finally said, "Don't look at the keyboard!"

Nadia Boulanger's approach to teaching was a far cry from what I had experienced in the United States. People who were "in the know" said that she was the most demanding of the students whom she had decided were worth her time. Even Aaron Copland, who studied with Boulanger from

1921–1924, quoted her in a 1967 *Los Angeles Times* interview: "I know I am exacting. I say to my students, 'So long as I am exacting you can have hope. If I am nice, that is a bad sign.'"

Many of my fellow students that summer were almost ignored by her. Sometimes I wanted to be! I tried to "hide" in harmony class—positioning myself in the back row or keeping my head down when Mlle asked a question. It didn't work. My complaints in letters to my parents referred often to her "picking" on me.

The private lessons continued. My diary entry for 14 July says, "I didn't cry! Hallelujah!" Still, I began to question my earlier success as a music teacher. Many times in my lesson when I did something incorrectly (such as doubling a leading tone). Mlle would rest her head on her arms, let out an exasperated sigh, and say, "My dear, I am sure that you are very successful in the United States, but *here*, this will not do!"

The harmonization we did in the lessons was similar, yet different from what I had encountered in first-year theory in the United States. Here, it was most important that each part have melodic interest—that the alto part, for example, flow as a musical line instead of just filling in a chord. In successive private lessons, I was to play my harmonizations that I had improved from the previous lesson. Each new harmonization was to be re-done and Scotch-taped (side-hinged) over the one I had previously presented so that she could see the improvements made week to week. I greatly missed the American custom of receiving letter grades for my work. Even a gold star would have been appreciated! No matter how hard I worked, there seemed to be no moment of final achievement. There always was more to learn.

By the fourth week, I was turning from depression to anger. I had come to Fontainebleau to study conducting, and it seemed all I was doing was harmony, sight-singing, dictation and keyboard. I felt I was being ignored in conducting class. Two persons were called upon frequently and there I sat! I was wondering about my future life in music. Should I continue? Should I go to graduate school? Had I made a mistake by quitting my job as a high school choral conductor? Finally, since I was doing very well in Annette Dieudonné's solfège class, I decided to confide in her and subsequently spelled out my frustrations.

Students of Nadia Boulanger were also students of Annette Dieudonné. The two were a wonderful team, musically and temperamentally. It was in the solfège class that my ear was strengthened by exercises in sight-singing and dictation. When I presented my concerns to Mlle Dieudonné, she was sympathetic and promised to speak with Mlle Boulanger, which she did. The very next day, I was called upon by Mlle Boulanger to conduct the Stravinsky *Dumbarton Oaks* in class. Not only did I get to conduct, I was also asked to play the transposed clarinet part in our "keyboard orchestra"—and was complimented for how well I did! Proud of myself and accepting of my esteemed professor's compliments, I breathed a sigh of relief.

The conducting students in 1959 were working on the Fauré Requiem and the *Dumbarton Oaks* in anticipation of the 17 August conducting competition, which was to be a kind of public final exam. In class, only three of us now were working on the Stravinsky. At the end of the previously-cited class period, Mlle announced that I would join the other two in conducting the Stravinsky in the competition. Needless to say, I was elated! I was floating on air as I went off to lunch with my friends.

A couple of hours later, in the day's second conducting class (where we worked on the Fauré Requiem) Mlle unexpectedly said that she had changed her mind and that I would *not* be conducting the Stravinsky in the upcoming competition—that the *Dumbarton Oaks Concerto* was too difficult for me. I was, of course, devastated.

It seemed to be part of Mlle Boulanger's pedagogical approach to keep students "off guard." Just when one thought he or she knew what to expect, there would come a "surprise." Again, the older and more experienced students would tell us that this was her way of determining the strength of our talent and motivation. Others said that she was just harder on the women in her classes.

I was quite upset by her announcement in front of the class that I would not be allowed to compete on the Stravinsky. I had spent many hours memorizing the difficult score. It now seemed pointless to continue that mental exercise. My partner in memorizing the Stravinsky was fellow-student Fiora Contino. Every morning the two of us had worked for at least an hour on it. Fiora urged me not to quit, because she was sure this was a test of my motivation and that Mlle Boulanger would probably call on me again. Therefore, I continued to work on the score, and Fiora was ultimately proven right. Ten days later, Mlle asked me in my 7:45 a.m. lesson if I had memorized the Stravinsky. I said, "Yes," with my fingers crossed behind my back. The entire lesson, then, was spent on conducting the *Dumbarton Oaks*—using the score, even though it was to be memorized for the competition. The experience was exhilarating. I was ecstatic. At the end of the lesson, Mlle told me that I would, indeed, conduct that work in the competition—a mere six days hence.

She didn't know that three of those days I was planning to spend on a holiday in Switzerland!

I arrived back in Paris at 7:10 a.m. on the day of the competition. Along with Swiss sight-seeing, I had continued to work on the Stravinsky—on the train, in the hotel room—wherever I could find a few minutes. The competition was scheduled for 4:00 p.m., which allowed a little time for rest.

We entered the Salle du Jeu de Paume shortly before 4:00 p.m. to see Mlle Boulanger, Mlle Dieudonné and several judges from Paris, including Jean Françaix and Jean Pasquier. The orchestra was seated onstage. We were given our instructions: first, conduct the *Dumbarton Oaks* straight through; then rehearse for five minutes, then conduct it straight through again. I would be the third contestant. "By the way," Mlle Boulanger said, "You may use your score." What a relief! No longer worried about memorization, we were free at last to make music.

By the time it was my turn to conduct, the orchestra was playing flawlessly. It was next-to-impossible to find something to fix. Nevertheless, it was an exhilarating experience for me. On that day, at age twenty-three, I felt I had truly "arrived" as a conductor.

The day wasn't yet over, however. Now, we were to sing the Fauré Requiem with the various movements conducted by other members of the conducting class. When it came time for the Sanctus, Mlle Boulanger, much to my surprise, called my name! "Mademoiselle," I protested, "I've already conducted the Stravinsky." "*So??*" she replied. Once again she had caught me off guard and once again I had to demonstrate that I was "always prepared."

That momentous day in 1959 is embedded in my memory. I knew then that my destiny was to be a conductor.

The experience of one short summer with Mlle Boulanger set me on a course from which I never looked back. I became more disciplined in my approach to making music. I became more secure in my conducting gestures. Mlle, in my final lesson, said I had made a lot of progress, and that my second beat had improved, but that I must have more "lead in my feet." She warned that I worked too quickly and that my conducting lacked "depth." Back in the USA I enrolled in graduate school. I tried to fill in the many gaps in my musical knowledge. From Boulanger I had learned to honor, always, the composer and to question, constantly, the interpretation I intended to bring to his or her music. Other fine professors taught me vocal and choral techniques. But the influence of *one* mentor remained above all the others, both pre- and post-Fontainebleau. To her I pay homage—Nadia Boulanger.

Biography

Dr. Harriet Simons retired in 1999 from her position as Director of Choruses and Professor of Voice and Conducting at the State University of New York at Buffalo (UB). An Honors graduate of Drake and Indiana Universities, Dr. Simons also studied with Nadia Boulanger, Helmuth Rilling, Wilhelm Ehmann, and Elmer Iseler.

In addition to preparing choruses for Robert Shaw, Pablo Casals, Lukas Foss, Pierre Boulez, and others during earlier faculty appointments at Oberlin College Conservatory and the State University of New York at Fredonia, Dr. Simons has guest-conducted and lectured at several colleges and universities.

Under the direction of Dr. Simons, the UB Choir won a Gold Medal in 1983 at an International Choral Festival in Canada, and presented concert tours of Europe in 1988 and 1995. The UB Choir also performed at New York state conferences of music educators and at an Eastern Division convention of the American Choral Directors Association. Dr. Simons has also conducted several operas with the University at Buffalo Opera Studio as well as the Greater Buffalo Opera.

As an outgrowth of her many articles and particularly her book, *Choral Conducting: A Leadership Teaching Approach*, she organized five highly successful biennial conferences in Buffalo beginning in 1987 entitled "The Preparation of Tomorrow's Conductors." She was also on the national boards of the Conductors Guild and Pi Kappa Lambda.

A member of the American Choral Directors Association, Dr. Simons has served as New York State President and as a long-time member of the Editorial Board of the *Choral Journal.* She has been a lecturer at national and regional conventions of ACDA, and in 1996, the New York chapter honored her as Conductor of the Year.

Biographies of Selected American Women Choral Conductors

Charlene Archibeque

(Born 15 July 1935)

Joan Whittemore

Charlene Archibeque did not intend to become a conductor. She wanted to be a teacher. The challenge for her was deciding what to teach—French, Physical Education, or Music. Fortunately for thousands of students who have had the opportunity to sing in her chorus, all state choir, honor choir, or choral workshop, or who have studied with her in a degree program, she chose music. In her early years of teaching in junior high school in San Diego, she discovered that she also loved conducting, relishing not only the teaching and rehearsing, but the performance as well. Conducting chose Archibeque.

At the time Archibeque began her teaching career in San Diego, the school system allowed women to direct choirs while men conducted bands and orchestras. Having studied with Elizabeth Green at the University of Michigan where students had the opportunity to conduct symphonic repertoire with the class members performing, she was somewhat disappointed not to conduct an instrumental ensemble. Nevertheless, she taught her singers to be the best musicians possible.

Archibeque learned from other conductors throughout her career. Jane Hardester, Charles Hirt, Roger Wagner, and Howard Swan taught by example and provided inspiration, and Lynn Whitten mentored her at the University of Colorado at Boulder during her doctoral studies. His maxim that conductors should strive for clarity, economy, and expressivity informs her performances to this day.[1]

In a Januray, 2007 interview, Archbeque discussed her mentors and what she learned from each of them:

> Early on they were all public school music and private piano teachers. At Oberlin there was Rose Marie Grentzer in Music Education, at the University of Michigan, Elizabeth Green, Marguerite Hood, Don Robinson, Gene Troth, and Sally Monsour who later served on my doctoral committee at the University of Colorado. Sally demonstrated beautifully that a teacher could be herself in front of a class and teach from her own personality, and was particularly helpful with *cheironomy*.
>
> In Southern California, we were very fortunate to have so many wonderful teachers and models like Charles Hirt, Roger Wagner, Howard Swan, Jane Hardester, and Paul Salamunovich. Paul's insights about early music and chant were so informative as were Don Neuen's techniques regarding diction and score preparation. I continued to learn Charles Hirt's techniques through Lynn Whitten and music history and performance practice with Alan Luhring. Participation in music conferences brought me in contact with Jean Berger, Lara Haggert, Harry Robert Wilson, Lloyd Pfautsch, Wilhelm Ehmann, and Helmuth Rilling.[2]

Archibeque also learned important aspects of conducting technique from observing orchestral conductors:

> I am very concerned that so many of our choral conductors have sloppy technique, that they do not conduct clearly, and make music in spite of this because they have good rehearsal techniques, or they are good singers, or they know what they want and accomplish it through other means; but good conducting technique saves so much time and puts the conductor in a more professional light with one's peers and with the audience. I learn from watching orchestral conductors—primarily Michael Tilson Thomas of the San Francisco Symphony and Seiji Ozawa—and I love to teach conducting.[3]

Her ability to practice what she teaches and teach what she practices is clearly evident to those who have observed Archibeque conduct and who have studied with her. Edwin Basilio, Director of Choral Activities at the University of San Diego and former student of Archibeque writes:

> I was blown away when I saw her conduct because—though I had observed many famous orchestral conductors—for the first time I could see a clear cause and effect connection between the manner with which directors use

> their physical attributes to elicit not only strategic responses but also make, interpret, and enjoy the "in the moment" creation of music.[4]

Archibeque highlighted score preparation as an essential part of creating music that is true to the composer's intentions:

> My approach to score study depends on the work itself, but often I begin by playing through the score at the piano. If it is a new work, I read through it first without playing at all. Then I decide which conducting patterns to use, highlight elements in the score to know what is there, translate terms, clarify how they apply to the music, and learn as fully as possible the composer's intent. Erich Leinsdorf's book, *The Composer's Advocate*, is such an excellent resource in this regard because of the emphasis on the responsibility to perform the music as closely to the manner the composer wanted to hear it as possible. There can be exceptions, for example, times when a composer sets a tempo that doesn't quite work and may need adjusting because of acoustics, but the composer's intent should be paramount.[5]

John Sutton, a former student of Archibeque and Director of Choral Activities at Azusa Pacific University relates how Archibeque shares the importance of score preparation with the students she mentors:

> She was the very first person in my choral education process to raise the questions: "What was the composer reading at the time? Who were the leading authors, painters, playwrights, architects, sculptures, etc. that were contemporaries of the composer? What were the financial and political situations that the composer lived within?"
>
> Charlene was the person who first introduced me to the idea of performance practice. She has been most influential to me in this regard. So, when I begin to study a composition, there's a whole new world waiting for me to explore. She taught me how to look at the piece in the total context of the world that it was created in, to look at the total DNA of a composition, and not just the obvious parts.[6]

Archibeque moves from the broadly analytical aspects of score study to the performance analysis, challenges, and intricacies of the piece. Her attention to each individual line and its relationship to the other lines and to the whole demonstrates the care she takes in her preparation as a conductor:

> Singing and conducting every part both instrumental and vocal, offsets the challenges of each line and enhances the conductor's ability to assist the singers to find a pitch or solve a rhythmic problem. Singing each part aloud helps to feel it in one's own voice. Playing some parts at the piano and singing others simultaneously clarifies the relationships among them along

> with the function of each line. Analyzing the piano part is essential because I want the pianist to play it really well, to know how much pedal to use, what kind of touch is appropriate, the length of the notes and the style of articulation. The piano can be a forgotten part of the choral performance, so demonstrating the style to the pianist when necessary enhances clarity. Oftentimes, a pianist needs to use more bass especially with treble choirs. Normally the left hand has to be really strong while in other works, playing lightly is required.
>
> Harmonic analysis is essential to determine where the climaxes are, where the emphasis is and why a note occurs in a particular voice. Is the note high in the tenor range or low in the bass range?
>
> If there aren't enough basses, it is helpful to have the baritones sing the bass line an octave higher using the overtones to create better balance in the chords. I often find that choir directors do not have a sense of the harmonic rhythm and the harmonic motion. If the work is performed so that every chord is equal, there is no relaxation and pull in the harmonic language.
>
> Analyzing the text and its meaning with word for word translations, accurate pronunciation, or even which pronunciation to use, particularly with Latin or German, is critical, as well as the timbre that brings out the inherent emotional quality of the music, the color of the language, the color of the emotions in the text that determine whether to use a bright, dark, warm, or harsh timbre. Poulenc's Mass, for example, should have a light clear ringing sound, rather than a style that is too legato.[7]

With regard to diction, Archibeque stated:

> Diction clarifies the text for the listener and gives the music meaning. It enables the conductor and singer to be absolutely accurate. Clarity in diction results in a precision that is not attained by any other means.[8]

Following the Missouri Music Educators Association All-Collegiate Choir Concert on 26 January 2007, Mark Jennings, Director of Choral Activities at Truman State University, wrote to Archibeque, observing:

> [The] clarity of your conducting brought out a sense of timing and clarity in diction . . . since you rehearsed with a sense of the importance of the text and its rhetorical declamation—i.e., having sopranos observe the commas in "I Loved a Lass" in the first rehearsal—the choir took that idea and began to realize the importance of being understood by an audience (diction-wise and meaning-wise). This manifested itself in the clarity of diction (as reinforced by clear gestures) that came out in the concert even though you hadn't "rehearsed" many spots with that in mind.[9]

Archibeque advocates using the International Phonetic Alphabet symbols even with very young singers and employing many different vocalises allowing them to exercise and rehearse all of the vowels. Her video "Daily Workout for a Beautiful Voice" featuring Charlotte Adams, produced as part of the Archibeque Choral Series, demonstrates this in a manner that enables other conductors to integrate these techniques into their own rehearsal routine. Ever the scholar and consummate teacher, she has often found it helpful when singing in foreign languages to have a native speaker who is a singer and who understands the poetic use of the language coach the singers and emphasize that many hours of practice are needed to ensure that everyone is singing exactly the same sound.[10]

The same responsibility Archibeque assumes for the sound and the vocal training of the choir she extends to their musical development:

> In speaking of singers' musicianship skills—the ability to hear, to actuate the page in their head and to be able to get from one note to the next without someone telling them how it sounds—I have observed many teachers assume that if someone else hasn't taught them, it is not their responsibility.
>
> No matter what a singer's background is, it is my responsibility to teach the skills needed. It doesn't take people that long to understand tonal relationships once someone explains it to them and they have the opportunity to practice hearing and singing intervals, starting with whole steps, half steps, whole tone, major and minor scales, every day. Make them cover their own part and watch another part as they sing their own. Notice when the two parts are together, or what the interval is between their part and another part, or their part and the melody. It is just a matter of calling singers' attention to it and teaching them to think about it, instead of always thinking their own part. Simply make the singers responsible for finding their own pitches.[11]

Daniel Hughes, a former student of Archibeque's and now conductor of The Choral Project, notes that Archibeque's rehearsals are "acclaimed for keeping singers intellectually involved, constantly inspired to achieve deep levels of communication with the audience, and magically tuned into their own highest capabilities."[12]

Another aspect of her methodology that affects both the development of musicianship and the blend of the ensemble is her approach to the standing positions of singers:

> Placing a leader next to a follower results in a division of an A choir and a B choir with the seating arrangement ABAB. In sight-reading new music

> some of the B singers couldn't sight-read and held back the A singers. So I would have the A singers sight-read and the B singers listen. The second time, the B singers could hum along. Whenever they felt really secure, they could sing. Still the A singers weren't getting enough support. Placing two As and two Bs together solved the problem because they had another good singer next to them to reinforce one other.
>
> The approach to seating then arose not so much from voice matching but from musicianship skills and how singers could learn from each other and learn the music faster. Singers with problems were in the front so that I could help them. At the same time, they could hear good readers behind them. At the university level, the main thing was how to achieve sound and blend so that I didn't have to spend a great deal of rehearsal time working on these aspects. They would blend naturally and normally if they were sitting next to the right singer.[13]

The ultimate result of Archibeque's detailed attention to the strengths and abilities of her singers is a unique and beautiful sound:

> Even though I have a model in my mind of how I want the ensemble to sound on one piece or another, that sound still comes from each singer using his or her own best voice. By developing their own voices, there is a richness and a freedom in the sound. Without this approach, the tone often sounds manipulated. I don't want them to sound like any specific choir, but rather to sound the way their own voices dictate that they should sing when they are singing correctly.[14]

Having conducted more than one hundred sixty works for chorus and orchestra and also prepared works for Seiji Ozawa, George Cleve, and Denis DeCouteau, Archibeque offered some insights on preparing choruses for another conductor:

> If I am preparing a chorus to sing with another conductor, I will often have some of my student conductors direct so the chorus becomes accustomed to another conductor. I often have the chorus sing the work without any direction at all by merely setting the tempo and saying, "Sing," so they don't rely on the conductor. I will also change *tempi*—much faster, then slower preparing them for any variations and enabling them to be vigilant of the subtleties of different conducting styles.
>
> Meeting with the conductor in advance whenever possible ensures greater clarity in the preparation of the chorus. Sometimes a conductor like Denis DeCouteau who conducted the San Francisco ballet orchestra had very precise *tempi* as ballet requires. When I prepared Beethoven's Ninth Symphony

> for him, he gave me the exact metronomic markings for each movement. We had one rehearsal with the orchestra. He told me exactly what he was going to do and that is what he did. It was wonderful. When a conductor knows and tells you clearly what he is going to do, it saves so much time.[15]

A visit to Archibeque's website (http://www.charlenearchibeque.com) yields a significant amount of information regarding her accomplishments and contributions to the field of choral music. Charlene Archibeque has an insatiable desire for knowledge equaled only by her determination to share it with others. This is evident in the acclaim she has earned in her thirty-five years as Professor of Choral Music at San Jose State University where she recruited scores of singers and mentored them through their studies. Under her tutelage, over eighty students completed Master's degrees in Choral Conducting and more than twenty entered doctoral programs and now serve in leadership positions throughout the United States as university conductors and Directors of Choral Activities.

Edwin Basilio sums up the impact of Archibeque's influence on him as teacher and conductor:

> What I learned most was that the technical precision with which one creates music e.g., instrumental skill, beauty of tone, dexterity etc., though vital, often does not culminate in a musical performance. However, with a skilled conductor, the previously mentioned elements can be focused and the musicians are encouraged to transcend the physical task of playing instruments and create Music. I perceive her ongoing contribution to be that she has raised the competence level of choral directors in education today.[16]

During Archibeque's tenure as Director of Choral Activities at San Jose State University, her choirs were selected to perform at twenty-five regional, divisional, state, and national conventions of the American Choral Directors Association, Music Educators National Conference, and the American Guild of Organists. The SJSU Choirs have appeared with the San Jose Symphony Orchestra, the San Francisco Symphony Orchestra, the San Francisco Concert Orchestra, the San Francisco Conservatory Orchestra, the Midsummer Mozart Festival, Sinfonia San Francisco and the San Jose Symphony Opera. Archibeque instituted and organized thirty Annual Invitational Choral Festivals, and established and conducted twenty-five Annual Scholarship Concerts with SJSU Orchestra and Choirs at St. Joseph's Basilica.

While serving as Guest Conductor for four Honor Choir European Tours and conducting the SJSU Choraliers on sixteen International Concert Tours, Archibeque conducted choirs in Carnegie Hall, Royal Albert Hall, St. Martin in the Fields, Queen Victoria Hall, the Hague Concertgebouw, the Berlin Philharmonic, and in cathedrals and churches throughout the European Continent including Notre Dame de Paris, Köln Dom, Salzburg Dom, St. Mathias in Budapest, and St. Peters in Rome. She has conducted All-State and honor choirs in forty-four states and six Canadian provinces.

Archibeque's service to the choral profession is legendary: she has served as Headliner for regional and national ACDA and MENC conventions; presented lectures, reading sessions, and clinics at festivals, colleges, and universities in the United States, Canada, and Europe; served as visiting professor and guest adjudicator; presented summer workshops; published articles; served as editor and board member for various arts groups in San Jose and San Francisco. Her numeous and varied contributions attest to her many interests and generous support to arts organizations.

Archibeque's teaching materials, articles, and previous interviews, as well as letters from her former students make it clear that she continually strives to improve, to learn more, to integrate, synthesize, and adapt. She is a role-model for her students as she constantly evaluates what is needed and how to achieve it. Her genuine concern for their development not only as musicians, but as people reveals itself in their reflections regarding what they have learned from her. She not only recruited and mentored students, but saw them through the next steps, assisting them in securing teaching positions and entrance to graduate schools, and celebrating their accomplishments. Through her own musicianship and through her ability to enhance and encourage musicianship in others, Charlene Archibeque shows that:

> Music has the ability to put people in touch with their own potential so that when they are making music they move from everyday life to a higher plane of existence . . . music helps them reach a level of humanity that very few other activities can . . . music opens up their senses and their feelings, and puts them in touch with their own core. I'd like them to know that they can find themselves through music.[17]

Bibliography

Charlene Archibeque Choral Series, Santa Barbara Publishing Co. 1990–1998.

Archibeque, Charlene. "A Rehearsal Check List," *Choral Journal*, June 1997, Vol. 38, No. 11, 2–3.

_____. "Making Rehearsal Time Count," *Choral Journal*, September 1992, Vol. 33, No. 2, 18–19.

_____ and Kerry Barnett. "Preparing Choirs for Orchestral Concerts and/or with Other Conductors," *Choral Journal*, February 1991, Vol. 31, No. 7, 15–21.

_____. "Daily Workout for a Beautiful Voice" Vocal Score, Choral Series Video No. 1, Santa Barbara Music Publishing, SBMP 40, 1990.

_____. "A Thanksgiving Concert." College of Music paper (D.M.A.) University of Colorado, Boulder, 1969.

_____. "Style characteristics and performance problems in the *Mörike-Chorallieder-buch* settings for women's voices of Hugo Distler." College of Music paper (D.M.A.) University of Colorado, Boulder, 1969.

_____. "The efficacy of vocalises in the choral rehearsal." College of Music paper (D.M.A.) University of Colorado, Boulder, 1969.

Hetzel, Lori and Kay Norton. "Women Choral Conductors at the Collegiate Level: Status and Perspectives," *College Music Society Symposium: Journal of the College Music Society*, 33/34 (1993/1994).

Discography

The Internet site http://www.worldcatlibraries.org lists sound recordings of all state honors choirs, San Jose State University A Capella Choir, Choraliers and Chamber Singers.

A Choraliers Christmas. (2002). The San Jose State University Choraliers. Johnson Digital Audio.

Encore: 1999 European Tour Performances. San Jose State University Choraliers.

Virtuosi: Performances of Rare 19th- and 20th-Century Virtuosic Choral Works. (1996). San Jose State University Choraliers.

Gaudete: The Songs of Christmas. (1995). San Jose State University Choraliers.

Vidu! Eastern European Concert Tour Performances, Summer 1994. (1994). San Jose State University Choraliers.

Together: A Collection of Choral Music from Renaissance to Contemporary. (1993). San Jose, CA: Johnson Digital Audio.

Videography

"Daily Workout for a Beautiful Voice," DVD featuring Charlotte Adams, Choral Series Video No. 1, Santa Barbara Music Publishing, SBMP 583, 1990.

Notes

[1] Charlene Archibeque, Personal Interview, St. Louis, MO, 22 January 2007.

[2] Charlene Archibeque, email, 5 August 2007

[3] Charlene Archibeque, Personal Interview, St. Louis, MO, 24 January 2007.

[4] Edwin Basilio, email, 24 July 2007.

[5] Charlene Archibeque, Personal Interview, St. Louis, MO, 22 January 2007.

[6] John Sutton, email, 22 August 2007.

[7] Ibid.

[8] Charlene Archibeque, Personal Interview, 22 January 2007.

[9] Mark Jennings, email to Archibeque, 26 January 2007.

[10] Charlene Archibeque, Personal Interview, 22 January 2007.

[11] Ibid.

[12] Daniel Hughes at http://www.danielhughesmusic.com

[13] Ibid.

[14] Ibid.

[15] Ibid.

[16] Charlene Archibeque, Personal Interview, 22 July 2007.

[17] Charlene Archibeque as cited in Leslie Guelker-Cone, *Choral Journal*, 1991, Vol. 31, No. 6, p. 3.

Tamara Brooks

I had to make peace with the fact that no one would make way for me, even people who love me.

Joan Catoni Conlon
with Joan Whittemore

Tamara Brooks has known enormous success in her more than thirty-five-year conducting career. She has conducted ensembles in Israel, Poland, Russia, Taiwan, Japan, Turkey, Greece, France, the Netherlands, Denmark, Austria, Germany, England, Wales, Italy and Bosnia. She held a Fulbright Professional Grant to conduct two bi-national festivals in Cyprus. She founded and was Music Director of Sequenza, a professional instrumental ensemble devoted to contemporary music. For many years she conducted the Mendelssohn Club of Philadelphia, with whom she earned a Grammy nomination. Yet this conductor-pianist-dean-educator also encountered resistance when she began to conduct. Like many women of her generation, she explains that her love of conducting had had a sacrificial side,

> because what I am capable of doing could not flower in the way it would have for a man. A woman was not even recognized for having the ability to conduct. When I conducted the Salzburg Mozarteum Orchestra, I heard from the person who engaged me . . . that the orchestra thought about not playing for me. They asked if they could send someone (literally, a spy) to the piano rehearsal. I said they could bring the entire orchestra. After the rehearsal, the man said in astonishment, "You know the music!"

Knowing the music—from its smallest detail to its largest form—has been at the core of Brooks' philosophy of conducting. She has believed that the work of the conductor is to discover, reveal, and present the composer's voice. To her, this discovery happens only when the conductor knows the score completely, and understands every aspect of the score. The conductor should be able to stop and start at any spot in the score, and then explain exactly what has happened, what is happening, and what will happen. The conductor then reveals the score when conducting gestures are informed by knowledge of the score. Lastly, the conductor presents the composer's voice when shaping each composition so that it takes on its own character.

Brooks' breadth and depth of interests are reflected in the appointments she has held throughout her career: pianist, conductor, professor and dean. In these different capacities, she has authored observations on conducting and on the entire music profession in precisely the same way she has taught conducting; i.e., grasp the larger picture, but also know the detail. Specifically, she has spoken eloquently on the role of music and arts in society. She further has investigated how music can bring together disparate communities. Moreover, she has embraced music as an art that transcends social and geographic boundaries. On the other hand, her writings demonstrate that she has had a keen understanding of the details of the mosaic of music in society. She has stood witness to the micro- and macro-elements that shape our engagement in music.

Concerning a conductor's specialization, Brooks has stated that she sees no difference between choral conducting and instrumental conducting.

> Conducting is conducting. Skill is skill. Choral conducting is an oxymoron. Conducting needs to be about the piece. My conducting is completely portable.

Yet, she has been most attentive to the one element that differentiates between orchestral and vocal music: the text. As conductor and interpreter she has been famous for her emphasis upon the text, for its pronunciation and enunciation, for its expressive value, and for its influence on the structure of the music. She then has worked to let the music speak for itself.

> I have no interest in power. My role on the podium is to allow the piece to speak. I have the architecture. I love the fact that I know that is going on everywhere, and that I can hear it. We can never prepare for great. Great happens. It is something extraordinary.

Tamara Brooks' friend and teacher Vincent Persichetti taught her that because every piece of music tells its own story, a conductor needs to know that story intimately. In fact, one of her foundational conducting exercise for her student Marguerite Brooks was to conduct eight bars of music written by the student herself. The lesson: know the music intimately.

> I make students write out the piece before they earn the right to rehearse it. They need to know what the harmonic rhythm is, or that the bassoon has the melody and that it is an octave lower. They need to learn every detail and put it back into the whole to make the architecture. If you know the piece,

> you should be able to come in at any point and know exactly where you are.

Brooks has conducted premieres of many of Persichetti's works, and was dedicatee of one of his works, Love. In fact, Brooks has asserted that today's conductors have a special obligation to the music of our time. In addition to working with Persichetti, she has worked with such legendary contemporary composers as Lutoslawski, Cage, Takemitsu, Sessions, Druckman, Tippett, Schuller, Adams and Ligeti.

On the importance of learning new music, she commented,

> When the Berg violin concerto was first played at Juilliard, it took an enormous amount of time to learn. It takes students much less time to learn the work today. After students play the Berg violin concerto, they play Mozart better.

In addition to her commitment to contemporary music, Brooks fervently has spoken out about art being of fundamental importance in contemporary lives and societies, and that the arts are an indispensable part of our culture.

> Art is central to any definition of what it is to be human. . . . Art is part of the life of our spirit.

As she said in her inaugural address as President of the New School, Philadelphia,

> I believe that the content of music is simple truth. That truth is revealed by the most gifted of us with a sense of enlightenment and emotional urgency. Music is the aural manifestation of the human spirit and its function is to broaden and enrich that spirit. Everything human (in the right hands and imagination) is the fit content of music.

She continued on the genesis, on the purpose, and on the performance of music.

> Pieces and performances are born of experience, frustration, defiance, horror, intolerance, grief, inhumanity. . . . Pieces and performances are also born of belief, hope, healing, love, or the challenge of a fresh idea. Music is not an extra-curricular luxury, an appended genteel frill. The music in each of us is fundamental to any definition we can fashion of humanity. Music is rooted in "real life." And the provocation to create is propelled by life itself. The musician joins eye, ear and to speak with ancient or new voice of idea, of feeling, of myths which are meant to be heard. Composer and performer have something to say, something important, something urgent, something private, something human. They must be heard. Old and new voices must have a chance to speak. The new ones may well help us see the

future. . . .

Finally, she articulated the ultimate reason for studying music.

> If we ask what education is for and we answer, "to make us better human beings," how can we exclude studies that hold . . . the broadening and bettering of mankind as central to their existence?

Another of Brooks' life concerns has been the role of music in transcending societal barriers, to "build bridges of peace among people of diverse ethnicities." In Atlanta, in December, 2006, she participated in one such event. Brooks worked with folk-music legend and actor Theodore Bikel who was screening his powerful film, "A Bridge to Peace," a film that featured the Mostar Orchestra. Brooks conducted this unique ensemble from Bosnia, an orchestra consisting of Christian and Muslim musicians who had survived the Bosnian war. This unusual ensemble regularly features music of all genres: folk, pop, classical, and rock.

In another international conference with Musicians Without Borders, Brooks conducted the Mostar Orchestra in a concert of Yiddish, Bosnian Sevdah and Sephardic songs: "Songs For the Soul." On yet two other occasions, she conducted at bi-national conferences that brought together Greek and Turkish Cypriot musicians in Cyprus, in an area of the globe that the world had known primarily for its long-lasting, bitter enmity.

Brooks does eschew conducting certain repertoire. She has chosen to conduct neither Bach's *St. John Passion* nor madrigals with texts about assaulting women.

Who mentored this extraordinary conductor, pianist, dean and educator? Her most important mentors, in addition to Persichetti, have included Eduard Steuerman, for whom the Webern piano concerto was written. Steuerman, she has explained, refused to perform the work because of its Nazi associations. Rather than perform the piece himself, he taught it to students. In her work with Steuerman, she also inherited his passion for the music of Schoenberg, a passion that she has shared with her students.

She has claimed that another important mentor who taught insights into life and music was her fourth-grade art teacher, who asked students to solve a problem of connecting dots with only four lines. She remembered,

> The solution was to go outside the lines!

Tamara Brooks graduated from Juilliard with Bachelor's and Master's degrees, and received an honorary doctorate from Villanova University. Before attending Juilliard, she had studied Philosophy, then Cheironomy and Gregorian Chant with a teacher from Solesmes. In the course of her teaching and conducting career, Brooks has taught at Syracuse University, New England Conservatory, Mount Holyoke, State University of New York at Albany, Haverford, Bryn Mawr, The New School, Hamilton, and the University of Iowa. She has been Consultant in Arts and Sciences at Syracuse University, New York.

ELAINE ISAACSON BROWN
(10 March 1910—6 September 1997)

JOAN WHITTEMORE

When Elaine Brown said, "Music is a great gluer; it holds us altogether," she wasn't just talking about her choir, the people in the room with her. She meant *us, all of us*—locally and globally, yesterday, today, and forever—people of every ethnic group, creed, age, rich, poor—the entire world. For many of us, the professional achievements of Elaine Brown as conductor and music educator alone would have been remarkable in themselves and certainly deserving of admiration and recognition of her as one who dedicated her life to the choral art. Her goals, accomplishments, and legacy, however, extended far beyond the choral profession.

Achievement of excellence in any field is always a difficult path. Consider the number of women who currently direct children's choruses, those who are conductors at the elementary, secondary, collegiate, and graduate levels, and professional organizations while simultaneously noting the concomitant decrease in those numbers at the higher echelons of the choral field. Such illustrious musicians as a John Finley Williamson and William Schuman sought her out to teach in and direct choral programs in prestigious institutions of higher education. That Elaine Brown was selected for posts at Westminster Choir College, Temple University, and the Juilliard School of Music in 1934, 1942, 1947, 1948, 1975 and that for the length of her professional career, colleges, universities, churches, seminaries, and professional organizations would continually engage her, attests to her remarkable abilities.

Even today, for a conductor to be requested to establish a community chorus *anywhere*, and for that chorus to become such an integral part of the community that it would earn local, national, and international recognition would be rare. In the case of Elaine Brown, that extraordinary musical organization had an equally remarkable mission: the members were to extend themselves to promote unity and understanding among diverse ethnic and cultural groups. Singing City, in 1948 co-sponsored by Temple University, Fellowship House, and the *Philadelphia Inquirer*, selected Elaine Brown as conductor for her unique strengths and leadership ability. With the commitment of the board and membership of Singing City, of its sponsors, and of Philadelphia itself, Elaine Brown's view was simply as follows:

> The choir represents every phase of Philadelphia, every community and way of thinking . . . every ethnicity and culture, all across religious, educational, and economic lines. . . . We are special in that our standards musically and human relations-wise must keep company. . . . We look for good people, not just good singers, who want to help others. I realize that may sound contrived or turn some people off, but that really is our *raison d'etre*.[1]

Born Elaine Isaacson on 10 March 1910 in Ridgway, Pennsylvania to John Reinhold Isaacson and Anna Anderson Isaacson, she was the eldest of three children. Her sister, Verna, was born in 1912, and her brother, Bruce in 1915. John Isaacson was an architect-builder who established his own business. Anna Isaacson was an organist and choirmaster of the Swedish Covenant First Mission Church in Ridgway. Elaine Isaacson's musical training began quite early when her mother carried her firstborn to choir rehearsals in a basket. Anna Isaacson was also Elaine's first piano teacher. Continuing piano studies with Kate Hamilton and May Curry, Elaine performed in school ensembles, at assemblies as accompanist, and with her mother in church throughout high school. Having graduated from Ridgway Centennial High School in 1927, she continued her music studies at Bush Conservatory in Chicago, completed the four-year curriculum in music education in two years, and graduated with a degree in music education with a major in piano in 1929.[2]

From 1929–1932 she taught music at Jefferson Junior High School in Jamestown, New York. During the 1930–1931 school year, John Finley Williamson brought the Westminster Choir to sing at the First Mission Church of Jamestown. The concert proved to be the spark Elaine Isaacson needed to impel her on the road she had already identified for herself: the choral profession. Following the concert, she met with John Finley Williamson, and then attended his summer session in Ithaca. After completing her third year of teaching in Jamestown, she enrolled at Westminster Choir College to earn a second bachelor of music degree in 1934. During her studies in Princeton, Dr. Herbert Haslam, then pastor of the Tioga Baptist Church in Philadelphia, hired Elaine Isaacson as a church musician. Both John Finley Williamson and Herbert Haslam proved to be great influences on the dual path that she would choose. While at Westminster, she met Hugh Brown, also a student. They were married in 1935 by Dr. Haslam at Tioga Baptist Church, and in 1937 had a daughter, Sonja.[3]

After her graduation, Dr. Williamson hired her to teach at Westminster Choir College. At the same time, she continued at Tioga Baptist Church, where Dr. Haslam was an administrator of Fellowship House which sought to bring people from different racial backgrounds together. In 1937 he approached Elaine Brown to enlist her in expanding the program for his congregation and particularly with an eye to involving young people and the choir. Much to the dismay of John Finley Williamson, Elaine Brown accepted Dr. Haslam's challenge. Fellowship House would later become the seed ground for Singing City. Elaine Brown recalls:

> The very earliest roots of Singing City were in taking turns as a white choir from a white congregation with a black choir from a black congregation in furnishing music for the experimental community services that Fellowship House was sponsoring.
>
> We soon realized that this was not the answer. Your turn, my turn—now black, now white. We knew that in order for the whole thing to work, we would have to put it together in some way.[4]

In 1939 Dr. Haslam was offered a pastorate at the Ashland Avenue Baptist Church in Toledo. He accepted and a year later offered a position to Elaine Brown to build a program in Toledo similar to the one that she had in Philadelphia. She accepted the position, but before leaving for Toledo in 1940, Dr. Vincent Jones invited her to teach a summer session at Temple University replacing Marjorie Jones who had become ill. Elaine Brown then organized an interracial, interfaith community chorus in Toledo. In her second year, Temple contacted her again, this time asking her to become director of choral activities. Leaving the fledgling program in Toledo was a difficult decision.[5]

Soon after returning to Philadelphia, Fellowship House, which already had a number of human relations activities in place, approached Elaine Brown expressing an interest in developing a music program—specifically an interracial, interfaith choir. Fellowship House agreed to sponsor the choir providing rehearsal space and a budget of fifty dollars. The first year the choir gave six public performances. By Elaine Brown's own account the choir was not very good, but she was committed to it because everyone felt there was a need for it in the community. The new choir had two basses, four tenors, and thirty-four women. The challenges of balance and repertoire were equally formidable for the choral program at Temple University during World War II. While teaching at Temple, Elaine Brown earned a Master of Science degree in Music Education in 1945. By the 1946–1947 season, the Fellowship House Choir had grown to sixty voices, had presented more than forty public performances, and had a budget of fifteen hundred dollars.[6]

William Schuman, then director of the Juilliard School of Music, offered Elaine Brown a faculty position in 1947. She taught choral literature, conducting, and she directed two choirs. In 1948 Temple University initiated the first baccalaureate degree with a major in choral conducting in the United States and wanted Elaine Brown to design and direct the program. She accepted. By this time, Temple University, Fellowship House, and the *Philadelphia Inquirer* now co-sponsored the Fellowship House Choir. This arrangement allowed Temple choral conducting majors to do community field work, afforded the program free publicity and advertising for the performances, and enabled expansion to involve many Philadelphia choirs. The name changed from Fellowship House Choir to Singing City in 1948.[7]

Elaine Brown completely reorganized the program of Singing City. She enlisted two voice teachers to audition all of the singers, resulting in a much better choir. Singing City had expanded to one hundred members and the budget grew from two thousand in 1940 to six thousand dollars annually by 1957. Elaine Brown's goal was always outreach: to build understanding among people through choral music. The First Annual Concert was held in the Spring of 1949, and has continued to be a highlight of the season. In 1952 the Fourth Annual Concert at the Academy of Music involved twenty choirs including church and school choirs, industrial choirs, ethnic folk singing and dancing ensembles, and over eight hundred singers. Later that same year, Singing City garnered national exposure with an appearance on Ed Sullivan's "Talk of the Town" television show on 22 June. The summer of 1953 brought Elaine Brown's Temple University Choir an invitation from UNESCO and the International Music Council to tour Europe with sponsorship from the United States Department of State. The Choir represented college choral music at the First International Music Educators' Conference in Brussels. Following the Conference the choir earned critical acclaim throughout England, France, Holland, Germany, and Austria for their performances.[8]

After her studies with the internationally renowned pedagogue Nadia Boulanger in the summer of 1951, the French government awarded Elaine Brown the *Prix d'excellence* for her remarkable achievements in conducting. In 1953, she was awarded the B'nai B'rith Interfaith Award, the Philadelphia Council of the National Council of Negro Women Honor for "outstanding contributions toward interracial and intercultural understanding through the medium of music," and the Distinguished Daughter of Pennsylvania, awarded by the Governor of the Commonwealth. Moreover, Sigma Alpha Iota inducted Elaine Brown in to the fraternity as an honorary member in 1954.[9]

After the United States Supreme Court's decision on integration in the public schools in 1954, Singing City embarked on its first southern tour from 2–13 May 1955. The choir traveled by bus to present concerts in Maryland, Ohio, Kentucky, Tennessee, Virginia, and North Carolina demonstrating that true integration was possible.[10]

As both Singing City and the Temple University program expanded, Elaine Brown realized that she had to make a choice. At the close of the 1955–1956 academic year, against the advice of nearly everyone, she relinquished her tenured position at Temple to devote her energies to Singing City. Soon afterward, Erich Leinsdorf engaged Singing City to perform the Verdi Requiem in June of 1956 with the Robin Hood Dell Orchestra, marking the chorus' first appearance with a professional orchestra. From that time, Singing City performed regularly in the Robin Hood Dell Summer Concert Series. That same year, Elaine Brown established the Singing City Chorale, numbering forty voices, whose membership was highly selective, and who performed even more sophisticated literature. Their first performance in 1957 was with the Bach Aria Group at the Philadelphia Academy of Music. Along with her responsibilities to Singing City, Elaine Brown taught part time at Union Theological Seminary School of Sacred Music until once again in 1959, Singing City's expansion necessitated her resignation. In 1957 the Philadelphia Conservatory of Music awarded Elaine Brown an honorary Doctor of Music degree. Ross Parmenter of the *New York Times* in an article lauded Singing City and the unique contribution of Elaine Brown. Sonya Garfinkle was hired as Assistant to the Director that same year, and the budget for the program increased to $25,000. Janet Yamron became the bookkeeper and librarian.

Singing City became autonomous and was granted a charter by the State of Pennsylvania as "a non-profit training and service center."[11]

Summer and Winter Workshops began. Some of the students attending those workshops became part of the Internship Program begun in 1959 and would stay from one to two years. Richard Bloesch was the first intern. Joseph Flummerfelt, Graeme Cowen, Jane Skinner Hardester, Robert Molison, Joann McGee, and Marge Scott were among the many others. Graeme Cowen and Joseph Flummerfelt would later serve as directors of Singing City following Elaine Brown's retirement.[12] Through the Intern program, Singing City was able to grow from one small choir to include more than a hundred choirs across the city of Philadelphia involving thousands of people.[13] Elaine Brown's own words best describe the program.

> Singing City is people. People who have a strong belief in the power of music as a carrier of meaning and direction in our society. I have seen three or four Singing City conductors, as a team, move down the aisles among an audience of more than a thousand foreign students, strangers to one another, and in a matter of minutes, transform these young people from every corner of the earth into one huge family of friends. I have seen crowds in many situations sing their differences away. It is then I know, once again, that Singing City's responsibility is to continue to develop leadership and singers who are concerned people.[14]

The full spectrum of Singing City's activities also included workshops, lecture-rehearsal- performance series with such notable scholar-performers as Julius Herford and Nadia Boulanger, premieres of new works performing with major symphony orchestras, and expansion of the program to extend participation in all neighborhoods of Philadelphia. In 1961, Singing City and the Philadelphia Conservatory of Music co-sponsored a lecture series with Julius Herford in the analysis of Bach's *St. John Passion*. That same year Singing City and the Philadelphia Orchestra participated in the one hundred fourth Anniversary Celebration of the Academy of Music with Leonard Bernstein conducting. Following that, Singing City performed Roy Harris's *A Folk Fantasy for Festivals* at the National Convention of the Music Teachers National Association in Philadelphia. A performance of Verdi's Requiem with Alfred Wallenstein conducting, Beethoven's Ninth Symphony with Erich Leinsdorf, and the first of a long tradition of *Messiah* concerts with Eugene Ormandy at the Philadelphia Academy of Music concluded the season.[15]

The next year, Singing City Chorale premiered Persichetti's Mass, Op. 84 while the combined choirs opened the Robin Dell 1962 season with Stravinsky's *Symphony of Psalms* under Erich Leinsdorf's direction, followed by Brahms' *German Requiem* with Hans Schwieger. *Messiah* performances followed in Philadelphia and New York at Philharmonic Hall and Lincoln Center in 1962 with Eugene Ormandy conducting.[16]

Further expansion of the program was facilitated through an anonymous donation for Sonya Garfinkle to establish the Singing City Youth Choir with forty to fifty high school students in 1962. The Youth Choir sang with the Philadelphia Orchestra on children's, students', and junior students' concert series and with the other Singing City Choruses.

Singing City celebrated its fifteenth anniversary in 1963 with a documentary, "The Singing City Story" that a CBS affiliate filmed and broadcasted. They garnered critical acclaim with Stravinsky's *Persephone*, in 1964 with the composer conducting, with the world premier of Ron Nelson's *What is Man*, and earned a performance at the American Choral Directors Association convention performing *Hello World* in Philadelphia. They performed Verdi's Requiem as a tribute to John F. Kennedy at the Robin Dell series. Fifty Singers from the Singing City Choir and Chorale went on their second tour of the South in 1964, marking the Tenth Anniversary of the Supreme Court Decision on integration. Maulton Leaman Baker who had been on the original tour, offered the following observation regarding both tours.[17]

> The first tour in 1955 was a rough tour. We rode in a bus half the day, or all day, and as you might suspect conditions were bad, but you learned how to cope with them. In 1964 we would fly into a town, like Louisville, Kentucky, and all of the officials and dignitaries would meet us at the airport. There was a different feeling entirely.[18]

"Caroling in the Neighborhoods" was also initiated in 1964, and Singing City, at the invitation of President Lyndon Johnson, was flown to the White House to participate in the tree lighting ceremony.[19]

Singing City worked, studied, rehearsed, and played together. The members were divided into interests groups, discussion groups, and planning committees. Another interest group including staff and ten elected members from the performing ensembles was established to evaluate Singing City's purpose and program.[20] The following incident recounted by Elaine Brown best describes the extent of involvement of Singing City in neighborhood Outreach.

> One May we held an outdoor folk festival. I got the Philadelphia Gas Works Company to give us their block square parking lot located in that same area as a location for the festival. I got the city itself to give us the equipment—microphones, loud speakers, johns, canopies, risers and platforms.

Our object in being there was to try to bring the Puerto Ricans and blacks together because they were living in the same neighborhood with the greatest of tension. They were living side by side, and for all the reasons we know, resenting it.

We thought that we could do something to bring these two groups of people together. There were costumes, and dances and folk music and the choir shared in that program, for our choir was right in the midst of it. I had a group of five boys, dropouts about whom I spoke earlier. They were very talented, had gorgeous voices, but had never been encouraged to use them. My role was to try to help them. First off, I had to learn rock and roll. They would listen all week long and then come in and imitate their favorite rock and roll groups. You know what a stickler we have to be for promptness when we're building choirs. My usual procedures were challenged, also. I waited as much as twenty minutes to a half hour every time I had a session with those kids. I would wait till they got ready to make an appearance and sing. At any rate, they were really looking forward to the day of this festival because they had worked up a couple of good numbers.

I had placed the big choir and was checking on some other things when one of the boys came to me. He pawed the ground and, never really looking me in the eye, said, "Jerry ain't here." "Jerry isn't here," I said. "Where is he? He's the top tenor." "He ain't gonna sing with us," he mumbled. Shocked, I replied, "He has to; he simply has to. Where is he?" "Look," he said. I looked, and there was Jerry, outside the parking lot on the other side of the high wire fence. He was walking up and down the street in hobo clothes with a stick with a bag on the end of it. He was demonstrating. He was usually quite nicely dressed, kind of spectacularly dressed sometimes, when he'd come for rehearsals. This was just the opposite. He couldn't have looked worse. But there he was, this big, strapping, six-foot kid, looking just ridiculous. The only thing that I could think of was to leave everything and to get him. The place was full of hundreds of people and those boys could not sing without him and he knew it. He was demonstrating about something and I couldn't piece it together. The only thing I could think of was to get to Jerry. So, I shot out of that lot and that gate toward the corner.

Now in the city, on that corner, anything can happen, on a Saturday afternoon. There was a bar on the other side of the street and it was just draped with people who spent Saturday afternoons so inebriated that they didn't have to worry about things for awhile. When they saw me dash after a black boy, they all lunged at me, and that second I knew I was really asking for it. Before I had time to think of what to do, I heard, "Hi, ya, Dr. Brown," said the nicest, loveliest, mellowest voice of a black woman who had seen what had happened. She was a counselor in the school. She was dressed in African garb with a high beautiful turban, for it was a very festive afternoon. She was a big, heavy set woman and she had pumped out of that lot behind me without my realizing it. She walked up to me like a long lost friend and the onlookers moved back. She said, "Now Jerry, is this any way to act?" trying to handle the situation. Jerry mumbled something and I begged him. I said, "Jerry, what is it? Is there anything I can do? What's bothering you?" He mumbled something and I gathered why he was demonstrating. It appeared that the boys had spent some money on getting up new garb. They were really going to have an act. He didn't think they should be bothered with how they looked, it was how they sang that concerned him. He had a perfectly good reason.

Well, we didn't seem to get to be able to influence him, so we returned to the festival. The other boys heard all of this, for they had followed us, and they were disappointed. All I could trust was that Jerry might put in an appearance. Well, one thing after another took place on the program, which included many things. There was dancing, and solos and combos, and small choirs, and Singing City. When it came time for these boys to sing we announced it and Jerry had decided to appear. He walked on stage, with this drab garb on, and the boys stole the show.[21]

From Outreach and community sponsorship, to workshops, and premieres of new works, Singing City thrived in its diversity at every level. Singing City's American premiere of Benjamin Britten's *Cantata Misericordiam* with Eugene Ormandy and the Philadelphia Orchestra in both Washington and New York occurred in 1965. An appearance at the New York World's Fair marked another milestone for Singing City, as did the premiere of Singing City's Chamber Choir. Singing City celebrated its twentieth season in 1967–1968 with Leopold Stokowski conducting Mahler's Second Symphony at the Academy of Music and Lincoln Center.[22] Donal Henahan of the *New York Times* wrote, "Elaine Brown's Singing City Choirs performed with extraordinary dynamic nuance, achieving the full range from deathlike whispers to roars entirely appropriate to the last Trump."[23]

The Samuel S. Fels Fund awarded Singing City a grant for eight thousand dollars in 1968 for the purpose of educational training, performance expenses, and the music library. With two hundred fifty members, Singing City celebrated the twentieth anniversary at their March concert with a Norman Dello Joio commission, *Years of the Modern*. Preceding the concert, Elaine Brown was awarded the Philadelphia Bowl of Honor in recognition of the work Singing City had done to further relations among interracial groups. Marian

Anderson and City Representative Harry Galfand, made the presentation. On 23 May 1968, Elaine Brown became the first woman to receive the Gold Medal Award of the Philadelphia Public Relations Association. In January of 1969 she received the Gimbel-Philadelphia Award, then was given a four-month sabbatical to return to France to study once again with Nadia Boulanger.[24]

Continuing the lecture-rehearsal performance series, Elaine Brown, Helmuth Rilling, and Sonya Garfinkle conducted a two week seminar at the Temple University's Summer Music Institute in 1970 with an analysis of Bach motets, Vivaldi's *Beatus vir* for double chorus and orchestra, and Stravinsky's *Symphony of Psalms* followed by a performance of the Vivaldi and Stravinsky at the Ambler Festival. In December of 1972, Elaine Brown became the first American woman to conduct the Philadelphia Orchestra in Stravinsky's *Symphony of Psalms*. The only other woman to conduct the orchestra had been Nadia Boulanger in 1939. For the 1972–1973 season Elaine Brown was appointed to the Choral Music Panel of the National Endowment for the Arts.[25]

At the invitation of Zubin Mehta and the Israel Philharmonic, Singing City served as Pennsylvania's Ambassadors of Music and Good Will for a Middle East Tour from 18 December 1974 to 2 January 1975. Performances were scheduled for Tel Aviv, Haifa, Bethlehem, Jerusalem, and Amman. The program included Messiah, the Bach Cantata, BWV 4, "Christ Lag in Todesbanden," and Stravinsky's *Symphony of Psalms*. Along with anonymous donations and Singing City's fundraising activities, the United States Department of State helped to sponsor the tour with a contribution of $15,000. They sang carols in Bethlehem, gave the first full length performance ever of *Messiah* in Israel, and received a twenty-minute ovation which was only quelled by another performance of the "Hallelujah Chorus." Though travelers who normally visited Israel were not allowed to cross into Jordan, by special arrangement of the United States Department of State, Singing City came to Ammam and performed for Queen Alis, catholic nuns, Arabs in traditional dress and Westernized Arabs.[26] Sonya Garfinkle and Janet Yamron noted that:

> What was so special about this trip was the education about the Mideast conflict for all of us before going. We became absorbed in the understanding about the experience we were to face. The performances reflected an understanding as the music making transcended the footlights.[27]

In September of 1975, Elaine Brown returned to Temple University as Director of Choral Activities. Singing City was invited to sing at the National Convention of the American Choral Directors Association in Dallas, Texas in

1977. The program included Helmuth Rilling conducting choruses from Bach's B Minor Mass, repertoire representing varying religious backgrounds, and audience participation of three thousand choral directors led by Sonya Garfinkle. The 1980s included another concert tour of the Middle East with a performance of Beethoven's ninth symphony conducted by Zubin Mehta in front of the Sphinx in Egypt.[28]

Though Elaine Brown retired from Temple University in 1981, she continued to be in demand for conducting, lectures, workshops, seminars, and residencies. Her ability to observe those who came to study with her attests to her gift of communication and was one of the hallmarks of her uniqueness as a musician, conductor, teacher, and humanitarian.

> I watch people in a workshop and I watch them get terribly discouraged when they realize how much they don't know, or how far there is to go. I say to them, "Look, it's far for everybody. The acquisition of knowledge about music, the building of musicianship is a life-long process. One needs to live at least twice to begin to grow. But we cannot wait until 'someday' to begin genuine creative teaching. The 'now'—this very moment in time—is all we have. We can recognize its potential, or we can waste it in procrastination. Realize that the grass isn't really greener someplace else. Make the most of your opportunities where you are." Quit making excuses and alibis like "If only I had better voices to work with, or more money for equipment (or more money for me!), or more appreciation for how hard I'm working, or just wait 'til I get a good situation. Then you'll hear what I can do!"
>
> Forget it! You will only do more or less of what you are now doing. Yours is the best job in the world. You may move from one set of circumstances to another, but each one is the best. This doesn't necessarily mean to be satisfied with where you are, or to stay put in a rut, but make where you are and what you do count. Stop feeling sorry for yourself. Get ready, grow, improve, extend, soak up all you can. Challenge yourself. When the time comes, when the time is ripe, *if you're ready*, there will be something, whether it's where you are or whether it's someplace else. And I really think that's true.[29]

She received four honorary doctorates from the Philadelphia Conservatory of Music, Villanova University, Westminster College and Holy Family College. The American Choral Directors Association honored her with the distinguished service award in 1985 at the national convention in Salt Lake City. Her final appearance with Singing City was the performance of Beethoven's *Choral Fantasia*, with the Philadelphia Orchestra on 13 July 1987 at the Mann Music Center. At her retirement, the City of Philadelphia bestowed on her the prestigious Philadelphia Award for her "extraordinary contribution to the Philadelphia community—making a real difference in the city's cultural life."[30]

Elaine Brown died 6 September 1997. At her memorial service, Joseph Flummerfelt captured the magnanimity of her spirit eloquently in the following tribute.

> Her incandescent spirit, her rigorous pursuit of the composer's voice, as well as her deep concern for the well-being of all people of whatever background forged Singing City into a powerful voice which not only stood at the center of Philadelphia's musical life, but reached into the larger world. . . . Everywhere she traveled she shared her deep conviction that only as we grow as human beings do we grow as musicians and that, as musicians, our human concerns need to reach far beyond the narrow parameters of our daily world. We all remember the deep personal losses she was called upon to endure. The tragic deaths of her husband and the prolonged life-snuffing illness of her only child was more than any one should have to bear. Yet devastated though she was, she drew strength from these trials and her intense passion to make a difference in the lives of others seemed only to increase. Elaine would always say "rise above it." What she well understood, of course, was that to reach high enough to overcome, one had to put down still deeper roots. In this respect, as in so many others, she was an example to us all.[31]

The following 31 March 1998, the Pennsylvania American Choral Directors Association, inaugurated the first "Outstanding Award for Choral Excellence in Pennsylvania" and made Elaine Brown the first recipient changing the name of the award to the "Elaine Brown Award for Choral Excellence in Pennsylvania." Always eloquent in the pursuit of excellence and deeply caring of those who traveled with her on that journey, Elaine Brown continues to urge us to do our very best in what ever situation we find ourselves. She remains the inspiration, the mentor, the energy to impel us on our own paths, and somehow convinces us that the impossible is possible.

> The music you make reflects what you are and how you function in a group . . . togetherness . . . consistency of attitude. You're not wearing one hat for one thing, music for another. The song remains in you. . . . As singers and conductors we need to ask: Does the music we make reflect integrity? Does it still relate to life, and where and how life is lived? Does it still possess the spontaneity and wonder of a child? Is it so permeated with sober awareness that it affects a musician who cares and relates to life around him so much that he can never again be invulnerable, immune, or oblivious? . . . What it comes down to as conductors, or ministers, or teachers, or parents or children. . . . We need to do a very simple thing. And that is to care more. It is

so simple that it is elusive. Not a saccharine caring, but a deep-down caring that is a part of commitment. It is the same care that makes you commit to the human race and to yourself.[32]

Bibliography

Drafall, Lynn. "The Elaine Brown Outstanding Pennsylvania Choral Conductor Award." 31 March 1998.

Ewing, James D. *Elaine Brown and Singing City: The Choral Art as a Communicative Social Force*, unpublished Ph.D. dissertation, University of Miami, 1976.

Obituary, *Choral Journal* (Vol. 38, No. 4, p. 58) November 1997, John Silantien, editor.

"Singing City: Celebrating 50 Years (1948–1998)" is a program booklet of the fiftieth anniversary concert to honor founder Elaine Brown. This booklet presents the concert program of Singing City and information about all those involved with this special event and also displays some beautiful photographs of Elaine Brown's career.

"A Celebration of Life for Elaine Brown" is a memorial brochure and a tape recording of the service. Included in a note from Helmuth Rilling in remembrance of Elaine and a poem for Elaine by Allen Lannon, past president of ACDA Eastern Division.

Notes

1 Elaine Brown as cited in Lynn Drafall's speech, "The Elaine Brown Outstanding Pennsylvania Choral Conductor Award," March 31, 1998.

2 James Ewing, *Elaine Brown and Singing City: The Choral Art As A Communicative Force*, unpublished Ph.D. dissertation, University of Miami, Coral Gables, Florida, 1976, 5–6.

[3] Ibid., 9–10.

[4] Ibid., 9–11.

[5] Ibid., 11.

[6] Ibid., 16–18.

[7] Ibid., 18–21.

[8] Ibid., 22–26.

[9] Ibid., 26.

[10] Ibid., 27.

[11] Ibid., 28–32.

[12] Janet Yamron and Sonya Garfinkle letter, Spring 2007.

[13] Ibid., 154.

[14] Ibid., 152.

[15] Ibid., 39.

[16] Ibid., 43–44.

[17] Ibid., 46–52.

[18] Ibid., as cited in Ewing, 53, 131.

[19] Ibid., 52.

[20] Ibid., 132–135.

[21] Ibid., 137–140.

[22] Ibid., 54, 62.

[23] Ibid., 62.

[24] Ibid., 64–65, 68–70.

[25] Ibid, 81, 89–90, 92.

[26] Ibid., 102, 305.

[27] Sonya Garfinkle and Janet Yamron, letter Spring, 2007.

[28] Ibid.

[29] Ewing, 109.

[30] Drafall, "The Elaine Brown Outstanding Pennsylvania Choral Conductor Award."

[31] Joseph Flummerfelt as cited in Drafall.

[32] Drafall, "The Elaine Brown Outstanding Pennsylvania Choral Conductor Award."

Fiora Corradetti Contino

(Born 17 June 1925)

Her presence would do honor to any opera house in the world.

Joan Whittemore

As a child Fiora Corradetti remembers hearing the typewriter at night as her father, Ferruccio, wrote his reviews of operas for Italian-language newspapers in New York. Now critics hail the elegant performances of the operas Fiora Corradetti Contino conducts. Then, she walked along the beach with her father, a prominent Italian baritone who had sung in operas conducted by Toscanini and Mascagni, as he and his students sang, discussed, and prepared their repertoire and roles. Now singers come to be coached by Maestra Contino in her New York Studio. As a young girl, Fiora substituted for her teacher playing for liturgies at St. Ignatius Martyr Parish in Long Beach, New York. When her teacher became too ill to continue, Fiora acquired her first position as an organist/conductor at the age of twelve. Through the recommendation of a friar, she studied Gregorian Chant with Mother Josephine Morgan, RSCJ at the Pius X School of Music at Manhattanville College. Although her father died when she was fourteen, his influence—what and how he taught, the sound, the inflection, the style, the conversation in Italian and French at home, the rich discussions about music with Arturo Toscanini, Ezio Pinza, Giovanni Martinelli—remains with her to this day.[1]

When Fiora Corradetti was ready to attend college, Arturo Toscanini's fidelity to his friend and recognition of Fiora's talent, appeared in the form of a letter of recommendation to Oberlin College on her behalf. Not many seventeen-year-old college freshmen are prepared to assume the role of directing a choir, but Fiora Corradetti was, and did so at Sacred Heart Church in Oberlin from 1942–1947 while she earned her degree in piano performance. During her studies at Oberlin, Fiora became a summer apprentice conductor to Cesare Sodero of the Metropolitan Opera, who convinced her that operatic conducting was possible for women.

Her first opportunity to conduct an opera came when she was twenty-seven. Fiora, then teaching at the University of Massachusetts, was approached by members of the Amherst community to become Founder and Director of the Amherst Community Opera. This was one of those fortuitous moments when the community desire was complemented by the resources in personnel, talent, facilities, financial and in-kind contributions of rehearsal and performance facilities, and for the first time, combined support from both Amherst College and the University of Massachusetts for such an endeavor. From 1953 to 1958, Fiora Contino conducted performances of *Cavalleria Rusticana*, *La Traviata*, *La Boheme*, *Amelia al Ballo*, *Amahl and the Night Visitors*, *Lucia di Lammermoor*, and *Madama Butterfly* with rave reviews from *The New York Times* and *Opera News*.

When Fiora went to study with Mademoiselle Nadia Boulanger at the Conservatoire Américain at Fontainebleau, the renowned teacher invited her to stay for two years. In 1960 the Conservatoire awarded Fiora Contino the *Premier Prix Hors Concours, cum laude* in the field of conducting. Two years later Fiora earned the Master of Music with Distinction in Choral Conducting from Indiana University, and in 1964, the Doctor of Music in Opera Conducting with Minors in Musicology and Harpsichord, also at Indiana University.[2]

Frivolous speculation abounds concerning what positions any male conductor with comparable gifts, expertise, and education to those of Maestra Contino would have achieved. The sheer number and diversity of her accomplishments demonstrate that there are few, if any, male or female conductors who have accomplished what Fiora Contino has as Founder and Director of the Amherst Community Opera, Director of Choral Activities at Bowling Green University (Ohio), Director of Opera and Choral Activities at Peabody; in her eighteen year tenure as Chairperson of the Choral Department at Indiana University where she also conducted opera and symphony and established Pro Arte, an early music group; as Department Head at the University of Texas at Austin where she also founded the Texas Bach Aria

Group; during her eighteen years as Director of the Choral Institute at the Aspen Music Festival; nineteen years as Director of Opera Illinois; seven years as director of the Anchorage Festival; as conductor for Teatro Grattacielo in New York; for the Memphis Opera Theatre and the San Antonio Opera Theatre; associate conductor of the New Orleans Symphony Orchestra; and guest conductor for the Baltimore Symphony Orchestra. Who else other than Maestra Contino knows, performs, and teaches repertoire from chant through the twenty-first century? How many conductors' curriculum vitae include opera, choral-orchestral literature, and symphonic repertoire, teaching conducting and performance practice, vocal coaching, and guest conducting for major symphony orchestras? Who else at the age of twenty-eight founded an opera company (Amherst Community Opera) that is in existence more than fifty years later? How many octogenarians still coach and conduct at all, or have yet another engagement to conduct *Madama Butterfly*? Maestra Contino has received critical acclaim for performances in Peoria, Philadelphia, Memphis, San Antonio, Baltimore, Anchorage, and at Alice Tully Hall at Lincoln Center in New York, and has mentored a legion of conductors and singers in the tradition in which she was so richly nurtured.[3] The chorus of critics is indeed in agreement. A critic of her performance of Puccini's *Madama Butterfly* with Dorothy Kirsten at the Ambler Festival in July 1973 wrote:

> Fiora Contino towered over everything as the conductor and music director. She held everything together with a baton that was sharp and in clear control of a magnificently coordinated performance. Her presence would do honor to any opera house in the world.[4]

For her performance of Alfano's *Risurrezione* at Teatro Grattacielo in 2001, *The New York Magazine* critic Peter Davies' wrote:

> Thank heaven for Teatro Grattacielo. Any opera lover who harbors a guilty passion for *verismo* opera—a vague term used to describe the florid music theater that flourished in Italy during the early 1900s—has precious few opportunities to see or hear these still-unfashionable, and virtually impossible to cast, operatic melodramas. For the past five years, Teatro Grattacielo has come to the rescue by offering a concert version of a choice work from the period, and this year's pick, performed in Alice Tully Hall, was Franco Alfano's *Risurrezione,* based on Leo Tolstoy's last novel and first seen in 1904. . . .
>
> That was mostly thanks to the supple and subtle conducting of Fiora Contino, an amazing musician in her seventies who may be the last conductor on earth with the music of Alfano and his generation in her bloodstream.[5]

In an interview with Fiora Contino on 2 September 2006, I had the opportunity to discuss the influences on her life and profession, her unique position as a conductor of opera, choral-orchestral literature, and symphonic repertoire, university professor, and vocal coach. Through observing her father teach, Maestra Contino reaped incalculable benefits by absorbing the tradition as she listened to him sing, when she performed with him in recitals, accompanied him to concerts, and as she listened to the rich conversations with his colleagues that followed. Her singular tutelage with these masters of late nineteenth-century and early twentieth-century Italian opera, followed by rigorous immersion into the gamut of music of Monteverdi, Bach, Faure, Poulenc, and Stravinsky with Nadia Boulanger, and the extensive collaboration with Julius Herford at Indiana University afforded Fiora Contino a uniquely international and multi-century vision that evoked and nurtured in her the remarkable gift that she possesses of enabling the composer's voice to be heard in a way that no other conductor does.

Maestra Contino began by explaining that her father, Ferruccio Corradetti (1866–1939) came to the United States because of the emergence of Mussolini as a power in Italy.

Contino: *My father had grown up in an atmosphere of politics. His father, Corrado Corradetti, had been a publisher involved with the freeing of Italy from Austrian rule in the late 1800s. He was a* capitano *of an entire province that had fought along side Garibaldi. His brother and he were rather important figures in their day for effecting change so that the poor were not necessarily pillaged in terms of their work. The two of them were in a position to do something, and it made them very marked people as far as Mussolini was concerned. All the signs led my father to emigrate because much of his property was confiscated since he was such an adamant enemy of Mussolini. When my father came to this country, he came the way an immigrant should come—just astonished at the freedom and at the openness of the government. He was the staunchest American one can find anywhere.*

My mother was twenty-two years younger than my father who was born in 1866. I was a child of his old age, so I am of a generation that shouldn't be here. He sang professionally until his death in 1939. He taught singing in New York and was the reviewer for many Italian newspapers: Il Progresso *in New York and* La Gazzetta di Massachusetts *in Boston.*

My older sister and I used to go to New York for lessons. My surroundings were a constant stimulation of things musical. We always had people on the weekend. When we lived in Long Beach, I can remember my father walking on the beach with his students following him, and they would be going through operas. He knew everything by heart. And they would speak the text among each other, or sing a little, and I was always in tow. I was more fortunate than I thought. It was just natural. From the age of four or five, I went with him to all the performances he reviewed. So it wasn't a teaching that he did, it's just that I was there among all of the musicians that knew him at the Metropolitan Opera. I remember falling asleep in his lap when we listened to the Toscanini performances every Sunday when the NBC orchestra would play the broadcasts. On a few memorable occasions, I remember going to those rehearsals in Studio Eight, once for a Verdi Requiem that Toscanini was conducting. Toscanini and he had worked together in the past, and they had kind of a mutual admiration society. They were old friends.

In Italy old friends are there for everybody. When my father died, I was only fourteen and became the beneficiary of that friendship. My mother just carried on. How I went to Oberlin was a miracle. When I graduated from high school which was three years after my father died, someone suggested to Toscanini that he write a letter of recommendation. He immediately wrote me a wonderful letter for Oberlin which might have been the reason that I got a scholarship. Edward Johnson, General Manager at the Met, did the same. Pasquale Amato and his friends helped me, too. All the people who were my father's generation who had some influence were real Italian old friends who took care of one another as they could.

I never had a daily regimen. No one ever forced me to do anything. I never studied solfeggio *with my Dad because he thought that if the schools were teaching "moveable do," that is what I should learn.*

Q: What is your preference, "moveable do" or "fixed do"?

Oh, absolutely "fixed do." I think "moveable do" is such a mistake. You can't use "moveable do" in Bach. There is not a composition of Bach that he is not in twenty-nine thousand keys before you leave two pages. What are you going to do—decide exactly when he decided he was going to a new key? It makes no sense. It also robs you of perfect pitch. I think I would have had perfect pitch if I had been left alone.

The whole system of the way the French transpose a score which is not taught in the United States was such an eye opener to me when I went to study with Mademoiselle Boulanger, because I always did a score in a relative fashion which is all right if it's a fifth. If you are talking about a Horn in D♭, it is hugely complicated, especially in Tchaikovsky when there are two horns in one key and two horns in another key. You could go crazy if you are thinking in a relative way; your brain can't manage it. Whereas with "fixed do," you read by clef and E♭ is E♭. You can't do the French transposition without "fixed do." We do a total disservice by not teaching "fixed do." So every time I teach score reading, I always make sure that they have the advantage of looking at music that way.

You began directing a choir at St. Ignatius at age twelve?

Yes, I studied with the organist and substituted occasionally. Then she became very sick. They asked if I could do it. I just stayed there all through high school. It's a strange thing, but the person who replaced me at St. Ignatius who is a doctor, is still there. When I went to college, he replaced me. At Oberlin, I also had a church job, too.

Did you learn the Solesmes Method?

I did.

Did Mademoiselle use the Solesmes Method?

She never talked about chant. I never ever even talked about chant with her. When I was at St. Ignatius, we lived on the ocean at Long Beach. Missionaries would come there for rest and relaxation. At one time when I was about twelve, a Franciscan Friar came up to the choir loft and asked if I would be interested in learning about chant, because he thought I really should learn the true music of the church. He arranged for me to go into New York every Saturday. At that time the Manhattanville College was the center for Gregorian Chant. They had this wonderful lady, Mother Josephine Morgan, who was a little short nun. She was a pistol! I used to stay in their classes in the morning from 9:00 to 12:00. They sang the Gregorian Chant every day and so the Saturdays were a preparation for what they were going to do for the rest of the week. She had one class where she started with the rudiments of the reading of neumes. I was fortunate enough to do that for two years. It gave me an understanding of chant that I don't think I could have ever had. She used to stamp her foot and say, "How can you be so stupid, beloved!" She was a wonderful musician who knew every rule, and explained it in such a way that it seemed easy. They teach chant so absolutely *wrong in the musicology books. I wish that I could teach it.*

When I was teaching at Indiana University, I tried to teach modes and the cheironomy *of chant to my students with the focus placed on the music of the chants as found in the* Liber Usualis. *One can immediately understand that the notation using neumes is the path to understanding the style. I found that that most students considered that the Dorian mode goes from D to D with the* Finalis *on D and the Dominant on A. It takes familiarity with the chants to see that although there is some truth to that, the wonderful interval from D to A is the essence of the Dorian Mode. One also understands that in practice, the B of the scale is usually altered to B♭ and that the melodies cluster around a as the reciting note. We have been discussing the Authentic Mode of Dorian. If one examines the Hypodorian Mode which is taught as a scale between A and A, it is of the utmost importance to understand that D is still the* Finalis *and F is the Dominant. The crux of hearing the Hypodorian mode is the tight interval between D and F and the importance of F as the Dominant note. The Dies Irae is the perfect example of Hypodorian. And so it goes. Every mode has a characteristic leap. There is no duplication. The trained ear can recognize each mode by its melodic orientation.*

What do you think chant has given you as a conductor?

It is a kind of music that is different from any other music, because I feel that in chant you are not living on this earth. In other words, high notes are not the goal. It has to do with the way the neumes are written. Because the descent begins with the highest note you generally will take some kind of an arsic motion that disappears before you reach the high note as though you strive for something which is not yet achievable now in this life. Chant has that other worldly quality of peace. And I don't know any other music that is like that.

The performance of the music of the Middle Ages oftentimes appears rather antiseptic compared to the sensuality of the chant. . . .

And it's harsh and rhythmic. I think it also depends on its origin. The French kept the original tradition that would not have been understood in Germany. When you look at Carmina Burana, *the sources are hugely rhythmic. Chant is not rhythmic; it's an eternal flow of supplication where it is a constant striving that is sensual, because in a way, the real Catholic receives gratification at a later time. It doesn't dry out the urge to be at one with someone, whether it is natural or spiritual. It has a human emotion in it that is palpable. The rhythmic tradition is perhaps later with Minnesingers, Meistersingers, Troubadours. I think it just depends on the tradition. If you are looking at the* Liber Usualis, *stay with the French tradition. If you are looking at something that is in four voices, it might be different. Even another language makes a difference.*

In terms of pronunciation of the Latin, what did Mademoiselle do?

We never did anything but ecclesiastical Latin.

How and when did you know you wanted to be a conductor?

It just happened because of the church experience.

How do you prepare a score you are to conduct for the first time?

I always start at the piano with the full score. Nadia Boulanger thought that if you couldn't play or sing it yourself, then you couldn't conduct it. She would have us sing and play it, play the clarinet part and sing the bass line, the horn parts and bassoon together, parts that were dissimilar, especially with the bass line, always in attempt to perform it ourselves.

Julius Herford said, "Analysis is preliminary work to open your heart to the inspiration of the moment to understand the spirituality of the composer—the imagination of something that is not tangible." You have to find the essence of the composer in the form and in the orchestration. Otherwise, the stylistic aspects are not understood.

With fugues, for example, each fugue is its own master. There is no such thing as a normal fugue. Julius Herford thought the subject in the fugue held more prominence and had a different quality than the answer. The opening notes don't tell you anything. You have to stay with it and see where the fugue is heading—to what word, for example—or if it is modulating, to which key it is going? In any fugue particularly of the Baroque period, whether it is instrumental or a soprano or an alto duet, for example, where one voice sings the subject matter and then the other sings it, when the two sing together, it has an emotional impact that surpasses what each has in the individual part. That is so simple that is seems ridiculous to articulate, but it makes such a difference in the way that you convey the mood.

How is your preparation different for an opera?

When possible, I prefer to coach all the singers. You have to be familiar with the language. I conducted those verismo *operas,* Iris, *etc. with Teatro Grattacielo with the understanding that I would coach all the singers.*

How did you prepare your students to deal with possible resistance from an orchestra because of their mindset regarding choral conductors?

That is a stigma in most places because of our educational system. When Dr. Herford and I directed the choral studies at Indiana University, we really endeavored to ensure that the education of our choral conducting students was the same as that of the orchestral conducting students. It seems provincial to think that choral conductors are not as well prepared as orchestral conductors. It is a question of repertoire rather than skill. A person trained as a choral conductor will know the choral-orchestral repertoire better than the orchestral conductor. An orchestral conductor will know the symphonic repertoire better than the choral-orchestral repertoire. When conducting the choral-orchestral repertoire, a person needs to be fully trained in terms of skills. The choral orchestral pieces are the greatest utterances. The Missa Solemnis *is probably as great a piece as Beethoven ever wrote.* The Damnation of Faust *is as great a piece as Berlioz ever wrote. Therefore, you need to know everything when you study these pieces.*

Did any orchestra ever make it difficult for you, and if so, how did you handle it?

I have never had any trouble, I can say honestly with any orchestral experience, except my first truly professional orchestra. A former acquaintance associated with the Ambler Festival, which in its day was a great festival right outside of Philadelphia with wonderful grounds, schools, and a full grown art colony, brought me there the first year to do a workshop. The next year they decided to do full operas and the Pittsburgh Symphony was in residence to play for these operas. I was in my early thirties, relatively inexperienced. I remember doing a Magic Flute *that I had never conducted before. When you stand up in front of the Pittsburgh Symphony to do the Overture you want to apologize. They have done this with the best. Steinberg, a great, great conductor, was their conductor at the time. The first rehearsal I had with that orchestra was for* Traviata, *a read through which we were supposed to do in three hours instead of the normal two rehearsals. This was, in effect, a two and a half hour rehearsal and this orchestra didn't want to do it. They didn't think they needed a read through on something that they had played probably a million times. So they were captives and not very thrilled with some unknown woman. We started the rehearsal. The prelude is one of the most heart searing works, and I didn't like the way they were playing it. I found that a woman rather sounds like a kindergarten teacher when saying, "I don't like this." I think that has to do with gender because a man sounds different when he complains about something. It came to a point where the second clarinetist, who I have since learned was a little bit goofy, turned his chair completely around making sure that he didn't see me. That was a hard rehearsal. I got through it; however, after that, there was one dress rehearsal. It was done with a minimum of rehearsal time because it was so expensive to produce, and because they were capable of doing it. There was no rehearsal with the soloists. The orchestra gave me a little bit of a rough time as long as we were rehearsing. When the performance came and when I could show them what I wanted with my stick, they were just terrific.*

Is there anything that you have not done that you would have liked to do?

I would have like to have had my own orchestra. By the time I concluded with Opera Illinois though, I felt it was mine.

Could you talk about your mentors and their influence on you?

I think the most fortunate influences in my life were threefold: first, my father and his legacy, his wonderful singing, and his intellect which was so very, very strong. Mademoiselle Boulanger, who never, ever *told us a thing, was the second. When we eventually came to a solution, she would say, "Well, of course," but she never told us* how *to do it. I can remember taking counterpoint with her in which we always did assignments in four clefs. Her idea of teaching harmony was to show how incredible composers did things that they weren't* supposed *to do. In other words, one is not supposed to go from Chord I to Chord ii,* not supposed to. *Then she would say, "In this Schubert quartet, listen to this. It's incredible," or "listen to this Mussorgsky." In counterpoint it was the same. She would set us a melody and then ask us to work with it contrapuntally writing in soprano, alto, tenor, and bass clef. They were like crossword puzzles. We would try to inch out this way in terms of what she had said to do and would struggle and come back with this piece of paper. She would put an "x" across this and an "x" across that and say, "This is not possible." Then she would show why it wasn't possible. Then we would struggle again, starting with those places where things had gone wrong and scotch taping the solutions on top of the errant measures. It got to the point where mine were this high [about half an inch], and I was still working on the first assignment. Meanwhile, she continued giving more assignments. It wasn't as though she stopped . . . it was a little like the angel with whom you are struggling who says "I will release you when you bless me." She never said what to do. She would only tell us what she liked or that something was good. Once she had assigned me* Threni. *Stravinsky had just written it, and he had sent her one of the first copies—*lucky *for all of us! There is a series of canons, particularly three canons that are rhythmically so complicated. She would expect us to sing any line and play the other two lines simultaneously. That was a typical "Nadiaism." I remember working to get two pages done, brought it into her, and it was reasonably all right. She then turned the page and said, "*Alors.*" [Let's go on.] I said, "I can't!" She taught in a way that was not for the faint of heart. You could lose your confidence really fast.*

Mademoiselle believed everything was voice leading which is something that I really learned from her that other people just don't see in a score. I remember a Master class at the Jeux de Pommes in Fontainbleau where she was fiendish in the way she worked with a Chopin Ballade *that starts with two fistfuls of notes at the top of the piano, and where every note of each hand then resolves three octaves lower in the very next chord. This poor child came up to play the piece. Mademoiselle had it in her head that every finger of one hand resolved to a specific note in the next chord. In other words she felt that the second finger here on this note should be balanced so that it led to the resolution in your other hand. This child tried it. As soon as she got two of them, then Mademoiselle would want the next one. . . . The girl just fainted dead away at the piano. People rushed up and laid her on the lip of the stage. Mademoiselle turned and said, "Next."* Totally unrepentant! *That's the way she taught. Mademoiselle Boulanger really taught me something the hard way.*

Dr. Herford was the greatest influence on me especially during the years when I conducted those first performances of major works. I was very young and though a professor, he mentored me. I thought it was a good role model for the students. He always wanted to tell us everything, everything he ever thought about anything. He wanted to make sure that we understood what he felt.

◆◆◆

In recent years Maestra Contino has served as Director of Opera Illinois, conducted performances for Teatro Grattacielo in New York, and served as one of the master conductors for the Chicago Choral/Orchestral Conducting Workshop sponsored by Chorus America. She maintains studios in New York and Indianapolis for vocal coaching, continues to conduct operas and present Master Classes as invitations present themselves, and has her own website (http://www.fioracontino.com). Fiora Contino still has much to teach us and willingly obliges those who come to study with her. She comes from a long and rich tradition of gifted and generous Corradettis who were writers, publishers, poets, opera singers, artists, and political activists. With great warmth, gratitude, and pride, she regards her four children and their productive lives as the "jewels in the crown" of her achievements.

A most generous teacher who indeed loves teaching, Fiora Contino has bestowed the rich legacy she inherited on her students, many of whom hold appointments as directors of choral activities in colleges and universities, opera theatre, symphonies, and sing with major opera companies throughout the world. Alan Harler, Music Director, Mendelssohn Club of Philadelphia, and Laura H. Carnell Professor Director of Graduate Choral Studies Boyer College of Music at Temple University, writes:

> I met and started working with Fiora Contino and Julius Herford at the same time in the early 1970s. My musical life was never the same. Combining Julius' score analysis with Fiora's unique ability to connect language to music was powerful stuff for a young conductor. Hearing Fiora prepare Italian repertoire, and especially Monteverdi, created a seismic revelation in

> my thinking about choral music. The uncompromising demands to shape the music to the text was never casual, it was passionate learning. In the late 1980s I was preparing to conduct my first Verdi Requiem, and Fiora agreed to meet with me for a coaching. While I had studied the score thoroughly and many times, I came away from that session with a clear idea of what I needed to do to "make the piece mine." An amazing quality of Fiora's teaching is that with her strength of musical personality, she doesn't overwhelm the musical personality of the student, but strengthens it. Her conducting is never about "technique." It is always about making music that sings and shapes and is expressing an emotional quality true to the composer.[6]

Jay Dean, Director of Orchestral Activities at the University of Southern Mississippi, another former student of Fiora Contino, observes that one of the exceptional benefits were the insights gained from the process of score study.

> Fiora Contino is a very special person and a very special musician. Probably the thing that I learned from her the most was to look "beyond" the music. I was always amazed by her ability to look at a musical score and see things in the score that no one else could see. Today when I look at a score, and I am trying to go to the level beyond what is merely on the page, I ask myself, "What would Dr. Contino see in this passage?" She also taught me to be practical, honest, and unpretentious when it comes to music making.[7]

Karen Keltner, Resident Conductor of the San Diego Opera, and former student of Dr. Contino, states:

> If I had not studied with Fiora, I probably would not be a conductor today. I was a piano major and a French major, and when I first saw Fiora in action it was the first time I had ever seen a woman conduct a full symphony orchestra. I had gone to a concert one evening in the old Music Building at IU. The orchestra filed onstage, then came the Concertmaster, and finally, the conductor—a *woman!* That woman was Fiora. I was astounded and thrilled. And it was during the course of that concert that I knew that conducting was what I had to do. It was a revelatory moment for me. I went in search of Dr. Contino the next day: she was graduate faculty and as an undergraduate I had only seen her in passing. I found her studio, took a deep breath, and knocked on her door and heard a "Come in." There I stood in front of this impressive woman, seated, pen in hand, working at her desk, and I somehow managed to blurt out, "I was at your concert last night, and I need to conduct." Fiora looked up at me for what seemed like a very long time, and finally said, "Well, you had better start."
>
> I think that what Fiora gave me was intangible in many respects. At the time that she was teaching me, she spoke to a part of me that made utter sense

> but which was not about any particular physical technique or "method". She would say to me, "Karen, come up here and make this Poulenc piece *sound* French." That would drive certain of my student colleagues crazy, but even though I wasn't sure *how* I was going to do it, I knew exactly what she wanted. I simply understood her on an intuitive level. And Fiora (Dr. Contino, I should say, because she wasn't "Fiora" to me until much later.) gave me confirmation that I *could* do this, that I could be a conductor. She calls me her "walk-on," like a sports "wanna-be" who just walks up to a coach and says, "I want to play!" I was older than the other students at that point, but I began taking beginning conducting classes, completed my undergraduate piano degree, and then entered the Master's program. When it came time to conduct my Master's project, I asked Fiora and Julius Herford to come and observe, and it was at the conclusion of that project that Dr. Herford invited me to join the doctoral program.
>
> I am grateful that Fiora was demanding as a teacher. One of the things she said to me that I often think about now is, "We have to toughen you up." She was so right. Conducting is a difficult profession. One must deal with all sorts of different personalities and contexts, and the politics are tricky, too.
>
> When Fiora speaks, when she makes music, we are treated to an amazing musical mind. I think she often sees and hears immediately how a work is put together harmonically. Fiora is also beautifully instinctive, and she understands what works best for the music. Who we are as individuals and what speaks to us individually are the elements we glean and elicit from a score. My hunch is that what Fiora sees in a score is probably immensely more than she ever thinks to articulate with words. Her words *are* the music.
>
> I have always admired and loved the way Fiora makes music. I still do. When I first began as a young conductor, people often told me that I reminded them of her. I took that as the highest praise. She and I agree that our styles of conducting are very different now, but as I often tell her, she is the reason I do what I do. She's to blame. And I am eternally grateful![8]

Like her mentor, Nadia Boulanger, who made a conscious decision to dedicate her life to the music of other composers transmitting not only their style through analysis, teaching, and performance to countless generations of students, Fiora Contino chose the process of teaching first, by example, in her unique position as a conductor of opera, choral-orchestral literature, and symphonic repertoire, as a vocal coach, and teacher. In doing so she has bestowed not one tradition, but the synthesis of three—her father, Ferruccio Corradetti's operatic legacy—the power of the text transcended through the music, Mademoiselle Boulanger's rigorous foundation of voice leading and the fierce independence born of contrapuntal mastery, and Julius Herford's insightful process of score analysis. Fiora Contino is that rare phenomenon who not only delivers the performance with grace, incisiveness, and authority, but generously enables her students to see, hear, comprehend, and perform masterfully.

There is yet one element missing from this account. I had not yet heard a performance in which Dr. Contino conducted. The reviews of critics and descriptions from former students were stellar, enthusiastic, insightful, and inspired more than a little envy and sadness for lost opportunities. Dr. Contino has been an interim conductor at Second Presbyterian Church in Indianapolis for a semester. I came to a service with camcorder in hand expecting to hear a beautiful performance of *Messiah*. What I did not expect was to be stunned having heard a legion of *Messiahs*. A new or unfamiliar work can sometimes evoke amazement and enchantment; these experiences are much more difficult to achieve with a familiar work. "Stunned" claims a mere a handful of life's experiences. *This* performance was one of those moments. Fiora's sopranos made "His Yoke is Easy" sound ethereal and effortless, and the proclamation of the text convinced me of its truth. The lightness and buoyancy of every entrance and melisma of "For Unto us a Child is born" was consistent from section to section sans the usual crescendo that obliterates the text, and yet it was still vibrant. How did she do that? This performance made me want to become a conductor all over again. I love the fact that I always learn something new from her and eagerly look forward to the next opportunity. Though I once said I could not listen to another performance of *Madama Butterfly*, not for lack of love of the opera, but because it is just too intense for me, I must attend one more because Fiora Contino will be conducting.

(Photograph of Fiora Contino by Delayne Spain, used by permission.)

INTERVIEWS

Duffie, Bruce. Interview with Fiora Contino, WNIB, 10 May 1990. http://www.bruceduffie.com/intst.html

Whittemore, Joan, CSJ. "Personal interview." 2 September 2006.

PUBLICATIONS

Contino, Fiora Corradetti, *Problems of Realization in Monteverdi's "L'Incoronazione di Poppea": An Excursion Into the Problems of Preparing a Practical Edition of "L'Incoronazione di Poppea," Together with a Proposed Solution of a Portion of the Opera.* Dissertation (Typewritten ms.), 1964.

______, ed. *Damigella tutta bella* (Maiden so beautiful), for mixed or male voices with accompaniment by Claudio Monteverdi; Macomb, IL, R. Dean Pub. Co., 1974. Baroque choral masterworks; C-101. Italian and English words.

______, ed. *Musica Dei donum optimi* (Music, gift of the highest God), for SSATTB chorus a cappella, Macomb, IL: R. Dean Pub. Co., 1974. Renaissance Choral Masterworks; CA-105.

______, ed. *Historia di Jepthe* (Latin oratorio), for soloists, chorus, and continuo by Giacomo Carissimi (1605–1674). (vi, 36 p.) + parts; 28 cm. Macomb, IL: R. Dean Pub. Co., 1976, *Harmoniae musarum* v. 7 CMC-107.

______. "Say, love, if ever thou didst find," Dowland, John, 1563?–1626, SATB chorus, *Songs or Ayres*, 3rd book. Macomb, IL: R. Dean Pub. Co., 1976, Pl. no. RD-CA-108.

BIBLIOGRAPHY

Davies, Peter. "Off-Peak Performance," *The New York Magazine*, 17 December 2001.

Deitz, Paula. "Reviving an Operatic Immortal," *The New York Times*, 22 November 1998.

Griffiths, Paul. "Shared Voyage of Discovery During an Opera in Concert," *The New York Times*, 28 November 1998.

____. "In the Style of Puccini, Up to a Point," *The New York Times*, 6 December 2001.

Hetzel, Lori and Kay Norton. "Women Choral Conductors at the Collegiate Level: Status and Perspectives," *College Music Society Symposium: Journal of the College Music Society*, 33/34 (1993/1994).

McPherson, Jim. "Before the Met: The Pioneer Days of Radio Opera Part 2, The NBC National Grand Opera." *Opera Quarterly*. 2000; 16: 204–223.

Midgette, Anne. "Giving Hidden Opera classics a Moment in the Sun," *The New York Times*, 29 November 2001.

Panetta, Gary A. "Director offers a rich connection to the greats," *Journal Star*, 8 September 2002.

Discography

The Internet site http://www.iucat.edu lists eighty four items including doctoral dissertation, sound recordings of Indiana Opera Theatre, Pro Arte, Indiana University Singers and Orchestra recordings, editions and publications of Fiora Contino.

The Internet site http://www.worldcatlibraries.org lists interview, sound recordings, editions and publications cited at Indiana University and additional concerts and interviews. Also listed are the recordings of Ferruccio Corradetti, Adriana Contino, cellist, Dr. Contino's daughter, Iris Adami, Corradetti, Dr. Contino's sister.

Videography

More Music From Aspen: Fiora Contino KQED-T, San Francisco; Public Television Library, 1975. ML38.A7 M6 Holdings University of Maryland, College Park OCLC Number 19272266. http://www.worldcatlibraries.org

Summary shows 135-voice, chorus, and 66-piece orchestra, under the direction of Fiora Contino, in rehearsal and in concert at the annual Music Festival held in Aspen, Colorado.

Notes

1 Fiora Contino, Private Interview, Joan Whittemore, CSJ, Indianapolis, 2 September 2006.

2 Ibid.

3 Ibid.

4 James Felton, *Philadelphia Evening Bulletin*, 13 July 1973.

5 Peter Davies, "Off-Peak Performance," Risurrezione, *The New York Magazine*, 17 December 2001.

6 Alan Harler, email 30 September 2006.

7 Jay Dean, email 15 October 2006.

8 Karen Keltner, email, 25 October 2006.

MARGARET HAWKINS

(28 January 1937—13 November 1993)

With music strong . . .
I hear the sounds, the sounds I love, sounds of the human voice. . . .
O give me to sing the songs of the great idea.[1]
—Walt Whitman

Remember, we exist to perform great music! That is our purpose.
—Margaret Hawkins

JOAN WHITTEMORE

Who knew that the kid back in the drum section of the Washington Parks High School in Racine, Wisconsin who wanted to become a band director would grow up to be Margaret Hawkins? The path to becoming Margaret Hawkins was one filled with parodox, dauntless determination, indefatigable dedication, insatiable scholarship, artistry, mysticism, integrity, razor sharp wit and boundless good humor combined with great love and suffering. The first responses to Margaret Hawkins' expressed intentions were always, "You can't do that! You can't be a band director because you are a girl; maybe you can be a choral director." She joined the chorus and loved it. At the University of Wisconsin—Milwaukee, she wanted to major in music and conducting, and was greeted with, "You really can't sing very well, and you're not a pianist, and you don't play the violin. Why don't you become an English Major?"[2]

She graduated from the University of Wisconsin—Milwaukee in 1959 with a degree in music education. "I had no talent and I got into UWM as an undergraduate with no talent. What I did have was a brain and I could play the piano sort of, and I could sing, sort of, so for some reason they thought, if I entered music education, that it would be okay."[3] In 1984 Margaret was honored with the Distinguished Alumnus Award of the University of Wisconsin—Milwaukee Alumni Association at the commencement ceremonies for her contributions to the development of musical life in Milwaukee and for her part in providing national exposure for city choral groups.[4] In 1993 the String Academy of Wisconsin presented its Arts Leadership Award to Margaret Hawkins. In accepting the award, she noted that "It's appropriate that all this is happening at UWM from which I graduated more than thirty years ago, when I probably didn't know the difference between a violin and a viola; but I do now."[5]

She began her teaching career at Pewaukee High School, Pewaukee, Wisconsin where she started with a chorus of nine girls that developed into one of Wisconsin's top rated choral programs. "For twelve years, Pewaukee High was a wonderful place to learn. I did anything I wanted. I learned how to conduct at that school—and of course, high school kids can do anything, anything at all except sing too high too long. I guess I kind of made that school a choral place. There had never been anything there before; the first year I was there I had nine girls."[6] She encouraged and challenged her high school students to have the courage to go beyond the limitations of their small town, and allowed them to travel to other countries and cultures through the music they performed and the art they studied.

During the summers, she earned a master's degree in conducting from Indiana University. Margaret observed that

> At Indiana they pioneered the very simple concept that choral conductors needed standard conducting technique because if you are ever going to do any real music, like Mozart and Haydn, you have to know how to handle an orchestra, too. So all of a sudden I saw the flaw in the choral conducting world: this thing of shaping music and never using beat patterns and never using a baton. . . . I trained myself to operate in a standard conducting way and discovered when confronted by an orchestra I was better off than most choral conductors, although I am still in the process of training myself to handle an orchestra.[7]

In 1964, she developed the Music for Youth Chorus. When it disbanded in 1969, Kenneth Schermerhorn, director of the Milwaukee Symphony Orchestra, having heard her Pewaukee Chorus perform, asked her to prepare a chorus to perform Stravinsky's *Symphony of Psalms* with the MSO. In 1971 the Wisconsin Conservatory of Music gave her the opportunity to form the Conservatory Singers.

At the same time, Margaret, with a minor in art, had taken over Pewaukee High School's art history course there, still chided by the naysayers with their worn out refrain, "But you're a musician, you can't teach art. In fact her course became so well known that Ohio and Michigan adopted her syllabus."[8] In 1971 she left Pewaukee and was asked to teach art history at the Layton School of Art from 1971–1974 and at the Milwaukee Institute of Art and Design in 1976–1977. Margaret owned that "I really learned art and history on my own through the years."[9] With art just as with music, she went to the original sources to learn, to see, study, and absorb in the galleries and the museums of Europe and the United States. "I love to travel, and when I go to a new city, I head first for the galleries before ever considering a concert. I've always found art to be a great help in understanding music—you can see it, touch it. In music, the political and other circumstances that shape the era of an artist are not so easy to see."[10] Her expertise as an art historian served her well in her approach to Stravinsky's *Symphony of Psalm*s in 1991. When Margaret recognized that the chorus didn't love the piece because of its difficulty, she came to the following rehearsal armed with the solution.

> The work is like a great piece of Greek architecture because everything is either vertical or horizontal. There are no scoops, nothing to get you from a high to a low note—no arches—nothing that will allow the voice to do what it does naturally. And I told them that the second movement is Bach, that all dissonances come out of long lines which are like the long lines in a Bach fugue. This helped them connect the lines to each other, rather than pouncing on downbeats and being ruled by the bar lines. Bar lines in Stravinsky are just there to provide information and not be responded to.[11]

Margaret founded the Wisconsin Conservatory Chamber Chorus, and was the Founding director of the Vocal Arts Consort. Again, in 1976, when Milwaukee Symphony Orchestra Director Kenneth Schermerhorn asked her to establish the Wisconsin Conservatory Symphony Chorus, the objections were legion with concern over how it would be funded, with the perceived competition with the other Milwaukee choruses, and there was even some benevolent banter about whether Milwaukee, like the Chicago Symphony Chorus, needed a Margaret.[12] The two hundred singers of the Wisconsin Conservatory Symphony Chorus made its debut with the Milwaukee Symphony Orchestra on 12 June 1976, in a performance of Berlioz' *The Damnation of Faust.* She prepared the choruses, but the orchestra directors would conduct the performances. "You can't conduct the orchestra, you are a choral conductor."

When the posters came out for the February 1979 concert in which she made her conducting debut with the Milwaukee Symphony Orchestra with Mozart's C minor Mass, MSO associate conductor, James Paul was listed as the conductor. Paul conducted part of the program but not the Mass. Margaret was furious at being allowed to conduct only half the concert. "I know. They say I have to prove myself. But I think I have been proving myself for a long time already."[13]

Louise Kenngott seems to agree in her review of the C minor Mass. "Ms. Hawkins made the musical experience simply breath-taking. . . . Her tempos were daredevil, incredibly dazzling. Her sense of the drama of the music was unfailing, it was a triumph."[14]

Lawrence B. Johnson celebrated her debut as guest conductor of the MSO with equal enthusiasm.

> As director of the Wisconsin Conservatory Symphony Chorus, Ms. Hawkins has earned celebrity status among symphony-goers without so much as lifting a baton onstage.
>
> At last, the woman who has waved magic over the two-hundred voice chorus backstage was given a chance to run the whole show. She seized upon it to create a magnificent production of Mozart's Mass in C minor—exemplary in style, impeccably constructed, full of life. Having honed the chorus to her usual high standards of precise ensemble, clear diction and expressive dynamic gradients, Miss Hawkins fused that element to a modest sized orchestra with invariably secure results. . . .
>
> [The] concert's first half was kept in the hands of Associate Conductor James Paul. This night, Paul found himself decidedly upstaged.[15]

Since that time the Wisconsin Conservatory Symphony Chorus has provided the choral forces for MSO performances on a regular basis. The MSO assumed the sponsorship and renamed the Conservatory Chorus the Milwaukee Symphony Chorus at the start of the 1985–1986 season.[16] The Chorus has twice appeared at both Carnegie Hall and Orchestra Hall in Chicago with the MSO. Margaret Hawkins became a regular guest conductor of the Milwaukee Symphony Orchestra.

During her tenure, Margaret Hawkins enjoyed an unprecedented and unrivaled relationship with the press. She was twice named "Musician of the

Year" by the *Milwaukee Sentinel.* No fewer than nineteen writers from four publications reviewed her performances, wrote feature articles about her, celebrated her triumphs both artistic and personal, mourned her passing, and counted themselves among her friends. Lawrence Johnson, reviewer for the *Milwaukee Sentinel,* reflected on a "lecture" he had gotten from Margaret.

> We were just talking in Magin Lounge at the Performing Arts Center before a concert, and I began to rhapsodize over some recital or other I'd heard, or maybe it was a recording. It seemed to me Hawkins wasn't quite listening. Anyway, this old friend and favorite conversationalist wasn't responding. Her face remained impassive. I stopped. Then she spoke:
>
> "Never lose your enthusiasm."
>
> That's all she said, but her words implied a clear and profound truth—that neither music nor life itself can flourish without passion. They were pointed words from a practicing preacher.[17]

The manner in which the reviewers recounted every milestone of her career and choruses speaks as eloquently of themselves and the community of Milwaukee as of the immensity of her contribution. Archbishop Rembert Weakland's memorial testimony to Margaret summarizes it most aptly. "She stood for art at its very best, and in the process had a profound effect on all of Milwaukee. She not only raised its quality, she became the measurement of it."[18]

Margaret's expertise and leadership in, and her dedication to the field of choral music extended far beyond Milwaukee. Within four years of establishing the Wisconsin Conservatory Chamber Singers, she conducted them in concerts at the American Choral Directors Association convention in St. Louis in 1975 and at the Kennedy Center for the Performing Arts. She served on the board of directors of Chorus America practically from its inception. Margaret Hillis noted that Margaret "made an incredible contribution when it came to time with her wonderful intellect and that sense of humor."[19] In 1991 Margaret Hawkins was given the Michael Korn Founders Award for Development of the Professional Choral Art from Chorus America.

Margaret was appointed a member of the Music Festival Panel for the National Endowment for the Arts (1979–1983), was Chairperson for the ACDA High School Standards and Repertoire Committee and published *An Annotated Inventory of Distinctive Choral Literature for Performance at the High School Level,* Monograph Series Number Two, for the ACDA.

National recognition of her conducting expertise brought invitations to guest conduct and even enticements to lure her away permanently from Milwaukee. She conducted the Handel and Haydn Society of Boston and the Cleveland Orchestra. Her Milwaukee Symphony Chorus performed with the Chicago Symphony Chorus at Ravinia. In 1989 Margaret was the first woman to conduct the Mormon Tabernacle Choir. Robert Page said, "I loved her because she let her singers sing. I'll never forget that. They didn't make little choral sounds or try to do little choral tricks, as some conductors get their choruses to do. Her people sang, and they knew the joy of singing from doing it."[20]

Even the manner in which she dealt with cancer was pure "Margaret." In June of 1986 at the age of forty-eight, she underwent a modified radical mastectomy. "I was afraid for my life and for my profession, for they are one and the same." Following the painful ordeal of surgery, an infection that left her right arm swollen and immobilized, physical therapy, and the fatigue of chemotherapy, she was once again greeted by the naysayer chorus of health care professionals who thought two hours of therapy a day should be the limit of her activity. "Impossible, they expect you to design your life around chemotherapy. After all, I have a season to live up to."[21]

Tom Strini, Music Critic for the *Milwaukee Journal*, reflected on the impact that Margaret Hawkins had from those who spoke at her memorial service at St. John's Cathedral.

> Their perspectives differed, but they had a common vision of Hawkins as devoted to music because she conceived of it as a kind of love. They testified that her music, and the courage with which she pursued excellence in music even in the face of pain and death, had an effect on their lives and the lives of everyone she reached, including her audiences.
>
> James Hawkins [Margaret's brother] recalled February 1992 at St. John's Cathedral. Hawkins was determined to conduct Rachmaninoff's *Vespers* despite being weak in her legs from cancer and the effects of chemotherapy.
>
> From his seat in the front pew, James Hawkins saw his sister struggle down the few steps of a half-concealed entrance and then stop to recover balance after every step. But when she rounded the last column and came into full view on the approach to her music stand, her back straightened and her stride quickened as she gathered all her strength for this music. It was the most inspiring moment I've ever had.[22]

In the last interview Tom Strini had with Margaret in 1991, she had expressed the hope that she would be alive to conduct the Rachmaninoff *Ves-*

pers the following February. "Remember, we exist to perform great music! That is our purpose." And that she did.

> Hawkins stood on the podium as unflappable and minimalist as ever as this strange mystical music formed in the air of St. John's Cathedral. The capacity audience was transfixed; at the end a long charged silence preceded an intense ovation.
>
> I will always associate that silence, that necessary delay for return from the spiritual to the normal world, with Hawkins. Forget the cancer, forget the heroic struggle with it. Margaret Hawkins was about the ineffable power of music.[23]

(Photograph of Margaret Hawkins courtesy of Christina Pruchra, Archivist of the American Choral Directors Association.)

Publications

Hawkins, Margaret. *An Annotated Inventory of Distinctive Choral Literature for Performance at the High School Level* (Monograph, American Choral Directors Association, no. 2). Chair, ACDA High School Standards and Repertoire Committee, 1976, 69 pp. ISBN 1-882648-01-3.

____. "The Exorcism of Boredom." *Choral Journal* 13 (No. 2 1972): pp. 9–10.

Discography

Ode for Orchestra. Lukas Foss, Milwaukee, WI, KC-1004, Koss Classics, c. 1990.

Obituary

Berger, Russell. "Dear Margaret: Chorus Leader Recalled in Weekend 'Requiem,'" *Milwaukee Sentinel*, 4 March 1991.

Lynch-German, Lauria. "Margaret Hawkins, Founder of Symphony Chorus, Dies at 56," *Milwaukee Journal*, 14 November 1993.

Senza Sordino, Official Publication of the International Conference of Symphony and Opera Musicians, December 1993, Volume 32, No. 2, p. 6.

Choral Journal, "In Memoriam: Margaret Hawkins," February 1994, p. 36.

Diapason, April 1994, p. 4.

Bibliography

"Hawkins to Receive Civic Music Award," *Milwaukee Journal*, 15 November 1987.

Blinkhorn, Lois. "Maestro Finds True Art at Rap Show," *Milwaukee Journal*, 10 October 1993.

Chute, James. "Margaret Hawkins to Reap Another Chorus of Approval," *Milwaukee Journal*, 12 June 1983.

Daniell, Constance. "She Conducted Singers to Top Competition" *Milwaukee Journal*, 21 January 1987.

Dennis, Cynthia. "Hawkins is Conducting a Battle against Cancer," *Milwaukee Journal*, 30 August 1986.

Gittleman, Neal. "Harmonium, Margaret and Me," *Encore*, January-March 1994, pp. 28–29.

Johnson, Lawrence. "Miss Hawkins a Maestro as Conductor," *Milwaukee Sentinel*, 5 February 1979.

_____. "Choral Leader to Advise US Panel on Grants," *Milwaukee Sentinel*, 1 November 1979.

_____. "Symphony Picks Choral Director," *Milwaukee Sentinel*, 6 December 1979.

_____. "Conductor Gives Life to Concert," *Milwaukee Sentinel*, 4 February 1980.

_____. "Symphony, 3 Choirs Perform," *Milwaukee Sentinel*, 21 February 1980.

_____. "All-Bach Performance Presented by Symphony," *Milwaukee Sentinel*, 28 March 1980.

_____. "Carnegie Hall Debut for Chorus," *Milwaukee Sentinel*, 19 May 1980.

_____. "Ms. Hawkins Scores Major Triumph with Symphony, Chorus," *Milwaukee Sentinel*, 13 April 1981.

_____. "Margaret Hawkins and the Music of the Voice," *Milwaukee Sentinel*, 3 January 1986.

_____. "Meet Margaret Hawkins, Musician, Artist, Scholar—She's All That—And More," *Milwaukee Sentinel*, 21 January 1987.

Joslyn, Jay. "Chamber Concert Exquisite," *Milwaukee Sentinel*, 22 January 1977.

_____. "Chamber Singers Serve Musical Feast," *Milwaukee Sentinel*, 17 November 1979.

Kenngott, Louise. "Back to Bach, With a Passion," *Milwaukee Journal*, 18 April 1976.

_____. "It was a Consummate Mozart Concert," *Milwaukee Journal*, 4 February 1979.

_____. "Margaret Hawkins: Portrait of a Renaissance Woman," *Milwaukee Journal*, 28 January 1979.

_____. "Orchestra Reaches a Tough Audience," *Milwaukee Journal*, 21 February 1980.

_____. "For Ms. Hawkins, a Triumphant Night," *Milwaukee Journal*, 27 March 1980.

_____. "A High Note at Carnegie," *Milwaukee Journal*, 4 May 1980.

Kincaid, Dorothy. "Docents Learn to Grab Child's Imagination," *Milwaukee Sentinel*, 22 October 1979.

Miller, Nancy. "Dramatic Spirit of Music is Explored," *Milwaukee Sentinel*, 1 October 1988

_____. "Milwaukee 'Treasure' Fine-Tuning Joint High School Choral Event," *Milwaukee Sentinel*, 1 February 1989

Murphy, Bruce. "Margaret Hawkins: Conquering the World of Milwaukee Music," *Milwaukee Magazine*, April 1980, pp. 82–83.

_____. "A Kind of Loving," *Milwaukee Magazine*, February 1994, pp. 66–72.

Orgill, Roxanne. "N.Y. Critics Laud Chorus," *Milwaukee Journal*, 19 May 1980.

_____. "Hawkins, Orchestra Team Well," *Milwaukee Journal*, 12 April 1981.

_____. "An Upbeat Trauma," *Milwaukee Journal*, 17 April 1981.

_____. "Conservatory Singers' Voices Fail to Fill Vast Area," *Milwaukee Journal*, 8 November 1981.

_____. "Much to Admire in Performance," *Milwaukee Journal*, 6 March 1982.

_____. "Facing the Music," *Milwaukee Journal*, 9 June 1982.

Raabe, Nancy. "Conductor Margaret Hawkins Relishes Her First *Messiah*," *Milwaukee Sentinel*, 6 April 1990.

_____. "Palestrina, Rare Saint-Saens Among Hawkins' Holiday Gifts," *Milwaukee Sentinel*, 14 December 1990.

_____. "Symphony Finds Substitute for Ailing Hawkins," *Milwaukee Sentinel*, 15 February 1991.

_____. "Hawkins Begins Work Again with Singing Group," *Milwaukee Sentinel*, 12 July 1991.

_____. "Chorus Puts New Vigor in *Nevsky*," *Milwaukee Sentinel*, 21 August 1991.

_____. "*Symphony of Psalms* Soars," *Milwaukee Sentinel*, 4 October 1991.

_____. "Challenge of *Vespers* Stirs Hawkins," *Milwaukee Sentinel*, 12 February 1992.

_____."Symphony Chorus' Hawkins is Honored," *Milwaukee Sentinel*, 19 May 1993.

_____. "Hawkins' Skills Show in Exquisite *Carmina*," *Milwaukee Sentinel*, 18 June 1993.

_____. "Loving Music: Hawkins Remembered as Passionate Artist," *Milwaukee Sentinel*, 13 November 1993.

_____. "Hawkins' Inspiration Will Live On," *Milwaukee Sentinel*, 15 November 1993.

_____. "Memories of Hawkins Inspire Musical Tribute," *Milwaukee Sentinel*, 24 November 1993.

Strini, Tom. "Finely Tuned Chorus Melds 200 Voices as 1,'" *Milwaukee Journal*, 1 October 1988.

_____. "Battle with Cancer Makes the Harmony Sweeter," *Milwaukee Journal*, 1 October 1991.

_____."Hawkins Worked Musical Magic," *Milwaukee Journal*, 15 November 1993.

_____. "Hawkins/MSO Chorus Conductor's Job Calls for Diplomacy, Humility," *Milwaukee Journal*, 20 May 1993.

_____ "The Power of Music was an Integral Part of Margaret Hawkins Life," *Milwaukee Journal*, 21 November 1993.

_____. "Tribute to Hawkins Lifts Voices 'With Music Strong,'" *Milwaukee Journal*, 24 November 1993.

_____. "MSO Getting Special Birthday Gift," *Milwaukee Journal Sentinel*, 30 October 2005.

Notes

[1] Lukas, Foss, *With Music Strong*, 1988 work dedicated to Margaret Hawkins and the Thirtieth Anniversary of the Milwaukee Symphony Orchestra.

[2] Louise Kenngott, "Margaret Hawkins: Portrait of a Renaissance Woman," *Milwaukee Journal*, 28 January 1979, p. 5.

[3] James Chute, "Margaret Hawkins to Reap Another Chorus of Approval," *Milwaukee Journal*, 12 June 1983, p. 8.

[4] "Hawkins to Receive UWM Alumni Award," *Milwaukee Sentinel*, 25 April 1984.

[5] "Symphony Chorus' Hawkins is Honored," *Milwaukee Sentinel*, 9 May 1993.

[6] Kenngott, p. 6.

[7] Chute, p. 8.

[8] Bruce Murphy, "A Kind of Loving," *Milwaukee Magazine*, 1994, p. 69.

[9] Kenngott, p. 6.

[10] Lawrence B. Johnson, "Meet Margaret Hawkins Musician, Artist, Scholar—She's All That—And More," *Milwaukee Sentinel*, 21 January 1977.

[11] Nancy Raabe, "*Symphony of Psalms* Soars," *Milwaukee Sentinel*, 4 October 1991, p. 13D.

[12] Raabe, "With Margaret Strong: Late MSO Director's Humanity Touched Many," *Encore*, Jan–March 1994, p. 17.

[13] Kenngott, p. 9.

[14] Louise Kenngott, *Milwaukee Journal*, 4 February 1979.

[15] Lawrence B. Johnson, "Miss Hawkins a Maestro as Conductor," *Milwaukee Sentinel*, 5 February 1979.

[16] Murphy, p. 69.

[17] Lawrence B. Johnson, "Margaret Hawkins and the Music of the Voice," *Milwaukee Sentinel*, 9 January 1986.

[18] Raabe, p. 17.

[19] Raabe, "Loving Music: Hawkins Remembered as Passionate Artist," *Milwaukee Sentinel*, 19 November 1993, p. 8D.

[20] Ibid.

[21] Cynthia Dennis, "Hawkins is Conducting a Battle against Cancer," *Milwaukee Journal*, 30 August 1986, p. 9A.

[22] Tom Strini, "Tribute to Hawkins Lifts Voices 'With Music Strong,'" *Milwaukee Journal*, 24 November 1993.

[23] Tom Strini, "The Power of Music was an Integral Part of Margaret Hawkins' Life," *Milwaukee Journal*, 21 November 1993, p. E8.

Iva Dee Hiatt

(14 September 1919—5 January 1980)

Joan Whittemore

Freshmen entering Smith College from the 1950s through the late 1970s joined a beloved Smith tradition created by Iva Dee Hiatt. Christmas Vespers in John M. Green Hall, conducted by Hiatt, began with a solo voice introducing "Veni, veni, Emmanuel." The Candlelight procession would swell to include the Freshman and Sophomore Choruses in the balconies, the Glee Club, and finally the audience. Each of the choruses performed individual portions of the concert, while the Glee Club, joined by one of the male choruses of a neighboring college or university—Harvard, Yale, Amherst, etc.—would then sing a major work under Hiatt's direction. At the close, all in attendance sang "Adeste fidelis." The Vespers then would conclude as they began, with a solo voice introducing the carol "Silent Night." This was the first of many events that Iva Dee Hiatt conceived, initiated, and brought to fruition in her thirty-one year tenure as "reigning musical genius" of Smith College.[1]

Iva Dee Hiatt was born 14 September 1919 in Terre Haute, Indiana, the only child of Frederick William Hiatt and Iva Lindley Hiatt. Her distinguished conducting career started at the University of California, Berkeley, when at the age of sixteen she entered as an English Major with a Music Minor. After she changed her major to music in her sophomore year, Randall Thompson chose her to be the "first chorister" (president) of the UC Chorus, a position she held for three years. She was the first undergraduate student conductor under Edward Lawton, and the first student to conduct the UC Chorus at Baccalaureate, graduating with honors in 1941. That same year she began her graduate work in musicology at the University of California, Berkeley, was awarded a teaching assistantship and studied with Arthur Bliss, Ernest Bloch, Curt Sachs, Roger Sessions, and Manfred Bukofzer.[2]

Along with her course work, teaching, and conducting, she earned a private pilot's license in 1940, and did war work from 1941 to 1945. During this period, she developed a course in the History of Jazz for the University of California Extension Division Music School. In 1947, while studying conducting with Hugh Ross and Robert Shaw, Iva Dee Hiatt was the first woman and the first choral conductor to direct a work for chorus and orchestra at the Berkshire Music Center at Tanglewood—Ralph Vaughan Williams' *Serenade to Music*. Serge Koussevitzky said to her following the concert, "You are a born conductor; never let anything stop you."[3]

In 1947–1948, she received the Gabriel Charlebois Scholarship in Music at the University of California, Berkeley, where she founded the Berkeley Chamber Singers, a small semi-professional chorus hailed by Darius Milhaud as "one of the finest small ensembles I have ever heard." The Chamber Singers performed premieres of Aaron Copland's *In the Beginning* and Stravinsky's Kyrie and Gloria from the Mass, the only two movements completed at the time. Hiatt coached singers and prepared the chorus in the world premiere of Roger Sessions' opera, *The Trial of Lucullus*, and completed her master's thesis, *An Introduction to the Sacred Music of Monteverdi*, earning a Master's degree at the University of California, Berkeley in 1948.[4]

Iva Dee Hiatt became the Director of Choral Music at Smith College, Northampton, Massachusetts, in 1948. She did not inherit a choral dynasty at the college; instead she created one. She would later advise her conducting students, "If you have limited resources, accept them and limit the repertoire. Make professional conditions out of your situation." She demonstrated by example not only how to accept limitations, but how to exceed them by inventing programs and establishing high musical standards. She designed the Smith College choral system of two Freshman Choirs and a Sophomore Choir of approximately eighty members each, a Glee Club of eighty Juniors and Seniors, and the Chamber Singers, a fifty- to sixty-member ensemble that toured during the summers or winter breaks. Not only did she create the Christmas Vespers program in 1950. She also started the November Thanksgiving and Praise Concert and the Rally Day concerts which featured a double chorus work, often a commissioned work by Gerald Finzi, Alvin Etler, or Edwin London.[5]

The Freshman and Sophomore Choruses sang for chapel each Sunday. Each would also give a concert with their male counterparts at Yale or Amherst. The Glee Club did not sing for chapel but had their own program of concerts that always included major choral-orchestral pieces performed with male singers from other colleges. They performed major works such as Heinrich Schütz's *Musicalische Exequien* and J.S. Bach's *St. John Passion*. In addition, there were the usual command performances for Convocation and Commencement, the POPS concerts for Fathers' weekend, and the yearly student-directed choral competitions for aspiring Smith conductors.[6]

Helen Stott Spencer, Director of Freshman Choirs from 1954–1956 and Acting Director of Choral Music, 1956–1957 recalls:

> When Dee arrived at Smith, choral music was almost at a standstill. In the fall of 1948, Iva Dee Hiatt hit the ground running.
>
> By the time I took over the freshman choirs in the fall of 1954 over five hundred students were auditioning each year to sing in one of the four choral groups. Competition was intense and the quality of those auditioning was, on the whole, tops. A system had evolved of two large freshman choirs (of equal ability) who graduated the following year to a college choir and the following year to a glee club of the most proficient singers. This was capped by the Smith College Chamber Singers who were drawn from the two upper class groups. The Chamber Singers were, I think, the first college choruses to sing in the major cathedrals of Europe: this to great acclaim. It was a real cachet in this college of twenty-two hundred women, and one which still resonates.[7]

Amy Kaiser, Director of the Saint Louis Symphony Chorus, recalls that Hiatt was a master in running a rehearsal, accomplishing the most music in the most efficient and engaging way. She had a great sense of timing, always starting and ending on time, concluding with something productive. She knew what she wanted and got it from the singers.[8]

"Keep giving the group something that's a little too hard for them," Hiatt said. "When they get the notes right, make them sing it legato with no accents. You have to watch the singers and develop an eye relationship with them," and she demonstrated how to engage that relationship with the singers.[9]

"Start each rehearsal with something different." Iva Dee Hiatt enjoyed beginning rehearsals with an excerpt from one of the pieces that the chorus was preparing: octave leaps, whole tone scale warm-ups, major thirds, major sevenths. "Unless a warm-up increases technical ability, don't use it. Make the warm-up accomplish two things at once. When you know something is wrong and don't know what it is, take it apart, but give them something more to do. Think of new ways to interest the chorus and yourself. A good conductor must try to recreate the compositional process starting with text. How would I set it?"[10] Iva Dee Hiatt's tenure at Smith was marked by an extraordinary number of "firsts." The Smith College Chamber Singers were the first group from a women's college to tour Europe. They were the first women ever allowed to perform in Canterbury Cathedral, St. Paul's Cathedral in England, and Chartres Cathedral in France, and gave a private concert for Pope Pius XII in 1952. Moreover, the Smith College Chamber Singers were the first college group to perform in such cities as Athens and Istanbul. In 1954, in the former Yugoslavia, they performed at a United States State Department reception for Marshal Tito.[11]

In 1958 they were the first American choral group to capture First Prize in the Adult Female Choir Division Competition at the International Choral Competition, Eisteddfod in Llangollen, Wales, against twenty-two choirs from both sides of the Iron Curtain. They also captured the Second Prize in the Youth Female Choir Division in the International Choral Competition at Eisteddfod in 1958.[12]

Subsequent awards garnered by the Smith College Chamber Singers under Iva Dee Hiatt's direction included four from the 1977 International Choral Competition at the Hague, Netherlands:

- First Prize Gold Medal: Youth Female Choir Division
- Audience Medal: Youth Female Choir Division
- Second Prize Silver Medal: Adult Female Choir Division
- Audience Medal: Adult Female Choir Division[13]

The Smith College Chamber Singers performed at Carnegie Hall, Lissner Auditorium (Washington, D.C.), Constitution Hall (Washington, D.C.), Symphony Hall (Boston, MA), Town Hall (New York), the Easter Sunrise Service from Radio City in New York. They sang with the Boston Pops; and toured the eastern and midwestern United States, raising $38,000 for scholarships. The Chamber Singers made twelve European Tours, a South American tour, another to the Azores, to Iceland, to Newfoundland, took two tours of the United States, four tours to Mexico, and joined Amherst and Princeton for European and South American Tours.[14]

Under Iva Dee Hiatt's direction, the Smith College Chamber Singers appeared in festivals in Spoleto, Holland, Aix-en-Province, Ljubljana, Split, Dubrovnik, Madallin (Brazil), Paris, and at the Brussels World's Fair as one of three choruses chosen to be official representatives of the United States. In 1965 the Chamber Singers were one of five United States choruses selected to appear at Lincoln Center in the First International University Choral Festival.

International adjudicators and critical reviews hail Iva Dee Hiatt as one of the most remarkable choral conductors of the twentieth century:[15]

> Miss Hiatt is a master of her craft and art. . . . Under her supple hand the chorus sounded well nigh flawless, secure, sonorous, and full of spirit. —*Christian Science Monitor*, Boston

> It was a wonderful example of what amateur singers can accomplish when they are inspired and instructed by a gifted conductor. —Henk Badings, International Judge, International Choral Festival at the Hague, 1977

> Where Iva Dee Hiatt steps up . . . the audience experiences something which is not only musical perfection and precision, but realizes that these young individuals have found in their devotion and passion in the concert a common goal or oneness. —*Suddentsche Zeitung*, Munich

> The quality and blend of the Smith Singers was at all times pleasing and well balanced, the intonation impeccable, while the dynamic range achieved was nothing less than remarkable. . . . Miss Hiatt has assembled an extraordinarily versatile group of musicians, both singers and instrumentalists, who perform with enthusiasm and polish, and who are indeed a credit to their college and country. She is to be further commended for choosing such a varied and challenging musical program which reflects the high standards of the performing arts in the United States today. —*The Athenian*, Athens

> This magnificent performance was conducted with complete mastery and elegance. —*La Gaceta*, Salamanca, Spain

Dee Hiatt influenced succeeding generations of conductors. Among her students are Catharine Melhorn, Smith (1963), former Director of Choral Activites at Mount Holyoke College and currently Director of the South Hadley Children's Chorus; Amy Kaiser, Smith (1965), Director of the Saint Louis Symphony Chorus and long-time freelance choral and opera conductor in New York City; Marietta Cheng, Smith (1974), Conductor of the Colgate University Orchestra; Barbara Schubert, Smith (1975), conductor of the University of Chicago Symphony Orchestra; Sheila Heffernon, Smith (1976), Northfield Mount Hermon School; and Julie Pretzat Merchant, Smith (1979), Professor of Choral Music, State University of New York at Oswego.

Richard K. Winslow, Professor Emeritus, Wesleyan University recalls the genius of Dee Hiatt as teacher and conductor.

> When I conducted at Wesleyan, I frequently teamed up with Smith College's Dee Hiatt to perform Bach's *St. Matthew Passion*, Stravinsky's *Symphony of Psalms*, etc. She was one of two genius-level choral conductors of my experience, the other being Robert Shaw with whom I worked closely. Each had exceptional native musicianship and each felt music as an extension of their very beings. Their quest was, by various and differing means, to coax and coach singers into identifying with that feeling. In this sense, each was a teacher and each turned out superb choruses.[16]

Truman Bullard, Professor Emeritus of Music at Dickinson College who on occasion served as accompanist for Dee Hiatt remembers that:

> Iva Dee Hiatt relished musical challenges, and she consistently chose repertoire that would give her singers the impression that they were singing far above their natural abilities, and the achievement of a good performance would represent a shared victory for singers and conductors. . . . Iva Dee Hiatt lived for, through, and by means of her work as a choral conductor . . . requiring every chorus to live and feel the meaning of every word sung. . . . I shall always treasure my memories of Iva Dee Hiatt, a person of the highest intelligence, firmest will power and artistic sensitivity. As a single woman in the 1960s, she was utterly comfortable in a commanding position as conductor, teacher, and leader.[17]

Iva Dee Hiatt's influence not only encompassed the individual students whom she taught and conducted, but extended to the local community, and to national and international venues. She was visiting professor at the University of California, Berkeley in 1963–1964, musical director for the Cambridge Society for Early Music from 1965–1977, Music Director for the Composers' Conference Choral Institute, Johnson, Vermont from 1976–1978. She held summer session professorships at Harvard, Stanford, University of Southern California, served on the conducting staff at the Aspen Choral Institute in 1972 and 1973, and at the Boston Symphony's Berkshire Music Festival at Tanglewood, preparing choruses for Erich Leinsdorf, Charles Munch, Pierre Monteux, and Leonard Bernstein. Hiatt was the first woman to conduct the Orquestra Sinfonica Nacional of Mexico.[18] In 1976, she was one of five United States conductors chosen by the American Choral Directors Association to present American Music Sessions at Interlochen, Michigan in the Bicentennial Celebration. On numerous occasions, Hiatt served as choral clinician, workshop director, and conductor of All State, and Regional High School Music Festivals and the American Guild of Organists' Choral Workshops.[19]

In addition to her early academic awards and subsequent honors achieved throughout her professional career, Iva Dee Hiatt has been lauded and remembered through various citations, a commission for a choral piece in her memory after her death, and scholarship funds in honor of her professional dedication and excellence. Additional honors were:

- 1978: Iva Dee Hiatt Choral Scholarships, Appalachian State University, Boone, NC.
- 1978: Smith College, Iva Dee Hiatt Endowment Fund.
- 1978: American Choral Directors Association, Massachusetts Chapter honored Iva Dee Hiatt for her long time devotion to excellence in choral music.
- 1979: The Smith Class of 1954 commissioned *Praising the Worth* from Edwin London sung by the Smith College Glee Club at the 9 April college choir competition.[20]
- 1979: Smith College Medal noted Dee Hiatt's "inimitable personal style" that has "helped to make us experience music without the casual pretenses or defenses which usually deaden the ear . . . to call out the best performance from others . . . and to teach us all what a calling means when lived with honesty, artistry, and true commitment."[21]
- 1979: Amherst College, 9 May awarded by John William Ward following an evening of Viennese Music sung by Smith College Glee Club and Amherst College Glee Club. The citation reads:

  Your professional worth is beyond question.
  Your human worth is beyond measurement.
  We applaud you. We pay homage to you.

- 1979: Honorary degree from the New England Conservatory of Music.
- 1979: Smith College, Iva Dee Hiatt Endowed Chair.[22]

Jill Kerr Conway, President of Smith College at the close of Dee Hiatt's tenure, recalls their friendship and the impact that she had on her students:

> Two years after we arrived at Smith, Dee told me she had been diagnosed with ALS, and that she planned to keep on conducting until the last possible moment. That she did. Her presence in a wheelchair, barely able to move her hands still compelled a dazzling performance.
>
> When she died the outpouring of affection and admiration for her career came from every corner of the globe—from former students, from friends made on concert tours, from fellow musicians, from dignitaries from all the great churches in Europe in which she had arranged for Smith touring groups to sing. Former students always reported the same things: "She taught me to take myself seriously, and accept nothing but the very best performance of which I was capable. She taught me discipline and concentration, how to find breath when I never knew I had it, and she showed me an unforgettable model of a woman who was a professional to the core."[23]

Dee Hiatt's final concert directing the Smith and Amherst Glee Clubs in Brahms' Motet, Op. 74, No. 1, *Warum is das Licht gegeben dem Mühseligen?*, took place on 4 March 1979 at Smith College to an appreciative audience. Sheila Heffernon, former student of Hiatt, questioned her about the choice of the Brahms while visiting with her the week of the performance, and learned that Hiatt had not conducted the piece previously because she thought the text was intimidating.[24] During the months prior to her death on 5 January 1980, students often came to sing for her at the Smith College Infirmary. Singers from Amherst and Mount Holyoke Colleges and Harvard University joined the Smith College choral groups in the Memorial Service tribute to Iva Dee Hiatt on 24 February 1980. Following the Benediction, they once again performed the final chorale from Johannes Brahms' *Warum is das Licht gegeben dem Mühseligen?* as the Choral Response:

> With peace and joy I pass over
> According to God's will,
> My heart and soul are comforted,
> Calm and still,
> As He hath given me His word,
> Death for me is turned to sleep.[25]

Colleagues and former singers took part in the enormous outpouring of love and respect in a choral service held at Trinity Church in Newton Centre, Massachusetts on 12 April 1980, where about forty singers participated, including many of Hiatt's close friends and conductor colleagues. This event led to a musical celebration the following year on 12 April at the Washington National Cathedral on Palm Sunday in a performance of Liturgical music from the fourteenth and fifteenth centuries. Based on the early liturgy for Palm Sunday, the program of Processional and Ceremonial Music moved the sound of five volunteer choirs from the choir and crossing, to balconies in the Nave, North, and South Transepts. Though organizers expected between forty and sixty singers, the number of performers swelled to approximately four hundred people who had traveled from all across the United States, Canada, and Europe. Conductors were Ruth Ring Harvie, Phyllis Isaacson, Mary C. Lunt, and Helen Stott Spencer. Joel Cohen conducted the Boston Camerata in Machaut's *Messe de Notre Dame* from the crossing, with interpolations of the chants, "Hosanna filio David," "Pueri Hebraeorum," "Vexilla regis," "Pange lingua," and "Crux fidelis" from the various choirs in the balconies. The pure chant melodies soared from choir to choir throughout the cathedral. Iva Dee Hiatt's physical voice may have been silenced in the sleep of death, but the tradition, the knowledge, the love of singing continued in each of the voices who participated in that tribute. The final hymn was not sung by a soloist, but each of the four hundred voices sang in unison the traditional hymn of triumph following victory in battle, the Te Deum Laudamus.[26]

Iva Dee Hiatt's legacy is not limited to the physical remains or performances of the pieces she commissioned; to her photographs, programs, or recordings; or to the memories of the thousands of students whom she taught and inspired through her performance. Her humor, wit, dynamic character, strength, and warmth of personality remain special treasures for those who knew her. Yet there is also an intangible legacy, one far greater than these, that endures because through her students and singers, her musical legacy is passed to succeeding generations of young singers.

(Photogrpah of Iva Dee Hiatt courtesy of Amy Kaiser.)

Bibliography

Hiatt, Iva Dee. *An Introduction to the Sacred Music of Claudio Monteverdi*, M.A. Thesis, University of California, Berkeley, 1948.

Iva Dee Hiatt faculty biographical file, professor and director of choral music at Smith College from 1948-1980.

Lawn, Constance E. *The Harvard Crimson*, "New Summer Chorus at Tanglewood at the Berkshire Festival Sunday," Published 16 July 1963. http://www.thecrimson.com/article.aspx?ref=249966

Memorial Service for Iva Dee Hiatt, John M. Greene Hall, Smith College, 24 February 1980.

Miller, Robert. *Smith College Alumnae Quarterly*, February 1980, Vol. 61, No. 2, 61–62.

Obituary, *Daily Hampshire Gazette*, 7 January 1980.

Processional and Ceremonial Music for Palm Sunday from the Fourteenth and Fifteenth Centuries, Washington National Cathedral, 12 April 1981, performed by The National Chamber Singers and the Boston Camerata presented in Memory of Iva Dee Hiatt.

NOTES

[1] Amy Kaiser, Director of the Saint Louis Symphony Chorus, in a personal interview, 14 March 2008.

[2] Iva Dee Hiatt, Curriculum Vitae, courtesy of Nanci A. Young Smith College Archivist, 20 February 2006.

[3] Ibid.

[4] Ibid.

[5] Ibid.

[6] Kaiser, 14 March 2008.

[7] Helen Stott Spencer in an email to Joan Whittemore, 8 March 2008.

[8] Kaiser, 14 March 2008.

[9] Hiatt, courtesy of Amy Kaiser.

[10] Ibid.

[11] Hiatt, Ibid.

[12] Ibid.

[13] Ibid.

[14] Ibid.

[15] Ibid.

[16] Richard K. Winslow in an email to Joan Whittemore, 23 January 2008

[17] Truman Bullard in an email to Joan Whittemore, 18 September 2007.

[18] Ibid.

[19] Hiatt, Curriculum Vitae.

[20] Ibid.

[21] Jill Ker Conway, President of Smith College, 18 May 1979.

[22] Obituary, *Daily Hampshire Gazette*, 7 January 1980.

[23] Jill Ker Conway, email to Joan Whittemore, 29 October 2007.

[24] Sheila Heffernon, Smith (1976), in an email to Joan Whittemore, 27 March 2007.

[25] Robert Miller, *Smith College Alumnae Quarterly*, February 1980, Vol. 61, No. 2, 61–62, and Memorial Service, Smith College, 24 February 1980.

[26] Ruth Ring Harvie in an email sent to Joan Whittemore, 24 January 2008.

Margaret Hillis

(1 October 1921—4 February 1998)

All music starts from score study.

Joan Whittemore

Consider the extraordinary achievements of Margaret Hillis: founder of the Chicago Symphony Chorus and its director for over thirty-seven years; winner of nine Grammy Awards; director of the Elgin Symphony Orchestra for fourteen years; guest conductor for the National Symphony, San Francisco, Indianapolis, Milwaukee, Saint Paul, Baltimore, Minnesota, Columbus, Peoria, San Antonio, Spokane, and Oregon symphony orchestras; and founder of the American Choral Foundation and Association of Professional Vocal Ensembles—known today as Chorus America. Yet, Hillis was not accepted as a conservatory conducting student because she would be taking the place of someone who could get a conducting job. A woman could not get such a job. Composition professor Bernard Heiden told Margaret Hillis not to attempt to become a conductor except perhaps through the "backdoor" of choral conducting. He offered the caution not for lack of recognition of her gifts, but in acknowledgement of the climate of the era.

When Margaret Hillis attended Indiana University, there was no conducting major. She studied piano, strings and wind instruments. She majored in composition because she thought that a conductor should know what goes on in a composer's mind. In her senior year at Indiana, some fellow students preparing a program of contemporary music needed someone to conduct the chorus. They had asked a student who had taken two semesters of conducting to be their conductor. When the student declined, Margaret Hillis stepped in to rehearse the chorus. Acknowledging that she had no rehearsal technique, but did have the sound of Kirsten Flagstad's voice in her ear, she achieved color, line, phrasing, relatively good intonation, and excitement in the music of Randall Thompson. Thereupon she announced to her composition teacher Bernard Heiden that she was a conductor. He agreed, but warned her that it was difficult even for a man and impossible for a woman to become an orchestral conductor. Margaret Hillis disagreed, "There's only one woman I know of who could never be a symphony conductor, and that's the Venus de Milo." (Benz, 2–3.)

Juilliard and New York

Following the advice of Bernard Heiden, Margaret Hillis went to Juilliard in 1947 to study conducting with Robert Shaw. In order to do that she had to have her own chorus. She managed to acquire a chorus of non-auditioned singers composed of six tenors, twelve basses, and too many women to number, sponsored by the Youth Division of the NAACP. An early Hillis rehearsal technique consisted of the entire chorus singing the tenor part, then the bass part, then rehearsing those two parts together until she was convinced that the tenors thought they were singing a tune, then adding the alto, and finally the soprano in order to prevent the tenors from singing the soprano an octave lower throughout the piece. Hillis early demonstrated her careful attention to and planning of every detail and moment of the rehearsal, a strategy for which she became renowned. (Benz, 2–3.) During that period she was assistant conductor of Robert Shaw's Collegiate Chorale. Singing in the Collegiate Chorale was her first experience singing in a chorus. She was a pianist, had played tuba and saxophone, and was principal chair of the double bass section in the orchestra at Indiana University. After a summer at Tanglewood in 1950, she established the Tanglewood Alumni Chorus of New York City, later called the New York Concert Choir and sometimes the Concert Choir and American Concert Choir. (Benz, 4; Villella.)

In 1954 Margaret Hillis established the American Choral Foundation and a concert series in Town Hall. At this time she began her association with Igor Stravinsky and, for a period of about six years, prepared the choruses for him in world premieres of his choral works She also conducted the premieres of choral works of Ned Rorem, Ezra Laderman, and Edgar Varese, and prepared choruses for other conductors, including choruses for at least one hundred twenty operas. (Benz, 4–6.) At the performance of Bellini's *I Puritani*, in Carnegie Hall, when Margaret Hillis was backstage for the bow following the concert, Maria Callas approached her and said, "You prepared the chorus didn't you?" When Hillis acknowledged that she had, Maria Callas, said, "It is exquisite and I thank you." (Benz, 4–6.)

Chicago Symphony Chorus

With her New York reputation as a conductor well established and a national reputation emerging through touring, Margaret Hillis was just the conductor Fritz Reiner was looking for when he came to New York to find a reliable professional chorus to perform with the Chicago Symphony Orchestra. Margaret Hillis' manager heard about the situation and sent Fritz Reiner to her rehearsal of the New York Concert Choir already in progress. When she stopped the basses for a poor entrance, Reiner said "How do you do?" and Margaret responded, "How do you do?" It was the first time she had met him. He then greeted the chorus in the same way and they responded in unison, "How do you do?" Reiner then asked if she had the Verdi Requiem. They did not have enough copies to go around. He asked if they had the *Missa Solemnis*. Again they did not have enough copies. Then, very impatiently he asked, "What *do* you have?" They had the Bach Magnificat. Reiner then asked if they had the B Minor Mass. They did and distributed the copies. Having earlier conducted a performance of the Mass with the chorus, Hillis noticed that the personnel had changed significantly and did not recall how many of them had sung the piece. She asked Reiner which movement he would like to hear. He requested the first Kyrie. After the first four measures, she saw Reiner's hand moving and took his tempo. She again saw his hand moving at the end of the piece and took his *ritardando*. The chorus sang absolutely beautifully. Reiner then said, "Fine, fine." Margaret Hillis saw him to the door, and he asked, "Tell me. Do they sight-read?" She said that they did, of course, very well, at the same time noticing and being grateful for the silence behind her in the rehearsal room. He told her that she would hear from him, and he closed the door behind him. When she turned around to face the chorus, they exploded in laughter. She then asked how many of them had sung the piece before. *Four* of the forty-four had. All the rest had sight-read it. (Benz, 4–6.) Reiner hired them and sixty singers performed with the Chicago Symphony the following year.

When Reiner wanted to do the Verdi Requiem, Hillis refused to do it with fewer than one hundred twenty singers. At the same time, she knew the fee for such a large chorus would be prohibitive and recommended that they use the funds to build a chorus in Chicago because it would cover a season of four or five concerts each year rather than one performance. Margaret Hillis thought she knew what was about to happen—that Chicago would establish its own symphony chorus and that would end the collaboration with her chorus and Chicago. She received a phone call. "Margaret!" She replied, "Yes." "This is Reiner. Where do we get the singers?" Hillis explained how to accomplish it and offered to come to Chicago to advise the manager on setting up the mechanics and to audition a conductor for the chorus. Reiner responded, "We don't have it unless you conduct." Taken by surprise, she asked to return his call the next day. She saw that she had nearly every Monday free and could catch a midnight plane to New York to be back for her eleven o'clock class Tuesday morning. Thus, in 1957, the Chicago Symphony Chorus—the first of its kind in the United States—was born, with Margaret Hillis commuting between New York and Chicago for the first five years. (Benz, 10–11.)

Carnegie Hall, 31 October 1977

Margaret Hillis, desiring to establish a high level of professionalism in her choirs, said that "Professionalism means 'commitment—a sense of calling,' almost a religious calling. The dictionary doesn't even mention money. I was looking for people who had this sense that they were in music because they couldn't live without it." (Benz, 12.) For the next thirty-seven years Margaret Hillis and the Chicago Symphony Chorus set the standard for professionalism and excellence in the choral-orchestral repertoire. She prepared her choruses to sing for Fritz Reiner, Jean Martinon, Georg Solti, Carlo Maria Giulini, Claudio Abbado, countless guest conductors, and European tours, while conducting her own Elgin Symphony Orchestra and guest conducting throughout the country.

On 29 October 1977 after having conducted the first performance of Mahler's Eighth Symphony on a Thursday in Orchestra Hall, and a Saturday morning rehearsal with orchestra and soloists, Georg Solti fell and was unable to conduct the Saturday evening performance. John Edwards called Margaret Hillis about 5:30 Saturday afternoon and asked if she could conduct that evening. Hillis knew Part I since it was all chorus, but not Part II. On Monday and Tuesday they were scheduled to perform in Carnegie Hall. She said she could be ready to conduct Monday evening if she were needed. They agreed and cancelled the Saturday performance. From Saturday evening through noon on Sunday, she prepared the score; then she called the soloists' accompanist, Betty Buccheri. Neither of them knew where the soloists breathed. Margaret's concern had been strictly with the chorus. After Betty left, the phone rang. It was Valerie Solti. The maestro offered to go over the score with her. She changed her plane reservation, met with Solti, and finished her score analysis on the plane to New York. No one but a few friends knew that she would be conducting and they kept quiet. Just before the concert on Monday, 31 October, Julius Bloom announced to the audience, "Mr. Solti has had an accident; however he is fine and will be conducting tomorrow night's concert. He has put this performance in the hands of the distinguished conductor of the Chicago Symphony Chorus." Before Bloom could even announce Margaret Hillis' name, the New York audience, with their long memory and admiration of her work, had erupted with shouting, yelling, and clapping. During the performance, her eyes in turn were continually focusing on the chorus, soloists, and orchestra, to the extent that she had to *remember* to turn pages. She was so busy concentrating that she was hardly aware of the audience except at moments such as the opening of Part II when she could sense the silence and the intense concentration of the audience behind her. Following the performance, the audience again erupted into applause and there were at least ten or twelve curtain calls. (Benz, 27–29.)

Not only did the audience receive Margaret Hillis' performance well, but the critics did as well.

> What an improbable scenario. Even a militant feminist editor might reject it as just too much. One of the world's most lionized conductors, scheduled to lead one of the great orchestras in a Carnegie hall performance of Mahler's most complex and philosophically ambitious symphony, His place is taken by his woman assistant, and she conducts a triumphant performance that wins her a standing ovation. . . .
>
> If the foregoing does not yet strike you as the fevered dream of a novelist, consider in addition that this is a symphony that closes with a Mystical Choir singing the final, famous words of Goethe's *Faust*: "Das ewig' Weibliche zieht uns hinan"—"The Eternal Feminine leads us on."
>
> Miss Hillis built her performance carefully, but she built it well. What her Mahler eighth sometimes lacked in Soltian fire and tension, it made up for in poise, clarity, and ethereal detail. . . .

> Wisely opting at first for certainty and control, which lent a rather metronomic feeling to much of Part I, Miss Hillis gradually loosened up, and by the last ecstatic pages she had her forces working for her and Mahler with a burning enthusiasm that radiated a fine glow of the Faustian finale.
>
> —Donald Henahan, "Woman Steps in for Solti, Wins Carnegie Hall Ovation," *The New York Times*, 1 November 1977.

Score Study

How does one memorize Mahler's Eighth Symphony in forty-eight hours? Fortunately, Dennish Shrock documented Margaret Hillis' process in his 1991 article in the *Choral Journal*, "An Interview with Margaret Hillis on Score Study." Her philosophy was, "All music starts from score study. Know the score. See everything on the page. When I teach conducting, I always start with score study. It is what determines everything the conductor will do—from rehearsal procedures to gestural technique. You have to get as near as you possibly can to what the composer had in his ear. That's the whole point of all score study." (Shrock 7, 11.)

Even as an undergraduate student Margaret Hillis understood that a conductor should know what goes on in a composer's mind. She built on that premise, developing her skills of seeing and hearing everything on the page during her studies with Julius Herford and Otto Werner Mueller. She would begin with a clean score and make three excursions through the piece without marking anything. From there, her process consisted of five steps to analyze phrasing, harmonic function, expression marks, melodic material, and then to mark the instrumental parts. (Shrock, 10.)

Example 1 illustrates Margaret Hillis' process of determining phrasing (bar line analysis) and harmonic function, and her color code system for expression marks, melodic material, and instrumental parts. (Shrock, 7–9.)

Example 1

1. Three excursions through score.	Make no markings yet in preparation for score study.
2. Score study to be certain of seeing and hearing everything that is on the page.	
3. Determine harmonic rhythm.	a. Write chord roots. b. Assign functions (tonic, subdominant, dominant) to determine cadences.
4. Bar line analysis.	Determine phrase groupings; black pencil, transparent ruler.
5. Color code system.	
Mark dynamics and principal material:	Red—anything strong, e.g., *ff*; →→in red above the score for *accelerando.* Blue—*p* or *mp.* Green—*pp.* Brown—to reinforce accents (>).
Tempo markings:	Blue—anything up to ♩ = 80, e.g., ♩ = 72. Brown—♩ = 80–100 , e.g., ♩ = 88. Red—♩ = 100 and above, e.g., ♩ = 120.
Meter markings:	4 is marked X , 3 is marked △ , 2 is marked V , 6/8 and 12/8 squiggles following arm directions. Diagonal line through score for slower tempo.
Melodic material:	Yellow—melodic material.
Solos:	Purple—e.g. alto soloist.
Score divisions:	Yellow—through clefs of choral staves to see score divisions.
Fugue subjects:	Orange—fugue subject.
Countersubjects:	Yellow—countersubject.
Voices are considered part of instrumentation and marked as such.	Augmentation—stronger shade of color. Diminution—lighter shade of color.
6. Mark instrumental parts. Knowing the orchestra parts is part of your learning.	Add rehearsal numbers at structural points (for long stretches between letters) if it will save time in rehearsal.

Over and above this process of preparing the score, Margaret Hillis demonstrated that in order for the conductor to hear and see everything on the page, one must know the function, range, color, strengths and limitations of each instrument and voice, as well as the context for the dynamic markings for a particular instrument or voice.

> You have to know the function of each instrument—does it function as coloring—you have to know this so you know how to treat the dynamic markings. A marking by itself means nothing. In the study of the score, you must *hear* not just the naked color of the sound but the function. If you don't *hear* it, it will never come out.

> The conductor must have considerable knowledge about instruments—that a flute player is always trying to get air while an oboe players always has too much and is trying to get rid of it—that an oboe gets softer as its pitch ascends while a flute gets louder. Brass instruments are in a sense like voices, the higher they go the more tension there is in their sound. If you have an F trumpet (which transposes up) play, say, the C above middle C, there's not going to be a lot of tension in that sound. If a B♭ trumpet plays that C, there's going to be more tension in the sound. As with voices, that C is a fairly low note for a coloratura soprano. For a lyric, it is middle territory. It begins to get high for a mezzo. And, for a contralto, it has a lot of tension. You cannot know what the score is going to sound like unless you know that the piccolo sounds an octave higher than what is written, etc. (Shrock, 10–11.)

She then made an instrumental chart to identify the movements in which the instruments played to plan rehearsals and maximize rehearsal time. She began rehearsing the movements with the largest number of instrumentalists first. When finished, they were allowed to leave. For an example of an instrumental chart, see Example 2. (Shrock, 12.)

Example 2

Movement Sections	Keys	Chorus	Piccolo	Flute	Oboe	Oboe d'Amore	English Horn	Clarinet	Eb Clarinet	Bass Clarinet	Saxophone	Bassoon	Contrabassoon	Horn	Trumpet	Trombone	Tuba	Harp	Keyboard	Timpani	Percussion	Violin I	Violin II	Viola	Cello	Bass

Then she prepared a home study chart including the page numbers of the orchestral score and the piano reduction score, the level of difficulty of each movement and the dates of rehearsals for sectionals, specific movements, orchestra rehearsals and performances for maximum rehearsal time. See Example 3 for a sample home study chart. (Shrock, 12.)

Example 3

Brahms *German Requiem*	Pages:			1	2	2	2	2	3	4	5	6	7	8	9	10	11	
Movements and sections of movements if the orchestration changes:	Orchestra Score	Piano-Vocal Reductions	Difficulty	Day-Date Full	Day-Date Soprano	Day-Date Alto	Day-Date Tenor	Day-Date Bass	Day-Date Full	Day-Date Full	Day-Date Soprano/Alto	Day-Date Tenor/Bass	Day-Date Full	Day-Date Ful	Day-Date Full	Day-Date Orchestra	Day-Date Orchestra	Day-Date Performance
1. Ziemlich Langsam																		
Selig sind die Toten		1	XXXXX	X					X	X	X	X	X	X	X	X	X	X
2. Langsam Märschmassig																		
Denn alles Fleisch	2	1	XX	X									X	X	X	X	X	X
Etwas Bewegter																		
So seit nun geduldig	2	9	XXXX	X									X	X	X	X	X	X
Tempo I																		
Denn alles Fleisch	3	3	XX	X									X	X	X	X	X	X
Un poco Sostenuto																		
Aber des Herrn Wort	4	1	XX	X									X	X	X	X	X	X
Allegro non Troppo																		
Die Erlöseten des Herrn	4	2	XXXXXX	X	X	X	X	X	X	X	X	X	X	X	X	X	X	X

REHEARSAL TECHNIQUES

Hillis' next step was to plan the individual rehearsal. Dr. Cheryl Frazes Hill, member of the Chicago Symphony Chorus for more than twenty years, appointed to the conducting staff by Margaret Hillis in 1987, and currently associate conductor of the CSC, presented a detailed account of Margaret Hillis' process of preparing the chorus in "The Rehearsal Techniques of Margaret Hillis: Their Development and Application to the Brahms *German Requiem*" in the *Choral Journal*, October 2002. She observed that, "Hillis' rehearsals were always strategic. She went from the general details of the score to the smallest details, returning, toward the end of a rehearsal period to the larger picture." (Frazes Hill, 12.)

Margaret Hillis articulated her goals for the rehearsal and performance.

> The pride of musicians is in the mastery of their craft . . . after the mastery of craft comes the spiritual commitment. . . .
>
> Mastery of the craft is what I rehearse for . . . in order that each chorister can master what he is doing—vocally and rhythmically . . . in diction in the sense of the text. . . . Once that is there—once the technical things are there, then they are free to make music—and until they put those chains on them-

> selves, they are not free. That freedom is what I try for. . . . There has to be a mastery of the craft so that then there can be improvisation . . . and so that things can be changed a little and that it ends up being flexible. . . . Without the mastery, there is no flexibility. (Benz, 20-21.)

Dr. Frazes Hill reported that Margaret Hillis first talked the chorus through the entire score. She would give each singer detailed markings for the score. Then she had the chorus sing through the work on a neutral syllable, in a slower tempo and at a *mezzo piano* dynamic level. In the initial process, Margaret Hillis emphasized linear direction, phrasing, stressed and unstressed syllables, and a sense of color and balance of the work.

Hillis elicited musicality from the chorus from the beginning of the process. She also identified difficult pitches and rhythms as part of this early stage. Once the chorus was familiar with the pitches, rhythms, and phrases of a work, Hillis would add the text, giving careful attention to the diction. After singing a section on a neutral syllable, the chorus would speak the text rhythmically. Sectional rehearsals followed a full rehearsal and focused on one or two issues: difficult intervals, dissonances, intonation, contrapuntal material, rehearsing language, dealing with rhythmic details. (Frazes Hill, 12–14.)[1]

Margaret Hillis' ultimate secret was her ability to teach the chorus to listen.

> My work is done through the ears of the Chorus. I make them listen. Do you like that sound?—Do it again! . . . You have to have the sound in your ear before you raise your arm. I insisted that the sound be different for each piece according to what it needs. We are there at the service of the music. You can't use a Verdi sound when it comes to Debussy. I just experiment with them until I get it . . . until the sound is right and I say "That's it! Listen to it." Then we reproduce it constantly. (Benz, 41.)

Hillis' diligence in preparation and rehearsal and her constant striving for excellence won her well-deserved recognition: nine Grammy Awards, honorary doctorates, appointment to the National Council on the Arts (1985–1991), the Governors' Award from the Chicago Chapter of the National Academy of Recording Arts and Sciences, a 1994 Distinguished Alumni Service Award from Indiana University and the Margaret Hillis Achievement Award for Choral Excellence established by Chorus America. Ironically one of the greatest acknowledgements of her expertise came when John Sudler, Chairman of the Chicago Symphony Board asked her opinion about the selection of the next conductor for the orchestra. She gave her reasons for not selecting Herbert Von Karajan, and he listened. A week later, Sudler called her again and asked her what she thought about Georg Solti as the new Music Director and Carlo Maria Giulini as the Principal Guest Conductor. She approved.

Margaret Hillis showed artistic integrity not merely through her mastery of craft, technique, and ability to teach, but through a sense of responsibility to composers, choristers, orchestras, and audiences.

> I could always teach conducting students to move properly . . . to analyze a score, but to get intuitively into that score is something that is un-teachable . . . at least to a conductor. I tried to do that intuitive thing when it comes to the Chorus, so that they would find real "joy" in singing. If the joy in singing isn't there, if the joy in any performance is not there, forget it, because an audience then cannot participate. The members of the audience, too, are musicians and are there to participate in a musical experience. Without the technical command and the intuitive element that comes from up above, it just doesn't work. (Benz, 22–23.)

> There has to be the sense of continuity dating back to the Gregorian chant. The continuity of the human condition—that's what the arts are all about. And, it is even harder, now, as I have found out with these young people—very few of them have any conception of history. Very few of them have any conception of the nobility of the human spirit. And to instill that nobility in them is a real job—that sense of nobility. Because there is nothing more noble than an artistic masterpiece whether it be by Van Gogh or by Verdi. The nobility is what life is all about. (Benz, 49.)

Acknowledgements

The author is indebted to Frank Villella, Archivist for the Samuel and Marie Louise Rosenthal Archives of the Chicago Symphony Orchestra, and Christina Prucha, Archivist for the American Choral Directors Association, for their assistance in providing research materials for this biography of Margaret Hillis.

Education

1947	Bachelor of Music in Composition, Indiana University
1947–1949	Juilliard School of Music Further study with Robert Shaw

Appointments

1950	Founder, Tanglewood Alumnae Choir which became the New York Concert Choir and Orchestra
1950	Founder and Director of the New York Concert Choir (American Concert Choir)
1951–1953	Juilliard School of Music
1950–1960	Union Theological Seminary
1952	Assistant Director of the Collegiate Choir (Robert Shaw) Chorus Master of the American Opera Society
1957	Founded Chicago Symphony Chorus
1958	Founder American Choral Foundation that issues *American Choral Review and Research Memorandum Series*
1961–1968	Music Director, Kenosha Civic Orchestra
1967–1991	Conductor, Civic orchestra of Chicago
1969–1971	Choral Director of the Cleveland Orchestra
1970–1977	Director of Choral Activities, Northwestern University
1971–1984	Music Director, Elgin Symphony Orchestra, Elgin, IL
1977	Association of Professional Vocal Ensembles, now named Chorus America
1978	Visiting Professor, Indiana University
1982–1982	Choral Director of the San Francisco Symphony Orchestra

Appearances as Guest Conductor

1957	First woman to conduct the Chicago Symphony Orchestra Baltimore Symphony Orchestra Civic Orchestra of Chicago Milwaukee Symphony Orchestra St. Paul Chamber Orchestra
1958–1959	Santa Fe Opera

1976 Conducted world premiere of Alan Stout's *Passion* with the Chicago Symphony Orchestra

1977 Conducted Mahler's Eighth Symphony, Carnegie Hall

Awards and Honors

Honorary doctorates, including degrees from Temple University, Indiana University, North Park University, Carthage College, Wartburg College, Adrian College, St. Mary's College at Notre Dame, Lake Forest College, Saint Xavier College, and Saint Mary-of-the-Woods College.

Recipient of the Governors' Award from the Chicago Chapter of the National Academy of Recording Arts and Sciences.

Chorus America established the Margaret Hillis Achievement Award for Choral Excellence. This award, which recognizes the late Miss Hillis for her more than forty years of professional achievement and outstanding contributions to the choral art, is presented annually to an ensemble that demonstrates artistic excellence, a strong organizational structure, and a commitment to outreach, educational, and/or culturally diverse activities. A cash award of $5,000 accompanies a plaque honoring the chosen ensemble. The award is given in alternating years to a professional chorus, a professional-core chorus, a volunteer chorus, and a children/youth chorus. (http://www.chorusamerica.org)

1985–1991 National Council of the Arts.

1994 Distinguished Alumni Service Award from Indiana University.

Grammy Awards

Margaret Hillis prepared the Chicago Symphony Chorus in forty-five recorded works. Under her choral direction, the Chicago Symphony Orchestra and Chorus won nine Grammy Awards for "Best Choral Performance, Classical."

1977 Verdi, Requiem, Georg Solti, conductor and Margaret Hillis, choral director.

1978 Beethoven, *Missa Solemnis*, Georg Solti, conductor, and Margaret Hillis, choral director.

1979 Brahms, *A German Requiem*, Sir Georg Solti, conductor, and Margaret Hillis, choral director.

1982 Berlioz, *La Damnation de Faust*, Sir Georg Solti, conductor, and Margaret Hillis, choral director.

1983 Haydn, *The Creation*, Sir Georg Solti, conductor, and Margaret Hillis, choral director.

1984 Classical Brahms, *A German Requiem*, James Levine, conductor, and Margaret Hillis, choral director.

1986 Orff, *Carmina Burana*, James Levine, conductor, and Margaret Hillis, choral director.

1991 Bach Mass in B Minor, Georg Solti, conductor, and Margaret Hillis, choral director.

1993 Bartók, *Cantata Profana*, Pierre Boulez, conductor, and Margaret Hillis, choral director.

Publications

Margaret Hillis' archival records of 286 items including scores, instrumental parts with her personal markings, books, Grammy Awards, photographs, papers, and correspondence are housed in the Samuel and Marie Louise Rosenthal Archives of the Chicago Symphony Orchestra. http://www.cso.org

Hillis, Margaret. *Choral Rehearsal Techniques: A Statement of Procedures Recommended for the Training of Choruses and Choirs.* N.A.T.S. 1959.

____. *Sample Application Form for Membership in a Chorus: An Outline of Procedures used for Auditioning Choristers, a Sample Anthem Rating Form, and Sample Acceptance and Rejection Letters for Auditionees.* New York: American Choral Foundation, 1960.

____. *At Rehearsals.* New York: American Choral Foundation, 1961.

____. *At Rehearsals.* Barrington, IL, 1969.

____. *A Select List of Choral Music for Festivals.* New York: American Choral Foundation, 1961.

Videography

Hillis, Margaret. *Brahms Requiem: A Master Class in Score Analysis.* Chicago: Hillis fellowship, 1984. OCLC 11445553.

_____. *Master Class Series.* Wheeling, IL. Master Class Productions, 1985.

_____. *Chorus Segment.* Chicago: U.S. Video 198- OCLC 22780205.

Artbeat Chicago: A Powerful Voice (Margaret Hillis), 20 May 1998, Samuel and Marie Louise Rosenthal Archives of the Chicago Symphony Orchestra. Archives Number AV-GEN-0302, Stack Number AV-GEN-0302 VC-185. http://www.cso.org

Memorial to Margaret Hillis, including historic photographs, recordings of Hillis speaking, of rehearsal and performance footage, and interviews with colleagues and Chicago Symphony Chorus members. Rehearsal and performance footage includes Hillis conducting the *Messiah* at Medinah Temple; Solti conducting the Chicago Symphony Chorus in *Damnation of Faust* (from commercial release); and Wolfe rehearsing the Chicago Symphony Chorus in *Fidelio* in Buntrock Hall.

Bibliogrpahy

Benz, Jon. "Interview of Margaret Hillis," Rosenthal Archives of the Chicago Symphony Orchestra, Oral History Collection G, NO. 611. 19 September 1989.

Chovanec, Sheila. "Conducting behind the old man's back: narratives of experience of Margaret Hillis," Master's Projects summer session 2005. VanderCook College of Music. 2005.

Dennen, Janel Jo. "Margaret Hillis and the Chicago Symphony Chorus: Perspective and Interview," *Choral Journal*, November 1982, p. 18.

Erickson, Raymond. "Miss Hillis Carries Her Baton Lightly." *The New York Times*, 2 November 1977.

Geiger, Peter, editor of transcript: "Anton Bruckner's Mass in E Minor: A Performer's Guide by Margaret Hillis," *Journal of the Conductor's Guild*, Vol. 21, No. 1 and 2, Winter/Spring-Summer/Fall 2000, p. 28.

Glenn, Carole ed., *In Quest of Answers*. Chapel Hill, NC. Hinshaw Music, 1991, p. 110.

Henahan, Donal. "Woman Steps in for Solti Wins Carnegie Hall Ovation," *The New York Times*, 1 November 1977.

Hill, Cheryl Frazes. "The Rehearsal Techniques of Margaret Hillis: Their Development and Application to Brahms' *German Requiem*," *Choral Journal*, October 2002, Vol. 43, No. 2, pp. 9–31. Online interactive video segment: http://www.acdaonline.org/cj/interactive/oct2002

Livengood, Stanley. "The History of the Chicago Symphony Chorus, 1957–2000," 2001, OCLC 48916972.

Pellegrini, Norman, "Interview of Margaret Hillis," transcribed, Rosenthal Archives of the Chicago Symphony Orchestra, Oral History Collection G, 6 October 1997.

Rosenberg, Deena. *The Musicmakers*. New York: Columbia University Press, 1979.

Samuelson, Jane. "For the Love Music," *Chicago Magazine*, April 1980, p. 194.

Shrock, Dennis, "An Interview with Margaret Hillis on Score Study," *Choral Journal*, 31, February 1991, p. 12.

Von Rein, John. "Hillis Stands on her Own as a Stand-In for Solti." *Chicago Tribune*, 3 Novemver 1977.

Obituary, *Choral Journal*, April 1998, p. 58.

INTERVIEWS

Margaret Hillis Interviewed by Duffie, Bruce. WNIB 30 September 1986, 8 March 1988, 3 April 1990, 8 May 1990, 26 February 1991, 5 October 1991, 5 October 1996, and 28 March 1998. http://www.bruceduffie.com/intst.html

_____. Interviewed by Benz, Jon. 19 September 1989. Rosenthal Archives of the Chicago Symphony Orchestra. Oral History Collection G. Archive Number: OHP-G.

_____. Interviewed by Pelligrini, Norman. 6 October 1997. Rosenthal Archives of the Chicago Symphony Orchestra. Oral History Collection G. Archive Number: OHP-G.

NOTE

[1] Margaret Hillis's score analysis techniques are described in much greater detail in Dr. Frazes Hill's article pertaining to the Brahms *German Requiem*. Hill's article has an online interactive video segment at: http://www.acdaonline.org/cj/interactive/oct2002

The Rosenthal Archives of the Chicago Symphony Orchestra, Oral History Collection, also includes a video of Margaret Hillis leading a master class in score analysis of Brahms *German Requiem*.

Eva Jessye

(20 January 1895—21 February 1992)

Joan Whittemore

"Whatever Ever Happened to Eva Jessye?" quipped a feature article in *Ebony* in May 1974.[1] Dr. Jessye told journalist Karen Ray,

> I don't want people to think my life was *Porgy and Bess*. It was not. You'd think I was dead before *Porgy and Bess*, then I came to life and since *Porgy and Bess* I died again.[2]

Indeed, Eva Jessye, born 20 January 1895 in Coffeyville, Kansas, came to be known as the "grand dame of Black Music in America."[3] She commented on her formal education in a personal interview with Doris Louise Jones Wilson that, "No training I have explains what I am able to do."[4] As a child she learned to play piano by ear, composed songs, and at age twelve organized a girls' quartet teaching them the parts by ear. The quartet was invited to sing in the Odd Fellows Hall in Coffeyville, Kansas.[5] At the age of thirteen, Eva's mother enrolled her in Western University in Quindaro, Kansas. Because she was too young to qualify for the choir, she entered a sight-singing class. R. G. Jackson, the choir director, soon discovered that Eva could read music, sing all the parts, and had a gift for harmony, thus qualifying her for the choir. Soon she became the director's assistant rehearsing the choir and girls sextet when occasions arose.[6] After four semesters in the choir, she discovered that some choir members were receiving free tuition for their participation in the choir. When she asked for tuition remission, she was refused. Her mother and other family members were making enormous sacrifices for her education, and this denial in view of her contribution to the chorus was very hurtful. She left the choir to devote time to piano, music theory, and her other academic subjects despite continued pleas (but no offer of tuition remission) from the choral director. She won first and second year awards for outstanding work in harmony class. The third year award was denied in retaliation for her having left the choir. Her gift for poetry was also recognized in 1914 when she was awarded first place winner in the James A. Handy Literary Society Contest in Fort Scott, Kansas.[7]

After graduation from Western University, she taught in Muskogee, Oklahoma, and entered the State University for Colored, later changed to Langston University. Upon earning her lifetime certification for public school teaching in 1918, she continued to teach in Oklahoma. During this period she was a church musician and also played piano in a movie house where she learned the Blues and became familiar with vaudeville music.[8]

William Pickens, Dean of Morgan College (subsequently Morgan State University), Baltimore, Maryland, advised Eva to apply for the position of music director at the college. She began her tenure at Morgan College in 1919. Eva asked permission to organize the first choir at Morgan. Permission was given, but support was not. There was no time allotted for the chorus in the schedule. When the students began skipping classes, etc. to be in the choir, she received the complaint that she put too much emphasis on music. Eva thought that the choir should not only learn traditional Black music, but classical repertoire as well. Dr. Spencer, the college president disagreed. This climate continued until Palm Sunday, 1920.

> On Palm Sunday, the choir marched into the chapel singing "Unfold, Unfold, Ye Portals Everlasting." It must have been twenty-four or thirty singers. It was beautiful. Dr. Ernest Lyons, Ambassador to Liberia, and Dr. Spencer were sitting on the rostrum. We sang spirituals and other things. Dr. Lyons turned to Dr. Spencer and said, "You and I have been friends for many years." Spencer answered, "Yes." Dr. Lyons continued, "Well, why didn't you tell me you had music like this at Morgan College?" Spencer puffed up and smiled broadly. The next morning, Eva walked into Spencer's office and handed him her resignation.[9]

The same day Eva resigned she returned to Oklahoma. When asked by Doris Louise Jones Wilson why she had resigned, Eva's comment was, "You can try for a thing so hard that, when you get it, to hell with it. It can take so much out of you that you don't value it. I was accepted, but the next day I resigned."[10]

In 1925, Eva having established a relationship with the paper through publishing her poetry while at Morgan College, returned to work at the Baltimore Afro-American newspaper as a proofreader, writer of musical reviews and feature articles.[11] While working for the newspaper, the Dixie Jubilee Singers, a local group of eight singers, asked her to be their conductor. They performed spirituals and popular songs in Baltimore. Phillip Patterson, one of the basses discovered that the Rivoli Theater on Broadway wanted a Black group to perform mood music before films. The Dixie Jubilee Singers auditioned and won the spot.[12]

Eva Jessye worked from 1926 to 1929 in radio at the Capitol Theater when she and the Dixie Jubilee Singers became regulars on the "Major Bowes Family Radio Hour" and the "General Motors Hour." She wrote scripts for her original programs and implemented her choir now known as the Eva Jessye Choir for which she arranged nearly all of the spirituals performed that aired on WOR and WJZ. One of her quartets, the Four Dusty Travellers, eventually had its own program on WJZ and performed what was thought to be one of the first singing commercials. Through her work at Capitol she met Eugene Ormandy, Leopold Stokowski, and Dmitri Mitropoulos with whom she and her choir later performed.[13]

Along with her work in radio, Eva worked with the National Council of Churches, performed concerts with the choir, and composed music. She asked to study with Percy Goetschius. He was reluctant to do so for fear of interfering with her spontaneity and intuition. His solution was for her to compose as much as she could and send the music to him for evaluation. The result was the collection of sixteen solo spirituals that she edited and arranged. Eva Jessye believed that the "Negro" spirituals of her ancestors were a distinct type of music unique to the African American heritage. *My Spirituals* was published in 1927 by Robbins—Engel, Inc.[14]

Gwendolyn B. Bennett in the November 1927 issue of *Opportunity*, noted

> She has done more than the mere gathering together a collection of spirituals; she has given them character, "body." Eva Jessye has compiled a volume that is an adequate merger of four arts: Music, Poetry, Decoration, and Bookbinding.[15]

Eva Jessye received a congratulatory note dated 21 September 1927 from the internationally known singer Paul Robeson upon publication of her Spirituals.[16]

My dear Miss Jessye:

I want to congratulate you upon your book, *My Spirituals*. I find the melodies most interesting, and different from the usual type of spiritual. I am looking forward with great pleasure to adding your "Who is Dat Yondah?" and "Gwine to March Down to Jordan" to my recital programs this year.

Very sincerely,
Paul Robeson

The Fisk Jubilee Singers had introduced Spirituals to the world. Eva Jessye introduced her own compositions to the National Broadcasting Company. Floyde J. Calvin noted that, "She brought the spirituals to their highest point—that of presenting international broadcasts composed of spirituals in a specific setting."[17]

Major Edward Bowes who was the Vice-President of MGM motion pictures, chose King Wallis Vidor (1894–1982) to direct the film, *Hallelujah* in 1929, the first talking film with a Black cast. He also selected Eva Jessye to be the music director. She and her choir were flown to Hollywood.[18] Doris Wilson reports that while King Vidor reputedly hired the best Black performers, he did not treat them professionally. They experienced discrimination, injustices, and embarrassments. Eva Jessye, attempting to protect her performers chastened them not to stay out late or perform for members of the set without pay. King Vidor overheard this and dismissed her from the film. Upon legal advice, Eva came to work each day and sat outside the studio. King Vidor had greatly underestimated her tenacity and the contribution that she made musically, in teaching, and in working within the necessary time frame. When Vidor saw that they were falling behind schedule, and that it was Eva who had been the force for "molding the singing and acting into a unit," he immediately rehired Eva and finished the film on time.[19]

Her next major opportunity came when she was selected to become the choral director for Virgil Thomson's and Gertrude Stein's opera, *Four Saints in Three Acts*, in 1934. The then fledgling playwright, John Houseman had been selected as producer-director.

After attending a performance of Hall Johnson's *Run Little Children*, Virgil Thomson decided that he wanted his opera to have a Black cast, because he stated, "They alone possess the dignity and the poise, the lack of self-consciousness that proper interpretation of the opera demands. And they are not ashamed of words."[20]

John Houseman and Virgil Thomson had originally wanted Hall Johnson's choir, but upon Edward Perry's recommendation that Eve Jessye's choir would be a better choice not only because of the quality of their singing and musical standards, but because Hall Johnson's choir sang principally by rote.[21]

Eva Jessye's account of the process was as follows.

> The first thing I did was get the score that night and get things in control for myself. The first thing is for the conductor to get things in control, have things figured out before he tells the choir. I had the choir to meet me for rehearsal at 8:00 the next morning. Thomson was to meet us at 10:00. We rehearsed until 9:30. Thomson arrived at 10:00. He started the rehearsal, not knowing they had seen the score, by saying something like, "now do the best you can." Thomson played; I conducted. When they started to sing, he was simply taken off his feet.[22]

Four Saints in Three Acts was successful financially and artistically. Thomson recalled:

> The negroes proved in every way rewarding. Not only could they enunciate and sing, they seemed to understand because they sang. . . . They moved, sang, spoke with grace and with alacrity, took on roles without self-consciousness, as if they were the saints they said they were. . . . The negroes gave meaning to both words and music by making the Stein text easy to accept.[23]

Conspicuous by its absence is Thomson's acknowledgement of Eva Jessye's role. Eva Jessye thought this to be in retaliation for her having insisted that her singers be paid for rehearsals. John Houseman concurred, and the singers were paid fifteen dollars a week from the first rehearsal. It was the first time that a Black chorus in Harlem was paid for rehearsals. Learning to protect herself and her singers, Eva Jessye did ensure that she and her singers were appropriately credited in the program.[24] The critic hailed her work.

The repertoire of the Eva Jessye Choir consisted of spirituals, work songs, blues, and jazz, many of which Eva wrote or arranged. Daniel Lyman Ridnut, Minister to the National Broadcasting Company wrote, "This choir is without a doubt the finest I have heard on the air, in the interpretation of Negro Spirituals."[25]

Etude in December 1934, listed Eva in their Historical Musical Portrait Series, in their serial collection of the "World's Best Known Musicians." She was hailed as an authority on Negro Spirituals and as Director of the Eva Jessye Choir, which had performed in Lewison Stadium in an opera, *Four Saints in Three Acts.*[26]

Eva's next great success was a folk oratorio, *Paradise Lost and Regained*, based on John Milton's epic, premiered on NBC. She saw spirituals on every subject throughout the work.[27]

All through the Depression, Eva was able to keep herself and her musicians employed. Following a tour of the South with her choir, she found an audition notice for George Gershwin's opera, *Porgy and Bess.*

Her contract with the Theater Guild, Inc. on 19 March 1935 stated that she was:

- to furnish her choir of sixteen and be responsible for the musical training of the entire chorus
- to play a small part in the production, without additional compensation
- to be announced on the program as Choral Director[28]

Eva Jessye would be associated with nearly every *Porgy and Bess* production worldwide for the next thirty years, becoming the "curator and guardian of the score."[29]

The first performance of *Porgy and Bess* was at the Colonial Theatre, Boston, Massachusetts on 30 September1935 with Todd Duncan as Porgy, Anne Brown as Bess, and the Eva Jessye Choir. The opera toured Detroit, Pittsburgh, Chicago, and Washington, DC.[30] Olin Downes, critic for *The New York Times*, wrote:

> When it came to sheer acting last night, certain operatic functionaries should have been present. If the Metropolitan chorus could even put one half the action into the riot scene in the second act of *Meistersinger* that the Negro cast put into the fight that followed the crap game it would be not merely refreshing but miraculous.[31]

With one hundred twenty performances in Boston, the three month tour, Merle Armitage's revival in 1938 in Los Angeles, Cheryl Crawford's revision in 1941 that returned to New York in 1942 with most of the original cast, huge box office successes and critical acclaim, an eight month run on Broadway followed by a forty-seven city tour, the one constant element was Eva and the Eva Jessye Choir. Another revival of *Porgy and Bess* came with new principals, William Warfield as Porgy and Leontyne Price as Bess and a second tour of Chicago, Pittsburgh, and Washington, D.C., included performances for President Truman and state officials. It is notable that for the first time Blacks were able to attend the performances at the National Theater without suffering the stigma of segregation.[32] During the State Department sponsored six month European goodwill tour of *Porgy and Bess*, the company garnered artistic and political headlines.[33]

Raymond Jack of *The New York Times* wrote, "The voices are admirable. It's simply wonderful how the voices fall from a screaming high pitch into a rich normal voice again. Every tone and every moment is full of discipline."[34] Max Graf wrote in *Musical America*, "The ensemble was flawless. The solo parts and the chorus, which had been trained by Eva Jessye, were consummately blended as the street of Charleston was revealed."[35]

There were two more European tours including a performance at La Scala and the Soviet Union, Canada, and Latin America. After three hundred and five performances on Broadway in 1953, touring all of the United States and twenty-six European countries, a tour of colleges in 1967, and a 1970 production in Israel, all of which involved Eva Jessye, she was named "guardian of the score" and was often called upon as an advisor in subsequent performances. There were times when directors thought they could employ her choir and dispense with her; but they soon discovered that Eva Jessye was the cornerstone on which the success of the performance depended.[36]

The European tours of *Porgy and Bess* also afforded the Eva Jessye Choir to perform for refugees, heads of state, and audiences in all the cities to which they traveled.[37] Following the first tour of *Porgy and Bess*, Eva Jessye continued to arrange performances for the Eva Jessye Choir, wrote her second oratorio, *The Chronicle of Job*, moved the choir's headquarters to Sumter, South Carolina, and devoted her time between her professional choir and her duties as visiting artist-in-residence at Claflin College in Orangeburg, South Carolina until 1940.[38]

During the forties she continued to seek performances with her professional choir, donated her services to the war efforts in the form of benefit conferences for which she received a government citation. Eva wrote the theme song, *Freedom is a Thing Worth Talking About*, for the Russian War Relief program that the Society for American-Soviet Friendship sponsored.[39] In the fifties Eva Jessye initiated her tour of Ten Thousand Miles performing in Oklahoma, Georgia, Missouri, Louisiana, and Texas all the while continuing with the revivals of *Porgy and Bess*. For the first time since childhood, she returned to her native town of Coffeyville, Kansas in 1952, and performed with her choir. In appreciation for the warmth of the reception that she and the choir received, she wrote a musical, *Heart of the U.S.A.*, which focused on the history of Kansas. She produced and directed the performance always with an eye for authenticity, and involved the entire community in the production. The production was a great success.[40]

In the mid-fifties Eva Jessye moved the choir to Lawrence, Massachusetts, and changed its name to the American Concert Ensemble. She produced her oratorio, *Paradise Lost and Regained.* Since the original Eva Jessye Choir was on tour with *Porgy and Bess,* the Lawrence choir consisted of members from surrounding towns and was sponsored by the Greater Lawrence Council of Churches. Not only did the performance enthrall the audience at the Fitchburg Church of Christ, but as a result, segregation in the worship services ceased. She wrote a radio script, *Following the Star*, which was aired in Lawrence. The Eva Jessye Choir performed the premiere concert for the Concert and Lecture Series on 3 November 1957. Her appearance in Kurt Weil's *Lost in the Stars* followed in 1958. She wrote and produced *The Story of the Black Wise Man*, which premiered in Brooklyn, New York in 1959.[41]

The Eva Jessye Choir headquarters moved to New York in 1960. Continuing in her tradition as champion of those experiencing injustice, she volunteered her choir for the 1963 march on Washington where it became the official choir for the Freedom March for Jobs.[42] At age sixty-eight she showed no signs of slowing down. John Gray Associates of Brooklyn, New York, honored her for her contribution to American folk music. She returned to college teaching and performed as an actress in films, most notably *Black Like Me* in 1964. She was choral director and singer for Pittsburgh's Civic Light Opera production of *Porgy and Bess* that ran for four weeks in 1965. There was another US tour of Porgy and Bess in which she and the Eva Jessye Choir performed to great critical acclaim.[43]

In 1972, Eva Jessye moved to Ann Arbor, Michigan looking to her future retirement. An invitation to conduct her oratorio, *Paradise Lost and Regained*, in the Washington National Cathedral came the same year. Although there had been performances of the work throughout the thirties, forties, and fifties, this was to be the first completed production anywhere. Lawrence Sears of the *Washington Evening Star* wrote of Eva:

> She turned out to be very much her "own woman." Showing perceptive taste, she avoided both the Broadway sheen Gershwin cast over DuBose Heyward's tale of Porgy, and the stylized simplicity of Thomson's treatment of the solemn nonsense in Gertrude Stein's *Four Saints in Three Acts.*
>
> Her treatment of spirituals is more than mere arrangements. The selection, individual scoring, and provision of threads of solo introduction and lead in devices turned out a revelation. Many may be surprised that out of the

thirty-some spirituals, two of the finest were entirely her own creation, "Lucifer, Son of the Morning" and "That Ancient City on the Seven Hills."[44]

Following this success, Eva Jessye returned to Ann Arbor, established a new Eva Jessye Choir, and conducted another production of *Porgy and Bess*. Through Willis Patterson, a University of Michigan faculty member, she learned that the University did not have a collection of materials on Black musicians and entertainers. For several years donating her own personal funds, she contacted Black musicians to contribute materials. The Eva Jessye Afro-American Music Collection at the University of Michigan was dedicated on 4 January 1974. The collection spans nearly one hundred years of manuscripts, photos, recordings, art objects, and Eva Jessye's personal library of countless materials of black writers, musicians, artists, dancers, and directors. She was honored by the university by having 19 January 1974 proclaimed as Eva Jessye Day.[45]

There would be many more days proclaimed for Eva Jessye: 10 October 1976 in Manhattan, 20 January 1978 in Atlanta, 1 October 1978, her eighty-third birthday, in Pittsburg, Kansas with a definitive production of *Paradise Lost and Regained*, which she produced, directed, and for which she played piano.[46]

Not surprisingly, Eva Jessye achieved a significant number of "firsts." Dr. Eileen Southern included her in *Music of Black Americans* published in 1971. It was the first time a writer had featured Eva Jessye in a historical textbook.[47] She was the first black woman to achieve international acclaim as a choral conductor.[48] She was admitted to the Songwriters Hall of Fame in 1973, and was awarded a degree in Determination by the Department of Afro-American Studies at the University of Michigan in 1976. The International Women's Year of 1976 cited Dr. Jessye for her contribution to the Arts.[49]

In 1976 Eva Jessye was featured in a PBS documentary, *Slices of Life*, in which she spoke about Black American folk music. The *Capital-Journal* of Topeka listed Eva Jessye among Kansans of distinction in December of 1978.[50] From 1978–1981 Eva Jessye was Artist-in-Residence at Pittsburg State University. Governor John Carlin declared Dr. Eva Jessye to be Kansas Ambassador for the Arts in 1981. Awarded honorary degrees from Wilberforce University, Allen University, and an honorary doctorate from Southern University, Eva Jessye received countless citations from government, educational, and musical institutions. She was a member of ASCAP and the Negro Actors' Guild.[51]

In 1977, Eva Jessye donated her papers: correspondence, photographs, newspapers articles, programs, music, writings including published and unpublished poems, rosters of her choirs, audio recordings, conversations, and scripts to the Leonard H. Axe Library Pittsburg State University, Kansas, that provided an excellent overview of her life and career. Arriving in Kansas in 1979, Eva Jessye determined to complete her writings so that the royalties and other income from her publications could be used for scholarships at Pittsburg State. The collections continued to grow until 1994 two years following her death.[52]

In the "biographical" series, Dr. Jessye included notes in preparation for her proposed biography with a working title "Red Carpet and Cold Linoleum." Of particular note in the Correspondence series are the letters of Jester Hairston during the period of 1953 to 1980 and those of Celia Cox, Dr. Jessye's aunt, from 1953 to 1980. A host of other correspondence is included with Eubie Blake, Ossie Davis, Ruby Dee, George and Ira Gershwin, Corretta Scott King, Langston Hughes, and Leopold Stokowski. Among the published and unpublished writings is the 1978 *Selected Poems by Dr. Eva Jessye*. Newspaper and magazine articles, book references, collected writings of other artists, Ora Williams' "Eva Jessye: The Musical Poet," and Eva Jessye's own "Rice and Roses: The Story of Celia Cox" form the "writing" series. The "photo" series includes everything from personal and family photos to publicity to artists and celebrities. Performance photos feature those of *Hallelujah*, *Four Saints in Three Acts*, *Paradise Lost and Regained*, and *Porgy and Bess*. Printed programs from her own Eva Jessye Choir as well as performances of other artists dating from 1919 to 1922 include concerts of the Dixie Jubilee Singers, a 1932 Major Edward Bowes radio program and a program from the 1963 Civil Rights March on Washington with Dr. Martin Luther King, Jr. The website for the Eva Jessye Collection is:
http://www.library.pittstate.edu/spcoll/indxjessye.html

In the 1980s, Eva Jessye became artist-in-residence at Pittsburg State University where she continued to write, direct, and produce musical performances. She was also free to accept invitations from other universities as well.[53] That same year the Wichita Chapter of Women in Communication chose Eva Jessye as one of six women in Kansas history to be featured in a series of illustrations. She was appointed Kansas Ambassador for the Arts, and named to the Senior Citizens Hall of Fame in Everett, Washington.[54] Following her three years in Pittsburg, Eva Jessye returned to Ann Arbor to complete her writings.

What is Eva Jessye's legacy? In her own words, she states that she did not want to be remembered as a one-hit-wonder. Eva Jessye was a teacher, conductor, poet, composer, arranger, scholar, impresario-manager who looked out for her singers and was particularly devoted to young artists by way of opening doors for them. "That's what I've been doing all of my life, opening doors for other people. And I plan to continue doing that."[55]

Dr. Jessye recounted an incident that gives great insight into her determination and ability to seize the moment in opening doors for others.

> Of booking agents . . . "I knew them all before I was through." She would be in New York and run across a booking agent she knew; he would say to her, "Come in and talk to me someday, I'll see what I can do." Eva would reply, "What's the matter with now? I'm here, you're here. Let's talk now." Then before she knew it, she would have a booking for the choir.[56]

Jester Hairston sang with the Eva Jessye Choir in the 1930s. In a letter to her he wrote:

> If I ever amount to anything in our field, it will be due to the inspiration I received from you, Miss Jessye. You did more for me than all the schools I attended, because you gave me a new concept of our people, through your sincere and artistic arrangements of the songs and your authentic interpretations of them. And because of the many happy experiences with you and your groups. I have devoted my musical knowledge and all my energy to carrying on this significant work.[57]

Eva Jessye, along with Hall Johnson, was a pioneer in professional Black Choir Movements in the United States, both of them predating the professional choirs of the next era of Fred Waring, Roger Wagner, Norman Luboff, and Robert Shaw.[58] Though her arena was primarily theatre and show business, she maintained a constant connection with college and university choirs, and church choirs through her artist-in-residence programs, and guest performances, enabling her to have an enormous influence and impact on succeeding generations of choral directors and singers. Eva Jessye was conductor of one of the longest living professional choruses, from 1926–1981.[59]

Whether through listening to performances of her choirs, singing the spirituals that she arranged, performing her oratorios, reading her poetry, or just having the courage to say, "What's the matter with now? I'm here, you're here. Let's talk now,"[60] Eva Jessye will continue to open doors for us for many years to come.

Bibliography

Black, Donald Fisher. *The Life and Work of Eva Jessye and Her Contributions to American Music.* Ph. D. Thesis, Ann Arbor: University of Michigan, 1986.

Blanding, Mary Catherine. *A catalogue of the Eva Jessye Afro-American Music Collection as of May 1, 1974.* Master's Thesis, Ann Arbor: University of Michigan, 1974.

Jessye, Eva. *I Dream a World.* 1989.

______. *My spirituals.* Illustrated by Millar of the Roland company, edited by Gordon Whyte and Hugo Frey. New York: Robbins-Engel, 1927.

Phillips, M Scott. *Theatre, War, and Propaganda: 1930–2005.* Tuscaloosa: Southeastern Theatre Conference and the University of Alabama Press, 2005.

Standifer, James. "The Complicated Life of Porgy and Bess." *Humanities,* November/December 1997, Volume 18, Number 6.

Wilson, Doris Louise Jones. *Eva Jessye: Afro-American Choral Director.* Thesis (Ed. D.) St. Louis: Washington University, 1989.

Eva Jessye Afro-American Music Collection at the University of Michigan, Ann Arbor, MI.

Contents: Books and periodicals, libretti, scripts of plays and motion picture productions, music programs, scores(well over one hundred musical scores), clippings, photographs (over six hundred), photographic display panels, correspondences, writings, papers, and numerous poems written by Dr. Jessye and her personal memoirs.

Kansas Historical Society, 6425 SW Sixth Avenue, Topeka KS, 66615. http://www.kshs.org/people/jessye_evea.htm

Leonard H. Axe Library Special collections Department at Pittsburg State University, Pittsburg, KS. http://www.library.pittstate.edu/spcoll/indxjessye.html

Maryland Historical Society. mdhs.org

Discography

Gershwin, George. Porgy and Bess (Original Cast Recordings, 1935–1942) Label: Naxos Historical, Catalogue No. 8.110219-20. Conductors: Greenwood, Clifford; Shilkret, Nathaniel; Smallens, Alexander; Wallenstein, Alfred. Orchestras: Decca Symphony Orchestra, Leo Reisman Orchestra, Los Angeles Philharmonic Orchestra. Choir: Eva Jessye Choir. Artists: Bay, Emmanuel; Brown, Anne; Dowdy, Helen; Duncan, Todd; Heifetz, Jascha; Jepson, Helen; Long, Avon; Matthews, Edward; Robeson, Paul; Tibbett, Lawrence.

Gershwin, George. *Porgy And Bess*. Original Soundtrack Audio CD (1 January 1997). Original Release Date: 28 April 1992. Number of Discs: 1. Format: Soundtrack. Label: MCA. ASIN: B000002OJM.

Eva Jessye Credits on Broadway from the Internet Broadway Database

Four Saints in Three Acts. (Original, Musical, All Black Cast, Opera) Choral Director: Eva Jessye. 20 February 1934–14 April 1934.

Porgy and Bess. (Original, Musical, Opera) Choral Director: Eva Jessye; Performer: The Eva Jessye Choir. 10 October 1935–25 January 1936.

Porgy and Bess. (Revival, Musical, Opera) Choral Director: Eva Jessye; Performer: The Eva Jessye Choir. 22 January 1942–26 September 1942.

Memphis Bound! (Original, Musical, Comedy) Staging assisted by Eva Jessye. 24 May 1945–23 June 1945.

Porgy and Bess. (Revival, Musical, Opera) Choral Director: Eva Jessye. 10 March 1953–28 November 1953.

Videography

Eva Jessye: Black American Folk Music (motion picture).

Slices of Life. Program 711. Original Airdate: 31 December 1976.

The Say Brother Collection Website is a production of the WGBH Archives, WGBH Educational Foundation.

Notes

[1] Doris Louise Jones Wilson. *Eva Jessye: Afro-American Choral Director.* Thesis (Ed. D.) St. Louis: Washington University, 1989, p. 58.

[2] Karen Ray, "Eva Jessye, Her Music and her Memories," *Michigan Journalist*, March 1976, p. 1, col. 1, as cited in Wilson, p. 47.

[3] The Eva Jessye Collection, Leonard H. Axe Library, Pittsburg State, Pittsburg, Kansas. http://library.pittstate.edu/spcoll/ndxjessye.html and Kansas State Historical Society. http://www.kshs.org/peoplejessye_eva.htm

[4] Wilson, p.12.

[5] Ibid., p. 13.

[6] Ibid., p. 14.

[7] Ibid., p. 15.

[8] Ibid., p. 17.

[9] Marie Howard, "She's a Musician Who Can't Recall When She Wasn't," *Morning Sentinel*, Waterville, Winslow-Maine, 20 September 1982, p. 1, as cited in Wilson, p. 20.

[10] Wilson, p. 20.

[11] Ibid.

[12] Ibid., p. 21.

[13] Ibid., p. 26.

[14] Ibid., p. 27.

[15] Gwendolyn B. Bennett, "My Spirituals," review of Eva Jessye (New York: Robbins and Engel, Inc.), *Opportunity*, V, November 1927 as cited in Wilson, p. 28.

[16] Note to Eva Jessye from Paul Robeson, The Eva Jessye Collection, Leonard H. Axe Library, Pittsburg State, Pittsburg, Kansas.

[17] Floyde J. Calvin, "Eva Jessye to Develop Folk Dances Along With Spirituals During the Year of 1933." Unidentified New York newspaper, 13 January 1933 as cited in Wilson, p. 27.

[18] Wilson, p. 31.

[19] Ibid., p. 32.

[20] John Houseman, *Run-Through: A Memoir*, (New York: Simon and Schuster, 1972), p. 105, as cited in Wilson, p. 33.

[21] Wilson, pp. 32–33.

[22] Ibid., p. 34, Eva Jessye interview, 11 September 1982.

[23] Virgil Thomson, *Virgil Thomson*. New York: A.A. Knopf, 1966, p. 31, as cited in Wilson, p. 35.

[24] Wilson, pp. 35–36.

[25] 16 February 1932, as cited in Wilson, p. 38.

[26] Ibid., p. 38.

[27] Ibid., p. 36.

[28] Ibid., p. 39.

[29] The Eva Jessye Collection, Leonard H. Axe Library, Pittsburg State, Pittsburg, Kansas. http://library.pittstate.edu/spcoll/ndxjessye.html and Kansas State Historical Society.

[30] Wilson, pp. 41–42.

[31] James Standifer, "The Complicated Life of Porgy and Bess.htm" *Humanities*, November/December 1997, Volume 18, Number 6.

[32] Wilson, p. 42.

[33] Ibid., pp. 41–43.

[34] Raymond Jack, "Berlin loves Bess as Much as Porgy," *The New York Times*, 18 September 1952, as cited in Wilson, p. 44.

[35] Max Graf, "Porgy and Bess Begin European Tour in Vienna," *Musical America*, Vol. 72, October 1952, p. 9, as cited in Wilson, p. 44.

[36] Wilson, pp. 44–47.

[37] Ibid., p. 44.

[38] Ibid., p. 47–48.

[39] Ibid., p. 48.

[40] Ibid., p. 49.

[41] Ibid., pp. 51–52.

[42] Ibid., p. 52.

[43] Ibid., pp. 52–53.

[44] Lawrence Sears, "Sermon Hit at Cathedral," *The Washington Evening Star*, 12 July 1972, as cited in Wilson, p. 56.

[45] Wilson, p. 58.

[46] Ibid., pp. 62–63.

[47] Ibid., p. 55.

[48] Ibid., p. 52.

[49] Ibid., pp. 58, 60.

[50] Ibid., p. 64.

[51] The Eva Jessye Collection, Leonard H. Axe Library, Pittsburg State, Pittsburg, Kansas. http://library.pittstate.edu/spcoll/ndxjessye.html and Kansas State Historical Society.

[52] Wilson, p. 65.

[53] Ibid., pp. 65–66.

[54] Ibid., pp. 66–67.

[55] Wilson, p. 76.

[56] Ibid., p. 37.

[57] Jester Hairston in an undated letter to Eva Jessye, as cited in Wilson, p. 76.

[58] Wilson, p. 71.

[59] Ibid., p. 72.

[60] Ibid., p. 37.

Colleen Jean Kirk

(7 September 1918—5 March 2004)

Teaching is about the students, not the teacher.
If not, it is just doing, not teaching.

Joan Whittemore

Communication through music, gesture, the spoken and written word, and nurturing students to become the best musicians and teachers possible were the foundations of Colleen Kirk's life and profession. The combination of solid musicianship, energy, and commitment to the fostering of students' development, dedication to the performance of the best literature, extraordinary communication and organizational skills culminated in a life of service to the choral profession and music education that is seldom achieved in any one lifetime.

Current and future teachers pondering the intricacies of balancing all the integral elements of performance, teaching, and organizational responsibilities of their profession, would do well to borrow a page or two from Colleen Kirk's vita. Born in Champaign, Illinois, she earned a bachelor's degree in music education from the University of Illinois, studied voice with Bruce Foote, and was a soloist at Wesley United Methodist Church in Urbana in the 1940s. Colleen Kirk had a lengthy engagement with both institutions that offered a unique opportunity in shaping her life's work. From 1947 until 1970, she served Wesley United Methodist Church as Director of Music, and earned her Minister of Music Certificate for the United Methodist Church. She conducted her choirs in major choral-orchestral works numerous times a year and made several recordings. Having earned both the bachelor's and master's degrees in Music Education at the University of Illinois, gaining experience teaching in elementary and secondary schools throughout the state, Colleen Kirk was invited to join the Music Education faculty of the University of Illinois in 1949 where she remained until 1970 completing her doctorate at Teacher's College, Columbia University in 1953, achieving the rank of Full Professor in 1964, and becoming Chair of the Music Education Division in 1967. Her focus at the University of Illinois was the preparation of student-teachers. Her 1953 dissertation, *Guides for Improving the Student Teaching Experience in Music Education at the University of Illinois*, served as the model for the student teaching program she directed.

Colleen Kirk's tireless efforts to expand and sequence the course offerings in a methodical process for students, visit the public schools where she established relationships with music teachers and the University of Illinois, design and implement evaluations for more effective learning, develop three-way communication with the student, cooperating teacher, and supervisor resulted in the improvement of the Music Education Division for a more effective teacher preparation, and a uniquely successful recruitment tool for the University of Illinois School of Music. (Chandler, 27.)

A former student of Colleen's, Doreen Rao, recalls:

> Colleen worked to engage the learners, cultivating a safe and caring climate. She was able to share herself through the music and would weave all of the essential components together to create a wonderful learning environment. She would create opportunities for success for all levels of learning . . . the undergraduate and the graduate. . . . The organization of the learning experiences with the student as the center of attention was a hallmark of Kirk's teaching. (Ch. 28.)

Encouraging future teachers to use music that is appropriate for the student's age level, teaching music fundamentals through the repertoire, and the combination of physical movement in music making were core to teacher preparation. Her now legendary note cards giving feedback to the student conductors regarding methods, techniques, and accomplishments of the individual rehearsals, and suggestions for improvements have served as a model for student conducting preparation nationwide.

In the conducting laboratory the students directed a chorus of graduate and undergraduate students. At the conclusion of the course, "each student would demonstrate leadership skills and the ability to test voices for choral placement, select appropriate literature and conduct effectively, plan for an aesthetically satisfying rehearsal, demonstrate the ability to pace a rehearsal, and would plan a concert program with attention to variety, contrast, and aesthetic satisfaction." (C. Kirk, Syllabus, Choral Techniques, Ch. 33.)

Every student completed one hundred cards for the semester that included pieces sung in the choral laboratory, discussed in class, and sung in choir, exposing the conductor to a variety of styles, periods, and voice classifications. The format included the information in Examples 1 and 2.

Example 1 (front)

	Solo ____________
Title ______________________	Unison SA SSA SSAA
Composer/Arranger/Editor ____________	TB TTB TBB TTBB
________________________	SAB SATB SSAA TTBB
Publisher ____________________	Other ____________
Edition number ________________	Year Published ________
Language ___________________	Source of Text ________
Type of Accompaniment _____________	Instrumentation ________
	________________

Range and Tessitura

S1 S2 A1 A2

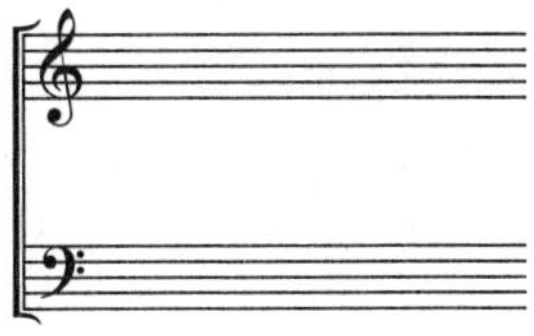

Specific Difficulties

T1 T2 B1 B2

Example 2 (back)

Dates Performed: ______________________

	Renaissance ________
	Baroque ________
	Classical ________
	Romantic ________
	20th Century ________
	Popular/Jazz ________
	Novelty ________
	Large Ensemble ________
	Small Ensemble ________
Possible Uses:	Program "Opener" ________
	Program "Ending" ________
	Special Occasion (specify) ____________
	____________
	Church Service ____________
	Teaching/Learning ____________
	Sight Singing ____________
	Expression/Text ____________
	Period/Composer ____________
Comments:	Other ____________

Always one to teach by example, Colleen Kirk served as administrator and director of the junior high chorus of the annual Illinois Summer Youth Music Camp in the early years and subsequently as director of the senior high chorus where the students could learn quality repertoire from one of the best known conductors in the state. (Rao, Ch. 38.)

In 1959 Henry Holt published her *Modern Methods in Elementary Education* which contained techniques for assisting the elementary music teacher in actively involving students in the music-making process. (Ch. 29.)

Harold Decker in 1962 sponsored Colleen Kirk for membership in the American Choral Directors Association. University of Illinois students who under Harold Decker's and Colleen Kirk's leadership attended the ACDA conventions long before the initiation of student chapters, and heard choruses from all over the country. ACDA would reap incalculable benefits through Colleen Kirk's leadership beginning in 1966 when the Executive Board asked her to serve on the Publications Committee, whose task it was read submissions to the *Choral Journal* that ACDA considered for publication. (Ch. 42.)

In 1970 Wiley Housewright, Dean of Florida State University, offered Colleen Kirk the position of Professor of Music Education and the Choral Union to direct. She continued the conducting laboratory techniques established at the University of Illinois improving the process through the use of video camera technology, team teaching with Clayton Krehbiehl, and subsequently providing graduate students the experience of conducting the Choral Union. In 1972 she was awarded tenure at Florida State University and was elected to the Faculty Senate in 1973. During that same year, Florida State University sponsored the First Annual Summer Institute for Choral Directors. Colleen Kirk and Clayton Krehbiel engaged Paul Salamunovich, Alice Parker, and Howard Swan for the program. Kirk also conducted the choral component of the Summer Honors Music Camp that included high school choral, band, and orchestra students from the region. (Ch. 33–34.) In 1978 she was the recipient of the President's Teaching Award for excellence in teaching at Florida State University. President Bernard Sliger wrote to Kirk:

> Your selection for this honor is cause for justifiable pride and reflects the high esteem the faculty and students of the University have for you. Colleen, you are to be commended for your contribution to higher education. (Ch. 34.)

Contributions to the American Choral Directors Association

Colleen Kirk placed her leadership, communication, and organization skills in the service of the American Choral Directors Association where she was called upon repeatedly throughout the next twenty years. Having served on the Publications Committee since 1966, as ACDA Southern President from 1971–1975, she was nominated but not elected for ACDA President in 1973, a little more than ten years after becoming a member. In attempting to respond to the national leadership's concern for closer collaboration among state, divisional, and national officers, Colleen Kirk with other state officers suggested the possibility of presenting leadership workshops for incoming officers. The national board approved the plan in June 1972 and the first workshop took place at the national headquarters in Tampa Florida. Working closely at the state level, Colleen Kirk with Phyllis Merritt, Florida Vocal Association President, instituted a reading chorus distinct from the All-State

Choir consisting of a hundred select singers who would read eight excerpts of six measures each of very difficult musical examples and be required to pass a musicianship test. Kirk chose the music for the session and was the first conductor. (Ch. 44.)

In 1973 Kirk led the Florida delegation and presided over an Interest Session at the national convention in Kansas City on "Classifying Young Voices." She was program chair for the convention in Charlotte, North Carolina in 1974 and again in 1975 for the National Convention in St. Louis, Missouri. With Wayne Hugoboom's retirement as ACDA's Executive Secretary, ACDA appointed Colleen Kirk chair of the search committee in 1976 resulting in the election of Gene Brooks.

With the constitutional revision in 1964 providing for standing committees for four membership categories consisting of college, high school, church and industry, the Repertoire and Standard Committee emerged. Prior to becoming an ACDA board member, Colleen Kirk was chosen to chair this committee, a position for which she was uniquely qualified. The board gave her the opportunity in asking her to reorganize the complete committee organizational structure to do what she did best: teach in a national forum the importance of introducing quality literature at every level of choral music education. (Mathis, Letter to Kirk, April 1977, Ch. 34.) In the process ACDA benefited from her extraordinary communication and organizational skills in rejuvenating and redefining the mission of these committees and strengthening their leadership.

In December of 1977 Colleen Kirk proposed and generated a new column in the *Choral Journal* for the September 1978 issue in which she wrote the first article to explain the purpose of the "Standing Committee Reports" column, wherein each chairperson would present information relative to the direction and accomplishments of each committee. She also served as editor of this column for subsequent issues. She saw the uniqueness of the role of these committees in influencing the choral art and was able to challenge the committee leaders to take their mission seriously and encouraged open communication at all levels of membership. As chair of the Standing Committee on Choral Standards and Repertoire, Kirk introduced and implemented a new "Committee Umbrella" structure consisting of the ten chairpersons of the national committees. (Ch. 46.) In the September 1978 issue of the *Choral Journal*, she reported a new and regular feature entitled "National Committee Report," outlined national committee structure, and introduced the personnel of the ten committees. Nominated and elected for the presidency of ACDA in 1978.

(Troop 1978, Ch. 48.) Colleen Kirk resigned as chair of the Repertoire and Standards Committee to assume responsibilities as national ACDA president-elect becoming the chairperson for the 1981 national convention in New Orleans. (Ch. 48.)

Among her many accomplishments as Chair of the Repertoire and Standards Committee was that she restructured committees and broadened their mission defined the role of the Repertoire and Standards leadership which had as its priority to study repertoire. (Ch. 45.) She was instrumental in the development of the summer workshops in leadership training for incoming officers at state and divisional levels.

While on sabbatical in 1979 and serving as president-elect of ACDA, Colleen Kirk co-wrote with Harold Decker of the University of Illinois, *Choral Conductors: Focus on Communication.*

By September of 1979 Colleen Kirk reported to the executive committee on the successes of the committee restructuring, made suggestions for continued improvement, and suggested that the ACDA divisions and states follow the same restructuring. (Ch. 46.) In 1980 after expressing her concerns to Royce Saltzman for the necessity for a handbook for state presidents, Colleen Kirk at Saltzman's request wrote the handbook which was ready for the 1981 national convention.

In November of 1979 as she prepared for 1981 convention, she set her goal of having quality choirs for performance, through choosing audition committee members with musical expertise and providing for the anonymity of choirs that were categorized by voice types and identified by number rather than school (Ch. 48.) She engaged Robert Shaw and the Atlanta Symphony Orchestra for Beethoven's *Missa Solemnis* with combined choirs from the Ohio State University, Loyola University of New Orleans, the University of Cincinnati, Howard University, and Florida State University forming the choir for the final concert. With Doug Anderson's assistance, she arranged for a late night interest session in which the show choirs performed on the riverboat, President. The proceeds from the ticket sales helped to offset the expenses incurred for the final concert. With Larry Wyatt, they were able to secure suitable performance venues for the concerts, specifically the Theatre of the Performing Arts for the Beethoven rehearsals and performance. Colleen Kirk planned an Ecumenical Service at the St. Louis Cathedral, with Paul Salamunovich conducting that is still memorable to this day.

Following the 1981 convention, Colleen Kirk became the first woman president of ACDA. This required her attendance at state, divisional, and national conventions, and executive board meetings, all the while serving as advisor to Florida State University undergraduate students in music education, and director for thirteen master's students and nine doctoral students' final projects. (Ch. 35.) During her term as ACDA President, Colleen Kirk continued to teach, inspire, challenge, and present ideas for growth and development always insisting that conductors choose music of the highest quality and appropriate level for a satisfying musical experience for their singers. Through her monthly column in the *Choral Journal*, she invited new members, and acknowledged the generosity of the members in contributing their expertise especially the *Choral Journal* editors.

In 1981 Colleen Kirk received the Harold Decker Award and was elected to the Board of Directors of the International Federation for Choral Music in 1982. After her term as ACDA President, she became Vice President and member of the Presidents Advisory Council, and provided guidance to the Repertoire and Standards Committee Chairperson. She once again chaired the nominating committee for ACDA president and treasurer. In 1985 the Florida State University student chapter led by David Frego was awarded the best student chapter at the Salt Lake City national convention. With Royce Saltzman and Gene Brook, she presented a policy to the executive board on inclusiveness in convention programming in 1986. She received the Wayne Hugoboom Award for the Florida ACDA in 1988.

Colleen Kirk assisted ACDA at the national, divisional, and state levels until her retirement as Professor Emerita at Florida State University in 1990. (Ch. 58.) In October of 1992, she returned as guest conductor of a choir of present and former members at a Homecoming Weekend at Wesley United Methodist Church in Urbana. At the 1999 San Antonio national convention, she received the Robert Lawson Shaw Award.

Doreen Rao commissioned a work in Colleen Kirk's honor. The work, *Irish Fantasies,* is an orchestral suite based on Irish melodies. Doreen Rao conducted the premiere at St. Luke Church in New York City on 5 November 2003. She expressed the essence of Colleen Kirk's legacy in an interview with her in July 2003.

> It is ever present because she taught that the best teaching is in the musical context, even though in other classes we were being encouraged to use the general music model for teaching. The fact is that I saw the choral music experience as the ideal environment for teaching and learning. It was a much more organic, natural model. She exemplified that in everything that she did. I think that had a profound influence on me. She was always teaching.

> She did not just conduct a rehearsal, there was teaching and learning at the deepest level. She cared enough in her rehearsals to empower every singer to know the music deeply and completely and to understand it.
>
> So when it came to performance of the music they had a wonderful, deep understanding. They were not just regurgitating what somebody had told them. This has become the philosophical basis for the years of work that I have done. So many people think that choral music rehearsals and music classes are two separate things. To think that a chorus is for singers and a class is for non singers is absolutely wrong. It flies in the face of Colleen's philosophy which was that every child should sing, every person should have that choral experience. I think she brought performance and learning together. I think that is her legacy. (Ch. 7.)

Colleen Kirk's many accomplishments and contributions to the American Choral Directors Association and generosity in implementing procedures and devising opportunities for others to create the best possible musical experiences for their students might at first glance appear to overshadow the fact that she was a consummate musician and music educator whose goals were always for the performance of music of the highest quality at every level. The key for her was to strive constantly for improvement, and engage the students. She worked tirelessly, selflessly toward that in every venue presented to her. Through her extraordinary ability to communicate with others, she was able to challenge us to do more that we ever thought possible with the added credibility of teaching by example. In her first column as president of ACDA, she capsulated her teaching philosophy and with these words continues to teach succeeding generations.

> I am grateful that in our remarkable art there is no possibility of achieving perfection. Regardless of our individual growth, there will always be room for improvement. . . . I am grateful that the sharing can be broad and can transcend barriers of race and nationality. (C. Kirk, *Choral Journal* 22.1:2.)

(Photograph of Colleen Kirk c. 1982 from the Colleen J. Kirk Papers, American Choral Directors Association Archive, reprinted by permission.)

Selected Bibliography

Chandler, Deborah Linn. *Colleen Jean Kirk (1918–2004): Her Life, Career, and her Influence on American Choral Music Education.* Chandler, Florida State University, Ph.D. Dissertation, 2004.

Decker, Harold A. and Colleen J. Kirk. *Choral Conducting: Focus on Communication.* Prospect Heights: Waveland, 1988.

Kirk, Colleen J. *Guides for Improving the Student teaching Experience in Music Education at the University of Illinois.* Diss. Teacher's College, Columbia University, 1953.

_____. *Modern Methods in Elementary Education.* Henry Holt, 1959.

_____. "Preparing the Next Generation of Choral Conductors." *Choral Journal* 19.2 (1978): 12–16.

_____. "Do You Hear What I Hear?" Southern Division MENC Convention. Mobile, AL. 1985.

Rao, Doreen B. "Personal interview." 11 July 2003.

Discography, Colleen Kirk, Conductor

Wesley Choir Presentation of "God's Trombones." Wesley Choir. Recorded 10 February 1963. L.P.

Wesley Sings. Wesley Choir. Recorded 1967. L.P.

ALICE PARKER

(Born 16 December 1925)

My pattern calls for forty years of education and self discovery,
and maturity beginning very late and lasting long.
As for retiring—I can't quite imagine it!

JOAN WHITTEMORE

In the spring of 1976, I decided to make a journey to determine whether I might really be a composer, or if what Garrison Keiller says were true in my case that, "To some, God gives the gift of music, but not to as many as think so." Alice Parker was teaching one of her week long courses in Composing and Arranging at Westminster Choir College. Before the end of the first day I was hooked. By Friday I asked Alice if I could enter the second week's course. Singing *Messiah* for eight hours a day with Robert Shaw could wait. I was entranced with the way Alice taught, the way she thought about music, and her approach to composition that changed the way I thought about music, and composed, and conducted my choruses. We sang, improvised, and composed using chant melodies, Psalter Hymns, Bach Chorales, spirituals, and folk melodies. We became engaged in what Alice teaches as the trinity of music: listener, performer, and composer, until it became one and informed our creative process. We sang our compositions for one another. We learned to write for our own ensembles rather than focus on being published. If a piece worked well with our own choruses, then we knew publication was possible. The challenge and the thrill was creating not merely the notation, but making music with our singers.

"Notation is an aid to remembered sound," Alice told us. That changes everything. All quarter notes are not equal. All syllables are not equal either. This syllable, this word requires more time, needs to open up. That may appear to be an elucidation of the obvious, but how often does one really hear that from a chorus! The marriage of text and tune (not the notation) is sacred. I learned to give the piece I was struggling to birth the appropriate gestation period it required. Life came from speaking and singing the text and the melody, constantly listening to what it wanted to do. The music is not shackled by the notation, but literally springs from it.

Alice had just completed the premiere performance of *Family Reunion*: a "backyard opera." Before I realized what I was saying, I asked Alice that if I were to schedule a performance of *Family Reunion* at my *girls'* academy in the coming year, would she come and conduct. What was I thinking? I had one hundred fifty girls! I needed adult men and women, teenage boys, little children, and a ten-piece orchestra. Alice agreed, and she came and conducted. I had been the only conductor that many of these singers had had for years. Alice Parker gave them and me an incredible gift. The singers had the opportunity to sing the music of a great American composer conducting her own opera, a composer who knows how to open up the world of beauty and creativity to singers at any age level. They allowed themselves to be shaped by her vision. They became listeners, performers, and composers with her and brought the piece to life under her direction.

Alice Parker's journey to composer, conductor, and teacher is well documented. Many are familiar with part of the story, and may think of her only in terms of hymn-singing or in the context of her choral arrangements for the Robert Shaw Chorale. They have yet to discover her operas, the recordings of Melodious Accord, a non-profit organization and chorus of professional singers, the composers' workshops, the SINGS, and the score study sessions in New York.

There are no fewer than seven dissertations and numerous articles written about her and her work. Alice, too, is a prolific writer. One can read the newsletters of Melodious Accord, discover when she will be conducting, giving a workshop, holding a SING, find information about the Melodious Accord Fellowship programs in Score Study, Melody Studies, Song Leading, Composers Workshop, find recordings, books, a piece that you want to program, and even email Alice at her website. In short, if you want to learn from her, Alice Parker is accessible. She has spent her life not only leading singers on an exhilarating trek to the mountains and the *Promised Land of Melody*, but also bringing the joy of singing to a rural town in Illinois or any major city on any continent.

Having written music from an early age and completing her first orchestral score while still in high school, Alice graduated from Smith College with a major in music performance and composition and earned a master's degree in conducting at the Juilliard School of Music where she studied with Robert Shaw and Julius Herford.

> I graduated from college thinking that I couldn't go on in composition—I was not attuned to the twentieth-century music aesthetic. So I changed to choral conducting and had the great good fortune to arrive at Juilliard while Robert Shaw and Julius Herford were there. I felt as though I had never truly listened before, and was challenged to learn and perform at a very high level. Intoxicating! . . .
>
> The arranging collaboration with Robert Shaw began while I was still his student and became my true education in the craft of composition—a medieval apprenticeship in renaissance vocal techniques. I've drawn on it ever since.
>
> I became mature enough to shake off the constrictions of my college years and to begin composing again, based strongly on what I had learned about melodies, singers, and concert life from Mr. Shaw. When he moved to Atlanta and stopped recording, Tom [Thomas Pyle, her husband] was home from touring and I was free to travel. I discovered that I loved meeting groups of students and adults and making music with them in brief workshops. I also discovered the ease of encouraging lovely music-making through improvisational SINGS. Somehow, composing and conducting and teaching had merged into one occupation.[1]

In 1999 following the death of Robert Shaw, Alice wrote of her first meeting with him, of studying conducting at Juilliard, and of the beginning of the twenty year collaboration with him on the music for the RCA contracts of the Robert Shaw Chorale.

> I met him when I was fresh out of college, at Tanglewood for the summer, singing the Mozart Requiem and the Beethoven Ninth with the "large" choir (no auditions) and with no inkling of how my life would change as a result. In photos of that summer we both seem impossibly young. . . .
>
> In the Fall, I enrolled at Juilliard to be a Choral Conducting student of his—accepted, I felt, only as the token female in the class. Maggie Hillis joined me the next year. Those years were like being on a roller-coaster: singing in the Collegiate Chorale (the Verdi Requiem with Toscanini; the

complete *Christmas Oratorio* at Carnegie on a full blizzard night); attending rehearsals of the Juilliard chorus (*The St. John Passion*) and the small group which became the nucleus of the Robert Shaw Chorale (radio programs, opera recordings, special performances); superb score study with Julius Herford (my other mentor: I started piano study with him that year); writing program notes, researching repertoire and doing all manner of odd jobs for Shaw.

This was the year of agonizing over whether to form the Robert Shaw Chorale: the first tour was in the Fall of 1948, with a few triumphs and many discouragements. I wrote a ridiculous *Cantata 1/2* to cheer them up at a low spot. There followed the recording contract with RCA, and the beginning of our twenty year collaboration. We found that we could work easily together, probably because our styles were so different. My function was to find melodies in the topic (suggested first by him or RCA) and make a whole set of sketches over the course of several months. Then, a week before the recording sessions were to start, we would work together: rewriting, polishing, rejecting-and-replacing, never accepting as-is, always wanting each piece to be just right, worthy of his singers. He said if we did our work right, the piece would sing itself: the excellent musician would have not a second's hesitation in following the flow of the line.

The memories are crystal-clear: his pointing at the coda of a sketch, saying: "That's the first idea you've had." Listening to my first play-through of the whole set, when I encountered more counterpoint than my fingers could handle, and began to sing: "For God's sake, don't crescendo!" Total failure on spirituals: he did them all at first.

Changing one note in a phrase; adjusting one duration; listening always to breathing so that it is built into the song; speaking text aloud to capture vowels, consonants, diphthongs, accents, colors; recognizing elements which would unite the whole; "one idea per verse"; enormous care with exact durations and cut-offs; learning that if you have a great melody to work with, you mostly need to stay out of its way (you can afford to be clever with the less-great). . . .

What did I learn? There's no holding back—throw yourself in, without counting the cost or time. Be your own harshest critic (I was never as good at that as he.) Listen all the time: the specific word, accent, mouth, voice, person, composer. Capture the sound on the page. In the last analysis (and the first), one can't separate the text, the melody and the setting: it's all one. In study and rehearsal one pulls them apart, but only to re-unite them. I learned that the spirit is in the details. That sharing ideas, bouncing them

> back and forth, is enormous fun, stimulating both players to greater achievement. That almost anything can be improved. That one is always walking a delicate balance-line between thought and action, intuition and craft, work and play, rehearsal and performance, life and art. And that music is one of the greatest gifts and sternest masters. When we enter its world, we must submerge our individuality in its surge and ebb, only finding our own voice through the mastery of its demands.[2]

The collaboration with Robert Shaw concluded when Shaw became music director of the Atlanta Symphony in 1967. Alice had begun composing again, traveling the country giving workshops, and teaching composing and arranging in Westminster Choir College's summer program. Alice's husband, Thomas Pyle, baritone and soloist for the Shaw Chorale, died in 1976. By 1984, Alice's five children had completed college. Having reflected about what she had not done that she really wanted to do, Alice's first priority was working with professional singers, and making a recording that would satisfy her ears. She envisioned a group that would not only perform, but also have a strong education component and connection to local and wider communities. The first meeting with friends to outline the corporation, set goals and procedures for accomplishing them took place in the summer of 1984 at Singing Brook Farm.[3]

> On Christmas Eve 1984, the State of New York issued the certificate of incorporation for a fledgling not-for-profit organization to be known as Melodious Accord, Inc. Eight music enthusiasts including professional and amateur musicians, educators, a real estate executive, a doctor, and Alice Parker were the initial directors. The name for the organization was taken from the second stanza of a James Montgomery setting of Psalm 100:
>
> O enter his gates with thanksgiving and song,
> Your vow in his temple proclaim.
> His praise with melodious accordance prolong,
> And bless his adorable Name. . . .[4]

The first concert, "Antecedents: Musical Bridges" was scheduled for the Cathedral of St. John the Divine in September 1985, but the threat of hurricane Gloria cancelled the performance. Melodious Accord produced a recording, *Sacred Symphonies*, which was released by the Musical Heritage Society in 1988. Nine more recordings followed, and two additional recordings are in preparation.[5]

In 1985 Alice introduced a series of six SINGS at the Cathedral School, open to the larger community at no charge as a means to make music that had almost no monetary cost, but that would provide a rewarding singing experience for family groups, older folks, foreign students and anyone who might wander in off the street.[6]

May 1986 marked the first performance of Melodious Accord, held in the Tower Room at the Riverside Church. "Love Songs for Johannes" featured the Brahms' *Liebeslieder*, op. 52, Alice Parker's *SongStream*, madrigals, and an audience SING of German folksongs. In January 1987, the first Spirituals Concert took place at the Cathedral of St. John the Divine with a choir of sixty voices including Melodious Accord's professional sixteen, a narrator, string quartet, the rhythm section from the Paul Winter Consort and two extended works, Alice Parker's *Sermon from the Mountain: Martin Luther King, Jr.* (1969), and her settings of some of Ellington's *Songs from the Sacred Concerts*.[7]

One of the most remarkable aspects of making music with Alice Parker whether as a composer, a singer, a participant in a workshop or SING, or as a conductor attempting to enrich one's music making with others, is that each person comes away learning how to listen more sensitively and intensely to the inflection of voice, word, direction and energy of the melody, the sonorities, lines, colors, textures, rhythms, and forms. The process evolves to the extent that one then approaches a piece of music as listener, performer, and conductor in a completely different manner. Alice never teaches just *one concept*. The quality of each individual's listening and awareness is heightened. Thereafter, nothing is ever the same. Even a conglomeration of singers that one finds at a SING—little children, high school and college age students, members of church choirs, and professional musicians combined, learn to listen with an intensity that is tangible under Alice Parker's direction that is then reflected in an extraordinary musical experience even in a relatively short period of time. With Alice Parker, one always learns something new, sees and hears the familiar in a new way, or discovers something about how to learn.

Alice Parker has captured the process in her book *The Anatomy of Melody* and in the video, *Alice Parker Folksong Transformations*, which demonstrate her teaching a group of adults, teenagers, and young children how to improvise. At first there is hesitation in the participants. Thoughts of "What does she want? Can I do this? I don't want to make a mistake. I'm scared," flood the minds of the singers. Then the transformation occurs through the joy of making music, first with small steps, and then more freely with Alice's coaching and coaxing. The energy in the room changes, and the attentive listening and enjoyment in the process becomes audible, palpable, and visible as each individual discovers the possibilities of learning to create music together spontaneously—a hidden gift utterly surprising and delighting each person. Alice is even able to engage individuals to join in a singing dialogue having one singer mirror the inflections, the mood, and articulation of another. The singers learn to hear what the melody wants to do. They learn to spin out a melody. The looks of satisfaction on the faces and their body language reveal that something extraordinary has happened here. They want to continue.

Fortunately, Alice is a masterful teacher on many levels and generous in sharing her experience as a lecturer, and writer. Along with the performances, recordings, and SINGS came the first Newsletter in 1985 announcing the purpose of Melodious Accord—to bring together composers, performers and listeners in the creation and re-creation of music. Melodious Accord would "look for composers who were engaged in a creative dialogue with their communities," and produce music "which is heard as an enriching process, not a product." There would be over the next ten year span the first composition contest (1986) for second performances, and concerts of music of thirty contemporary composers. The first grant from the New York State Council on the Arts was awarded in 1987. The first Fellowship Program began in 1988 which now can boast of over one hundred Fellows, and the Melodious Accord Symposia, Poems, and Songs took place in 1990. Chorus America's recognition of Melodious Accord as a "vital force in choral music in the United States," five honorary doctorates, the Eastern Division of ACDA surprising her with the dedication of their 2006 convention to her are only a few of the many tributes to Alice, who has been named the first lady of American Choral Music.[8]

Alice offers observation and diagnosis of the challenges that present themselves to conductors, composers, performers, and listeners in not only preserving the legacy of melody and song, but of spinning it out. Together we improvise preparing ourselves and the musicians with whom we make music, to explore the intricacies of our own folk music, hymnody, and world music, and take a fresh approach to the music we are preparing for our next concert.

In her *Melodious Accord Newsletters*, Alice addresses the issues confronting music teachers and conductors who have been prepared to teach from a model that no longer or rarely exists in our culture.

Children today have less experience of making music than ever before. They wear their Ipods, cell phones, and game players as though they were life sustaining devices, and receive their music education from commercials, film, television, videos, and pop icons who offer nothing in the way of role modeling for healthy singing. The impact of this electronic tuning out and turning inward creating a perception of music as coming solely from electronic sources rather than making music with and for others, affects and impairs their growth, and renders the school music teacher's task of teaching children to sing and make their own music nearly insurmountable. Music teaching from the elementary to post graduate level first must pry children, teenagers, and adults from their electronic stranglehold in order to free them to recognize their own creativity and spontaneity through singing, improvisation, and making music with others. Alice writes:

> Children come to school at all levels with no musical background whatsoever except what they have gleaned from the TV—much of that advertisements and videos. They have never heard an adult they know well sing for pure pleasure; have never sung around the house while doing chores or in a car on a long journey. Their idea of music is founded on electronics, at a high level of volume, and sales techniques which promise immediate gratification with no effort. What does this mean at the primary level? Children cannot match pitches; singing with their own age group without accompaniment is unheard-of; a folk or community repertoire is entirely foreign to them; the idea that music is an "extra," not important, is preserved by before-school or after-school rehearsals and a congenital lack of community support. It takes superhuman effort and much time to get these youngsters far enough into the process so that they can begin to join mainstream educational thinking and musical enjoyment.
>
> At junior high and high school ages, the young people come with no firm background to build on. Again, they can't sing, and the elements of reading music have never been presented to them, or have been discussed in such a brief time-frame that no mastery follows. What is the teacher to do? He or she wants to get these students to experience some of our great choral/vocal music, but with their lack of skills has to fall back on lesser literature, spoon-fed.
>
> And at college, we see the inevitable result. A good friend teaches at a community college, where students come with many backgrounds, ages, levels of ability and experience. They stay for only two years; they are a transient population with none of the opportunities for extended time together that the traditional, live-in, four-year institutions enjoy. What is the teacher to do? They not only have no training—they don't know that they have none! "We had a great chorus in high school, and I learned a lot of songs"—but in many cases it was pop songs taught by rote and sung in a manner injurious to the vocal chords.[9]

Improvisation is one solution and is essential to every aspect of what Alice Parker teaches through the Melodious Accord Fellows Program, the SINGS, and the Composing and Arranging Seminars. She demonstrates that the best thing that we can do for our children, students, and choruses at every level is to engage them first in just singing for pleasure, then in the process of listening, composing, improvising and performing with others in formal and informal settings that strengthen the communal experiences with one another and our audiences. Alice challenges all of us with very simple and achievable goals and always teaches us how to begin with a single melody and sustain the process with our own voices and creativity. Alice takes this a step further in making the connection with learning to sing a melody. Becoming familiar with our rich heritage of folk music and hymnody offers us the best preparation for learning the intricate rhythms, inflections and sonorities, of world music.

> Since our western world's inventions of musical notation and the printing press, we have been imposing severe limits on this world of sound—almost making it a visual art. Reading the page, being faithful to it, studying books and taking courses about music are all secondary to living, actual sound. What music can we make together, here, now?
>
> Look what we can do without reading music or even playing an instrument: sing songs alone or with others, remember old ones "by heart," make up new ones and learn more "by ear," trade them with others, vary them. Anything other than a simple repetition of the song may be called "improvising"—the game of playing with tones and rhythms. It is the gateway to composition. Children do it very naturally. They change the words, sing higher or lower, ornamenting with high spirits and imaginative energy. It is natural to improvise: it is unnatural to repeat as if in a carbon copy, with no variants. Our human invitation to music begins with melody and expands to musical conversations—call and response—more easily than to the world of harmony.
>
> Somehow when we go through our traditional, page oriented courses of study we get less proficient at these "ear" responses. Here's a quick quiz: if someone sings an unfamiliar tune, can you remember it? And imitate it (the actual voice, not the written representation)? Can you play with this tune: vary it, make up new words, ornament it, extend it? Or can you make up an answer to it responding to its mood, dance and verbal cues? Can you keep the song going when you run out of words? Can you "spin" the moment out until the energy is gone? . . .

> One must learn to trust the medium (the song will never let you down), and to give up conscious control (analytic thinking) for a surrendering to the ear and an intuitive response.
>
> Singing a single-line melody is much the easiest way to relearn this skill, and it is what I teach every summer in my Writing for Voices class at Westminster Choir College, and at all the SINGS that I lead as I travel around the country. I was delighted to learn this spring that new guidelines established for college music departments this year include requirements both for improvisation and for "world music."
>
> These are more closely related than you might think: the non-visual relationship to music is the norm in non-western cultures. (Many cultures) have no traditional notation, and often defy translation into ours. So we have to learn them "by ear," and learn too, the kinds of responses that are customary in their own surroundings. We need to listen better, twist our tongues around new words, our pitch sense around quarter-tones and sliding "off-key" sounds, and learn rhythms more complex than any that we are used to. (Yes, in this sense, both pitch and rhythm have been enormously simplified by notation.)
>
> Learning to swim in the sea of sound is important for us Westerners. It opens cultural gateways as we trade songs with people from all over the world who sing for the same reasons (and with the same equipment) as we do. Moving into a culture through its folk melodies is immensely rewarding, as well as horizon-expanding. And it is truly basic to an understanding of what a page of music is: in its first and last sense, an aid to remembered sound, to a rich musical experience—never just a collection of black marks signifying abstract pitches and rhythms. Let us all re-study our art to have this free relationship with it, so that we can open our ears and mouths and become ambassadors of song wherever we go.[10]

So, then, how does a composer, such as Alice Parker, approach the music of other composers—whether white, European, and dead, or those still very much alive? In an editorial in 2004, "Musical Analysis: Discovering What's There," Alice addressed her process of score preparation and analysis.

> The student begins with imagined sound and ends with ten to one hundred pages of written symbols. The composer is erecting a structure in sound which has not previously existed; the student's aim should be to determine that structure, thereby retracing the composer's path.
>
> The architecture is the skeleton of the music. When I conduct, I need to be clear about this structure: not only the large divisions of the work, but how

each single phrase relates to the next. I begin not by playing the music, but by looking at the first page, noting the title, composer, tempo, key, meter, performing forces, and any markings which help me to place the work in time and place, in intent and function. Then I turn all the pages quickly, noting changes in tempo or performers, and places where the motion stops: fermatas, movement ends, etc. (In a multi-movement work, I go through the whole piece at this stage.) I like to end up with a list (including page numbers) which shows me at a glance the mega-structure of the whole.

The next task is to flesh out that beginning, to discover the phrase structures within the whole, to find where the music "breathes" (Julius Herford's term). I place a tiny check-mark beneath the staff at each clear cadence point. This is easy with homophonic music, but can be really difficult or confusing in polyphonic passages, where each voice seems to breathe at a different time. The student must try and re-try to find where the aggregate sound coalesces into an implied ending, or a new surge of energy. Now I go back and count the measures between each check-mark. This shows instantly whether phrase lengths are symmetrical (i.e. 4 + 4) or odd (i.e. 4 + 5), which in turn reflects the amount of energy needed to go from cadence to cadence. When the measures are numbered throughout the work, one can diagram the relationships from phrase to section to movement to whole. Again, this does not yield an exact equivalent: for one thing, it fails to account for changing meters within a phrase. But added to the information above, it yields increasing information about the structure of the work.

Now, I begin a search for the meaning of the music: what is its affect or mood, and how is this produced? With any vocal or choral music, the text must be the beginning point: I must study its own structure, poetical devices and meaning. Then, how does the music relate to the words: is the setting sympathetic to the spoken and/or sung syllables? Does it reflect, intensify, comment on or reveal those things that the text hints at but can't say?

I believe that melodic analysis is essentially far more meaningful than harmonic. What is the structure and affect of the melody, or thematic material? How is it extended: which musical devices of color or structure or voicing are used, and to what effect? The melody is what we remember, and looking for its statements and transformations leads one quickly into the heart of the piece.

But any analysis is of far greater value to its maker than to any subsequent reader: the search through the score is its own reward. It should be a conversation with the creator, leading to deeper insights with each new exchange. And the resultant understanding must rest on an uneasy balance

> between what can be stated and what is implied. Far more is going on than meets the eye. What is seen and written must be translated into an inner-ear audialization (step one) which must then be translated into actual sound (step two). If human beings are making that sound, there is a scrim of infinite variety (step three) between the vision and the reality. The heard music is different each time, but the architecture remains the same. The great conductors reconstruct the composer's vision; the great listeners co-construct (in Hindemith's phrase) the work as it flows into their ears.
>
> All of which is to say that the craft of composition and the craft of analysis are opposite sides of the same coin. The writer's creative journey should be just as fascinating and revealing as the reader's re-creation of it. We balance each other, and need each other for a complete musical experience.[11]

A journey that began thirty years ago yielded far more than an answer to a single question. Literally thousands of composers, conductors, teachers, students, lovers of music have allowed themselves to be captivated by the power of a single melody through a teacher who invites them to listen, to ask what the melody wants to do, and respond. According to Alice, it would appear that God does give the gift of music to as many as think so—different degrees and functions, perhaps, but as at the "Welcome Table" of her "backyard opera," *Family Reunion*, something to nourish each of us. Alice Parker has nurtured our minds and hearts with great music, song, food, and much laughter and just as importantly, has taught us how to do that in their churches, schools, and communities with melodious accord.

> I find that I consider music a humanity rather than an art (for humans' sake, rather than arts'). Music is basic to our lives, giving us a language for our emotions and a healing sense of order. Singing is the quintessential bringer-together: Songs and choruses unite us in unique and mysterious ways. The union of words, rhythms, and pitches is an inexhaustible spring. Composition is as functional as cooking: I'm feeding people's ears. Folk music is the fountainhead of song, and improvising and arranging teach us about the nature of melody. Conducting is the ability to make music with a group. Orchestral conducting is one part of the discipline; choral is similar in its professional guise, but that's still only half. A true conductor should be able to lead song in churches and homes, in classrooms and hospitals—wherever song can bring its healing. And my kind of teaching is the verbalization of musical process: discovering what is going on in one's own ear, mind, and voice, and opening others to discover their own abilities. It's passing along the whole-life experience, seeking to unite disciplines rather than separate them.[12]

Bibliography

Bellinger, Karen. *Alice Parker—America's Treasured Folk Song Arranger.* Master of Music, Southwestern Oklahoma State University, 2002.

Breuer, Sammy Jo. "Alice Parker's Integration of Text and Musical Elements in *Songs from the Dragon Quilt.*" 2002.

Fleming, Gail. *Alice Parker: American Choral Composer, Arranger, and Educator.* ProQuest/UMI, 2006.

Gresham, Mark. *Choral Conversations: Selected Interviews from Chorus! Magazine.* San Carlos: Thomas House Publications, 1997.

King, Jennifer, Sue. *Three Choral Compositions by Alice Parker: A Conductor's Analysis of Songstream, Angels and Challengers, and Songs from The Dragon Quilt.* Doctoral thesis, Louisiana State University, 2005.

Long, Janice Elaine Miller. *Alice Parker, Analytical Notes on the Cantatas: An Annotated Catalogue, A Complete Works lLst, and a Biography.* Ph.D. thesis. (Musical Arts), University of Cincinnati, 1979.

Parker, Alice. "Podium Time Alice at 80—A Life Lived in Song," *The Voice of Chorus America,* Winter 2005/2006.
http://www.chorusamerica.org/publications.cfm

Roberts, Connie Day. *The Ponder Heart: An Opera by Alice Parker Adapted from the Novel by Eudora Welty.* Graduate School, University of Southern Mississippi, Hattiesburg, Mississippi, 2001.

Shive, Kimberly. *A Study of Choral Works of Alice Parker, Gwyneth Walker, and Libby Larson for Women's Voices.* Music Education, Meredith College, Raleigh, North Carolina, 2002.

Yarrington, John Charles. *A performance analysis of "Martyrs' Mirror," "Family Reunion," and "Singers Glen": Three Operas by Alice Parker.* 1985.

Books by Alice Parker

Anatomy of Melody. Chicago: GIA Publications, 2006.

Reflections on Song: My Musical World. 2006.

The View from Here: Living in Hawley. 2006

Folk Song Transformations. (Revised to accompany video.) Hinshaw Music, Inc., 2000.

Melodious Accord: Good Singing in Church. Liturgy Training Publications, 1991.

Folk Song Transformations. Galaxy Music Corp., 1986.

Creative Hymn Singing. Hinshaw Music, Inc., 1977.

Music Reference Crammer. Doubleday, 1962.

Alice Parker's Hand-Me-Down Songs. (With James Heiks.) Chicago: GIA Publications, 2005.

Discography

The Musicians of Melodious Accord, conducted by Alice Parker

2005 *O, Sing the Glories.* GIA Publications.

2004 *Listen, Lord.* Gothic Records (G49219).

2003 *Family Reunion.*

2001 *Angels and Challengers.*

2003 *My Love and I.* Gothic Records (B0000C0FMJ).

1999 *Sweet Manna.* GIA Publications (ASIN B00002Z86l).

1998 *SING!* Association of Lutheran Church Musicians, a collection of hymns, Congregational Song Series, No. 3.

1998 *New Song from Old Hymns.* Liturgy Training Publications, based on *Creative Hymn Singing*, a demonstration of musical hymn singing.

1998 *King and the Duke.* Ethereal Enterprises.

1993 *Take Me to the Water.* GIA Publications.

1991 *Transformations.* Musical Heritage Society, Inc., includes the cantata *Melodious Accord: Thirteen Wonderful Shape-Note Hymns Arranged for Chorus, Harp, and Brass Quartet.*

1989 *Spiritual Songs.* Musical Heritage Society, Inc.

1988 *Sacred Symphonies: Melodious Accord Recording.* Musical Heritage Society, Inc., sixteenth- and twentieth-century sacred motets.

Alice Parker's Compositions with Lucy Shelton and the Manhattan String Quartet

2006 *Songs for Eve* (Archibald MacLeish), re-release on CD of the LP from Musical Heritage Society, Inc., 1985.

1985 *Songs for Eve* (Archibald MacLeish).
Echoes from the Hills (Emily Dickinson).

Arrangements and Recordings

With Robert Shaw for the Robert Shaw Chorale, 1951–1962

1962	*I'm Goin' to Sing*	(16 arr.)	RCA Victor
1961	*Sea Shanties*	(16 arr.)	RCA Victor
1961	*Deep River*	(2 arr.)	RCA Victor
1960	*What Wondrous Love*	(18 arr.)	RCA Victor
1960	*A Chorus of Love*	(15 arr.)	RCA Victor
1959	*Stephen Foster Song Book*	(16 arr.)	RCA Victor
1958	*A Mighty Fortress*	(6 arr.)	RCA Victor
1957	*Christmas Hymns and Carols Vol. II*	(17 arr.)	RCA Victor
1956	*My True Love Sings*	(15 arr.)	RCA Victor
1954	*With Love from a Chorus*	(9 arr.)	RCA Victor
1952	*Christmas Hymns and Carols Vol. I*	(22 arr.)	RCA Victor
1951	*A Treasury of Easter Songs*	(13 arr.)	RCA Victor

Alice Parker Arrangements for the Robert Shaw Chorale

1967	*Irish Folk Songs*	(16 arr.)	RCA Victor
1965	*Sing to the Lord*	(16 arr.)	RCA Victor

Videography

Folk Song Transformations. Chapel Hill: Hinshaw Music, Inc., 2000.

The Reason Why We Sing. Chicago: Liturgy Training Publications, 1995.

When We Sing. Chicago: Liturgy Training Publications, 1994.

Yes, We'll Gather. Chicago: Liturgy Training Publications, 1993.

Complete Works List

Alic Parker's original compositions and arrangements are listed on her website at http://www.aliceparker.com. Click on "works list," then "musical form": opera, choral, song cycle, chorus/full orchestra, etc.

Notes

1 Alice Parker, "Alice at 80—A Life Lived in Song," Podium Time, *The Voice of Chorus America*, Winter 2005/2006.

2 Alice Parker, "Remembering Robert Lawson Shaw," *Melodious Accord Newsletter*, February 1999, Vol. 13, No. 1.

3 Parker, "Looking Back—and Ahead," *Melodious Accord Newsletter*, October 2005, Vol. 21. No 1.

4 Marilyn Pryor, "Twenty Years and Counting," *Melodious Accord Newsletter*, November 2004, Vol. 20, No 1.

5 Parker, "Looking Back—and Ahead," *Melodious Accord Newsletter*, October 2005, Vol. 21, No 1.

6 Ibid.

7 Ibid.

8 Ibid.

9 Parker, "Music Ed 2001," *Melodious Accord Newsletter*, October 1997, Vol. 12. No 4.

10 Alice Parker, "Improvising and World Music," *Melodious Accord Newsletter*, October 1998, Vol. 12, No. 7.

11 Alice Parker, "Musical Analysis: Discovering What's There." *Melodious Accord Newsletter*, July 2004, Vol.1, No. 3.

12 Podium Time, "Alice at 80—A Life Lived in Song," *The Voice of Chorus America*, Winter 2005/2006.

Lorna Cooke deVaron

Lori Wiest

Conductor and educator Lorna Cooke deVaron, known to her friends and students as "Cookie," has been one of the nation's strongest leaders in choral music.[1] As conductor of the New England Conservatory Chorus for forty-one years and the Longy Chamber Singers for seventeen, Lorna has devoted a lifetime to choral singing and performing music by contemporary choral composers. Through her teaching at New England Conservatory and Tanglewood, she has inspired generations of musicians from around the world.

Born in 1921, Lorna received the Bachelor of Arts from Wellesley College in 1942 where she studied theory and harmony with composer and pianist Nadia Boulanger. In 1943 she completed the Master of Arts from Radcliffe College studying with conductor G. Wallace Woodworth and theorist Walter Piston, while serving as assistant conductor of the Radcliffe Choral Society and the Radcliffe Choir.

Lorna was appointed to the faculty of music at Bryn Mawr College in 1945, a position she held for two years until 1947, when she became the founder and director of the New England Conservatory Chorus. At NEC, she served as Chair of the Choral Department, taught choral conducting and also conducted the New England Chamber Singers and Alumni Chorus. Through her leadership conducting the NEC Chorus and through their association with the Boston Symphony Orchestra, Lorna had the opportunity to work with some of the world's leading orchestral conductors including Leonard Bernstein, Claudio Abbado, Aaron Copland, Robert Shaw, and Seiji Ozawa. Joint recordings of NEC Chorus with the Boston Symphony Orchestra have been released under the labels of RCA, Deutsche Grammophon, Composers Recordings Inc., and Columbia.

After World War II, Lorna studied with Robert Shaw at Tanglewood, rehearsing six hours a day and, following dinner, reading through Bach Cantatas in the evenings. Lorna was the only female conducting student studying with Shaw during that time and later reflected on her earlier career stating: "I got my first job at Bryn Mawr when I was twenty-three and hadn't even finished up my studies at Harvard,"[2] just as the war was ending. This was a remarkable achievement at the time: a woman holding a collegiate position in choral music. In an interview with Richard Dyer for *The Boston Globe*, Lorna stated that she felt "Women do well with choruses because they understand the intimate emotions the choral literature expresses, and they know how to deal with people."[3] In 1953, Lorna became the Director of the Tanglewood Festival Chorus and taught conducting. Ten years later, she became the head of the choral department of the Berkshire Music Festival at Tanglewood.

In addition to conducting the NEC Chorus on numerous performance tours including Soviet Union, Romania, Bulgaria, and China, Lorna was invited to be guest conductor in various cities around the world. In 1977, she conducted the Kibbutz choirs and a choral workshop in Israel as a guest of the Israeli Government. The following year, the New England Conservatory, under her direction, participated in the thirtieth anniversary celebration of the founding of Israel. She was also invited to direct the Cameron Singers in Israel and the Broadcasting Chorus of Beijing, China.

In 1988, Lorna retired as Chair of the Choral Department at New England Conservatory but she continued to conduct the New England Conservatory Camerata, the choral ensemble of the NEC Continuing Education Department. The same year, she began to conduct the Longy Chamber Singers, a position from which she retired in 2005.

Lorna Cooke DeVaron received many awards and honors throughout her career including the Boston Medal for Distinguished Achievement in 1967 for the chorus's concert tour of the Soviet Union as part of the Cultural Exchange Program. In 1978, the Wellesley College Alumnae Association honored her with the presentation of their Alumnae Achievement Award. During her tenure at New England Conservatory, six of the seventeen recordings of the New England Conservatory Chorus prepared by Lorna with the Boston Symphony Orchestra won the Grand Prix du Disque of France, including their recording of *Romeo et Juliette* of Berlioz. The National Academy of Recording Arts also gave them several award nominations. New England Conservatory bestowed upon her an honorary doctorate in music, and the Harvard Glee Club and American Choral Directors Association both honored her for Distinguished Service to Choral Music.

Lorna's commitment to contemporary choral music is seen through the recordings and the programming of her ensembles. In a press release for her final concert of the Longy Chamber Singers, Lorna commented, "Championing new American music has been the main purpose of my life as a choral director."[4] The NEC Chorus performed many American and world premieres of composers such as Leonard Bernstein, Alan Hovhaness, Daniel Pinkham, and Randall Thompson.

In his review of Rodion Shchedrin's *The Sealed Angel* performed by the NEC Camerata and the Longy Chamber Singers, both conducted by Lorna Cooke deVaron, Henry Fogel states "the choral singing is lovely, well balanced, secure, warm, and impassioned."[5] He continues to praise Lorna's interpretation and skills, stating her "conducting has shape, direction, and variety of intensity—in short, it seems ideal."[6]

Following her noteworthy academic career, Lorna's strategy has been to continue to conduct long into retirement. In a phone interview with Richard Dyer in 2006, she said, "I have no plans to stop working while I can still raise a hand in the air."[7] Her musicianship and devotion to music has passed to her son, Alexander deVaron, a composer, and to her daughter, Tina deVaron, a jazz musician.

Notes

1 Dyer, Richard, "De Varon ends NEC era with concert," *The Boston Globe*, 12 May 2006.

2 Ibid.

3 Ibid.

4 Ratterree, Alice, "Longy Bids Farewell to Choral Conductor Lorna Cooke de-Varon." Longy School of Music, press release, www.longy.edu, 22 February 2005.

5 Fogel, Henry, *330 Fanfare,* November/December 1998.

6 Ibid.

7 Dyer, Richard, "DeVaron ends NEC era with concert," *The Boston Globe*, 12 May 2006.

Jane Skinner Hardester

Lori Wiest

"Alas for those who never sing, but die with all their music in them." This quotation by Oliver Wendell Holmes—a favorite of Jane Skinner Hardester—probably best represented this conductor's devotion to choral music. She sought to insure "that all who met her through the choral art would have experienced the joy of singing and expressing all of the music within them," as written by Ginger Covert Colla in the Southern California Vocal Association Newsletter.[1]

Jane Skinner Hardester was born on 3 October 1922. After receiving the Bachelor of Arts degree from College of the Pacific in Stockton, California, she served in the U.S. Navy. There, she taught recruits at Hunter College, New York, she directed the Glee Club of Waves in Washington D.C., and she performed as a member of the radio chorus of navy personnel under the direction of Dr. Lara Hoggard.

In her first teaching position, Jane was choral director at Mountain View School District in El Monte, California, from 1949–1958. In 1959, she received the Master of Music degree from the University of Southern California. Her thesis, titled "A suggested vocal music program for high schools with special reference to El Monte High School," demonstrated her desire to inspire and educate youth through choral music in the school system. Jane assisted with Pacific Music Camp at College of the Pacific and lectured during the summers in the School of Music at University of Southern California. She then had a one-year internship with Elaine Brown's Singing City in Philadelphia. In 1962, she became a full-time faculty member at El Camino College in Torrance, California, and director of the Lyric Singers, a women's community choir. The latter group appeared at the ACDA North Central Division Convention in Lincoln, Nebraska, and at the Western Division Convention in Reno, Nevada.

As part of her championing music education, Jane led a committee of members of the American Choral Directors Association in developing "Suggested Guidelines for the Junior College Choral Program as Prepared by the ACDA Committee on Junior College Choral Problems" which was presented at the National Convention of the ACDA in Seattle in 1968. This project, a suggested program designed for junior college (community college) students, included a graded music curriculum, discrimination in selecting quality choral literature, and development of materials for choir festivals.

Jane Hardester was one of the original eighty-one charter members of the American Choral Directors Association. When ACDA was originally being organized, some choral seminars and choral performances had been held in conjunction with MENC conferences. From 1961–1969, Jane was one of four choral conductors who chaired those sessions in the Western Division. After ACDA became a separate organization, Jane continued her leadership role by serving as Western Division President between 1971 and 1975, during which time she organized and hosted the second Western Division Convention in Coronado, California. This conference featured presenters such as Elaine Brown and Sonja Garfinkle from Singing City in Philadelphia, Paul Salamunovich, Jester Hairston, Frank Pooler, Albert McNeil, Morris Hayes, and Howard Swan. Importantly for ACDA, as Western Division President, she developed a division board represented by fourteen high school, university, community, and church choral groups from the states comprising the Western Division. She then appointed the first Western Division President Elect, Ginger Covert Colla, who created a division board structure consistent with that of the ACDA National Board. Jane was known as "a great organizer, and had a unique talent for delegating duties and involving others in the planning process."[2]

Following her two terms as president of the Western Division, Jane completed the Doctor of Musical Arts from University of Southern California in 1976, *magna cum laude*. Throughout her career, Jane credited the mentors with whom she studied choral music and conducting: Charles Hirt, Harold Decker, Elaine Brown, Lara Haggard, and Jester Hairston.

In 1978, Jane founded the Jane Hardester Singers, a semi-professional ensemble that toured Europe on several occasions and performed at regional and national conventions of ACDA. Although she retired from full-time teaching in 1990, Jane continued as conductor of the Jane Hardester Singers until 1992. In the Fall of 1993, Jane was the guest conductor of the Los Angeles Gay Men's Chorus, and the following spring served as the clinician for the Korean Choral Conductors Symposium in Seoul. From 1995 to 2000, she served as choir director for the El Segundo Methodist Church. Together with Diane Simons, Jane founded the South Bay Children's Choir in 1996. This organization, sponsored by El Camino College, is comprised of one hundred twenty-five girls and boys ages seven to seventeen. She retired from her position as co-director in 2000 but the South Bay Children's Choir continues to flourish.

Jane received numerous awards for her achievements in choral music. California ACDA awarded her the Howard Swan Award for her "outstanding contribution to the choral art" in 1993. In 1998, she received the Distinguished Woman Award from El Camino College and during the same year was recognized by the South Bay Master Chorale for her commitment to the choral art. In 2000, she received the Katy Geissert Award from the Cultural Arts Commission in Torrance.

Jane spent her professional career and her lifetime teaching singers from all backgrounds about choral music. While her conducting and teaching positions centered in California, the impact of her devotion to choral music education transcended boundaries. After her death, the Western Division of ACDA established the Jane Skinner Hardester Memorial Award "in recognition for her outstanding leadership and contributions to ACDA and her dedication to the choral art."[3] This annual award supports two aspiring choral conductors with ACDA membership to attend a workshop or conference to assist them in their professional development.

Jane Hardester passed away 24 October 2006. A memorial service on 26 November in Davis, California, was followed by a memorial concert at the First United Methodist Church in Glendale on 20 December. Both events celebrated the life of an esteemed teacher and colleague to music educators throughout the choral world.

NOTES

[1] Covert Colla, Ginger. "In Memoriam-Jane Skinner Hardester, October 3, 1922-October 23, 2006." *Southern California Vocal Association Newsletter* (December 2006).

[2] American Choral Directors Association, Western Division, www.acdaonline.org/Western/Division%20History.html

[3] American Choral Directors Association, Western Division, www.acdaonline.org/Western/

Biographies of Biographers

Joan Whittemore, CSJ, DMA, is the founding director of the Carondelet Women's Chorus and the Carondelet Children's Chorus. She is a noted composer, editor, guest conductor, and has served as clinician for the College Music Society, the American Guild of Organists, and the American Choral Directors Association. She holds both the master's and doctoral degrees in conducting from the University of Illinois at Urbana-Champaign, a Bachelor of Music in Music Education from Fontbonne College, and serves on the National Committee for Research and Publications for American Choral Directors Association.

Joan Whittemore's interest in treble-voiced music led her to research the music of the Ospedali Veneziani while at the University of Illinois. Her dissertation, *The Revision of Music Performed at the Venetian Ospedali in the Eighteenth Century* (1986), established that more than eight-hundred *figlie del coro* (daughters of the chorus) had performed the music in the choruses and orchestras fostered at the Ospedali. The key to this discovery lay in the founding documents that gave the four Ospedali the same canonical privileges to have women perform the music of the liturgy that were afforded to women in convents. Thirteen composers, Johann Adolph Hasse, Niccolo Jommelli, Nicola Porpora, and Antonio Vivaldi, to name a few, were among those who had either written music for the Ospedali (SSAA), and subsequently revised that music for other institutions (SATB, TTBB, etc.), and vice versa. *The Choral Journal* published Joan Whittemore's article detailing the revision process in "Revision Repertoire of the Ospedali Veneziani," in March 1994. In 2007, Joan Whittemore directed the Carondelet Women's Chorus and St. Cecilia Academy's Singers of Nashville, Tennessee, in two performances of the Music of the Ospedali including Antonio Vivaldi's Magnificat (RV 611) for SSAA, soli and strings (1739) and Baldassare Galuppi's Nunc Dimittis (1772) at Church of the Pietà and the Ospedale degli Derelitti in Venice, Italy.

Winner of the prestigious Gladys Krieble-Delmas Award for Venetian Studies in 1986, Joan Whittemore returned to Venice to complete research on *Music of the Venetian Ospedali Composers, a Thematic Catalogue*, (Pendragon Press, 1995) that consists of excerpts of nearly thirteen hundred titles of music principally of Ospedali *maestri*, but also includes other contemporary composers. Together with Dr. Jane Baldauf-Berdes, she is editor of the forthcoming *Guide to Ospedali Research*, a two volume companion to Jane

Baldauf-Berdes's *Women Musicians of Venice Musical Foundations, 1525–1855*, Clarendon Press, 1993, that will serve as an invaluable research tool for the more than two-hundred topics still to be explored on the Ospedali, the musicians, and the repertoire.

Marie-Thérèse Bouquet-Boyer invited Joan to be a contributing author to the series, *Musique à Venise De Maddalena Laura Lombardini Sirmen à Jane Baldauf- Berdes*, Cahier de l'IRHMES, Publications De La MSH-Alpes 2006, juin, which resulted in "The Jane Berdes Archive at Duke University: a Legacy," 113–131. Joan Whittemore continues to edit, perform, and publish music of the Ospedali composers, and is currently writing a book on the teaching legacy of Fiora Contino.

Joan Whittemore's own compositions have been performed widely throughout the United States. Alice Parker designated Joan as a Melodious Accord Fellow in 1997 and 2001. Alliance Music, Inc. and Boosey and Hawkes publish her original compositions and editions of the sacred music of Antonio Vivaldi, Nicola Porpora, and Baldassare Galuppi. She is a regular contributor to *Springtime of the Soul*, a publication of Ministry of the Arts. Joan Whittemore is listed in *Who's Who of American Women*.

Lori Wiest is Associate Professor of Music at Washington State University in Pullman, Washington, where she is Director of Choral Activities and the conductor of the WSU Concert Choir and Madrigal Singers. She teaches Choral Conducting and graduate courses in Choral History and Literature and in Choral Conducting. Currently, Dr. Wiest also serves as Associate Dean of the WSU Graduate School and the conductor of the Spokane Symphony Chorale. Prior to her present position, Dr. Wiest taught Music Theory at Mesa Community College in Arizona and at the University of Arizona.

Dr. Wiest has worked with composers Eric Whitacre, John Corigliano, Morten Lauridsen, Chen Yi, and Libby Larsen. Her two ensembles, the WSU Concert Choir and Madrigal Singers, have performed in St. Petersburg, Russia, in Italy, Austria, the Czech Republic, Hungary, Germany, throughout the state of Washington and the western United States, and at Lincoln Center in New York. They have been featured performers with the Spokane Symphony and the Washington-Idaho Symphony.

Dr. Wiest is active as an adjudicator, All-State conductor, clinician, and guest conductor. She was adjudicator and clinician at the Australian International Music Festival, and has been frequently invited to present for the Northwest American Choral Directors Association, the Washington American Choral Directors Summer Institute, Washington ArtsTime Conference, Washington Music Educators, the Northwest Music Educators Association, the College Music Society, the Rocky Mountain Modern Language Association, and the MENC Biennial In-Service Conference. She was the organizer and facilitator of the ACDA National Conducting Awards and Choral Conversations presentations in 2003 and 2005 at the national conventions. Her article, "Techniques for Vocal Health," was published in the February 1997 issue of *Teaching Music*, a publication of MENC. Additional articles by Dr. Wiest have been published in *The Choral Journal*.

As a featured soloist, Dr. Wiest has performed with the Washington-Idaho Symphony and the WSU Concert Choir. She was a member of the Robert Shaw Festival Singers and has also performed as a solo recitalist in Italy, Switzerland, and Germany.

In 1990, Dr. Wiest received the Doctor of Musical Arts in Choral Conducting and Music Theory from the University of Arizona, in 1986 the Master of Music in Choral Music from Arizona State University, and in 1984 the Bachelor of Science in Music Education and Piano Performance from North Dakota State University. She has sung with conductors Robert Shaw, Charles Dutoit, Maurice Skones, Douglas McEwen, and Edwin Fissinger.